POX AMERICANA

POX AMERICANA

THE GREAT SMALLPOX EPIDEMIC

OF 1775–82

ELIZABETH A. FENN

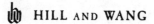 HILL AND WANG

A DIVISION OF FARRAR, STRAUS AND GIROUX

NEW YORK

Hill and Wang
A division of Farrar, Straus and Giroux
19 Union Square West, New York 10003

Copyright © 2001 by Elizabeth A. Fenn
All rights reserved
Distributed in Canada by Douglas & McIntyre Ltd.
Printed in the United States of America
First edition, 2001

Library of Congress Cataloging-in-Publication Data
Fenn, Elizabeth A. (Elizabeth Anne), 1959–
    Pox Americana : the great smallpox epidemic of 1775–82 /
Elizabeth A. Fenn.
        p.   cm.
    Includes bibliographical references and index.
    ISBN 0-8090-7820-1 (hardcover : alk. paper)
    1. Smallpox—United States—History—18th century. I. Title.

RC183.49 .F46 2001
614.5'21'097309033—dc21

                                                    2001016886

Designed by Jonathan D. Lippincott

Maps by Elizabeth A. Fenn

3   5   7   9   10   8   6   4   2

FOR PETER

CONTENTS

Foreword ix

Introduction 3

1. Variola 13

2. Vigilance 44

3. Control 80

4. Surrender 104

5. Entierros 135

6. Traders 167

7. Connections 196

8. Passages 224

Epilogue 259

Notes 279

Index 359

FOREWORD

My interest in the events recorded in this book developed piecemeal, over the course of twenty years. I first encountered the great smallpox epidemic of 1775–82 in 1980, when I was an undergraduate writing a senior essay on Native Americans in the Hudson Bay fur trade. Scattered throughout the writings of fur traders working for the Hudson's Bay and North West companies were descriptions of a terrible smallpox outbreak that swept the Canadian interior in 1781–82. The descriptions were at once dreadful and captivating. They impressed me enough that I used a brief account of this local episode to conclude my essay, but my exploration of the topic stopped there. I had no concept of the vastness of the outbreak. Nor did I understand that the experience of Indians in what is now Manitoba and Saskatchewan was shared by hundreds of thousands of other people across the North American continent from 1775 to 1782.

I let it lie. I never forgot about the epidemic entirely, but I didn't think about it either. Instead, I pursued other interests. A brief stint in graduate school in the early 1980s was followed by a longer stint working as an auto mechanic for eight years. It was during those years that I found the time to read broadly and eclectically, savoring words the way some savor fine food and drink. Although I do not recall the precise date, it was probably in 1994 that a friend loaned me a thick little novel titled *The Horseman on the Roof*, by the great French writer Jean Giono. It told the story of Angelo, an Italian nobleman making his way through nineteenth-century Provence as cholera erupted around him. The book enthralled me. I marveled at its physical expressiveness, at its juxtaposition of beauty and fear. It also transported me, not just to nineteenth-century France but (much to my surprise) to eighteenth-century Canada as well. Even as I labored at brake jobs and engine repairs, I found myself carried back to the Native Americans whose suffering was described in those Hudson Bay smallpox documents I had read more than a decade before. Eventually I could not stand it anymore. I wanted to write a story of my own, a story about smallpox.

My preliminary research yielded many surprises. The most stunning was simply that I was on to something big. At the start, I envisioned doing a sort of microhistory, a tightly focused study of a terrible epidemic in the Canadian fur country. But soon I realized that the Canadian outbreak was just one piece of a much larger puzzle, one missing many pieces but still breathtaking in scope—and huge. The pestilence had swept not only North America but parts of South America as well. Why didn't we know about it? Why wasn't this a part of our core knowledge of the era of the American Revolution?

Then I discovered that some people, a few people, *did* know about portions of it. Arthur J. Ray's work on Canada and Marc Simmons's work on New Mexico had appeared in print even before I discovered the epidemic in college. During my years turning wrenches, exciting studies by Jody Decker, Robert Boyd, Cole Harris, Robert Jackson, and Thomas Pearcy all had been published, works that shed light on the pestilence in specific locales, often with vague but tantalizing references to a larger background pandemic. What about this larger pandemic? I wondered. Surely it was a story that needed telling. Could I possibly write about the whole thing? In the end, I decided to try, and the result is this book.

Between the decision and the book was the research. My greatest discovery was the marvelous records kept by priests and friars in Catholic parishes throughout the Spanish empire in North America. These records consist almost solely of lists—of baptisms, of marriages, of burials—and quite naturally it was the burial records that interested me. I soon found that these lists of buried people all over Mexico and what is now the American Southwest had two seemingly contradictory qualities. Their sheer volume seemed overwhelming at first, and even now I admit that compiling the data they contain was as tiresome a research task as I have ever undertaken. They are, after all, simply lists. But in the months I spent on them, they became much more than that. Like the AIDS quilt or the Vietnam Memorial, the sheer volume of names and monotony of form made them monumental. The only time in my research when I found myself moved to tears was as I went through these lists of thousands and thousands of names. And my greatest regret is that I have found it impossible to write about these names in a way that does justice to the lives they represent.

Many people helped make this book possible. Kevin Clayton, Scott Clayton, Tommy Cutts, Jim Dewar, Daniel Emory, Stuart Gregory, Colin Hogan, Greg Marzen, Justin Meddock, Mark Painter, Erik Rahimtoola, Eddie Sain, Gene Sull, Henry Tate, and Brian Yeargan all have influenced my life more than they will ever know. Without their acceptance I would never have left the world of spark plugs and camshafts to pursue this project. Likewise, the cheerful flexibility of Wayne and Monie Clayton in the unforgiving world of automotive repair made it possible for me to earn a living even while I pursued the preliminary research that brought this book to life. For their support I am grateful. Florence Thomas, Ingrid Walsøe-Engel, David Montgomery, and Frank Snowden also provided valuable encouragement in the early stages of this project.

Many generous scholars responded to my queries and shared their own thoughts, ideas, and research with me, including Barbara Belyea, John Brooke, Robert Cain, Colin Calloway, Max Edelson, Jay Gitlin, David Hancock, Don Higginbotham, Marjoleine Kars, Steve Langdon, Wayne Lee, Michael McDonnell, Jim McMillan, Matt Mulcahy, John Nelson, Elizabeth Perkins, Paige Raibmon, Claudio Saunt, Marc Simmons, David Steinberg, Linea Sundstrom, Robert Tórrez, the members of the Triangle Early American History Seminar, and the members of the Columbia University Seminar on Early American History and Culture. Jack Nisbet encouraged my interests from the start and helped put me in touch with resources that shed light on the explorer David Thompson's accounts of smallpox. Likewise, Sean Peake was kind enough to send me his own transcription of Thompson's jumbled-up manuscript and to enlighten me regarding important issues of authorship within it. In the medical profession, Drs. D. A. Henderson, Sam Katz, Anne Nicholson-Weller, and Walter Rogan all helped me with important questions, and the immunologist Karen McKinnon patiently (and repeatedly) coached me in the intricacies of human immune response. Francis Black, a specialist in the epidemiology of isolated populations, likewise made valuable suggestions on more than one occasion.

Friends and family have provided more assistance than they can possibly know. Buzz Alexander, Janie Paul, Peter Hinks, Jason DeParle, Nancy-Ann DeParle, Michele Hoffnung, Eileen Roche, and Robert Broom all welcomed me into their homes during research trips that spanned the continent. Anne Nicholson-Weller encouraged me at every turn and gave me access to a reclusive writer's paradise at a crucial time. To Marjoleine Kars I am grateful not only for introducing me to *The Horseman on the Roof,* but also for more than twenty years of steadfast friendship. My dear friend Florence Kuster did not live to see this book in print, but her enthusiasm for it shows in every page. My parents, Bob and Ann Fenn, and my brothers, Jon and Tim Fenn, all encouraged my work and expressed lively interest in its progress. By introducing me to the world of Geographic Information Systems, Tim dramatically changed the way I approached my research. I am grateful for his assistance in many, many ways.

For financial support, I would like to thank Yale University for the Marion C. Sheridan Fellowship that funded my first year of full-time research in 1996–97. I also benefited from a Jacob M. Price Visiting Research Fellowship from the William L. Clements Library that funded a research trip to Ann Arbor. To the Clements Library staff—John Dann, Brian Dunnigan, Rob Cox, John Harriman, Mary Pedley, Arlene Shy, Adolfo Tarango, and Don Wilcox—I am grateful for abundant encouragement, advice, and camaraderie. In the summer of 1997, a Mayers Fellowship from the Henry E. Huntington Library gave me the opportunity to utilize that repository's collections. Peter Blodgett, Bill Frank, and Tom Lange all gave me valuable assistance during my time there, and Roy Ritchie's enthusiasm for my work was undying. I would also like to thank Dale Harmon and his staff for allowing me to make the Durham Stake Family History Center of the Church of Jesus Christ of Latter-day Saints my home away from home for many months. Their patience with my requests never ceased to amaze me. At the History Collection of the New York Academy of Medicine, Michael North kindly answered my questions about the John Cochran Letterbook, and at the William Andrews Clark Memorial Library, Suzanne Tatian's initiative rescued me from a disastrous day of research. George Miles at Yale University's Beinecke Library provided helpful suggestions at several stages in this project. In addition, a Charlotte W. Newcombe Doctoral Dissertation Fellowship from the Woodrow Wilson National Fellowship Foundation gave me the luxury of writing for a year without outside distractions.

In a seminar in 1982, Edmund S. Morgan encouraged my wide-ranging interests and inspired me with his crystal-clear prose. Many years later his advice and his friendship remain true, and I am grateful for both. My editor, Elisabeth Sifton, delighted me with the grace and clarity of her editorial suggestions. Thanks to her, I now know for certain that the rules of automotive engineering also apply to the written word: The best solution is always the simple one. Additional thanks go to John Demos not only for his interest and enthusiasm but also for his thoughtful critiques and literary suggestions. My debts to John Mack Faragher are too many to count. Johnny instantly and intuitively understood the significance of this work, and in the years since our first meeting in 1996, he has read this manuscript in many forms and provided incomparable advice, good cheer, and support.

My last and greatest debt is to Peter H. Wood, whose very being is woven into the fiber of these pages. Since I cannot begin to detail his contribution to my life and this work, I shall simply say thank you, from the bottom of my heart.

EAF
Hillsborough, North Carolina
July 2001

POX AMERICANA

INTRODUCTION

The story that follows is about *Variola major*, the virus that causes smallpox. From 1775 to 1782, *Variola* ravaged the greater part of North America, from Mexico to Massachusetts, from Pensacola to Puget Sound. For the virus, the great pestilence represented a phenomenal success: It found countless new hosts, it multiplied rapidly, and it traveled vast distances. But in its wake it left death and despair, killing more than a hundred thousand people and maiming many more. With no respect for boundaries of race, class, or nationality, the opportunistic microbe swept an astonishing array of people and events into its maelstrom: missionaries, mariners, fur traders, explorers, planters, fishermen, hunters, farmers, homemakers, warriors, neophytes, trappers, soldiers, prisoners, and runaway slaves. By the time the pestilence was over, it had reshaped human destinies across the continent.

Today, it is hard to imagine the havoc that *Variola* once caused, for an entire generation has now come of age without knowing its ravages. In 1979, after a monumental campaign against a virus that had plagued humankind for three thousand years, the World Health Organization (WHO) certified that it had eradicated smallpox from the world. It was an enormous humanitarian triumph. But if eradication was a triumph, it was also a punctuation mark. It marked the close of an optimistic era in which public health officials had envisioned the imminent end of infectious disease itself. Already, at the time the eradication of smallpox was announced, the still-unknown and unidentified human immunodeficiency virus (HIV) had begun its silent transit around the world, representing only the deadliest of many new or resistant "emerging" diseases. Thus the elimination of one plague in 1979 was only replaced by the fear of new ones.

Even the conquest of smallpox may not be secure today. Here the failure is not medical but political. In the post-eradication world, the WHO had intended that only two repositories of *Variola* exist: one in the United States and one in Russia. The supplies of virus held in these locations were to be destroyed on June 30, 1999. Had everything proceeded as planned, it would have been the first time that humankind had knowingly and deliberately annihilated another species from the earth. But the much-anticipated rendezvous with the autoclave never took place. Instead, on April 22, 1999, some two months before smallpox was scheduled to meet its end, the United States announced that it would retain its stores of the virus. The decision was controversial. It came in response to new intelligence indicating that clandestine supplies of *Variola* were now at large in a world in which the virus was both coveted and feared as an agent of biological terror.

Beneath the pronouncements and posturing lies a profound tragedy. The eradication of smallpox came about through two decades of dogged "shoe-leather" epidemiology, as public health workers around the world went door to door, sometimes under extraordinary conditions, to track down and eliminate the *Variola* virus. In its final, "intensified" phase alone—from 1967 through 1979—the campaign cost the funding nations nearly $1 billion.[1] It was marked, moreover, by extraordinary international cooperation despite the bellicose rivalries of the Cold War era. Considering this background, the reemergence of *Variola* as a threat to humankind today represents a failure every bit as great as the success that preceded it.

The last naturally occurring case of smallpox in the world

appeared in Somalia in October 1977. The victim, a twenty-three-year-old cook named Ali Maow Maalin, was successfully quarantined, and all his contacts were quickly vaccinated. A three-thousand-year chain of transmission had been broken. The WHO workers who had labored so hard for so long had cause for celebration. But ten months later, a shocking report came out of Birmingham, England. A woman named Janet Parker had mysteriously taken ill with full-fledged smallpox. Parker was a medical photographer. Her studio at the Medical School of the University of Birmingham was in the same building as a smallpox laboratory, albeit upstairs and several rooms away. Somehow, in what is known as a laboratory outbreak, Parker had picked up the virus. She gave it to her family as well. At the age of seventy, Parker's mother came down with smallpox and survived. Her father, aged seventy-seven, also showed symptoms, but before the disease could be diagnosed, he died of a heart attack, even while his daughter remained alive. In the midst of the chaos, the head of the laboratory from which the virus had escaped committed suicide. Janet Parker herself died of smallpox on September 11, 1978. Hers was the last known death from the disease.

Today, despite rumors and intelligence reports, we live in a smallpox-free world. The pages that follow make our good fortune clear.

Variola's relationship to humankind is both parasitic and paradoxical. To thrive and multiply, the virus has to have a host. But for the host species—unlucky *Homo sapiens*—*Variola* is the most unruly of guests. It inflicts unspeakable suffering upon its victims. It blinds, scars, and maims. In the end, it also confers either immunity or death. For the parasite, this presents a problem. *Variola* consumes its human hosts as a fire consumes its fuel, leaving spent bodies, dead or immune, behind. To survive, the virus has to find a constant supply of new victims. In a large urban population, such individuals might become available through immigration or childbirth. But elsewhere, if *Variola* is to succeed, it has to travel. It has to find more hosts and then, inexorably, still more.

Variola has no animal vector. It is not transmitted by insects like malaria or by water like cholera. It passes only from one human being to another. As a result, *Variola*'s story is necessarily a story of connections between people. As it ravaged North America in the years 1775–82, the virus showed that a vast web of human contact spanned the continent well before Meriwether Lewis and William Clark made their famous journey to the Pacific in 1804–06. Smallpox highlighted these contacts, illuminated their nature, and added a new dimension to their consequences.

In many regions of North America, *Variola* was by the late eighteenth century an old enemy with a well-established place in the annals of colonial conquest. The natives of Mexico—to choose only the most famous example—had endured a horrific epidemic of smallpox in conjunction with Hernán Cortés's triumph over the Aztecs between 1519 and 1521. Repeated bouts of Old World pestilence occurred in the years that followed. Smallpox may have been the most deadly of these plagues, but others too earned the respect and fear of America's indigenous peoples. Measles, influenza, mumps, typhus, cholera, plague, malaria, yellow fever, scarlet fever, whooping cough, and diphtheria all wreaked havoc in the two and a half centuries between Cortés's conquest and the American Revolution. By the time the first shots sounded in the great anti-imperial conflict that has come to epitomize the late eighteenth century, this Pandora's box of disease (with comparatively minor assistance from warfare and alcohol) had decimated the natives of the Western Hemisphere many times over.

The smallpox pestilence of 1775–82 was thus a relatively late development in a region (North America including Mexico) that had already witnessed considerable depopulation thanks to a plethora of Old World diseases. Four things, however, make this huge wave of sickness worth studying. First, it may well constitute the first continental episode of disease in the history of North America. (If not, it is certainly the first that is clearly identifiable.)

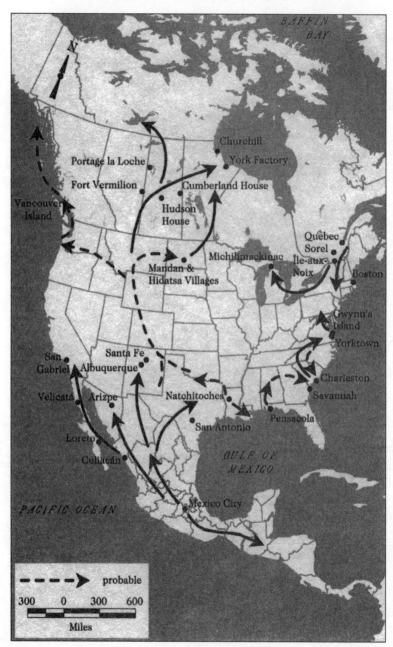

Smallpox transmission through North America, 1775–82

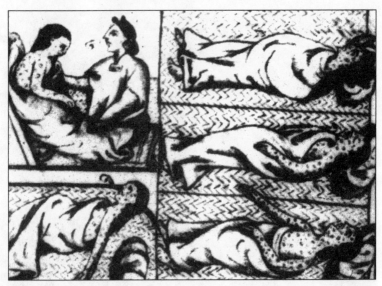

Aztec record of the first smallpox epidemic, from the *Codex Florentino*. Courtesy Library of Congress

Two versions of an Aztec image of smallpox, 1520, possibly representing an Aztec ruler who died of the disease. These are copies made by scholars of the original *Codex en Cruz*, which is so damaged that it is barely legible. Courtesy University of Utah Press

Second, although the smallpox scourge of 1775–82 coincided almost perfectly with the American Revolution and took many more American lives than the war with the British did, it remains almost entirely unknown and unacknowledged by scholars and laypeople alike. Third, unlike so many earlier outbreaks of contagion, this one is extensively documented in the historical record. And fourth, by directing our attention to events elsewhere on the continent in an era in which historians have previously focused largely on the eastern seaboard, the plague highlights the geographic and demographic gaps in our historical canon. While colonial independence reshaped global politics forever, the contagion was the defining and determining event of the era for many residents of North America. With the exception of the war itself, epidemic smallpox was the greatest upheaval to afflict the continent in these years.

It was an upheaval that left telltale signs behind. In 1792, an English sea captain named George Vancouver led an expedition to America's northern Pacific seaboard. His charge was twofold: He was to establish British dominion in the region after a diplomatic squabble with Spain, and he was to survey the coastline for an entrance to the elusive, indeed mythical, Northwest Passage. But in May 1792, it was neither Spain nor the Northwest Passage that preoccupied the famous British navigator. It was his observations of Indian villages along the shores of the Strait of Juan de Fuca, the waterway that separates what is now British Columbia's Vancouver Island from Washington State's Olympic Peninsula. Something, he believed, was terribly wrong. He had first noticed it after setting up camp at what he called Port Discovery (Discovery Bay), on the strait's southern shore. There, wrote Vancouver, "we found a deserted village capable of containing an hundred inhabitants." The houses had crumbled, and once-worn paths had given way to weeds, "amongst which were found several human sculls, and other bones, promiscuously scattered about."[2] Where, the captain wondered, were all the people?

Vancouver was no newcomer to the region. In 1778, he had

landed at Nootka with Captain James Cook and spent several months cruising the spectacular mountainous shoreline of British Columbia and Alaska. He thus had a touchstone of sorts for judging what he saw.

The mystery soon deepened. Just a few miles from their campsite, on a neck of land marking the entrance to Puget Sound, Vancouver and his men found another "deserted Indian village, much in the same state of decay as that which we had examined at the head of port Discovery." Elsewhere too, "the scull, limbs, ribs, and back bones, or some other vestiges of the human body, were found in many places promiscuously scattered about the beach, in great numbers." The country was abundant. It had salmon and fresh water "sufficient to answer all purposes" in supporting "a very numerous body of inhabitants." Any one of the deserted villages the men had seen could have contained the whole sum of the Indians they encountered. Something had happened, Vancouver concluded. A land "this delightful" should not have been so "thinly inhabited." In his view, all the evidence indicated "that at no very remote period this country had been far more populous than at present."[3]

Perhaps Vancouver was misguided. Perhaps he was, as one writer has suggested, "mildly obsessed by the idea of depopulation."[4] If so, he was not alone, for the navigator's crew confirmed his perceptions. Officers from the expedition found Discovery Bay so littered with human remains that it seemed "a general cemetery for the whole of the surrounding country." The pilot Peter Puget observed "Several deserted Villages" to the south as he explored the sound that bears his name today. And on a survey to the northward, the midshipman Thomas Manby noted "a great many deserted Villages," some "capable of holding many hundred Inhabitants." Where domestic life had once reigned, "brambles and bushes" now grew. For Manby, as for Vancouver, the conclusion was obvious. "By some event," he wrote, "this country has been considerably depopulated, but from what cause is hard to determine."[5]

There were clues among the few Indians the visitors saw. As they probed the narrow confines of Washington's Hood Canal, Vancouver and his men encountered a group of sixty natives, probably a party of Twana-speaking Coast Salish. The Indians received the Englishmen hospitably, offering them fish and receiving in return trinkets "which delighted them excessively." One of their hosts "had suffered very much from the small pox," the captain noted, and scars from the disease "were seen on many." Several of the Indians had even "lost the sight of one eye," Vancouver added, most probably a consequence of that "baneful disorder."[6]

A similar report came from the botanist Archibald Menzies. Menzies had already served as an expedition scientist to Captain Cook, a position once turned down by a young English physician named Edward Jenner. Now, just a few years before Jenner was to stun the scientific community with his development of a smallpox vaccine, Menzies bore witness to *Variola*'s ravages nearly halfway around the world. On May 21, 1792, as he and his companions charted the intricate coastline of Puget Sound, Menzies recorded an encounter with three Indians. The men were "stout fellows," he wrote, "two of them were much pitted with the small pox & each destitute of a right eye."[7]

Smallpox could explain the blindness, the scars, and the other disfigurements. But could it explain the desolation of the coastline? George Vancouver was not sure. As he pondered the bone-littered landscape around him, he acknowledged the constraints that time and perspective placed on his understanding of events that had preceded him. It was not "very easy," he wrote, "to draw any just conclusions on the true cause from which this havoc of the human race proceeded: this must remain for the investigation of others who may have more leisure, and a better opportunity, to direct such an inquiry."[8] Today, with "more leisure" and "a better opportunity" than Vancouver had in 1792, we turn to the tumult, and the virus, that shaped his times.

1

VARIOLA

September 28, 1751. *Time has left the early pages of his diary so damaged that the exact date remains uncertain. But it was probably on this day that nineteen-year-old George Washington set sail from Virginia to the island of Barbados with his older half brother, Lawrence. If their departure date is unclear, the brothers' purpose is not: The trip was intended to ease Lawrence's persistent cough and congested lungs, symptoms of the consumption that was to kill him within a year. In the eighteenth and nineteenth centuries, travel abroad was a favored treatment for consumption, the contagious disease that today we call tuberculosis. Early Americans understood consumption to be an ailment of heredity and climate, alleviated by salt air, mountain breezes, or whatever atmospheric conditions best suited a particular patient's constitution. It was the Washingtons' hope that Barbados would suit Lawrence.*

The trip was difficult. Hurricanes regularly strafe the Caribbean in the early fall, and 1751 was no exception. The brothers and their shipmates endured a week of stiff gales, rain squalls, and high seas in late October, the effects of a nearby storm. They disembarked at Bridgetown, Barbados, on November 2, 1751. Although the purpose of the journey was to ease Lawrence's consumption, it was soon George who lay seriously ill—not from tuberculosis, but from smallpox.

On November 3, the day after landing, the two brothers begrudgingly accepted an invitation to dine at the home of Gedney Clarke, a prominent merchant, planter, and slave trader with family ties to the Washingtons. "We went,—myself with some reluctance, as the smallpox was in his family," George wrote in his diary. His misgivings were justified. For a fortnight afterward, the two Americans plied the Barbadian social circuit, unaware of the virus silently multiplying in George's body. Then, on November 17, when the incubation period had passed, the infection hit hard. "Was strongly attacked with the small Pox," Washington wrote. Thereafter, his journal entries stop. Not until December 12, when he was well enough to go out once again, did George Washington return to his diary.

The brothers' stay in Barbados was brief. "This climate has not afforded the relief I expected from it," wrote Lawrence. On December 22, the brothers parted ways, George returning to Virginia and Lawrence opting for the more promising climate of Bermuda. Lawrence's health was failing fast. He spent the spring in Bermuda and then hurried desperately to his home at Mount Vernon, Virginia, where tuberculosis took his life on July 26, 1752.[1]

On Sunday, July 2, 1775, a much-older George Washington stepped out of a carriage in Cambridge, Massachusetts, to take command of the Continental army, newly established by the Congress still meeting in Philadelphia. Already, an American siege of nearby Boston was under way. The standoff was the outcome of the battles of Lexington and Concord in April 1775, when an angry throng of New England militiamen had routed a column of British troops attempting to seize a stash of munitions at Concord. Exhausted and humiliated, the king's soldiers had staggered sixteen miles back to Boston under relentless American sniper fire. Here they were trapped. The armed patriots were to besiege them in the city for the next eleven months.

By the time Washington arrived to command the American army in July, the confrontation had taken on an added dimension: It was not just military but medical as well. Smallpox was spreading through Boston. Washington knew how debilitating the disease could be, and he knew that the New Englanders who formed the core of his Boston-based army were among those most likely to be vulnerable. It was a vulnerability they shared with a great many others in late-eighteenth-century North America.

When smallpox struck George Washington in Barbados in 1751, his diary entries stopped for twenty-four days. If this was not inevitable, it was nevertheless predictable. Rare was the diarist who kept writing through the throes of the smallpox. The void in Washington's diary is thus telling; its very silence speaks of a misery commonplace in years gone by but unfamiliar to the world today.

Although the route of infection is impossible to determine, it is most likely that Washington picked up *Variola* through direct contact with a sick member of the Gedney Clarke household. The contagious party may have been Mrs. Clarke herself, who was "much indisposed" at the time of the brothers' visit. If Washington had a face-to-face meeting with her, he might have inhaled tiny infectious droplets or his hands might have carried the contagion to his mouth or nose. Such an encounter is the most likely mode of infection, but it is by no means the only one possible. Even scabs and dried-out body secretions can transmit smallpox. If someone had recently swept the floors or changed the bedclothes in a sickroom in the Clarke home, desiccated but dangerous particles may have circulated aloft. Finally, one last form of transmission bears mentioning. *Variola* can survive for weeks outside the human body. Carefully stored, it retains its virulence for years.[2] Thus it is conceivable that George Washington caught smallpox from an inanimate object (often cloth or clothing) contaminated with the virus.

How do we know that Washington caught smallpox in the Clarke household? The acknowledged presence of the disease there is one clue. Timing is another. The incubation period for smallpox usually ranges from ten to fourteen days. A twelve-day incubation is most common, with the first symptoms appearing thirteen days after exposure.[3] George Washington's case was thus fairly typical. He dined at the Clarke home on November 3, and according to his diary, his first symptoms appeared fourteen days later.

We have no firsthand description of Washington's bout with the pox. But to judge by the experience of other victims, his early symptoms would have resembled a very nasty case of the flu. Headache, backache, fever, vomiting, and general malaise all are among the initial signs of infection. The headache can be splitting; the backache, excruciating. Lakota (Sioux) Indian representations of smallpox often use a spiral symbol to illustrate intense pain in the midsection. Anxiety is another symptom. Fretful, overwrought patients often die within days, never even developing the distinctive rash identified with the disease. Twentieth-century studies indicate that such hard-to-diagnose cases are rare. But eyewitness accounts suggest that in historical epidemics, this deadly form of smallpox may have been more common among Native Americans, who frequently died before the telltale skin eruptions appeared.[4]

To judge by the outcome of his illness, George Washington's "pre-eruptive" symptoms were not nearly so grave. The fever usually abates after the first day or two, and many patients rally briefly. Some may be fooled into thinking they have indeed had a mere bout of the flu. But the respite is deceptive, for relief is fleeting. By the fourth day of symptoms, the fever creeps upward again, and the first smallpox sores appear in the mouth, throat, and nasal passages. At this point, the patient is contagious. Susceptible individuals risk their lives if they come near.

The rash now moves quickly. Over a twenty-four-hour period, it extends itself from the mucous membranes to the surface of the skin. On some, it turns inward, hemorrhaging subcutaneously. These victims die early, bleeding from the gums, eyes, nose, and other orifices. In most cases, however, the rash turns outward, covering the victim in raised pustules that concentrate in precisely the places where they will cause the most physical pain and

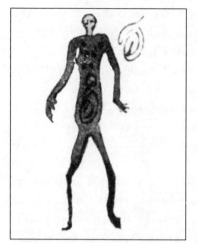 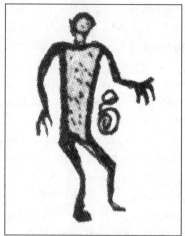

Two images of smallpox from the Sicangu Lakota winter count of Battiste Good. The figures include dots for pustules as well as the spiral symbol for pain—indicated here in the midsection. The image on the left represents the first documented smallpox outbreak on the northern plains in 1734–35. The image on the right represents an outbreak more than a century later, in 1860–61. Garrick Mallery, *Picture-Writing of the American Indians*, Tenth Annual Report of the Bureau of Ethnology to the Secretary of the Smithsonian Institution, 1888–'89 (1893; rpt., New York: Dover, n.d.), 1:300, 325

Smallpox. World Health Organization photograph, National Library of Medicine, Bethesda, Maryland, A014034

psychological anguish: The soles of the feet, the palms of the hands, the face, forearms, neck, and back are focal points of the eruption. Elsewhere, the distribution is lighter.

If the pustules remain discrete—if they do not run together— the prognosis is good. But if they converge upon one another in a single oozing mass, it is not. This is called confluent smallpox, and patients who develop it stand at least a 60 percent chance of dying. For some, as the rash progresses in the mouth and throat, drinking becomes difficult, and dehydration follows. Often, an odor peculiar to smallpox develops. "The small-pox pustules begin to crack run and smell," wrote a Boston physician in 1722. A missionary in Brazil described a "pox so loathsome and evil-smelling that none could stand the great stench" of its victims.[5] Patients at this stage of the disease can be hard to recognize. If damage to the eyes occurs, it begins now. Secondary bacterial infections can also set in, with consequences fully as severe as those of the smallpox.

Scabs start to form after two weeks of suffering, but this does little to end the patient's ordeal. In confluent or semiconfluent cases of the disease, scabbing can encrust most of the body, making any movement excruciating. The Puritan leader William Bradford described this condition among the Narragansett Indians in 1634: "They lye on their hard matts, the poxe breaking and mattering, and runing one into another, their skin cleaving (by reason therof) to the matts they lye on; when they turne them, a whole side will flea of[f] at once." An earlier report from Brazil told of "pox that were so rotten and poisonous that the flesh fell off" the victims "in pieces full of evil-smelling beasties."[6]

Death, when it occurs, usually comes after ten to sixteen days of suffering. Thereafter, the risk drops significantly as fever subsides and unsightly scars replace scabs and pustules. After four weeks of illness, only the lesions encapsulated in the palms of the hands and soles of the feet remain intact. Unlucky sufferers whose feet have hardened from years of walking barefoot sometimes shed the entire sole of the foot at this time, delaying recovery

COMMUNICABILITY	DAY	SYMPTOMS & PATHOGENESIS	
not contagious	1	no symptoms	virus introduced to respiratory tract
	2		
	3		
	4		appears in lymph nodes
	5		
	6		replicates in lymph system
	7		
	8		
	9		
	10		
	11		
contagious	12	first symptoms	fever, backache, headache, nausea, malaise
	13		
	14		
	15	rash	macules
very contagious	16		papules
	17		
	18		
	19		vesicles
	20		
contagious	21		pustules
	22		
	23		
	24		
	25		scabs
scabs contagious	26		
	27		
	28		
	29		
	30		
not contagious	31		scars
	32		

Smallpox: communicability, symptoms, and pathogenesis

considerably. But in most cases, the usual course of the disease—from initial infection to the loss of all scabs—runs a little over a month. Patients remain contagious until the last scab falls off.

Although the timing and progress of George Washington's bout with smallpox appear typical, his infection may have been milder than most. According to one of his biographers, he escaped the disease with "only several very light scars on his nose."[7] Most survivors bear more numerous scars, and some are blinded. But despite the consequences, those who live through the illness can count themselves fortunate. Immune for life, they need never fear smallpox again.

The case fatality rate of a disease is an indication of the number of deaths that occur among those who contract it. For the historical study of smallpox, these figures can be elusive, deceptive, and downright confusing. The reasons are various. For one thing, most twentieth-century surveys included both vaccinated and unvaccinated individuals. Because vaccinated persons tend to have mild forms of the disease if they catch it at all, studies that include them provide no usable comparison to mortality in the days before Edward Jenner's earth-shattering development of 1796. To confuse matters further, a new, much less virulent smallpox virus named *Variola minor* appeared in the 1890s, quickly supplanting *Variola major* in many parts of the world. This milder bug was not present in George Washington's day, and its emergence makes many twentieth-century studies unsuitable for assessing death rates in earlier times.

Given these problems with relatively modern data, one might expect appraisals of epidemics in centuries past to be more helpful in assessing the historical impact of the disease. Unfortunately, this is not the case. In outbreaks of smallpox before the emergence of *Variola minor* and before the development of vaccination, case fatality rates appear to have fluctuated wildly. The differences could be due to the particular vulnerabilities of a given population, the changing virulence of the virus, the availability of nursing care, or even the widespread presence of immune systems compromised by such factors as famine.

Despite these disclaimers and caveats, one historical trend is clearly identifiable in the documentary record. In general, *Variola* appears to have become *more* virulent in the three centuries leading up to 1800. In Florence, Italy, between 1424 and 1458, officials recorded only eighty-four smallpox deaths despite three epidemics of the disease in the same years. In mid-seventeenth-century London, the case fatality rate from *Variola* hovered around 7 percent. A famous outbreak in Boston, Massachusetts, in 1721 yielded a much higher rate of 15 percent. By 1792, in another outbreak in the same city, the rate reached 30 percent. A Scottish smallpox epidemic in 1787 also took the lives of a third of its victims. Just a few years later, a "virgin soil" epidemic—an outbreak in a population with no prior exposure to the disease—struck an isolated village on the Japanese island of Hachijo-Jima. Of the 86 percent of villagers infected, some 38 percent died. Finally, in what may be the only modern study with relevance for epidemics in the pre-Jenner era, an analysis of seven thousand unvaccinated smallpox cases in Madras, India, during the 1960s revealed a frightening case fatality rate of 43 percent.[8]

Another story lies beneath these broad, population-based figures. When attacked by *Variola*, certain individuals consistently fare worse than others. Here two recent studies *are* valuable. They show that the very old and the very young die in disproportionate numbers when smallpox erupts. The highest case fatality rates appear among those under the age of one and over the age of forty-five or fifty. The lowest rates occur in the five- to fourteen-year-old age group. The difference is dramatic: In one study, *Variola* took the lives of 29 percent of its victims under one year old and 32 percent of its victims over forty-five, but among five- to fourteen-year-olds, the case fatality rate was only 8 percent.[9] Although both these studies included vaccinated individuals, there is no reason to think that similar age-related patterns (with higher case fatality rates) would not be detected in a wholly unvaccinated population.

Pregnant women, like infants and the elderly, fare badly under *Variola*'s assault. Here again, modern studies include both vaccinated and unvaccinated individuals. They nevertheless show that the impact of smallpox on pregnancy is dire. Of early-term pregnancies, almost 75 percent end in spontaneous abortions or stillbirths. Of late-term pregnancies, nearly 60 percent terminate in the same way. While some babies are born alive, 55 percent of them die within two weeks, usually within three days of birth. The maternal prognosis is similarly grim. In the prevaccination era, it is likely that half of all pregnant women infected with *Variola* developed what is called hemorrhagic smallpox, the most deadly form of the disease known, with a case fatality rate exceeding 96 percent.[10]

Finally, smallpox sufferers in the throes of famine not surprisingly do worse. Blindness in particular seems more common among malnourished victims, but other complications may occur more frequently as well. Ironically, because scarcity causes people to circulate broadly in their search for food, it may help spread contagious pathogens such as *Variola*. A recent study of America's northern plains Indians indicates that historically, epidemic smallpox often appeared after times of starvation.[11]

Age, pregnancy, and nutritional status all influence the impact of *Variola* on particular individuals. Are these the only variables? Probably not. Entire populations of people seem to die in disproportionate numbers when smallpox strikes. Nowhere has this been more apparent, or more catastrophic, than among Native Americans. For the indigenous residents of the New World, Christopher Columbus's famous voyage of 1492 brought an abrupt end to thousands of years of isolation from the infectious diseases of Europe, Africa, and Asia. No one—not a single individual—had acquired immunity to *Variola* or any other Old World pathogen. Everyone was susceptible.

With its first New World landfall, *Variola* gained access to millions of potential victims with no acquired immunity. It was as though a spark had landed in a forest laden with thousands of years of dried timber. The results were explosive; the consequences, unspeakable. In horrific virgin soil smallpox epidemics, the rate of infection could be higher than 80 percent, and the death tolls ghastly. Eyewitness estimates of mortality in early New World smallpox outbreaks routinely approached and often exceeded 50 percent. "In some provinces half the people died, and in others a little less," wrote a Franciscan friar of an epidemic in Mexico in 1520. William Bradford reported that when *Variola* struck the Indians of the Connecticut River valley in the winter of 1633–34, it caused "such a mortalitie that of a 1000" who contracted the disease, "above 900. and a halfe of them dyed, and many of them did rott above ground for want of buriall."[12] Such numbers point to case fatality rates that far surpassed those found in Old World populations.

Why was case fatality so high among Native Americans? It is possible that in fact it was not. The temptation to overstatement may have proved irresistible for eyewitnesses trying to convey the horror of the nearly universal sickness in virgin soil smallpox epidemics. Yet the consistency of the reports is striking. A fur trader, Samuel Hearne, estimated that the epidemic of 1781 "carried off nine-tenths" of the Chipewyan Indians northwest of Hudson Bay. A North West Company servant charged the same wave of pestilence with "sweeping off three fourths" of the natives on the Canadian plains. In a minor outbreak at Sandusky, Ohio, in 1787, four out of six Indians who caught the smallpox died. Similarly, of a party of forty Indians who visited the Missouri River post of Fort Union during the plains epidemic of 1837, "more than one-half" reportedly died.[13]

These reports are merely representative examples. Though exaggeration no doubt existed, the sheer number of such accounts suggests that the pox was indeed more deadly among Native Americans than among Old World peoples. Some observers even said so directly. "Although many Spaniards die also, smallpox kills incomparably more Indians," wrote a missionary in northern Mexico's Sonoran Desert. A similar report came from Louisiana: "Two distempers, that are not very fatal in other parts of the world, make dreadful ravages among them," wrote a Frenchman of the local natives; "I mean the small-pox and a cold, which baffle all the art of their physicians."[14]

Definitive explanations for *Variola*'s peculiar virulence among Native Americans remain elusive, but historical evidence and modern science both yield clues. As entire Indian communities succumbed to *Variola* in the early epidemics, mortality stemmed not just from the pestilence itself but also from famine and thirst as the raging contagion left no one well enough to care for the ill. Fear justifiably compounded the problem. "They are frightened of going nigh one to another as soon as they take bad," wrote a Hudson's Bay Company trader in 1781. "So the one half for want of indulgencies is starved before they can gather Strength to help themselves." In faraway Baja California, a Dominican friar echoed these words, attributing the high case fatality rate there to factors that included "lack of proper care among the heathen" and a subsequent "lack of food." Victims of later outbreaks reaped a significant benefit from *Variola*'s earlier ravages, for survivors with acquired immunity could tend to their needs as they battled the disease. "Good nursing care," in the words of one distinguished smallpox scholar, "is of far more importance than any other form of treatment."[15] This was always true of the disease.

Native American healing customs may also have exacerbated the effects of *Variola*. "Their injudicious treatment of that infectious malady, generally renders it fatal," wrote an observer in 1784. Perhaps the most universal practice was the sweat bath. "For a relief, in nearly all of their diseases, they resort to their grand remedy, sweating," wrote an observer of the tribes of the northern plains. The English traveler Nicholas Cresswell saw a sweat lodge in use among the Delawares in 1775. The sick Indian, he observed, entered the lodge "wrapped in his Blanket," after which "his friends put in large stones red hot and a pail of water, then make up the door as close as possible." The patient then doused the stones with water, filling the chamber with steam. "He continues in this little hell as long as he is able to bear it," Cresswell explained.[16]

If the heat of the sweat bath worsened the effect of smallpox's fever, what followed could have even more serious consequences: "Whilst reeking with sweat, and dissolving in streams of warm moisture, they rush out into the open air, quite naked, and suddenly plunge into the deepest and coldest stream of running water that can be found, immersing their whole body in the chilling flood." A Salish Indian woman named Mourning Dove described the results of this practice as she recounted her grandmother's story of the first smallpox outbreaks in the American Northwest. "Some tried to use the sweat lodge, but when they jumped into cold water after sweating, they got worse and died faster," she explained. If the victim was too weak to swim, drowning could result. Contemporary accounts often reported drownings among Indians who sought relief from the heat of the pox in the cooling waters of lakes and streams. "The unfortunate Indians, when in the height of the fever, would plunge into a river, which generally caused instant death," remarked one fur trader.[17]

Jumping into cold water while desperately ill was indeed a dangerous practice. But despite the gibes of literate observers, it must be said that in many ways native medical care differed little from that of European colonists. "The Indian, when he falls ill, has recourse first to his roots and sacredly regarded herbs; he purges and sweats inordinately; fasts for days together," wrote J. D. Schöpf. So too did colonists utilize sweating, fasting, bleeding, blistering, vomiting, and an array of medicines that ranged from mercury to laxatives to human excrement itself.[18] It is possible that the difference was one of degree, expressed in Schöpf's use of the word "inordinately" in his litany of Indian cures.

Beyond issues of care and custom, genetic factors may also have contributed to the demographic catastrophe that resulted from the arrival of *Variola* and other Old World microbes in the

Americas. Some have speculated that thousands of years of isolation from the plagues of Europe, Africa, and Asia meant that Native Americans were not genetically selected to survive infections
such as smallpox.[19] Instead, evolution would have favored traits
that enhanced life in the relatively disease-free New World environment. Amerindians therefore may lack what is known as innate
immunity to smallpox. Innate immunity, as opposed to acquired
immunity, encompasses a broad array of mechanisms the body can
use to fend off disease. Examples include not only the receptors
of certain immune cells but also such traits as blood type, stomach
acidity, and mucus in the respiratory system, all of which influence
the body's vulnerability to various pathogens. As a barrier to infection, even the skin itself can be part of one's innate immunity.[20] It
is not likely, however, that we shall ever learn the precise ways in
which these mechanisms dealt with *Variola*. Today, there are neither medical nor moral reasons to conduct human studies with the
virus.

In fact, research now points in a different, although related, direction. Medical tests show that when Native American peoples
are exposed to most pathogens, their immune response is fully as
robust as that of other populations. "In no instance was the level
of induced antibody inferior to that usually observed elsewhere,"
wrote the epidemiologist Francis L. Black after measuring the immune response of several Amazonian tribes.[21] Upon initial exposure to a given microbe, a New World native probably has as good
a chance of survival as a European, an African, or an Asian.

All this changes once the bug starts circulating. Studies indicate that compared with Old World populations, indigenous
Americans possess little diversity in immune system antigens. In
other words, despite a healthy, vigorous response, the immune
systems of American Indians are strikingly similar to one another.
This homogeneity may make indigenous Americans more vulnerable when contagion strikes. Studies of measles in Old World populations indicate that the disease is much more virulent when
transmitted by a consanguineous family member than when trans-

mitted by an unrelated person. Mortality nearly doubles when the measles virus passes between cousins and nearly quadruples when passed between siblings. This occurs because measles and other viruses mutate constantly, adjusting quickly to the immune systems of individual hosts. When the contagion passes from one family member to another, much of the adaptive work is already done. The virus is tailor-made for attacking the unlucky victim.[22]

The implications for indigenous Americans may well have been profound. The immune system antigens found in Native American populations are so homogeneous that in the case of measles, transmission of the virus between two random individuals in a New World population is comparable to transmission between family members in an Old World population. Historically, as measles made its way through a community, American Indians may well have confronted a virus uniquely equipped to circumvent their immune systems.[23] Small wonder that the results were so dramatic.

Granted, smallpox is not measles. Yet it is probable that a similar process of mutation and transmission occurred not just with smallpox and other viruses but to a limited extent even with bacteria.[24] Thanks to the eradication of smallpox from the world, it is not likely that we shall ever know precisely how *Variola* adapted to its genetically similar New World hosts. But anecdotal accounts indicate that the adaptation may have been successful indeed for the virus. As it stands, immune system uniformity is one of the best explanations to date for the extraordinarily high case fatality rates among American Indians in successive waves of smallpox. The years to come may yield added insights into this phenomenon, as medical science is only beginning to appreciate the significance of genetic diversity in fending off infectious disease.

Regardless of genetics, the most important single determinant of vulnerability to smallpox was prior exposure. In the towns and cities of England, smallpox was endemic—that is, constantly present—by the middle of the eighteenth century. This meant that exposure to *Variola* was likely early in life, and as a result, immunity prevailed among grownups. Even in rural market towns where the pox was not endemic, outbreaks tended to occur in five-year cycles. Here too, immunity was common by adulthood.[25] It is probable, if not inevitable, that similar patterns existed throughout Europe.

In America, by contrast, neither smallpox nor immunity was nearly so widespread. By the time musket fire marked the historic turn of events at Lexington and Concord, *Variola* had been present in North America for more than two and a half centuries. One scholar has counted twenty-three separate smallpox epidemics of varied extent and impact that left their mark on Indian groups ranging from the Coahuiltecans of Texas to the Montagnais-Naskapis of Quebec and Labrador. At times the pestilence affected colonists as well as Indians. By the late eighteenth century, only western Canada, Alaska, and Alta (upper) California appear to have escaped the pox entirely, and even in these regions, early episodes may simply have escaped documentation.[26]

Despite their impressive number and extent, these early American epidemics do not mean that either smallpox or immunity was common. They were not. *Variola* needs an endless train of new victims to survive. In eighteenth-century Europe, these victims became available thanks to closely packed cities, immigration, natural increase, and rapid communication between regions. But eighteenth-century North America was different. It had neither the population density nor the transportation networks needed to sustain the ongoing, endemic presence of the virus. The result was that years could pass between outbreaks, allowing the number of susceptibles to balloon as native-born Americans across the continent came of age without exposure to the virus. When epidemics then occurred, they could be catastrophic, affecting grownups as well as children and crippling entire communities.

Because smallpox leaves not just death but also immunity in

its wake, prior outbreaks influence the shape of those that follow. For Americans on the eve of the Revolutionary War, the most recent epidemics had occurred in the late 1750s and early 1760s, often in association with military campaigns. In New York, eastern Canada, and the Great Lakes region, many Indian allies of New France had caught smallpox during the Seven Years' War. Many others had suffered from it in 1763, in the Ohio country, where British soldiers tried to spread the disease among their enemies during Pontiac's Revolt. In the South, *Variola* had infected Indians involved in the Cherokee War of 1759, and during 1760 it spread not just to the Cherokees' neighbors the Catawbas and Creeks but also to the white and black colonists of South Carolina and Georgia. Mexico likewise had endured a serious outbreak in 1761–63 that extended from the central highlands into Baja California and northern Sonora. In western Texas, smallpox had struck the Lipan Apaches in 1764, and in the lower Mississippi Valley, it struck the Chickasaws and Choctaws at approximately the same time. Finally, the cities of Philadelphia and Boston had also witnessed epidemics in this period.[27] All these smallpox outbreaks left pockets of immunity behind.

Prior epidemics were not the only influence on patterns of susceptibility and immunity. By the mid-eighteenth century, many Americans had learned ways to control the pox's spread. This was particularly true in the English colonies, where smallpox was probably better understood than any infectious disease other than syphilis. For Anglo-Americans who wanted to protect themselves against *Variola* then, two options existed: isolation or inoculation. Each had risks, and each had advantages. Both were used regularly and at times effectively. Both also revealed that while no one had yet viewed a virus through a microscope, the contagious nature of smallpox was widely understood.

In theory, isolation was simple. It meant preventing contact between susceptible individuals and the *Variola* virus. One way of doing this was quarantine. Even though they often attributed epidemic disease to supernatural intervention, Americans of all stripes did not hesitate to impose quarantine when smallpox broke out. "Whoever is accidently attacked by the small-pox," wrote a French traveler through eighteenth-century Virginia, "is carried to a lonely house in the middle of the woods and there he receives medical assistance." Infected towns, he explained, were likewise "cut off from all communication with the rest of the country." The Puritan settlers of the Massachusetts Bay Colony had implemented quarantine as early as 1647 in an attempt to keep ships arriving from Barbados from spreading disease. Later, the provincial assembly passed "An Act to Prevent Persons from Concealing the Small Pox," which ordered that a red warning flag be flown outside any infected household. A South Carolina ordinance called for sentinels outside pox-infested homes and required householders to post notices to warn susceptible citizens. In Virginia, guards turned people away from infected residences in both Williamsburg and Winchester. Rhode Island colonists, who condemned smallpox as "a contagious and most dirty disease," set up quarantine at "Pest, or Smallpox Island" (now Coasters Harbor Island) off Newport. Similarly, South Carolina officials established a "Pest House" on Sullivans Island to quarantine occupants of incoming ships, particularly those carrying slaves from West Africa. By the late 1700s, Pennsylvania stood out as the only English colony that did not enforce local quarantine laws.[28]

English colonists were not the only Americans to impose quarantines. Devastated by successive epidemics since the sixteenth century, some Indian groups also utilized the practice, indicating that they too recognized the pox's infectious nature. In 1759 and 1760, when *Variola* struck the inhabitants of the "lower" Cherokee town of Keowee, their kinsfolk in the "upper" towns implemented a quarantine to keep the contagion at bay. "The People of the Upper Towns are in such Dread of the Infection," reported a Georgia correspondent for the *Pennsylvania Gazette*, "that they will not allow a single Person from the above named Places to come amongst them."[29]

Another isolation strategy was flight. It lacked the organization and state sanction of quarantine, but it too represented an effort to keep susceptible and sick people apart. Wherever smallpox broke out, vulnerable individuals took to their heels in the hope of avoiding it. In South Carolina in 1698 and 1699, the pox reduced one band of Indians "to 5 or 6 which ran away and left their dead unburied." During Boston's horrible epidemic of 1721, some 900 of the town's 10,700 citizens took to the countryside. When the disease struck again a generation later, nearly 2,000 out of 15,000 fled. Many Cherokee Indians did the same during the 1759–60 outbreak at Keowee, whence it was reported that those who had "not yet had that Distemper, were gone to the Woods."[30]

The strategy of isolation, especially by running off, had risks. The greatest was that by fleeing, fugitives from the pestilence would in fact spread it. Because of smallpox's asymptomatic incubation period, infected individuals could easily escape with others, not knowing they already carried the plague. When South Carolina's Keowee Cherokees took to the woods, they "carried smallpox into the Middle Settlement and Valley," where they infected others in their tribe. Likewise, refugees from Boston in 1751 may have started the outbreaks that afflicted Concord and other outlying towns.[31] In all, flight may have done more to spread smallpox than to prevent it.

The other drawback to the strategy of isolation, whether by quarantine or by flight, was quite simply that it did nothing to address the issue of susceptibility. Those who successfully dodged one outbreak remained vulnerable when the next one struck. In the busy world of the late eighteenth century, marked by an expansion of commerce among communities around the globe, chance encounters with the *Variola* virus were increasingly likely. Continued susceptibility to smallpox meant living a life of incessant dread.

Inoculation offered the risky alternative to a life of fear. Utilized for hundreds of years in parts of Asia and Africa, the procedure was nevertheless unknown among Europeans until the early eighteenth century. Shortly after 1700, word of the practice reached Europe from a number of sources. One was the Puritan minister Cotton Mather. In a famous letter from Boston in 1716, Mather described to his London colleagues an interview he had conducted with his "Coromantee" slave, Onesimus. The cleric had asked the African whether he had ever had smallpox. "*Yes*, and, *No*," came the response, and Onesimus proceeded to tell Mather "that he had undergone an Operation, which had given him something of yᵉ *Small-Pox*, & would forever præserve him from it." Simultaneously, other accounts of this peculiar practice were arriving in Europe from Asia, as travelers abroad sent word of it home. The most famous of these correspondents was Mary Wortley Montagu, who observed inoculation in Constantinople, where her husband was the British ambassador. "The small-pox, so fatal, and so general amongst us," she wrote to a friend in 1717, "is here entirely harmless, by the invention of *ingrafting*." [32]

The procedure, both frightening and fascinating, consisted of deliberately implanting live *Variola* in an incision, usually on the patient's hand or arm. The result of this inoculation (also called variolation) was predictable: After an abbreviated incubation period, smallpox ensued. But the symptoms were surprising. Patients who took the virus by inoculation had fewer pustules, less scarring, and a much-reduced case fatality rate compared with other victims of *Variola*. Why? By the late eighteenth century, a partial explanation could be found in some inoculators' deliberate efforts to derive their infectious matter from less severe cases. But this was not always the practice, and for the most part, the lighter symptoms of inoculated smallpox have yet to be fully explained.* Regardless of the reasons, the reward was enormous: Inoculees, like others who survived smallpox, acquired immunity for life.

While inoculation and variolation refer to essentially the same thing, neither should be confused with vaccination, introduced to

_____

*It cannot simply have been that the virus was introduced through the skin rather than the usual respiratory route. In Asia, variolation was accomplished by inhaling ground scab material through the nose, apparently with the same mild effects.

the world by Edward Jenner in *An Inquiry into the Causes and Effects of the Variolae Vaccinae*, published in 1798. In Jenner's now-famous experiment of 1796, the English physician deliberately infected an eight-year-old boy, James Phipps, with cowpox, a much milder disease that was closely related to smallpox. Several months later, Jenner inoculated Phipps with smallpox and found that he could not produce an infection. Thanks to his exposure to cowpox, the boy was immune. It was, in the words of one historian, "as if an Angel's trumpet had sounded over the earth."[33] Unlike variolation, vaccination did not oblige patients to endure an actual case of smallpox to acquire immunity. But in George Washington's day, vaccination was not an option. Jenner's tract on the subject appeared in print only a year before Washington died. Throughout the eighteenth century, Americans seeking immunity to *Variola* had only two choices: to contract the disease naturally or to contract it by inoculation. Either one meant going through smallpox.

Inoculation was risky business, and many did die from the illness they inevitably (and necessarily) contracted through the procedure. But in the midst of a severe epidemic, the hazards of variolation paled by comparison to the hazards of catching the disease naturally. When Cotton Mather convinced Zabdiel Boylston to try the operation during Boston's 1721 outbreak, death from naturally contracted smallpox occurred in 15 percent of cases, while death from inoculated smallpox occurred in only 2 percent of cases.[34] Smallpox "received by Inoculation," an opponent of the experiment later admitted, "is not so fatal, and the Symptoms frequently more mild, than in the accidental Contagion."[35]

The procedure was grueling despite its promising results. It began with a dietary regimen that many practitioners imposed on patients before the operation took place. The experience of the Massachusetts patriot John Adams was typical. In 1764, when another in a series of epidemics struck Boston, Adams decided to undergo inoculation rather than chance natural infection. Several doctors, including the radical Dr. Joseph Warren, attended Adams and his brother. They "prepared me, by a milk Diet and a Course of Mercurial Preparations, till they reduced me very low," Adams wrote later. In good spirits nevertheless, the two brothers took regular "Vomits," stimulated by syrup of ipecac. "Did you ever see two Persons in one Room Iphichacuana'd together?" John wrote to his wife-to-be, Abigail. "I assure you they make merry Diversion. We took turns to be sick and to laugh. When my Companion was sick I laughed at him, and when I was sick he laughed at me."[36] Ingestion of milk and mercury continued apace, Adams said. It "salivated" him "to such a degree" that he soon suffered from classic signs of mercury poisoning: "Every tooth in my head became so loose that I believe I could have pulled them all with my Thumb and finger." Other food was closely regulated. For breakfast the doctors allowed "Pottage without salt, or Spice or Butter," and they enforced "abstinence from all, but the cool and the soft."[37]

After a week of preparation, the inoculation took place. "Dr. Perkins demanded my left Arm and Dr. Warren my Brothers," John reported. "They took their Launcetts and with their Points divided the skin for about a Quarter of an Inch and just suffering the Blood to appear, buried a Thread . . . in the Channell."[38] The thread bore on it the *Variola* virus, collected from the pustules of an earlier victim.

Adams took his inoculation in a house with nine others undergoing the procedure under the care of different doctors. While he and his brother could eat "as much Bread and as much new pure Milk, as much Pudding, and Rice, and indeed as much of every Thing of the farinaceous Kind as We please," the others faced many more restrictions. "No Bread, No Pudding, No Milk is permitted them," Adams wrote, noting that only "a Mixture of Half Milk and Half Water" was allowed. Beyond this, he said, "every other Day they are tortured with Powders that make them as sick as Death and as weak as Water."[39] The effect of this nutritional regimen (not to mention mercury poisoning) on the outcome of inoculated smallpox remains unknown. But given the general correlation of malnutrition and poor outcomes in modern cases of the disease, it was most likely negative.

When the incubation period had run its course and Adams finally broke out in the smallpox, his letters to Abigail virtually ceased. He had an "Absolute Fear," he told her, of sending "Paper from this House, so much infected as it is, to any Person lyable to take the Distemper but especially to you."[40] Despite his light symptoms, the rigors of smallpox must also have constrained him from writing, just as it had constrained George Washington a dozen years before. Few were the writers who kept to their routine through the discomfort of smallpox, even in mild cases taken by inoculation.

Once he had emerged from the worst of it, Adams wrote that he had suffered little, especially compared with others in the house: "None of the Race of Adam, ever passed the small Pox, with fewer Pains, Achs, Qualms . . . than I have done." In fact, he bragged, he only had eight or ten pockmarks to show for the ordeal. Not all were so lucky. "Pretty high Fevers, and severe Pains, and a pretty Plentiful Eruption has been the Portion of Three at least of our Companions," he told Abigail. In spite of his own good fortune, he gave her a stern warning: "Don't conclude from any Thing I have written that I think Inoculation a light matter."[41] Abigail did not undergo variolation herself until 1776.

The twelve years that separated John's and Abigail's inoculations saw notable advancement in the procedure. In England, the inoculator Robert Sutton and his sons worked through the 1760s toward a new, modified technique that became known as the Suttonian method. Under the Suttons' influence, the grueling preparatory regimen first waned and then disappeared entirely. Deep incisions also fell by the wayside as the Suttons found that shallow ones yielded good results with fewer complications. In addition, following a technique practiced in South Carolina as early as 1738, the Suttons acquired their infectious matter from another inoculee, not from a victim of the natural smallpox. Finally, while acknowledging that inoculees required "air," the Suttons insisted that they seek it in private, quarantined from the community at large.[42]

Because of the profits to be made, the Suttons for years tried to keep their methods concealed. Not until 1796 did Daniel Sutton, one of Robert's six sons, publish *The Inoculator; or, Suttonian System of Inoculation.* Fortunately, those they trained were not so secretive. As early as 1767 Thomas Dimsdale published a tract in London outlining the basics of the modified technique. A New York publisher reprinted it in 1771, and word of Dimsdale's improved procedure, basically the same as the Suttons', spread gradually through the English colonies. By July 1776, when Abigail Adams and her children went through inoculation in Boston, some of the changes were already evident. "I now date from Boston" she wrote to her husband, "where I yesterday arrived and was with all 4 of our Little ones innoculated for the small pox."[43] She mentioned no milk diet, no mercury, no preparations whatsoever.*

Controversy attended inoculation from the start. When Cotton Mather supported Dr. Zabdiel Boylston's experiments in Boston in 1721, the result was uproar and shock. Was it not, asked one minister, "a distrust of God's overruling care" to inoculate? Dr. William Douglass (who later had a change of heart) reckoned it a sin "to propagate infection by this means." The furor culminated in the firebombing of Mather's house on November 13, 1721. "COTTON MATHER, *You Dog, Dam you,*" said the note attached to the bomb: "*I'l inoculate you with this, with a Pox to you.*"[44] Regardless of God's will, critics of inoculation had legitimate cause for concern. The practice might impart immunity to those who went through it, but it could also spread the disease and spark new epidemics. While sick, inoculees were active carriers of *Variola.* They

---

*In a letter of July 21, Abigail Adams did say that "Mr. Cranch," who was undergoing inoculation at the same time, had "passed thro the preparation."

were capable of infecting others until the last scab fell off, and they often showed little regard for the contagious nature of the disease or for those they put at risk. Five days after her inoculation on July 12, 1776, Abigail Adams attended "a very Good Sermon" and "went with the Multitude into Kings Street to hear the proclamation for Independence read and proclamed."[45] When she began experiencing the "many dissagreable Sensations" of the pox three days later, she nevertheless went "out to meeting" yet again. In early August, still under inoculation, she proclaimed proudly: "I have attended publick worship constantly, except one day and a half ever since I have been in Town."[46]

Such conduct did not stem from ignorance of the pox's contagious character. A few months earlier, "fearfull of the small pox," Abigail Adams had avoided traveling into Boston from Braintree.[47] She had used smoke to sterilize the letters she received from her husband-to-be while he went through variolation in 1764. Indeed, this was the very woman whose future husband had avoided even letter writing at the height of his own infection for fear of contaminating her. Abigail Adams did not know about viruses or the way they worked, but like most colonists, she was clearly aware that smallpox was contagious.

In fairness it should be said that there is no evidence that she infected anyone as a result of her actions. Nor can it be said that her behavior was unusual. As early as 1722 and 1723, colonial observers noted that many patients under inoculation continued "to do all Things, as at other times." Among bedridden inoculees, visitors were common: "Ordinarily the Patient sits up every Day, and entertains his Friends, yea ventures upon a Glass of Wine with them." Even if these callers were themselves immune, they could carry active viral particles into the streets when they left. The Boston doctor James Thacher was no more responsible than Abigail Adams when he had himself inoculated during the very same outbreak that prompted her to go through the procedure. "I . . . have passed through the disease in the most favorable manner," he wrote in his journal, "not suffering one day's confinement."[48]

As a medical man he certainly knew what the consequences of not "confining" himself could be.

Not surprisingly, it was largely for fear of contagion that inoculation often elicited protest and apprehension. In 1767, when the inoculator John Smith set up shop in Yorktown, Virginia, some residents objected "to his bringing the Infection into a Country or Neighbourhood that is free from it." He brought with him contagious "matter enough to infect the world," and Virginians feared he might open "A second Pandora's Box." It took less than a year to confirm their fears. "Mr. John Smith hath rendered himself very blamable," wrote William Nelson in February 1768, by "suffering some of his Patients to go abroad too soon: so that the Distemper hath spread in two or three Parts of the Country." Among those released prematurely were some college students who carried the smallpox to Williamsburg, where it proved to be a most dangerous strain. Of those who caught it, Nelson said, "two out of three have died." Only "the Care of the Magistrates" brought the epidemic to a halt.[49]

It was cases like this that so frequently made inoculation unpopular in the English colonies. Riots and other crowd actions characterized much of the Anglo-American political scene from the 1760s until well after the Revolutionary War. Although the protests usually targeted royal authority, they also struck at inoculation hospitals when public health seemed threatened. Even as John Smith set up his ill-fated inoculation business at Yorktown, riots broke out over a similar venture in nearby Norfolk. There, despite local objections, two doctors, John Dalgleish and Archibald Campbell, had begun inoculating patients at Campbell's home. When they refused to desist, an angry crowd torched the house and forced the patients within to flee in a downpour of rain. Massachusetts colonists likewise took matters into their own hands when they felt threatened by variolation. After inoculation hospitals opened in Salem and Marblehead in 1774, rioting residents razed one institution and closed both. They also tarred and feathered four Salem men caught stealing clothes that had been hanging outside one hospital, clothes that might well have contaminated the community.[50]

Because the practice was so controversial, inoculation often came under legal restriction. In response to the Williamsburg outbreak of 1768, the Virginia legislature received numerous petitions "setting forth the destructive Tendency of Inoculation with the Small-Pox; and therefore praying that no such Practices may be allowed in Virginia." While the House of Burgesses never banned inoculation entirely, the regulations it imposed in 1770 were so restrictive that the effect was nearly the same. In Charleston, the first inoculation control law came in 1738, when the city passed "An Act for the better preventing of the spreading of the infection of the Small Pox." The ordinance imposed a hefty fine of five hundred pounds on anyone giving or receiving inoculation within two miles of the city. New York followed suit in 1747, with an executive proclamation "strictly prohibiting and forbidding all and every of the Doctors, Physicians, Surgeons, and Practitioners of Physick, and all and every other persons within this Province, to inoculate for small pox any persons or person within the City and County of New York, on pain of being prosecuted to the utmost rigour of the law."[51]

Nowhere was inoculation more restricted and unpopular than in New England. Most New England cities imposed very strict quarantines and banned all smallpox inoculation except when epidemics broke out. Some years after the American Revolution, the physician Benjamin Waterhouse wondered at the restrictions New Englanders had tolerated in order to avoid infection from smallpox. "New England," he wrote, was "the most democratical region on the face of the earth," yet the people there had "voluntarily submitted to more restrictions and abridgments of liberty, to secure themselves against that terrific scourge, than any absolute monarch could have enforced."[52]

By contrast, regulations were lax in the middle colonies, where exposure and immunity to *Variola* were common. Perhaps this was due in part to the large proportion of foreign-born settlers in the region, many of whom had had smallpox as children. With less to fear from the disease, residents of the middle colonies seemed downright cavalier in their attitudes. In Pennsylvania, officials rarely enforced the province's lone quarantine statute, and only once did they enforce it against smallpox. Inoculation hospitals flourished not only here but also in Maryland, New Jersey, New York, and even Connecticut. Statutory restrictions in New England and the South meant that elsewhere, variolation could be a profitable business affair. Enterprising physicians from the middle colonies cast their nets broadly in the quest for patrons from regions where the procedure was banned. In 1769, a Baltimore inoculator named Henry Stevenson ran an advertisement in Rind's *Virginia Gazette* promising that clients would be "carefully and tenderly dealt with" and extending reduced prices to slaveowners seeking to have their black laborers immunized. (Cut-rate prices very likely meant cut-rate care.) Other inoculators from the middle colonies ran similar ads in the Virginia papers, "knowing," in the words of one, "that the legislature of your Colony have prohibited Inoculation."[53]

In New England, contingents of wealthy friends traveled to the middle colonies together to undergo the procedure in "classes." So lucrative was the practice that when some Rhode Island residents sought to establish an inoculation hospital in 1763, they cited among other reasons the "Large Sums of Gold and Silver Money" that would be "Saved and Kept within the Colony." When New Yorkers got wind of the plan, they worried that it would "stop one Source of Profit to this City and East Jersey, whereto Numbers are constantly resorting from the above mentioned Colony."[54]

Despite variolation's growing visibility in the English colonies, the operation nevertheless remained inaccessible to most North Americans in the late eighteenth century. There were several reasons for this. Obviously, some people lived in colonies where inoculation was banned. But in any case, settlers in the English colonies represented only one portion of North America's vast human population. Even by the time of the Revolutionary War, most Americans, including Indians across the continent and nearly everyone in New Spain, still had not heard of inoculation. It is likely that African slaves in the Spanish colonies, like Onesimus in New England, had some knowledge of the procedure, but if they utilized it among themselves before 1779, it probably went unrecorded. Variolation did not see common use in Spain until the 1770s, and there is no known evidence of the practice in Spain's North American empire prior to 1779. In Canada, inoculation appears to have won more widespread acceptance—probably because of its gradual implementation in France in the 1750s and 1760s.[55] Still, the extent of variolation in the former French colony should not be exaggerated. It was very likely an urban phenomenon.

Economics imposed limits on the accessibility of inoculation. Even where the practice was known and permitted, price placed it beyond the reach of most Americans. One inoculator in an unnamed locale charged two pounds per person for the procedure in 1764. In Philadelphia, the fee was around three pounds. At the short-lived hospital off Marblehead, Massachusetts, it was a whopping five pounds, fifteen shillings. These sums are huge—the equivalent of hundreds of dollars today—but in the midst of an epidemic they may have been even higher. Accusations of price gouging were not unknown.[56] Benjamin Franklin, a staunch advocate of inoculation, recognized that cost was an enormous obstacle for most people. "The *expence* of having the operation perform'd by a Surgeon," he wrote, "has been pretty high in some parts of *America*." For a tradesman with a large family, "it amounts to more money than he can well spare." The time requirement was likewise prohibitive. Neither artisans nor the working poor could afford three to four weeks away from their families and labors. Thus it is hardly surprising that in 1774, when smallpox spread through Philadelphia and claimed the lives of some three hundred souls, "the chief of them were the children of poor People."[57]

These economic constraints go far to explain the public outcry and crowd actions against inoculation. For the well-to-do, the operation represented a chance to avoid the dangers of smallpox caught in the "natural" way. But for those who could not afford it, variolation put them at greater risk than before, since wealthy individuals, such as Abigail Adams, might expose them to the disease while undergoing the procedure. Thus it was often affluent Americans who championed inoculation and laboring Americans who fought against it. The opposition point of view can be easily misunderstood. It stemmed not from "fear and superstition," as one historian has suggested, but from a realistic appraisal of working-class risks and opportunities.[58]

The introduction of Suttonian inoculation in the 1760s dropped the price somewhat and made the procedure a little more accessible. In addition, poor and working people sometimes gained access to variolation in crisis situations. During the Boston outbreak of 1764, for example, at least five hundred of Boston's poor eventually received inoculation for free. Likewise, during the 1774 epidemic in Philadelphia, a group of twelve well-to-do citizens established a Society for Inoculating the Poor.[59] But for the most part, the practice remained too expensive and too time-consuming for common folk to afford. Immunity thus tended to concentrate in the upper classes, for whom variolation was an established and affordable protocol. When an epidemic broke out in the English colonies, its victims were most likely to be the uninoculated, nonimmune poor.

By July 1775, when Washington surveyed the Continental troops arrayed before Boston for the first time, a complicated patchwork of immunity and susceptibility had emerged across North America. *Variola*'s ravages in the early 1760s meant that people living in New Spain and in the East were the likeliest to have acquired immunity from prior exposure. Yet even in these regions, susceptible individuals were in the clear majority. Among the indigenous peoples living west of the Mississippi and north of New Mexico, immunity (like smallpox itself) was practically unheard of.

Other immunological trends can also be discerned. Because importations of *Variola* were more frequent in bustling seaports and commercial hubs, acquired immunity was more common among city dwellers than among country folk. Similarly, thanks to the availability of inoculation, denizens of the middle colonies were less likely to be vulnerable than residents of New England or the South. Inoculation had the additional effect of concentrating immunity among the well-to-do. Even age could make a difference, for older people stood a better chance of having lived through the disease than their younger neighbors and kin. Finally, Native Americans, like anyone else, won immunity if they survived *Variola*'s ravages, but they appear to have suffered extraordinarily high case fatality rates when the virus struck.

The New Englanders of Washington's army at Boston were only one piece of this elaborate patchwork, but most of them were vulnerable. As the commander in chief contemplated the danger posed by the smallpox now spreading through the besieged city, he must have thought back to his own youthful encounter with the disease. He knew all too well that it incapacitated its victims and often killed them. If *Variola* got loose, the impact on the Continental forces could be devastating. The storm clouds building over Boston that summer signaled the onset not just of war but of pestilence.

VIGILANCE

April 19, 1775. *The word spread like wildfire: British troops had fired on American militiamen at Lexington and Concord. The redcoats were besieged in Boston. Men were needed to keep them there.*

In Bedford, New Hampshire, less than sixty miles away, the news arrived the very night of the battles. There, as in hundreds of other New England towns, hasty meetings convened and men gathered arms. The next day, according to the diarist Matthew Patten, twenty men from Bedford marched "Directly off from the Meeting house" to assist the American rebels. Others, like Patten's son John, determined "to Sett off for our army" the following morning. "Our Girls sit up all night bakeing bread and fitting things for him," his father wrote. The scene repeated itself across New England, as men, eager to defend their rights and test their military mettle, flocked to the American lines.

The men were volunteers. Hard experience with the British had taught them that professional standing armies with long tours of duty enslaved both soldiers and civilians. Thus in this first phase of the Revolutionary War, enlistments were short, and soldiers at times seemed to come and go as they pleased. On May 1, just ten days after he had departed for the patriot lines outside Boston, John Patten returned home to Bedford for the first time. The visit appears to have been brief. He was back with the army by June 17, for on that day he was shot in the arm at the Battle of Bunker

Hill. He soon came home on furlough, perhaps because of his wound. Then, on July 5, he was off to Boston once more.

Even while away, Patten stayed in close touch with his family. In September, he sent some rice home by way of a traveler going toward Bedford. Likewise, as the weather turned cool in October, his parents sent him some much-needed winter clothing via a neighbor headed for the army. Patten probably returned home soon thereafter. We know this not because his father mentioned his arrival but because on December 9, 1775, he noted that John had "set off for the Army" yet again. The young soldier may well have been responding to a new call for two thousand men to strengthen the American lines around Boston.

John Patten returned home for the last time on March 2, 1776. He did not stay for long. Some of his neighbors had long since marched off to Quebec in a daring military attempt to add a fourteenth colony to the mounting rebellion against Britain. But by early 1776, the Canadian campaign was faltering, and appeals for reinforcements for the Northern Army were ceaseless. Sometime in March or early April—the date is not clear—twenty-three-year-old John Patten trekked northward to take his place alongside his fellows.

John Patten typified the Continental soldier caught up by the rage militaire *early in the Revolutionary War: He was a rural New Englander. He was a volunteer. He signed up for short tours of duty. But Patten was typical in another way as well. Like most others in the newly formed Continental army, he had never had smallpox. The campaign against Canada would be the last military adventure of John Patten's young life.*[1]

As John Patten and his companions consolidated their siege of Boston in July 1775, no one, not even George Washington, could have known what a significant problem smallpox would become. The war had barely begun. Congress had yet to declare independence from Britain. Most people assumed that some sort of reconciliation was imminent. But over the course of the next year, the conflict escalated. Armies were formed. Meetings were held. People gathered and dispersed repeatedly. When they did so, they carried plans, news, and information from one place to another. They also carried microbes. It is no coincidence that smallpox and independence fever erupted together or that contemporaries wrote of republicanism itself spreading "l[i]ke a Contagion, into all the other colonies."[2] For a virus that needs a constant supply of new, unexposed human beings to thrive, conditions were perfect.

From July 1775 to July 1776, Washington's first year as commander in chief, *Variola* intervened implacably in the opening hostilities of the Revolutionary War. It seemed to be everywhere. In Massachusetts during the siege of Boston, in Virginia during the mobilization of Lord Dunmore's Ethiopian Regiment, and in Canada during the siege of Quebec, smallpox wreaked havoc as people and microbes came together in explosive combinations. By the time bells pealed in Philadelphia to announce independence on July 4, 1776, the pox had emerged as a distinctly American affliction. All the evidence indicated that it could bring the Continental army to its knees.

The first ominous cases of smallpox had shown up in Boston and outlying towns in 1774, just as Britain's Parliament passed a series of Coercive Acts intended to chastise the American colonies, particularly Massachusetts, for a decade of escalating protest. The northerly town of Ipswich had proclaimed a fast "on account of small-pox" as early as February 1774. By December, Cambridge and Charlestown had reported incidents of the disease, and Boston was also infected. The new year saw no change: Smallpox continued its gradual but inexorable spread as the political insurrection mounted. Roxbury, Cambridge, and Mendon all felt the disease's impact in the early months of 1775.[3] Finally, the military deadlock that emerged from the battles of Lexington and Concord trapped at least thirteen thousand residents in the town of Boston.

Landfill has today rendered Boston's eighteenth-century contours unrecognizable. The city now sprawls along a man-made shoreline that funnels the Charles River efficiently into Massachusetts Bay. But in 1775, Boston was a peninsular harbor town, situated at the end of a spit that extended into the bay like a short-handled spoon. Only a narrow neck of land connected the city to the mainland; without it, Boston would have been an island. With the siege under way, American troops blockaded the neck and dug in on the heights encircling the harbor to make sure that British troops made no further sallies. Within the city proper, Tory patrols scoured the streets and docks day and night, making flight impossible for Whig sympathizers. It was a standoff. Bostonians were trapped, with nowhere to go and nowhere to hide. As time passed, hunger and filth heightened vulnerability and made the transmission of *Variola* more and more likely.

For much of the summer of 1775, smallpox festered in the besieged city. According to a civilian who escaped on July 10, the population was "very sickly: from ten to thirty funerals a day, but no bells allowed to toll."[4] The citizens of Boston, like their countrymen who invested them, were primarily New Englanders. Few had acquired immunity to the *Variola* virus. This was an immunological vulnerability that translated into misery within Boston. But for the Continental army, it translated into a military weakness that posed a thorny dilemma for George Washington. Epidemic smallpox, he knew, might be highly dangerous if it gained a foothold in his crowded camps. But inoculation also posed problems. Doing it piecemeal would take months, and if just one inoculee was released too early—if the virus escaped quarantine—a full-blown epidemic could result. By the same token, inoculating the whole army at once would incapacitate so many men that the British might well seize the opportunity to attack.

In the end, Washington decided that variolation was simply too risky. Instead, prevention was the order of the day. Anyone even suspected of carrying smallpox had to be kept from the American lines until the danger of infection had past. Civilians with symptoms faced quarantine in the town of Brookline. Military cases went to a smallpox hospital established at Fresh Pond near Cambridge, where official instructions kept vulnerable soldiers away. "No Person is to be allowed to go to Fresh-water pond a fishing or on any other occasion as there may be a danger of introducing the small pox into the army," ordered Washington on July 4, 1775, only his second full day on the job. He had a guard posted as well, "at a certain distance from the small pox Hospital." Explaining the situation to the congressional president John Hancock, the general promised to continue exercising "the utmost Vigilance against this most dangerous Enemy."[5]

Events soon tested this vigilance. Even as Washington penned his letter to Hancock, a new threat of infection loomed. Conditions had grown grim within Boston. Fresh meat and vegetables were hard to come by, and conditions for the poor were dire. On July 21, the Massachusetts House of Representatives, controlled by patriots and meeting outside the British-held city, heard a petition from the selectmen of Boston "purporting the distress'd situation of the Poor & others" trapped within. Whig sympathizers felt especially beleaguered, trapped along with the British by their very own Continental army. Many patriots were "desirous of being removed from their cruel confinement," and they begged the house for permission to leave.[6]

The government was receptive. But before it allowed any departures to take place, it imposed two conditions: First, the British were to have no say in who left and who stayed behind; all who wanted to leave had to be permitted to do so. Second, provisions for the control of smallpox had to be both implemented and honored, for if refugees infected the vulnerable Continental line, the patriot cause might crumble. "Considering the Hazard of propagating the smallpox, the Inhabitants of the Town of Boston are to be removed by Water to the Port of Salem," resolved the House. At Salem, the House would provide both hospital care and lodging for the refugees "untill they shall have been so cleans'd as to remove all apprehensions of their communicating that infectious Distemper." In other words, a quarantine was in order.[7]

Soon nearby Chelsea was also open to citizens fleeing Boston, apparently with similar restrictions. Here, however, the operation was short-lived. As cool weather set in, the smallpox hazard seemed too great, control too difficult, and contagion too likely. Furthermore, in defiance of American policy, the British began making up their own rules, prohibiting certain citizens from leaving while allowing others to go. On October 5, recognizing "that the Small-Pox prevails in the Town of *Boston*," and fearful of "spreading that distemper through the country," the Massachusetts House ordered the Chelsea ferry shut down.[8]

Still, the danger continued to grow.

In November, as the dispirited inhabitants of Boston turned indoors to fend off the winter's chill, smallpox attacked with renewed fierceness. Even the British garrison felt the epidemic's wrath. On November 18, 1775, the British general Sir William Howe asked his officers to poll the ranks to find all those who had never had the disease. They were then "to have such of their Men Enoculated as have not had it & that as soon as possible." At first, variolation was mandatory for susceptible British soldiers. Any who refused were to be reported immediately. Later, General Howe eased his hard-line policy, making the procedure highly recommended but voluntary.[9]

The strategy worked, and Howe's actions exemplified the British approach to smallpox control: When *Variola* threatened, officers immediately polled their men and inoculated vulnerable soldiers. For a European army dominated by soldiers who had dealt with the virus in childhood, the policy was practical. There were few susceptibles among the English-born troops. The British were thus free of the concern that kept the Americans from inoculating; even if smallpox escaped quarantine, the infection would not incapacitate large numbers of men and undermine military readiness. In the spring of 1774, the army had had special "Small Pox Vessels fitted up" to house sick or inoculated soldiers. Now, after a summer more preoccupied with plagues of scurvy and dysentery, British doctors finally put their floating smallpox hospitals to good use.[10]

At the same time, the British command added a new dimension to the seven-month-old military standoff. On November 24, 1775, General Howe granted permission for the residents of Boston to initiate their own inoculations. Simultaneously, as *Variola* raced through the city, he began *ordering* selected citizens to leave. Whether the timing was deliberate is not known. Either way, the result was the same: Washington now faced a flood tide of castaways who might well infect the American lines. He professed his anxieties to Congress on November 27, 1775. "General Howe has ordered 300 inhabitants of Boston to Point Shirley in destitute condition," he wrote. "I have ordered provisions to them until they can be moved, but am under dreadful apprehensions of their communicating the Smallpox as it is rife in Boston."[11]

Hoping to prevent the pox's spread, Washington took steps to secure the American quarantine. First, on November 28, he banned the refugees from the Continentals' camp. Then, a few days later, he implemented still more stringent measures, requiring even letters coming out of the city "to be dipped in vinegar" before they were read. A special Smallpox Committee appointed by the Massachusetts House assumed responsibility for the exiles now coming out of Boston. The committee's charge was to detain on the spot any who "may have been in the way of receiving the Small-Pox" for as long as it took "to determine whether they had the infection." Even those deemed smallpox-free were to be "smoked and cleansed" before they could receive written certification "that they are of the poor of *Boston*, and quite free from infection."[12]

As the siege of Boston continued through the cold months of winter, smallpox remained a constant preoccupation. Dr. John Morgan ran the Continental army's Hospital Department. Frederick Ridgely, one of his assistants during the siege, recalled "that during the winter, the Small-Pox frequently made its appearance among the Soldiery; to prevent the spreading of which, D^r. Morgan continued a small-Pox Hospital, beyond the line of Encampment, and in a proper, retired place, with Guards &c." In the end, these efforts had what Ridgely described as a "most happy effect": The disease stayed at bay for the duration of the standoff. The American line found "Violent Colds" far more troublesome than smallpox.[13]

All of this changed on March 17, 1776. On this date, hungry, tired, and frustrated, William Howe and his British troops gave up the city. New American fortifications on Dorchester Heights had made the occupation untenable, as the British fleet could no longer anchor safely in Boston Harbor. By sunset, nearly eight thousand men, joined by more than a thousand Tory refugees, had boarded British vessels. Five days later they sailed for Halifax, in the loyalist province of Nova Scotia. There, a relentless flow of soldiers and Tory exiles had fostered epidemic smallpox in the previous months.[14] For the veteran troops now arriving at Halifax from Boston, the disease environment, at the very least, was familiar.

The redcoat evacuation from Massachusetts, far from alleviating the perils of smallpox, actually renewed them. Now, Washington knew, the pox would have more opportunities than ever to take hold among his men. To diminish the risk, he sent a vanguard of one thousand immune troops into Boston as the British pulled out. Among them was Richard Wallace of Thetford, Vermont, selected like the rest because he had already lived through an encounter with *Variola*. "I was drafted to go into Boston to cleanse the town from the smallpox and guard the town," he recalled later. People had once clamored to get out of Boston, but now they clamored to get back in. The city was springing to life. Civilians flooded into town, even as the army exercised caution. Apologetically, Washington broached his fears of the consequences to the Massachusetts legislature on March 21: "Notwithstanding all the precaution, which I have endeavoured to use, to restrain and limit the Intercourse between the Town and the Army and Country for a few days, I greatly fear that the Small Pox will be communicated to both."[15]

For the general and most of his troops, the concern was short-lived. Many had already headed home. Others focused on Howe's next move, for as the king's forces pulled out of Boston, the Americans had no way of knowing where they might turn up next. Washington guessed they would attack the strategically important middle colonies of New York or Pennsylvania, and he had men marching in that direction even before the British ships set sail.[16] On April 4, 1776, he headed south himself, leaving two regiments behind. His instincts soon proved themselves sound, as the first sails of a great British armada came into view off New York Harbor in June.

The armies had departed from Massachusetts, but the smallpox had not. In fact, as Washington had feared, the British departure breathed new life into the epidemic. With Whig sympathizers crowding into town and Tories fleeing in terror, both helped spread the pestilence. On Cape Cod, for example, a sloop went aground carrying loyalists who had left Boston with the British. The passengers had departed "in a most dismal Ciutation," said one witness, "not haveing even Water sufficient and crowded and some sick with the small pox." The Massachusetts General Court charged a special committee with preventing the contagious prisoners from "communicating the infection of the Small Pox, to any of the Inhabitants" of Provincetown. Elsewhere, when Continental forces captured a Tory vessel carrying "two Women & Sum Children" sick with smallpox, susceptible soldiers were so frightened that they refused to transport the ailing prisoners. In Boston proper, the Council of Massachusetts directed the selectmen to seek out anyone sick with smallpox and "cause them to be collected in some several house or houses, in the most westerly part of the town" where the infection might be contained. In the revolutionary spirit of the day, the council urged the selectmen to keep the people informed, asking them "very particularly to advertise the publick state of the small-pox during its continuance there."[17]

Boston was alive with action in the spring of 1776, however, and efforts to check the contagion proved useless. "The town is open for all who wish to go in," Dorothy Dudley recorded on March 23, "and yesterday an immense concourse of people from all the surrounding country crowded the streets. Many went from curiosity, others to see again the friends and relatives they had so long been parted from." In a March 31 letter to her husband, John, away at the Continental Congress in Philadelphia, Abigail Adams captured both the excitement and the anxiety of the moment. "Do not you want to see Boston?" she asked. "I am fearfull of the small pox, or I should have been in before this time." Eager to see loved ones or to survey property left behind, many could not resist the temptation. By mid-April, the scourge had begun to extend itself. "Went to Boston," wrote Ezekiel Price, a former selectman in the Massachusetts town. "Nothing remarkable, save probability of the small-pox spreading."[18]

Inoculation, although permitted at times during the British occupation, had been banned by civil authorities, who feared it would spread the pestilence further. But people inoculated anyway, hoping to preserve themselves as others fell ill. James Thacher, a surgeon's mate at the provincial hospital in Cambridge, explained in May 1776 that he "was advised by my friends to have recourse to inoculation for my own safety, though contrary to general orders." Thacher "was accordingly inoculated" by his friend Dr. John Homans. In fact, many medical doctors favored the practice. They included the Continental army's John Morgan, who spent part of the spring of 1776 editing a brief tract to encourage acceptance of the operation.[19]

It was not long before the Massachusetts legislature came around to Morgan's point of view. Smallpox had gotten out of hand, and as spring turned to summer, no end was in sight. On July 3, 1776, with independence looming in Philadelphia, the legislators lifted the statutory ban on inoculation for twelve days. Ezekiel Price recorded the moment in his diary: "Liberty given for to inoculate for the small-pox: many began upon it this afternoon." Traditionally fearful of the practice, Bostonians went inoculation-mad. General Artemas Ward had the remaining Continental troops inoculated. Harvard College postponed commencement while students had themselves inoculated. Ezekiel Price had his family inoculated. This was the time when Abigail Adams had herself and her four children inoculated. And at the last minute, the attorney-preacher Manasseh Cutler likewise made the decision on Sunday, July 14. "*Lord's Day*," he wrote in his diary. "Preached. Sacrament. Pretty full meeting. Concluded to go to Boston to be inoculated." The procedure, according to Hannah Winthrop, now was "as modish as running away from the Troops of a barbarous George was the last year." In all, nearly five thousand people underwent inoculation. "*Boston*," wrote Moses Morse, "is become a hospital with the small-pox."[20]

To contain the pestilence, guards monitored the roads and ferries leaving Boston. It was another siege, in effect: Only those clear of smallpox could leave, and only those immune to it could enter. True to their mandate, the town selectmen monitored and publicized the state of the epidemic. By August 22, 1776, it had begun to wane. "Only seventy-eight persons are now under the distemper of the small-pox," reported the selectmen in a newspaper advertisement. The following week they anticipated that Boston would "be clear of that infection in the course of a fortnight, or three weeks at farthest." Soon thereafter they ordered all infected houses smoked and cleansed. On September 14, only eighteen remained sick. Finally, four days later, the selectmen withdrew the sentinels from the roadways and restored free commerce with the countryside.[21]

For the time being, smallpox had been eliminated from Boston. Moreover, thanks to Washington's decisive actions, the Continental army had generally stayed clear of the infection. *Variola*, however, had emerged as an influential player on the revolutionary stage. Soon reports from other theaters indicated how very lucky Washington's Boston army had been. The American commander had only to look south, to his home province of Virginia, to see how smallpox could ravage a vulnerable army. The army in question served the king of England, but the soldiers, like Washington's Continentals, were primarily Americans.

"If the Virginians are wise," an indignant George Washington had written from Cambridge on December 15, 1775, "that Arch Traitor to the Rights of Humanity, Lord Dunmore, should be instantly crushd, if it takes the force of the whole Colony to do it." The object of the slaveholding general's wrath was the royal governor of Virginia, John Murray, Lord Dunmore. With the stroke of a pen, Dunmore had just turned the American Revolution on its head. Determined to quell the escalating colonial rebellion in his tobacco-growing province, the governor had declared free "all indented Servants, Negroes, or others (appertaining to Rebels)," so long as they were "able and willing to bear Arms" for "his Majesty's Troops."[22] Written on November 7, 1775, and published a week later, Dunmore's proclamation thrilled Virginia's unfree laborers just as it galled the colony's revolutionary elites.

The reaction to Dunmore's proclamation was powerful and immediate. Within a month of its publication, the governor's fighting force had doubled from three hundred to six hundred men. One who served among these loyalist troops was George Washington's own servant, Joseph Wilson, a white painter who absconded from Mount Vernon in September, when rumors of Dunmore's plan preceded its announcement. At the commander in chief's enormous Virginia plantation, other unfree laborers also took heart. "There is not a man of them, but woud leave us, if they believe'd they coud make there Escape," reported Lund Washington to his cousin George on December 3, 1775. "Liberty," he added, "is sweet."[23]

Dunmore's limited "emancipation proclamation" came as a

surprise to no one. The governor had contemplated such an action for months, and he had long equated slavery with military vulnerability in North America's southern colonies. As early as 1772, he had postulated that in the event of a war with Spain or some other power, Virginia's slaves "would join the first that would encourage them to revenge themselves," enabling "a Conquest of this Country" to "be effected in a very Short time." With so many slaveholding planters among Virginia's prominent Whig leaders, Dunmore believed he could turn the colony's deep social divisions to the advantage of the crown. As early as April 1775, Dunmore had reportedly declared that if violence erupted, he would "have a Majority of white People and all the Slaves on the side of [the British] Government." The governor had by this early date already received a clandestine offer of services from one group of slaves, whom he had bidden to "go about their business" for the time being.[24]

While Dunmore's proclamation thrilled servants and slaves everywhere, it outraged Virginia's revolutionary elites. "If my Dear Sir that Man is not crushed before Spring," wrote Washington to fellow Virginian Richard Henry Lee on December 26, 1775, "he will become the most formidable Enemy America has—his strength will Increase as a Snow ball by Rolling." Andrew Lewis, soon to be named a brigadier general in the Continental army, referred to the royal governor as "the detestable Lord Dunmore." To Lee, he was "Our Devil Dunmore" and (derisively) "our African Hero." And to the aging Landon Carter, one of Virginia's most prominent slaveholders, Dunmore was not just an "accursed enemy" but a "monster" as well.[25]

For Virginia's black residents, some 40 percent of the colony's population, Dunmore bore more resemblance to Moses than to a monster. Estimates of the number of slaves who joined the governor's Ethiopian Regiment are speculative at best, but by one appraisal, roughly eight hundred black laborers found their way to Dunmore. Another estimate puts the count closer to a thousand. Neither of these numbers includes the many slaves—women and children as well as able-bodied men—who fled from their owners but failed to reach the loyalist force because of insurmountable obstacles in the form of patrols, geography, scant provisions, and hard luck. Eyewitness accounts make it clear that Dunmore's proclamation drew freedom-loving African Americans like a magnet. "Slaves Flock to him in abundance," wrote the Virginian Edmund Pendleton to Richard Henry Lee.[26] The fugitives came by foot, by boat, and by sheer force of will, even though capture could mean whipping, exportation, or execution.

The Ethiopian Regiment saw only limited action against Virginia's patriot forces, who bore the appellation shirtmen for the hunting shirts they chose as their uniform. What fighting there was centered on the western shore of lower Chesapeake Bay, where for much of the fall of 1775, Dunmore made Norfolk his base of operations. Although members of the Ethiopian Regiment fought "with the intrepidity of lions," as one sailor reported in a letter, wearing the words "Liberty to Slaves" emblazoned across their chests, they met with defeat at a battle near Norfolk on December 9, 1775.[27] Forced out of the little harbor town and onto ships offshore, Dunmore cruised the Chesapeake coastline for two months. His loyalist flotilla served as a sort of portable base camp. From it, he and his men launched guerrilla attacks on rebel plantations, pilfering provisions, burning storehouses, and continuing to draw eager bondsmen into the loyalist ranks.

Smallpox, however, could destroy even the most determined freedom fighter.

In early 1776, even as it simultaneously plagued Boston, *Variola* found its way on board Dunmore's fleet in the Chesapeake. The precise timing of the initial outbreak is uncertain, as is the source of the infection. But the connection to the political and military turmoil of the day is clear: The very act of assembling the Ethiopian Regiment had brought together in one place a large, vulnerable population. Once the virus gained a foothold among the men crowded into the governor's vessels, further infection was inevitable, and a constant influx of susceptible newcomers kept the contagion alive. The crisis unfolded on shipboard through January 1776. Then, on February 9, the British warship *Roebuck* sailed into Chesapeake Bay. With the help of her captain and crew, Dunmore's loyalist army established a tiny camp onshore, at Tucker's Point near Portsmouth, Virginia.[28]

From February until May, the combined black and white army hung on to its shoreline toehold while *Variola* coursed through the camp. It struck the black troops particularly hard. Finally, according to the *Roebuck*'s captain, Andrew Snape Hamond, "in order to save them, the Surgeons recommended that the whole should be inoculated." The loyalist band faced the same dilemma that Washington had just faced at Boston: Inoculation might protect soldiers in the long run, but it would incapacitate them in large numbers for weeks at a time. The vulnerable Tucker's Point camp would be untenable. "Therefore on considering every circumstance, we thought it adviseable to move the Fleet imediately," wrote Captain Hamond. The new position would be at Gwynn's Island, fifty miles north at the mouth of the Piankatank River. In some ninety vessels large and small, Dunmore's men made the move in the closing days of May. They destroyed all the buildings at Tucker's Point as they left, but the graves of almost three hundred men remained to mark the site of their former encampment.[29]

Only a few details survive from the Gwynn's Island affair. The pox-infested army, including what a Whig sympathizer described as "the Shattered remains of the Ethiopn. regiment," arrived at its new campsite on May 27. So sickly were Dunmore's 650 men that Captain Hamond had to send marines from the *Roebuck* ashore to "do the Common duty" and assist with entrenchments. Still, despite the pox and the difficulty of reaching the island, new recruits poured in. The Ethiopian Regiment gained "six or eight fresh Men every day" at the new location. These newcomers succumbed to smallpox almost as fast as they arrived, and the presence of the disease could only have discouraged others from joining up. "Had it not been for this horrid disorder," Dunmore wrote in June, "I should have had two thousand blacks; with whom I should have had no doubt of penetrating into the heart of this Colony."[30]

At Gwynn's Island, as at Tucker's Point, black soldiers seemed to suffer much more from disease than white soldiers did. According to a prisoner who escaped by swimming from the island to the mainland on June 6, it was "particularly Negroes" who died in the loyalist lines. This may well have been due to the establishment of segregated camps, which kept smallpox isolated among the black troops. The number of inoculations undertaken is not clear. An account by Captain Hamond indicates that most of the black troops "had been inoculated before they left Norfolk" and that they "got thro' the disorder with great success" only to be assailed by a fever, perhaps typhus, when they reached Gwynn's Island. Yet other reports, including another one from Hamond, imply that it was only when the loyalist army moved to the island that mass inoculations took place. It seems likely that variolation on a large scale did proceed there, but mortality failed to abate, perhaps because another disease—the "fever" mentioned by Hamond—attacked the beleaguered army even as it struggled against smallpox.[31]

The results were ghastly. "Dozens died daily from Small Pox and rotten Fevers by which diseases they were infected," wrote one eyewitness on June 23. Under a relentless microbial attack, the black forces languished in their huts. "Lord Dunmore still remains on Gwin's Island," wrote Richard Henry Lee on July 6. "Caterpillar like, We hear he has devoured everything in that place, so that it is probable force of some kind or other will shortly drive him thence." The little army, "reduced by the small Pox and an epidemic Fever," was now "too weak to resist any considerable force," wrote Captain Hamond. As Virginia shirtmen gathered and mounted cannons on the mainland shore, the loyalist troops prepared to withdraw, finally abandoning the island when the anticipated assault began on July 9. "Ld. Dunmore has had a most compleat Drubbing," wrote the Virginia patriot John Page to

Thomas Jefferson. Aboard what a newspaper labeled "Lord Dunmore's pestilential fleet" were roughly three hundred blacks, the
sole remnants of the Ethiopian Regiment.[32]

The fleet sailed north first, landing briefly at St. George Island
in the Potomac River. From there, deserters from Dunmore carried smallpox wherever they went. "We have several Deserters
from the Enemy most of them in the small Pox," wrote Major
Thomas Price to the Maryland Council of Safety on July 23. The
Maryland militia lieutenant Bennett Bracco appealed to the council three days later for permission to inoculate his men when "a
man that called himself a deserter from Lord Dunmore" broke out
with smallpox after "a day and night in company with all the soldiers here." In yet another incident, Dunmore's men inadver-
tently carried *Variola* ashore when the wind drove two of their
boats aground near the Maryland town of St. Inigoes. "On board
of one of them was three Whites & two Negroes, three of which
now have the small Pox on them," reported an American officer to
the Maryland Council of Safety.[33] Dunmore's stay in the Potomac
River basin was brief. In the first week of August, his fleet split up
and departed Chesapeake Bay entirely, sailing for St. Augustine,
New York, and England.

At Gwynn's Island, so hastily evacuated by the governor's
troops, the Virginia shirtmen discovered a grim scene. "On our arrival," wrote one, "we found the enemy had evacuated the place
with the greatest precipitation, and were struck with horrour at
the number of dead bodies, in a state of putrefaction, strewed all
the way from their battery to *Cherry-Point*, about two miles in
length, without a shovelful of earth upon them." Others lived still,
"gasping for life; and some had crawled to the water's edge, who
could only make known their distress by beckoning to us."
Among the corpses were many who had burned to death, too sick
to move when fire had engulfed their brush huts during the frantic
evacuation. At least 130 graves, "many of them large enough to
hold a corporal's guard," lay close together near the site of the
camp. The death toll was stunning: "By the small-pox, and other

malignant disorders which have raged on board the fleet for many months past, it is clear they have lost, since their arrival at Gwin's Island, near five hundred souls." Other eyewitnesses concurred.[34]

For the conquering patriots, the gruesome camp presented a serious threat of contagion. Dunmore's men "had a dreadful fever amongst them, and the small-pox," wrote one worried observer. "I wish our Army may not catch the infection." Such luck was elusive. Within a month of the landing on Gwynn's Island, pestilence of some kind—perhaps smallpox, perhaps "fever," perhaps both—began making inroads among Virginia's patriot troops. "Our men are sickly and die but too fast," wrote an officer on August 6. Two months later, according to another witness, the unnamed illness still flourished: "The troops in the lower parts of the country have been extremely sickly these two months past, especially at Williamsburgh."[35]

In the aftermath of Dunmore's brief visit to the Potomac, smallpox made inroads throughout northern Virginia, hitting especially hard at the province's northern neck, the long peninsula of land between the Potomac and Rappahannock rivers. Here, as smallpox spread, the Westmoreland County Court heard numerous requests for inoculation licenses. On October 29, it granted Magdalen M. Clanaham "leave to innoculate her family for small pox." A month later, it licensed Reuben Jordan to inoculate his family and gave Robert Carter "leave to inoculate his Negroes at his Forrest Quarter where the Disorder now is." The applications kept coming in until the overwhelmed court took more drastic action in December, waiving the license requirement for all those "in whose families the disorder hath already appeared."[36]

By February 1777, homeward-bound troops had "drop'd" the disease in Caroline County, on the south bank of the Rappahannock. One Virginian feared that from there, the soldiers would "Spread the disorder thro' America." Evidence indicates that the northern neck continued to struggle with the pox through early 1777 and that the pestilence moved farther up the Potomac as well. In April it occurred in Leesburg, and by May it had taken hold at Mount Vernon, where George Washington's wife, Martha, tried to keep it in check. Mrs. Washington had undergone inoculation a year before in Philadelphia, so she was not vulnerable to the spreading infirmity, but others were, including many of the slaves on the Washington plantation. Writing to the Continental army's medical director, Dr. William Shippen, on May 3, 1777, the commander in chief explained that he expected "not less than three hundred Persons to take the disorder" at his Virginia home. His wife was desperate for medicine, the general said, particularly "Jallop and Calomel"—both "purgatives" (laxatives) used to treat a broad array of maladies including smallpox. "I must beg you to furnish the bearer with so much of the above Articles for my use as you shall judge necessary," he wrote.[37]

Simultaneous events in Massachusetts and Virginia had highlighted the way political turmoil and military upheaval enhanced the circulation of microbes. People were traveling about as never before, meeting, dispersing, and regrouping, silently exchanging pathogens at every turn.

Even as the twin dramas unfolded in Boston and Tidewater Virginia over the winter of 1775–76, a third war-related episode of smallpox occurred in the loyalist colony of Canada, where eleven hundred Continental troops had set up camp outside the walled city of Quebec in the late fall of 1775. The camp's location was auspicious: It sat on the Plains of Abraham, site of the fatal encounter between the Marquis de Montcalm and General James Wolfe in the Seven Years' War (1756–63). Once again, the drama here was to be fatal, but this time, smallpox would bear most of the blame. Events in Canada eventually eclipsed those in Boston and Virginia and forced Washington to confront his army's debilitating vulnerability to *Variola*.

The American army had converged on Quebec from two directions in late November and early December 1775. Some six hundred men arrived with General Benedict Arnold, after courting dysentery, drowning, and starvation on an extraordinary march up Maine's Kennebec River. Arnold's men had been reduced to eating dogs and shot pouches on their desperate trek. Some faced the impending Canadian winter without shoes.[38] Another five hundred men arrived with General Richard Montgomery, commander of the entire expedition. They had an easier time of it, proceeding northward on Lake Champlain to the Richelieu River and the St. Lawrence, pausing briefly to capture Montreal along the way.

For smallpox, conditions were ideal. After long, stressful marches, more than a thousand men had assembled in one place from disparate provinces from Maine to Virginia. If their home colonies were diverse, so were the microbes, infections, and medical histories they carried with them, now conjoined on the Plains of Abraham. The men were exhausted. Many were weak from starvation. They lived in close, unsanitary conditions, and with winter setting in, lodgings only became more crowded and contact more familiar. Very soon after arriving, a Massachusetts-born fife player made an ominous journal entry. "The small pox is all around us," wrote Caleb Haskell on December 6, 1775, "and there is great danger of its spreading in the army." The disease had appeared in Quebec before the Americans' arrival, but now, the exhausted and vulnerable Northern Army added fuel to the smoldering fire.[39]

A tiny spark was all it took. *Variola* began to spread among the troops very shortly after they arrived. Among the first to suffer were the men in Samuel Ward's Rhode Island company. "The small pox [is] very plenty among us," wrote Jeremiah Greenman in mid-December. Isolated in a location some three miles outside camp, Greenman's messmates went through the travails of the ailment. "I am very ill," Caleb Haskell noted in his journal. On December 22, he described his plight directly: "Poor attendance; no bed to lie on; no medicine to take; troubled much with a sore throat." Haskell and the Rhode Islanders were not alone. In those closing days of 1775, the soldiers camped before Quebec made daily note of the spreading contagion. "The small pox [is] very breaf [rife] amung our troops," wrote one. "Maynard is looked upon very Dangerous with the Small Pox and Brigham has it very favorably," wrote another. Haskell recovered, but others died, and cases multiplied.[40]

In command of the expedition, General Montgomery watched his forces dwindle as men fell ill one by one. His own pockmarked face revealed that, like General Washington, he knew firsthand how debilitating smallpox could be. Yet quarantine came piecemeal, too little, and too late. By Christmas, the epidemic had led to the creation of a dedicated smallpox hospital, but many sick men stayed elsewhere. "All the houses in the neighborhood," wrote Caleb Haskell on December 28, "are full of our soldiers with the small-pox." The liberty-minded Americans, moreover, felt free to disobey orders when they saw fit. "John McGuire is ordered to the Small Pox hospital but Declines at going," noted the army surveyor John Pierce on December 23.[41]

Smallpox was by no means the only problem facing Montgomery. Determined to protect their personal freedom, many of the New England troops had signed up for very short tours of duty. Some were due to end on New Year's Day, which was anticipated with glee. A soldier from Massachusetts wrote in his journal: "*December ye 30th 1775* The Last Day of Service all rejoice—again I Say rejoice."[42]

As smallpox spread and the enlistment clock ticked down, General Montgomery knew he had to take action. Finally, with many soldiers bound for home at sunrise, he made his move against Quebec under the cover of a blizzard at midnight on December 31, 1775. The assault failed dismally. Montgomery died sword in hand as the fighting began, and the men he led turned back. Virginia's Daniel Morgan scaled the city walls with his men and performed heroically, but he eventually surrendered as the sun rose. Some thirty Americans died, and more than four hundred became prisoners of war. The remainder straggled back to their camp on the Plains of Abraham, where those whose enlistments did not expire continued their wintry siege of the city. For both groups of men—the soldiers in camp and the prisoners in Quebec—the *Variola* virus became harder and harder to avoid.

In accordance with accepted protocol, the British held captured officers and enlisted men in separate quarters. The pox struck the enlisted men hardest. It erupted among them after only a week of confinement, indicating that some had incubated the virus even as they launched their ill-fated midnight offensive. "Some of our people taken with the small-pox," wrote the imprisoned James Melvin on January 7, 1776. "We expect it will be a general disorder." The first wave struck ten or twelve prisoners. They were removed to a hospital but did not stay long. A Massachusetts private explained: "The survivors, as soon as the fever left them and the scabs began to come off, were brought back and, without any cleansing, were thrust in among us." The consequences were unavoidable. "Of course, all who had not had it took the disease," wrote a soldier named Simon Fobes, nineteen years of age.[43]

Before long, eighty prisoners were sick, and predictable patterns emerged: New Englanders and southerners were far more likely to be susceptible than soldiers from the middle colonies, who tended to have immunity thanks to earlier encounters with the disease. In prison with the others, a sixteen-year-old Pennsylvanian mourned the effect smallpox was having on Daniel Morgan's Virginia riflemen, who had impressed him deeply with their character and marksmanship. They were "as elegant a body of men as ever came into my view," he wrote later, "adroit young men, courageous and thorough-going." Yet more than others, they "became the subjects of death by that virulent disease."[44]

Living conditions in captivity facilitated contagion. The accommodations changed frequently, but overcrowding was consistent. "This day to pleas us we ware [shut] up in a smaller part of ye house than before," reported Jeremiah Greenman in mid-January; "the Small pox very breaf [rife] among us." At one point sixty men spent twenty-four hours crammed "into a room so small that we could not lie down without lying on one another." Spiking fevers as high as 103° F, the sick prisoners were at times desperate for water. "With no water to drink," wrote Simon Fobes, "some of the men drank of their own urine, which made the fever rage too violently to be endured."[45]

Imprisoned officers suffered less than their enlisted men. Indeed, the contrast is striking. "We were treated with the greatest humanity," wrote Lieutenant Francis Nichols. "Gen. Carleton allowed us to send for clothing and money." Money, even in prison, gave the officers a decided advantage in coping with smallpox since it allowed them to purchase the services of an inoculator. "Some of the New England officers not having had the small pox, petitioned the General for permission to be inoculated," Nichols wrote. They engaged the services of one Dr. Bullen, who inoculated sixteen of the thirty-four imprisoned officers on January 3 and January 4. The remainder either took their chances or had immunity from exposure at some earlier time.[46]

Beyond Quebec's walls, in the freezing and forlorn American camp, a parallel drama unfolded. With smallpox spreading and provisions running thin, many whose enlistments expired left for home the day after the unsuccessful attempt on the city. According to one eyewitness, "neither art, craft, nor money" could keep them from going. Their comrades watched jealously. "Our men march off Daily," wrote a despondent John Pierce on January 3, 1776, "and I entend to march as Soon as my health will allow . . . I am left as it were all alone."[47]

The death of General Montgomery had left the wounded Benedict Arnold in charge of the Northern Army. With his forces dwindling daily, Arnold struggled to control the spreading pestilence. By February 11, his frustration was palpable. The American troops were steeped in the rhetoric of liberty and revolution, and they readily disobeyed instructions they disliked. Arnold complained that his "repeated orders given to prevent the spreading of that fatal disorder the Small-Pox" had been "in a great measure disregarded." He ordered all sick men to the hospital at once. Soldiers who knew of smallpox cases but failed to report them would "be treated as neglecting their duty, and guilty of a breach of orders."[48]

Strong words could not stop the virus. By February 15, Arnold believed the continued spread of "Small-Pox at this juncture" would lead to "the entire ruin of the Army." The epidemic was out of control, and he broke the bad news to Washington. "Notwithstanding every precaution that could be used," Arnold wrote, "the smallpox has crept in among the troops; we have near one hundred men in the Hospital." Other reports indicated that as many as two hundred were sick.[49]

From the very beginning of the showdown at Quebec, both the Americans and the British had sent out calls for more men. Now, as the Americans succumbed to smallpox, the siege of Quebec became little more than a waiting game to see whose reinforcements would get there the fastest. The Americans had a clear geographical advantage. On January 25, fresh troops began trickling in, but their numbers were few, and in February the call went out for more. "We have been reinforced with only one hundred and seventy-five men," wrote Arnold to President John Hancock; "our whole force is about eight hundred effective men." Despite Arnold's plea, fresh troops were of dubious benefit: As fast as the new men arrived, so they also fell ill. By March 30, reinforcements had swelled the American ranks to 2,505 men, but 786 of these were sick and unfit for duty.[50]

The size of the American fighting force dropped by five to six hundred men in April, thanks to expired enlistments, desertion, and the ravages of *Variola*. When Major General John Thomas finally arrived to replace Montgomery in the first week of May, only nineteen hundred American soldiers remained. Nine hundred of them were sick, and Thomas himself, according to one eyewitness, was "an utter stranger in the country, and much terrified with the small-pox."[51] It was not a good sign.

By the time Thomas arrived, a fleet carrying British reinforcements had been battering its way up the icy St. Lawrence River for days. It anchored at Quebec on May 6. "Immediately upon

landing," wrote Dr. Isaac Senter, the British "rushed out in parties
. . . upon the plains of Abraham." Pandemonium erupted in the
American camp. Surprised, unprepared, and burdened with an incapacitated army, General Thomas gave the command to retreat.
The men raised their siege in a panic, fleeing in a "most irregular,
helter skelter manner" toward Montreal, leaving equipment, ammunition, and clothing behind.[52]

The abandoned matériel was impressive, but the abandoned
people were more so. "We were obliged to escape as we could,"
wrote Dr. Senter, "the most of our sick fell into their hands." At
the American hospital, the British found men so ill with smallpox
that they could barely move. In the woods and along the St.
Lawrence shoreline, they found more—pox-ridden, abandoned,
unable to walk or rescue themselves, even thrown overboard by
their desperate companions.[53]

Moved by their plight and eager to show the compassion of the
British crown, General Sir Guy Carleton commanded his men to
search out the abandoned sick and "convey them to the general
hospital, where proper care shall be taken of them." In the days
that followed, the British rescued between two and five hundred
men, nearly all in the throes of smallpox.[54] A tiny virus had proved
far more ferocious than the British troops these men had come to
fight.

If some American soldiers were glad to put the Plains of Abraham behind them, their relief was short-lived, for even the hasti-
est withdrawal could not outstrip *Variola*. The retreat from
Quebec brought an instant end to all efforts at quarantine, feeble
though they were. At every juncture, sick men now mingled with
healthy troops, and others unaware they incubated the virus
trudged alongside them as well. "I crawled to the boat and got under a seat," wrote Captain Lemuel Roberts, who had hoped that
others would row him upstream. His comrades, however, could
not overcome the current, and Roberts reluctantly took an oar.
"My pock had become so sore and troublesome," he recalled,
"that my clothes stuck fast to my body, especially to my feet; and

it became a severe trial to my fortitude, to bear my disorder and assist in managing the boat." Spring rains had swollen the St. Lawrence and its feeder streams, and "the river had overflowed its banks in many places to the distance of several miles." The deluge posed an obstacle to Captain Roberts and his companions in their rowboat, but it posed an even greater one to the bulk of the army scrambling along the riverbank, forced into long, tedious detours by the flood and the shortage of watercraft.[55]

By May 11, after five days of pox-plagued marching through rain-sodden woods, the vanguard of the retreating forces reached the little fur-trading village of Sorel, strategically situated at the confluence of the Richelieu and St. Lawrence rivers. Here the soldiers collapsed in exhaustion, and here they met a delegation of commissioners sent by Congress to investigate the unraveling Canadian debacle. The delegation was a distinguished one, including such prominent patriots as Charles Carroll, Benjamin Franklin, and Samuel Chase, all of whom were stunned at the sight of the disheveled army. "We are unable to express our apprehensions of the Distress our army must soon be reduced to from the want of provisions and the Small pox," they reported on May 11. If they feared for the fate of the army in general, they had more specific concerns about one man in particular. Ten days earlier, they had forwarded an ominous message to Congress at Philadelphia. "The small pox is in the army," they wrote, "and General Thomas has unfortunately never had it."[56]

As the retreating Americans tried to regroup in Sorel, their numbers were bolstered by the arrival of long-sought reinforcements, who had followed the spring weather northward. Among them was John Patten, the New Hampshire patriot who had taken part in the siege of Boston and the Battle of Bunker Hill. Sorel, however, was not Boston. Circumstances were dire, and Patten and his fellows did little to help. Not only did they come without provisions, but nearly all of them were susceptible to smallpox. With *Variola* coursing through the army, the arrival of new troops was akin to throwing gasoline on a fire. "Three-fourths of the

Army have not had the small-pox," the commissioners noted as new recruits poured in. In early June, Philip Schuyler made a special appeal to General Washington from his post at Albany. "If the Militia ordered into Canada from the New England Colonies should not have had the small Pox," he wrote, "they will rather weaken than strengthen our Army."[57] It was better to have no reinforcements at all than to bear the burden of more sick men.

The sights and sounds of Sorel terrified the newly arrived troops. For those susceptible to smallpox, infection seemed unavoidable. Many contemplated inoculation. The procedure was off-limits, however; from the early days of the siege at Quebec, military officials had prohibited variolation out of fear that it would spread the insidious pestilence. "The Surgeons of the Army are forbid, under the severest penalty, to inoculate any person," read General Arnold's orders of February 15, long before the calamitous withdrawal. Penalties for violators were severe: Officers would be "immediately cashiered," and privates would be "punished at the discretion of a Court-Martial." The American command had reiterated these orders regularly. "Inoculation is in the most peremptory manner prohibited," General Thomas proclaimed just three days prior to the evacuation. "And any officer or Soldier who shall be Detected receiving the Small pox by Inockulation will be surely Punished."[58]

Yet the forces in Canada scoffed at military regulations. As the congressional commissioners saw it, there was "little or no discipline" among the troops. This was especially true where smallpox was at issue. Long before the precipitous retreat up the St. Lawrence River, soldiers had violated quarantine flagrantly on the Plains of Abraham. Illegal inoculations had taken place as early as Christmas Day 1775. "Scarce any of the New England recruits had ever had the disorder," Dr. Isaac Senter explained, and they had real "apprehensions of taking it in the natural way." Many years later, a Quebec veteran named John Joseph Henry recalled how "great numbers of the soldiers inoculated themselves . . . by laceration under the finger nails by means of pins or needles." The practice went on in secret, for according to one witness, "it was death for any doctor who attempted inoculation." The threat of punishment failed to deter the terrified troops. As one eyewitness explained, "they were willing to run any hazard" to avoid catching smallpox in "the natural way."[59]

Officers ignored or quietly sanctioned rank-and-file inoculations. Among the reinforcements that arrived at Quebec before the retreat were 373 Green Mountain Boys under Colonel Seth Warner's command. Deeply concerned for the welfare of his men, Warner earned the regard of his troops wherever he served. When he reached the American camp on the Plains of Abraham in March 1776, the pox-smitten scene appalled him. According to the slightly garbled recollection of his son, the colonel called his men together and told them: "I do not wish to Countermand the General Orders, but if you should take it [smallpox] in the Thigh and Diet for it, it would be much better for you, and they will not find it out." Thus, with Warner's blessing, the Green Mountain Boys inoculated themselves. Among those who did so was Josiah Sabin, a Massachusetts volunteer who gathered contagious material at the camp smallpox hospital and then variolated himself and others. To protect Sabin's identity, soldiers "were sent into his room blindfolded, were inoculated, and sent out in the same condition." By implanting the infection in the thigh rather than the arm, the men hoped to escape detection.[60]

As sick soldiers and vulnerable reinforcements poured into Sorel in May 1776, American officers increasingly questioned the army's inoculation ban. Infection, it seemed, was unavoidable, and surreptitious inoculations could not be stopped. With the commissioners' approval, Benedict Arnold even lifted the prohibition for one brief day before General Thomas came. But as soon as Thomas arrived in camp, he immediately "gave Counter orders, that it should be death for any person to innoculate."[61] For Thomas himself, however, it was too late. Inoculation or no inoculation, *Variola* already circulated in his bloodstream.

Even before the retreat from Quebec, rumors had spread of a combined force of Indians, French-speaking habitants, and British soldiers preparing to assault the American-held city of Montreal. In late April 1776, General Arnold countered the threat by dispatching Colonel Timothy Bedel and four hundred soldiers some thirty-five miles up the St. Lawrence to a site called the Cedars. Their instructions were to build and arm a stockade that would establish an American presence and intercept any enemy approach from the backcountry. "The Cedars," wrote a young New Hampshire soldier, "is a very pleasant country, possessing a very rich and fertile soil."[62]

However pleasing to the eye, the countryside could hardly have made smallpox easier to endure. Many of the troops sent to the Cedars already incubated the *Variola* virus. Some, like Colonel Bedel himself, had contracted it by inoculation.[63] Others had caught it through incidental contagion. Ill though they were, the men completed a respectable breastwork by May 6, the very day their compatriots at Quebec took flight from their camp on the Plains of Abraham.

Colonel Bedel did not supervise the barricade's construction. Instead, he left Major Isaac Butterfield in charge and sought to wield his influence among the Kahnawake Mohawks nearby. The Mohawks were part of the great Iroquois Confederacy, also known as the Six Nations. Although the war between Britain and the American colonies was soon to split the famous Indian alliance, the Six Nations still clung to an official policy of neutrality in 1776. Bedel knew, however, that the British had been lobbying the Iroquois, he knew that groups as well as individuals might act autonomously, and he knew how fragile the Six Nations' policy was. According to those familiar with him, Bedel "had the greatest influence over the Indians of any man." The colonel thus saw it as his personal duty "to attend to the Cultivation of a friendship with the savages."[64]

It is tempting to speculate on the outcome of Bedel's talks. Politically, he was apparently successful: The Kahnawakes remained neutral for the time being. But Bedel had recently undergone in-oculation, and he was sick with the smallpox even as he met with the Indians. "I was but a man and a Sick man at the time," he re-called later. Duty alone, he said, "led me to Comply with the Re-quest of the Savage Chiefs in meeting them in Council at Coughnawaga even at a Time when I was Ill with the Small Pox." Did Bedel pass the infection on to the Kahnawakes? Did the tra-ditional calumet circulate at these councils in a ritual very likely to communicate the virus? Specific evidence is elusive, but the num-ber of funerals surged upward at Kahnawake in both 1775 and 1776, especially for infants, the most likely to be susceptible to *Variola*.[65]

What occurred at the fortress at the Cedars is more certain. Be-del returned to the post on May 6 so riddled with smallpox that he feared he might die. Others at the Cedars were also sick, and ille-gal inoculations continued apace. "On the 10th I took the Small Pock," wrote Frye Bayley; "11th took Medicine, 12th took Jalap, and so continued until my pock came out." Bayley's companions followed suit. Bedel himself did not die, and by May 15 he was well enough to leave once again, returning to negotiations at Kah-nawake.[66] Now it was Major Butterfield, again in command, who suffered from smallpox.

Within hours of Bedel's departure, the ailing Butterfield "had News by Some Indians" of an approaching enemy force of 400 men. In truth there were nowhere near that number; under the command of Captain George Forster, the British force consisted of about 160 Native American warriors supplemented by a few habi-tants and regular soldiers. But the pox-afflicted Continentals at the Cedars had no way of knowing the report was exaggerated, and the Indian troops were particularly disquieting to Butterfield and his men. The Indians came primarily from the western tribes eager to reopen trade with the British at Montreal. Fearful that they could not defend themselves, some of the sick Americans fled the post immediately. On May 18, before the fighting began, Captain Forster advised his foe that he would be unable to restrain his warriors from acts of cruelty unless the garrison surrendered at once.[67]

The two forces exchanged sporadic gunfire through the afternoon. A band of Continentals even ventured out to burn an outbuilding in which some of the attackers had taken refuge. Overnight, however, the prospect of Indian atrocities sank in among the ailing Americans. Unaware that reinforcements had already set out from Montreal to assist him, Major Butterfield surrendered the post in the morning. Some attributed his capitulation to cowardice, but in the eyes of one witness, "a majority of the Officers were greater cowards than Butterfield, for he was in fact, very sick with the Small Pock."[68] In a negotiated surrender, Butterfield turned over everything to Forster and the Indians—everything except the clothes on the backs of his men.

The incoming relief party—approximately 120 Continental soldiers under Major Henry Sherburne—was not so lucky, nor was the force that ambushed them. The "British" attackers consisted largely of Native Americans, who easily overcame Sherburne's column. In an unconditional surrender, the Continentals "were made prisoners by the savages without any stipulation." The victors had absolute rights over their captives. Angered over the loss of several chiefs, the Indians laid claim to everything, "stripping and leaving stark naked those who had clothes on fit for anything." It was a fateful act. The clothes, like the soldiers who wore them, carried the *Variola* virus. The Bostonian John Adams, otherwise distraught over the havoc smallpox had wrought in Canada, took solace in the infection of the Indians. "It is some small Consolation," he wrote to his wife, Abigail, "that the Scoundrell Savages have taken a large Dose of it. They plundered the Baggage, and stripped off the Cloaths of our Men, who had the Small Pox, out full upon them at the Cedars." Captain Forster's force hailed from Oswegatchie, New York, and it included men who came from as far west as Detroit. Indians returning from Quebec carried the pox beyond Detroit all the way to Michilimackinac.[69]

For General John Thomas, there would be no going home. His

Canadian nightmare was nearing its end. At Sorel on May 20, the physician Lewis Beebe noted that the general "remained poorly" and had "many Symptoms of the small pox." His condition deteriorated quickly. The next day he gave up his command and "was carried" south to Fort Chambly, some forty-five miles farther up the Richelieu River, while General William Thompson, the fifth officer to lead the Northern Army since December, took charge at Sorel. At Albany on May 31, Philip Schuyler heard that Thomas was "rather in a dangerous way." Two days later, just after dawn, the general died. According to a witness, his pox-ravaged body "was obliged to be interred that day—he was so mortified."[70]

Thomas's death epitomized the miserable state of affairs in the Northern Army in the spring of 1776. So careworn were the American forces at Sorel and Montreal that the enemy they fought against had become a mere afterthought. But in the second week of June, the sight of British sails on the St. Lawrence prompted another hasty, disorganized evacuation. " 'Retreat! Retreat! the British are upon us!' " was the cry at Montreal. "Down we scampered to the boats," wrote one soldier, who recalled seeing sick men "from the hospital crawling after us." In the rain, encumbered by as many as twenty-nine hundred invalids, the troops struggled southward to Chambly and then St. Jean. At St. Jean, which he labeled a "dirty, stinking place," Dr. Beebe set up a makeshift hospital consisting of several "Large barns filled with men in the very heighth of the small pox." "It is a very dying time," wrote Frye Bayley in his journal.[71]

The British continued their pursuit. They had followed their usual protocol for smallpox prevention, inoculating the few susceptibles in their ranks as soon as the disease threatened. Now they had little to fear from their ailing American foes. They pursued the pox-ravaged Northern Army with impunity, forcing it to flee Chambly and St. Jean just as it had left Sorel a few days before. Among the Americans, decorum and duty both fell by the wayside. The "Vast No of Men sick & in the most distressing condition with the Small pox is not to be discribed," wrote Jeduthan

Baldwin, "& many officers Runing off Leaving there men by the Side of the river to be taken care of by me or others."[72] By foot, boat, and stretcher, between fifteen hundred and two thousand ailing soldiers made their way to Île-aux-Noix, a swampy, low-lying island near the Canada–New York border.

John Patten of Bedford, New Hampshire, now sick with small-pox, was among them. The particulars of Patten's case do not appear in the historical record, but it is clear that for him, as for others, the misery peaked at Île-aux-Noix. "Oh the Groans of the Sick," wrote Bayze Wells on June 17. "What they undergo I Cant Expres." Lewis Beebe noted that there was "Scarcely a tent upon this Isle but what contains one or more in distress and continually groaning, & calling for relief, but in vain!" He described a barn full of vermin-covered men who could not see, speak, or walk: "One nay two had large maggots, an inch long, Crawl out of their ears." If Beebe's description bears the marks of hyperbole, even its most gruesome details are confirmed in the accounts of others. "My eyes never before beheld such a seen," recalled the Pennsyl-vanian John Lacey, "nor do I ever desire to see such another—the Lice and Maggots seme to vie with each other, were creeping in Millions over the Victims; the Doctors themselves sick or out of Medicine."[73]

Those healthy enough to dig opened two mass graves. To each were consigned fifteen to twenty bodies per day so long as the army remained on the island. On June 20, the corpse of twenty-four-year-old John Patten joined the others in one of these pits. It was a month before his father learned of his demise. When he did, he vented his rage in his diary. John had died "defending the just Rights of America" against "that wicked tyrannical Brute (Nea worse than Brute) of Great Britain," Matthew Patten wrote. The day before, while still unaware of his son's death, he had bought a few odds and ends in Chester, New Hampshire, among which were "2 £ of tobacca a rub ball for my breeches and a Declaration for Independence."[74] The date was July 20, 1776.

The occupation of Île-aux-Noix was brief. So unhealthy was

the island that General John Sullivan feared any more time spent there would destroy his army entirely. Orders to evacuate came on June 20, the day John Patten died. Now the army traveled southward the length of Lake Champlain, first to Crown Point and then, by mid-July, to Ticonderoga. Accounts make it clear that in both places smallpox continued to take a toll. "I can truly say that I did not look into a tent or a hut in which I did not find either a dead or dying man," wrote the artist John Trumbull at Crown Point. When torrential rains struck Ticonderoga on July 17, many "tents were ancle deep in water," and the sick lay immersed. One soldier drowned, "having the small pox bad, & unable to help himself . . . being in a tent alone."[75]

Despite the obstacles, the diminished British threat in this more southerly lake region allowed American officers to establish discipline, order, and most important, quarantine. Healthy troops set up quarters on the east side of Lake George, while those with smallpox congregated on the lake's western shore. Orders enjoined the sick "by no Means to Stop at Tyconderoga or at any house on the East Side of Lake Champlain" as they made their way southward. Major General Horatio Gates commanded all reinforcements to halt at a distance "untill Obliged by the most pressing Emergency" to come closer. "Every thing about this Army is infected with the Pestilence; The Cloaths, The Blanketts, The Air, & the Ground they Walk upon," he explained. Because clandestine inoculation continued to be a problem, new smallpox victims had to "swear solemnly by the Ever living God" that they had not acquired "the Infection of the Small pox by enoculation." Any man refusing to take the oath was expected to name his inoculator so that punishment could be imposed.[76]

All these efforts combined with the passage of time to yield improvement. In mid-July, when smallpox peaked in postsiege Boston to the east, it began to wane among the Continental troops in New York. "The small-pox has almost gone through our Army," reported an eyewitness on July 10; "they are in much better health than they were." Dr. Beebe noted two days later that the men were "on the gaining hand." By the middle of August, dysentery, malaria, and "Bilious Putrid Fevers" had begun to supplant smallpox among the American forces, although the threat from smallpox remained real. "I am straining every nerve to annihilate the infection," General Gates wrote on August 19. Before long his efforts paid off. He passed welcome news on to Washington on August 28. "The Small-Pox is now perfectly removed from the Army," he reported, much relieved. On the very same day, Dr. Beebe visited the army's "burying place" nearby and "counted upwards of 300 graves" dug in just five weeks' time. It "was melancholy indeed," he observed, "to see such desolation made in our army."[77]

For the rebellious colonies and their armed forces, these opening episodes in the war had revealed a serious military vulnerability: Any army containing large numbers of native-born Americans might be easily brought down by smallpox. In the case of Virginia's Ethiopian Regiment, the primary army affected was a loyalist one, but the lesson was the same. In a tumultuous time characterized by a mobile and susceptible populace, *Variola* was very likely to find its way into any large group of people gathered in one place. For the British, this was not a major concern beyond the native-born loyalists (including African Americans and Indians) who joined their ranks. But for General Washington and the Continental army, it was a significant obstacle with dire military implications.

Success at the siege of Boston had briefly led patriot leaders, Washington among them, to believe that quarantine alone could keep smallpox from taking hold among susceptible American soldiers. "If proper precautions are taken, the small-pox may be prevented from spreading," wrote Washington as late as July 7, 1776. "This was done at Cambridge, and I trust will be continued by Generals Schuyler and Gates." Yet it was clear by this time that the conditions at Boston were not easily replicated. Quarantine might confine the contagion, but it did so only as long as it could be enforced. Cold weather, close quarters, and rank-and-file insubordination all could undermine efforts to keep smallpox isolated. More important, in the heat of battle or chaos of retreat the contagion could never be controlled. As the colonies moved toward independence in the summer of 1776, a huge question loomed for the American army. "The small Pox! The small Pox!" wrote John Adams to Abigail. "What shall We do with it?"[78]

The question was to reverberate throughout North America in the six years to come.

3

CONTROL

November 1777. *In a dilapidated house in Alexandria, Virginia, three men lay shivering on pallets of straw. Two wore some tattered "old Cloth[e]s" to ward off the late autumn chill; the third had only an "old shirt and half an old Blankitt." They were weak. They were starving. They had smallpox as well.*

The men were members of the Continental army's Ninth North Carolina Regiment, newly assembled over the previous summer. Much had changed since young John Patten had so enthusiastically joined the service in 1775 and gone to his death in 1776. Gone was the hopeful anticipation that the conflict with Britain would be short. Gone too was the idealism of the early days of the war. The rage militaire *had subsided, and the short-term citizen-soldier had become obsolete. After 1776, the Continental army was a poor man's military force, populated by landless and jobless men recruited not for brief tours of duty but for a year, three years, or "the duration." Many were hired substitutes, paid by rich men to fight in their stead. These were professional soldiers who served to fulfill a contract: They would supply the government with labor, and the government would supply them with food, clothing, and wages, sometimes accompanied by a cash bounty or a promise of land. In this regard, the members of the Ninth North Carolina Regiment were typical, for they took their contract seriously. In August 1777, they had re-*

fused to march to Virginia until they received the wages the army owed them.

The labor action brought results. Money in hand, the men of the Ninth Regiment set out for Virginia on September 1. They halted at Alexandria several weeks later. Here, by the time they arrived, Dr. William Rickman had put hundreds of southern recruits through inoculation, immunizing them to smallpox before they went on to join General Washington and the main army. The once-banned procedure was now required under official military policy. As autumn took hold in Alexandria, susceptible members of the Ninth North Carolina and Fifteenth Virginia regiments rolled up their sleeves and bared their arms for Dr. Rickman and his staff.

The inoculations did not go well. The soldiers complained that after giving them the smallpox, Rickman abandoned them, forcing them to go through the disease without medical support. The men of the Fifteenth Virginia Regiment claimed they had "very little care and attention paid to them while under Inoculation," and one of their officers said he "never saw Doctor Rickman in the Barracks where his men were sick." The North Carolinians protested as well. Colonel John Williams charged Rickman with "great neglect & mismanagement," saying he had left the care of the soldiers "to his assistants, all of whom was negligent and cruel."

Languishing in their quarters throughout the town, the pox-ridden soldiers did their best to look out for one another. When the three men in the cold, run-down house were discovered, Colonel Williams was called to the scene. He was horrified by what he saw. Dr. Rickman, characteristically, could not be found, so Williams sent for one of the doctor's subordinates, Mr. Parker, to help his men. Parker "refused to attend, until he was brought by Force." There are two different accounts of Parker's response when he was finally confronted with the three abandoned soldiers. According to one, he denied any knowledge that "the men were in so bad a situation." According to the other, he admitted knowing of their condition but said he had provided no assistance since there had been no official report.

For the men who lay on the floor, help had come too late. Two died the night they were discovered, and the third died a few days later. Their names were not recorded.[1]

By July 4, 1776, smallpox had established itself as a major danger in what was now a revolutionary war. It had been central in three of the opening salvos of the conflict: the siege of Boston, the siege of Quebec, and the mobilization of Dunmore's Ethiopian Regiment. All these episodes had highlighted the vulnerability of native-born American troops to infection with *Variola major*, a vulnerability that did not bode well for George Washington's army. Even though the overall level of immunity increased with the growing proportion of foreign-born men in the American service after 1776, huge numbers of native-born soldiers kept the army at risk. Everything indicated that unless checked, smallpox would wreak havoc among the Continental forces.

If the signs were ominous, they were nevertheless easy to set aside. In July 1776, the American army had other things to worry about, notably General William Howe and his redcoats. This British force had landed on Staten Island in New York Harbor on July 2, and in the months that followed, it chased Washington and his men out of New York and across the rolling hills of New Jersey to the far side of the Delaware River. Only the stunning American victories at Trenton and Princeton had resurrected the patriot cause. In the first week of January 1777, Washington's exhausted men set up camp at Morristown, New Jersey, where those soldiers who did not head for home nursed their wounds and savored their recent success. But even as they built their huts and settled into their winter quarters, smallpox was knocking at the door. Soon it knocked so loudly that Washington and his medical staff had to take heed.

Nowhere in North America was smallpox more persistent than in the city of Philadelphia. By the time of the Revolutionary War,

Pennsylvania's thriving commercial hub may well have been the only place on the continent where *Variola* had become endemic. Records indicate that after several serious outbreaks during the French and Indian War (1754–63), the disease had a constant presence in the Quaker metropolis, ebbing and flowing cyclically, as it did in British cities.[2]

In part, the high incidence of smallpox in Philadelphia stemmed from the reluctance of authorities to regulate inoculation. Whereas officials elsewhere were cautious or opposed to the operation, officials in Philadelphia were cavalier. Quarantines were rare, and restrictions on variolation were virtually nonexistent. As a result, the practice flourished in the city. Medical practitioners had long urged the public to adopt inoculation, and affluent Americans seeking immunity flocked to Philadelphia from other locales where the procedure came under closer regulation. Thomas Jefferson, for example, underwent inoculation in Philadelphia in 1766, and ten years later, George Washington's wife, Martha, did the same, even as her husband grappled with news of the smallpox's ravages in his Northern Army. The city's variolators included such prominent physicians as John Morgan and Benjamin Rush, and advocates of the practice included the leading citizen and newspaper publisher Benjamin Franklin.[3]

It was Franklin who took the initiative in trying to address the economic inequality that marred Philadelphia's open inoculation policy. For those who could afford it, the procedure was a great boon, but for poor and working-class Philadelphians, it was far too expensive and time-consuming to be practical, and its secondary consequences could be deadly. As well-heeled inoculees circulated through the city streets, they readily passed on the infection to those susceptible in its more dangerous "natural" form. Not surprisingly, in Philadelphia, the children of the poor suffered the highest mortality from the disease. Franklin had lost one of his own children, four-year-old Francis, to smallpox in 1736. Nearly four decades later, in 1774, he and others solicited donations to a society dedicated to the free inoculation of the poor. Although it is hard to say what the overall effect of the program was, it apparently had some success: On May 29, 1776, according to the *Pennsylvania Gazette*, the charitable "Innoculating (or Small Pox) Hospital" housed twenty poor children, "all happily coming through the Disease under Innoculation, and several in the natural Way."[4]

While the continuous circulation of smallpox made Philadelphia a dangerous place for anyone susceptible to *Variola*, it did not keep the city from becoming the nominal capital of the thirteen states during the Revolutionary War. This posed a particular danger to members of the Continental Congress, many of whom came from states where smallpox was rare and inoculation banned. During the congressional sessions in Philadelphia, susceptible delegates were at considerable risk for contracting the infection. John Adams, inoculated in the 1760s, even suggested that immunity to *Variola* was the primary reason for his appointment to Congress. Worn down by his duties, he sarcastically celebrated the spread of epidemic smallpox in Boston in 1775–76. "I rejoice at the spread of the Small Pox on another account," he wrote to James Warren from Philadelphia; "having had the Small Pox, was the merit, which originally recommended me to this lofty Station. This merit is now likely to be common enough & I shall stand a chance to be relieved. Let some others come here and see the Beauties and Sublimities of a Continental Congress."[5]

But smallpox was no joke. To reduce the chance of contagion for vulnerable delegates, Philadelphia physicians agreed to halt all inoculations while the First Continental Congress met in 1774. This was done because "several of the Northern and Southern delegates" were "understood not to have had that disorder." There is no indication, however, that the inoculators halted their activities during later years. The Rhode Island delegate Samuel Ward, chairman of the Congress's powerful Secret Committee, contracted smallpox and died during the Second Continental Congress in 1776. Thomas Burke, a North Carolina member, "was averse to proceeding to Philadelphia" because of "his apprehension of the Small pox" in 1777.[6]

Many susceptible delegates sought inoculation upon their arrival in the pox-plagued metropolis. "The Small Pox is in the City," wrote New Hampshire's Josiah Bartlett to his wife in September 1775. "Some of the members of the Congress are now under Innoculation." Others simply risked the disease, and Bartlett himself was undecided on the matter. "Which I Shall Do I am not fully Determined," he continued, concerned that the operation would keep him "at least a fortnight" from his duties at Congress. Soon, however, he submitted to the inoculator's knife. "Tell Polly I received her letter and Shall be very Carefull not to Bring home the Small Pox to my family as Col. Moulton did to his," he wrote. "I think my Self & Cloaths Clear of it at this time."[7]

Bartlett was not alone in his decision. This in itself may explain why physicians no longer halted inoculations after the First Continental Congress gathered in 1774; fear of smallpox ran so deep that many delegates actually sought out the procedure. Patrick Henry of Virginia went through variolation in the able hands of Dr. Benjamin Rush. Matthew Thornton of New Hampshire took the pox from an unnamed physician. "The 3d instant we arrived safe in this city, and the 8th inoculated for the smallpox," Thornton wrote in November 1776. Another New Hampshire delegate submitted to inoculation in 1780, and Connecticut's Samuel Huntington, who had already chanced catching the disease while attending earlier meetings, went through it in the same year.[8]

Nonetheless, the persistent contagion established Philadelphia as a sort of distribution center from which the pox could spread far and wide. In January 1776, the Continental fleet under Commodore Esek Hopkins set sail from the city. Because of ice in the Delaware River, it took more than a month for his ships to reach the Atlantic. By February 17, when they finally put to sea, smallpox had become rampant among the men. "We had many Sick," wrote Hopkins, "and four of the Vessels had a large number on-board with the Small Pox." By one account at least, it was the commodore's fear of spreading the disease to his fellow Americans that prompted him to shun the continental coastline for the time being. "The Small-Pox," according to the *Connecticut Gazette*, "rendered it imprudent to cruise on this Coast." Instead, the fleet sped southward and took the British fort at Nassau, in the Bahamas, replete with much-needed ammunition. Whether Hopkins's sailors and marines communicated smallpox to the residents of Nassau remains unknown, but the plague almost certainly continued within the fleet when the men landed on March 3, 1776. Six months later, pox from Philadelphia also turned up in the South Carolina backcountry, where it threatened inland plantations in the region of the Lynches River.[9]

Once the war was under way, no single group of people was more likely to carry smallpox away from Philadelphia than soldiers in the Continental army. Because of its central location on the Atlantic seaboard, the city was a logical stopping point for newly enlisted southern recruits on their way north to join Washington and his men. Southerners of course were among those most likely to be vulnerable to *Variola*. But the lives these fast-moving enlistees endangered were not just their own. A soldier could pick up smallpox in Philadelphia and then march for nearly two weeks before showing symptoms and infecting his messmates. Hence in August 1776, still reeling from the debacle in Canada, President John Hancock ordered regiments marching from Virginia to New Jersey to go around "Phil[a]. on Acc[t]. of the Small Pox." Six months later the problem remained, and Virginia troops once again received instructions "to avoid Philadelphia where the Infection now prevails." The contagious city exasperated Washington. "I would wish to have the small Pox intirely out of Philadelphia," he wrote, but he acknowledged that it simply could not be done.[10] Only if the troops were immune could they pass through the Quaker city without risk.

Obviously, smallpox presented a significant obstacle to the enlistment of new soldiers in the Continental service. In Connecticut, as news spread of the pestilence in Canada, Governor Jonathan Trumbull observed the pox's detrimental effect on local recruiting efforts. "Our people in general have not had that Distemper," he told Washington on July 4, 1776. "Fear of the Infection operates strongly to prevent Soldiers from engageing in the Service, and the Battallions ordered to be raised in this Colony fill up slowly." Two days later, again in a letter to Washington, he went further, reminding the general that patterns of immunity to smallpox varied widely among the Anglo-American provinces. "Probably not one in twenty of our Men have ever had that distemper," he wrote of his Connecticut constituents, "when the New York, Jersey, & Pennsylvania Men have generally passed thro' it." In New York in 1776, Major General Schuyler found militiamen from New England "extremely apprehensive of being infected with the small pox, and not without Reason as it proves fatal to many of them."[11]

Fear of the pox also hindered enlistments in the South. On February 8, 1777, as smallpox raged in the army's Virginia encampments, the politician Edmund Pendleton feared it would "much retard our inlistments." The "terrors of the smallpox added to Lies of Deserters &c, &c, deter but too many," wrote Patrick Henry in March. Recruitment continued to lag, and a month later Washington himself admitted "that the apprehensions of the Small pox and its calamitous consequences" had "greatly retarded the Inlistments" from Virginia.[12]

With a relative abundance of time and money at their disposal, many of Virginia's revolutionary elites had undergone inoculation in provinces where the procedure was unfettered by legal restraints. Often immune themselves, some argued that popular fears of the pox were exaggerated. "Some evil disposed people," according to Richard Henry Lee, had "industriously propagated" rumors "that the plague rages in our Army—In consequence of which, it is said, the recruiting business stops, and desertions are frequent." By 1778, popular resentment of military conscription had resulted in violence in several Virginia counties. As George Washington's younger brother John Augustine described it, the common folk of Virginia took a skeptical view of the Continental service: "Whether it proceeds from the fear of the Small pox, and those other dangerous disorders they are told prevail in the Camp, or whether it is from disaffection to the cause I cannot determine, but in all probability partly to all three." Nevertheless, he added, "I know the dainger of the small pox and camp fever is more alarming to many than any dainger they apprehend from the arms of the enemy."[13]

Potential enlistees were put off not just by the prospect of catching smallpox but also by the prospect of discipline if they inoculated against orders in an effort to protect themselves. When the Continental army docked Seth Warner's pay because "his men went into Inoculation contrary to order" at Quebec, the Connecticut congressional delegate William Williams warned that Warner's being treated with "impolitic Severity" would "have a very ill Effect" and would "disaffect Men" from enlisting. The disease environment in Canada had been extraordinary, he said, and under such duress, "allowances ought to be made and Faults winked at, especially when the Men are so much wanted etc."[14]

Nothing instilled fear in American soldiers and civilians so much as the prospect that the British might use smallpox as a weapon of war. The concern may seem farfetched and sensational, but it was not without merit. British officers had already demonstrated their willingness to use biological warfare in 1763, when Indians organized under the Ottawa leader Pontiac had threatened the safety of Fort Pitt, on the Pennsylvania frontier. "Out of our regard to them," wrote a trader on the scene, "we gave them two Blankets and an Handkerchief out of the Small Pox Hospital. I hope it will have the desired effect." This act had the sanction of an impressive array of British officers, including Sir Jeffery Amherst, commander in chief at the time, and General Thomas Gage, who replaced Amherst and signed off on reimbursements for the "Sundries" used "to Convey the Smallpox to the Indians." But would the British use germ warfare against their own subjects? Would they use it against individuals of European descent? American colonists seemed to think that they would. It was Gage, after all, who commanded the British army during the first months of the colonists' siege of Boston. Seth Pomeroy was an American officer who had served under Gage during the French and Indian War. "If it is In General Gages power," Pomeroy wrote in May 1775, "I Expect he will Send ye Small pox Into ye Army—but I hope In ye Infinight Mercy of God he will prevent It, as he hath don In Every attempt that he has made yet." Rumors of germ warfare at Boston had circulated as early as March 1775.[15]

By the year's end, Thomas Gage had turned over his command to Sir William Howe, but talk of germ warfare had failed to subside. Instead, the evidence mounted. On December 3, shortly after the British began to force selected citizens to leave Boston, four British deserters arrived at the American headquarters in Cambridge. They brought with them a sinister report. General Howe, they said, had deliberately infected several of the exiles "with a design to spread the Small-Pox among the [American] Troops." General Washington found the accusation so astonishing that he could "hardly give Credit" to it. But the danger was too great to ignore, and he took it seriously, immediately informing local authorities and President John Hancock.[16]

December 10, 1775, brought more evidence, albeit circumstantial. "The small-pox has broke out in two families that came out of *Boston* in the first vessels," wrote a man named Thomas Crafts. Even worse for the Americans, the pestilence had not been contained to one place. "Two persons have it at *Point Shirley*," Crafts reported, "and one at *Malden*." An obviously concerned Washington expressed dismay to the Massachusetts House of Representatives. "Should it spread," he wrote, the smallpox would be "very disastrous & fatal to our army and the Country around it." The outbreak caused him to reappraise his earlier skepticism about the deserters' report of germ warfare. "I now must give Some Credit to it," he said, "as it [smallpox] has made its appearance on Severall of those who Last Came out of Boston." Months later, a youth named Thomas Francis swore under oath that at his master's orders he had boarded a ship out of Boston after being inoculated with the disease. The intention, he implied, had been to spread it.[17]

Whether or not the British deliberately employed biological warfare at the siege of Boston, the rising tide of smallpox there certainly helped thwart any American plans to attack. Washington described the disease as "a weapon of Defence, they Are useing against us." An assault upon the city might mean casualties well in excess of those suffered on the battlefield, he knew. To Joseph Reed on December 15, he reiterated the point. "The Small Pox is in every part of Boston," he wrote; the sick, he believed, were "consider'd as a Security against any attempt of ours."[18]

Even as the British departed, Washington believed they were leaving a pestilential trap in wait for his men, as he warned them as early as March 13, 1776. No one was to enter Boston without permission, he said, "as the enemy with a malicious assiduity, have spread the infection of the smallpox through all parts of the town." The subject came up again in the army's orders for the following day: "The General was informed Yesterday evening, by a person just out of Boston, that our Enemies in that place, had laid several Schemes for communicating the infection of the small-pox, to the Continental Army, when they get into the town."[19]

Boston was not the only place where such charges were leveled. At Quebec rumors had circulated hand in hand with the smallpox, and American eyewitnesses pointed their fingers at their British adversaries. "The small pox," the rifleman John Joseph Henry later told his daughter, was "introduced into our cantonments by the indecorous, yet fascinating arts of the enemy." At congressional hearings held even as the Canadian campaign unraveled in July 1776, several witnesses made the same accusation. "The small pox was sent out of Quebeck by Carleton," said Cap-

tain Hector McNeal. It "was said but no proof that Carleton had
sent it," said another officer. Such testimony convinced Thomas
Jefferson of British culpability. "I have been informed by officers
who were on the spot, and whom I believe myself, that this disorder was sent into our army designedly by the commanding officer
in Quebec," he wrote to the French historian François Soulés.[20]

The charge arose in Virginia as well, after Lord Dunmore's
move from Tucker's Point to Gwynn's Island in May 1776. Noting
that many of the governor's black troops were in the throes of
smallpox at the time, a local newspaper went on to give the following account: "His Lordship, before the departure of the fleet
from Norfolk harbour, had two of those wretches inoculated and
sent ashore, in order to spread the infection, but it was happily
prevented." The story seems to have circulated widely, for it came
up in an interview with a man named James Cunningham, who
deserted from Dunmore's service in the Potomac in July. "How
long were they inocul[ated] & was it done to communicate it to
the People on shore?" asked the interrogators. "By no means,"
was Cunningham's ambiguous response; "every one in the Fleet
was inoculated, that had it not."[21]

The next spring, whispers of biological warfare circulated far to
the north in New Hampshire. Returning soldiers had already
spread smallpox across New England in the aftermath of the Quebec fiasco, heightening concerns over the disease. But in April
1777, these concerns took a new tack when rumors surfaced in
Kingston, New Hampshire, of a secret "Tory plan" allegedly involving "great numbers of people bound together by the most
solemn oaths and imprecations." Josiah Bartlett described the pur-
ported plot to his fellow congressional delegate William Whipple:
"It seems their design is, this Spring to spread the small pox
through the country." Leading New Hampshire patriots were
"certainly concerned and we have reason to think most of the Tories in New England are in the plan."[22]

Eruptions of the pox did occur in New Hampshire and the
New Hampshire grants (modern-day Vermont) in 1777 and 1778.

Among those who died was young Joseph Allen, described by his bereft father, the American patriot Ethan Allen, as "My only son, the darling of my soul." The New Hampshire suspicions seem to have subsided quickly, but the threat of biological warfare would not go away.[23]

By January 1777, Washington and his men had encamped for the winter in the rich farmland around Morristown, New Jersey. They faced uncertain prospects. Their recent victories at Trenton and Princeton had somewhat compensated for the earlier loss of New York and the dismal episode in Canada, but huge problems remained. Just south of them, Philadelphia seemed vulnerable. To the north, on Lake Champlain, the British general John Burgoyne seemed poised to finish off the Americans' Northern Army at Ticonderoga. Ominous too was the British position at New York City, whence the king's forces might sail up the Hudson River, possibly joining Burgoyne and cutting off New England from the rest of the colonies. But on January 6, 1777, Washington had another problem to tackle, a problem as old and persistent as the war itself. Smallpox had again appeared in the Continental army. "We should have more to dread from it, than from the Sword of the Enemy," wrote Washington.[24] The time had come to inoculate the troops.

Inoculation had long been standard procedure in the British army, rarely endangered by *Variola* unless native-born American loyalists enlisted. When the virus did threaten, British regimental surgeons simply polled the ranks and inoculated the few soldiers who had never had the disease. This was what they had done in Boston and in Canada as well. Because the king's forces contained a much smaller proportion of vulnerable soldiers, the procedure presented neither logistical nor strategic difficulties. Attendants with immunity were easy to come by. Quarantine was easy to maintain. If the virus did escape isolation, the small number of susceptibles kept the pox from broadening its base in the army itself. Thomas Dickson Reide, surgeon to the First Battalion of Foot, indicated how insignificant the problem was for the king's troops as they chased the pox-ridden Americans out of Canada. "The Americans having left some sick in the small-pox on their quitting Montreal," he observed mildly in June 1776, "the commanding officer ordered that all those who had not had that disease should be inoculated immediately." A survey of the troops yielded only a handful of susceptible soldiers. Reide and another surgeon "performed that operation on twelve or fourteen men, all of who[m] did well."[25]

For the Americans, by contrast, inoculation presented formidable obstacles. It is true that by 1777, the number of foreign-born soldiers was growing in the Continental army, and there can be little doubt that these men were less likely than others to be vulnerable to *Variola*. But there were still huge numbers of native-born susceptibles. To cite but one example, it was estimated that in one unit of North Carolina soldiers who marched northward in the spring of 1777, only 23 percent had ever had smallpox. Inoculating all the vulnerable soldiers in the Continental army was an enormous undertaking with significant military risks. So treacherous was the task that on January 28, 1777, three weeks after he told Dr. Shippen to begin mass inoculations of the troops in Philadelphia, Washington had a change of heart. The inoculation of these men, he now informed Shippen, "would be a very Salutary Measure, if we could prevent them from bringing the Infection on to the Army; but as they cannot have a change of Cloaths, I fear it is impossible." He told Shippen instead to devote his attention to those already sick, making sure they were "perfectly cured" and disinfected before sending them to join him.[26]

Washington's indecision reflected the complexity of the problem. On February 5, only a week later, he changed his mind yet again. The inoculations would go forward, he told President Hancock. "The small pox has made such Head in every Quarter that I find it impossible to keep it from spreading thro' the whole Army in the natural way. I have therefore determined, not only to innoculate all the Troops now here, that have not had it, but shall order Doc^r. Shippen to innoculate the Recruits as fast as they come in to

Philadelphia." Within days, the Congress's Medical Committee, chaired by Dr. Rush, affirmed Washington's new policy. The decision could not have come soon enough. The disease was making inroads at Morristown, and the commander in chief had already sent Dr. John Cochran to Newtown, Pennsylvania, to combat another outbreak among troops quartered there.[27] Soon reports came in of smallpox spreading in army camps in Virginia and New York, where the malady had again infected Ticonderoga.[28] If fresh recruits with no immunity to *Variola* joined the soldiers already in these pestilential camps, the disease would once again bring the army to its knees. Inoculation was the only solution.

It was a daunting task for the Continental army's medical department. At camps and enlistment centers from Virginia to Connecticut, medical personnel now had to ascertain which soldiers had never had smallpox, proceed with variolation, ensure quarantine, provide immune attendants, nurse the inoculees through the disease, disinfect the recovered patients, and finally, in most cases, send the men on to the main army. Moreover, all this required the utmost secrecy, for if the British got wind of it, they might capitalize on the temporary indisposition of thousands of American soldiers. "I need not mention the necessity of as much secrecy as the nature of the Subject will admit of," wrote Washington, "it being beyond doubt, that the Enemy will avail themselves of the event as far as they can."[29]

The inoculations took place in Virginia at Alexandria, Fairfax, and Dumfries; in Maryland at Georgetown; in New Jersey at Morristown; in Pennsylvania at Newtown, Bethlehem, and Philadelphia; in New York at Ticonderoga and the Hudson Highlands near West Point; and in Connecticut at an undetermined location.[30] Other sites too may have witnessed the inoculations of soldiers during 1777. For the better part of a year, until Washington ordered a procedural change in March 1778, veterans went through the procedure wherever they camped with their comrades, while new enlistees faced inoculation before they set out to join the army. "Inoculate your men as fast as they are enlisted," wrote

Washington to Colonel George Baylor in Virginia on March 28, 1777. Running the new recruits through smallpox before they marched was a preemptive measure. Protected by their recently acquired immunity, reinforcements would not pick up natural smallpox en route or upon reaching the army, which, Washington hoped, would thus remain free of the infection and unburdened by sick men. Above all, he wanted to avoid a repeat of "the deplorable and melancholy situation, to which one of our Armies was reduced last Campaign by the Small pox."[31]

Thousands of soldiers received variolation in 1777, and in most instances the procedure went well. Limited resources and the advances attending Suttonian inoculation meant that few had to endure a grueling preparatory routine, a change that must have saved lives. At the Hudson Highlands, Private Joseph Plumb Martin went through the procedure with some four hundred other Connecticut troops in the summer of 1777. Housed in an old set of barracks and attended by a guard of previously immunized troops from Massachusetts, the men came through variolation with great success. "We lost none," he observed. "I had the smallpox favorably as did the rest."[32]

Only in the Virginia hospitals were there complaints of poor treatment and neglect. The Virginia operation was supervised by several prominent physicians, but it may simply have been too large to ensure quality control. On a single day in May 1777, for example, a Caroline County observer watched as some twenty-two hundred "healthy and Spirited" North Carolina troops passed by on their way to an inoculation hospital. Only five hundred of them had previously acquired immunity; the rest faced the inoculator's knife. Nicholas Cresswell, a traveler who was in Alexandria in the midst of the inoculations, gave an idea of the scale of the undertaking in a journal entry of April 20, 1777. "All the townspeople and a Regiment of soldiers that are quartered here all inoculated for the Smallpox," he wrote. "Such a pock-eyed place I never was in before."[33] Here, where Dr. William Rickman inoculated the three doomed North Carolina soldiers in the fall of 1777,

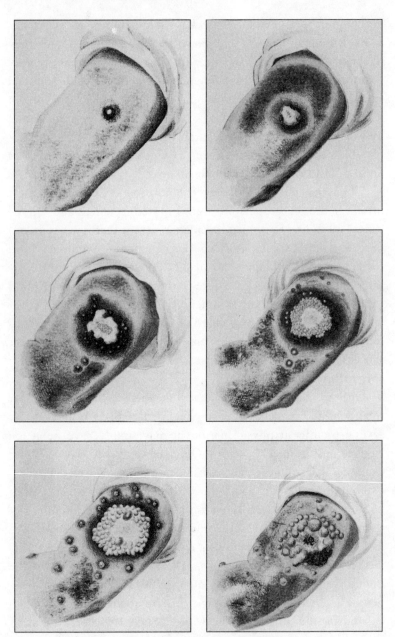

The progress of inoculated smallpox. Composite image from the chromolithographs of George Kirtland. Courtesy the Wellcome Library

complaints also emerged of abuses so severe that the army eventually investigated.

The investigation was a serious one, in which eyewitnesses gave sworn depositions regarding events at the troubled inoculation center. Those who supported Rickman appear to have been colleagues, officers, and acquaintances, some of whom stayed in the doctor's home during their immunizations. "As I lodged with Rickman when I was at Alexandria his diligence necessarily came under my observation," explained a deponent named Jacob Walker. Not only had Rickman "paid the strictest attention to the sold[i]ers under his care in the small pox," but on at least one occasion he had even "left his bed when called by a soldier." Another witness lucky enough to have "lodged in the Doctors House" was a man named Richard Randolph. "As far as I was capable of judging the Doct^r. payed the greatest attention to the soldiers under his care," he testified. Rickman, he recalled, was in "constant motion," visiting his inoculees "every morning & evening, & whenever he was call'd on." Asked about the three freezing North Carolina soldiers found dying unattended, one of the doctor's assistants claimed the men were deserters who had imprudently "confined themself in an open House." Rickman himself—in an unsworn document—said the three North Carolinians had had poor prospects from the start. "They were not stout men," he explained, "but poor emaciated Creatures" even when they arrived.[34]

Others saw the entire affair quite differently. Colonel Williams described the three men as "stout likely persons," and a lieutenant from the Third North Carolina Regiment said that after his own inoculation, the doctor "never came to see him" again. Thomas Wells of the Fifteenth Virginia Regiment said that "physick" was given only to those who requested it. And Lieutenant William Murry of North Carolina testified that he and his fellow inoculees were so desperate for care that they eventually hired another doctor and "paid him out of their own pockets." Local residents were reportedly appalled: "It was said by the Inhabitants that they had never known any persons have the small pox so severely before that were inoculated." The evidence against Dr. Rickman seemed overwhelming, and the Continental army eventually suspended him for mistreatment of the soldiers in his care.[35] If soldiers at other variolation centers had similar complaints, they apparently went unrecorded. Alexandria alone emerged with a reputation for being a particularly hard place to undergo inoculation.

The winter of 1777–78 was the famous "Valley Forge" winter, symbolized by the bloody footprints that shoeless Continental soldiers left in the snow around the army's Pennsylvania headquarters. The previous autumn had yielded mixed news: At Saratoga, in upstate New York, American forces had scored a stunning victory over General Burgoyne's army of British and Hessian soldiers, but in southeast Pennsylvania, at Brandywine Creek and Germantown, the Americans had lost, and British troops under General Howe had taken Philadelphia. Internal dissension rocked Washington's officer corps, and extraordinary physical hardship threatened his fighting men.

Desperate though his soldiers were for food, clothing, and shelter, Washington clung to his vision of a smallpox-free army. He was therefore dismayed to find that the troops at Valley Forge, by this time mostly veterans on long-term enlistments, still included susceptible men who had somehow escaped smallpox inoculation. "Notwithstanding the Orders I had given last year to have all the Recruits innoculated," Washington wrote to Connecticut Governor Trumbull, "I found upon examination, that between three and four thousand Men had not had the Small Pox; that disorder began to make its appearance in Camp, and to avoid its spreading in the natural way, the whole were immediately innoculated." Beginning in the first week of January 1778, inoculations thus went on in winter quarters at Valley Forge just as they had the year before at Morristown.[36] Already laden with soldiers suffering from dysentery, "fevers," and other camp disorders, the sick rolls now expanded further as susceptible men took the *Variola* virus. "Our numbers of Effectives is so reduced by inoculation, that it is impossible to spare the few Men of the 13th Virginia Regiment just at this time," wrote Washington on March 25, 1778. Army doctors went about their work "with all possible secrecy," and by one account, "nearly one-half of the troops had gone through the disease before the enemy became apprised of its commencement."[37]

As spring crept across the Pennsylvania countryside, the enemy was a growing concern. The British seemed to be up to something in Philadelphia. But because of desertions and the expiration of enlistments at the close of 1777, Washington faced any move with a mere shell of an army. The number of troops "present fit for duty & on duty" dropped from 14,122 in December 1777 to 8,095 in January 1778 and 7,316 by March.[38] Recruiting had the utmost urgency, but inoculation seriously delayed the activation of new enlistees, who spent three to four weeks at it before marching to join the army. In the spring of 1778, Washington desperately needed men.

Increasingly "suspicious that General Howe" was "drawing his reinforcements together to attack," the American commander in chief had to weigh the benefits of remote inoculation against the delays it caused. Not only did the current policy postpone the arrival at Valley Forge of the new enlistments, but it also tied up the many immune men who nursed the inoculees in the distant hospital camps. In Virginia, Richard Henry Lee complained of "inconsiderate Officers" who, rather than forward immune soldiers to the army, insisted that they remain in camp to serve "as Attendees upon those who are to undergo inoculation."[39] In March, Washington consulted with his medical staff. It was time, they decided, to change their policy.

The first set of revised orders went out on March 20. In a letter to the commanding officer at Alexandria, Virginia, Washington explained that after much consultation, he had "determined that it will be more convenient to innoculate all the Levies that have not had the small pox, at or near the Camp [Valley Forge]." Therefore, he continued, "I desire that you will suffer none of them to be detained at Alexandria or George Town for that purpose." The new drafts should march directly to Valley Forge without undergoing variolation. But, he added, "They are to make diligent enquiry whether the small pox be at any Houses upon the Road, and if it is to avoid them carefully." Physicians at Valley Forge would inoculate the men as they arrived.[40] Army officials in Massachusetts, Connecticut, New York, Pennsylvania, and North Carolina received similar orders.[41] Haste had replaced immunization as the highest priority.

"I beg you will exert yourself in forwarding on the Recruits," wrote Washington to Major General William Heath in Massachusetts. "They need not remain to be innoculated as that can be done conveniently upon their arrival in Camp." Medical opinion now suggested that as long as the recruits avoided smallpox on the trek to Valley Forge, in-camp inoculations might promise an even better outcome than the earlier protocol: "As they will not have a long march to undergo after they have recovered, they will in all probability do better than if they had taken the small pox before they set out." In addition, he could call upon the patients if necessary in a military emergency.[42]

The new policy meant new procedures. As long as variolation continued in and around Valley Forge, the threat of unchecked contagion loomed large: If quarantine was not secure, inoculated soldiers could easily infect vulnerable newcomers. Washington enjoined all officers "upon the arrival of recruits or return of absent soldiers to make immediate and strict inquiry whether they have had the Small Pox, and order such as have not to be innoculated without loss of time." The new arrivals, for their part, got instructions to halt two to three days away from the American camp and to send word ahead, in order "that proper accommodations may be prepared for them."[43]

The grueling inoculations continued through May, as dog-woods dropped their blossoms and new enlistments bolstered the size of the Continental army to 15,061 men.[44] The onset of spring brought good news as well as fresh men: France had taken up the American cause, Washington learned, and the French fleet had already set out across the Atlantic Ocean. In Philadelphia, where the British had wintered, changes were also afoot. General Sir Henry Clinton had replaced Howe at the head of Britain's North American forces, and he had brought with him a new set of orders from Lord Germain, the man ultimately responsible for crown strategy. Largely in response to France's entry into the war, the new orders called for two significant moves: The British were to withdraw from Philadelphia and return to New York, and they were also to launch a major expedition against the French colony of St. Lucia, a tiny but strategically important island in the Caribbean.

As Philadelphia sprang to life, General Clinton's intent to depart became clear, and the American camp also made preparations. A British march across New Jersey might give Washington the chance to test the mettle of his newly reorganized and freshly drilled troops. Urgency therefore set the tone. But as the Continental army scrambled to respond to the impending British move, the sick remained to be dealt with. In May 1778, they amounted to nearly thirty-eight hundred men, including "Men in the Small Pox or under Innoculation." Instead of marching with the army, these invalids would remain behind until well. "A sufficient number of Camp Kettles must be left for the use of the sick," Washington ordered, and a commissary had to stay to provision them. Medicine chests were to go with the army, but brigade surgeons would remain in camp " 'till relieved by Surgeons from the General Hospital." To assist them in their duties, orderlies were "also to be left, one to every twenty sick men."[45]

For nursing care, Washington drew upon one of the Continental army's least appreciated resources, the little-known group of

patriots whom he called the Women of the Army. It has been estimated that on the American side, about twenty thousand women
served in this vaguely defined capacity over the course of the Revolutionary War. Now, as Washington prepared to take off after the
British, he enlisted some of these women to stay behind to tend to
smallpox patients at the Valley Forge camp. He had his officers
and surgeons recruit "as many Women of the Army as can be
prevailed on to serve as Nurses." They would be paid at what
Washington termed "the usual Price." It was hazardous duty, un-
appealing indeed for anyone susceptible to *Variola*. But the general's strict admonition "that no Women be suffered on any
Pretence to get into the Waggons of the Army on the march" no
doubt encouraged female attendants to remain with the sick in
Pennsylvania.[46]

On June 18, 1778, Clinton's Philadelphia-based British army
set out north across the Delaware River, and Washington's troops
crossed in pursuit almost immediately. It is unclear exactly how
many ailing men remained behind, but after reporting thirty-
eight hundred ill the previous month, the sick rolls showed only
nine hundred indisposed in June. Given the mass inoculations of
March and April and the remarkable improvement in June, it is
clear that a great number of the inoculees had recovered.[47] Now,
with men freshly drilled and largely invulnerable to this most
terrifying disease, Washington must have set off through New
Jersey's piney woods with new confidence. Within days, his
smallpox-free army squared off against Clinton's force of British
and Hessians at the Battle of Monmouth. The showdown ended
in a draw.

The Battle of Monmouth was inconclusive, and the ultimate
effect of George Washington's massive inoculation operation also
remained unclear. The inoculations themselves, despite the
lapses in Alexandria, can fairly be called successful. The army had
pulled off the first large-scale, state-sponsored immunization campaign in American history. But only the future would tell what difference it would make, for the war was far from over. Over the

next three years the conflict moved south to Georgia, the Carolinas, and Washington's home state of Virginia. Smallpox followed it like a shadow. In an ongoing maelstrom of people and microbes, the southern theater proved the ultimate test for the general's newly inoculated army.

4

SURRENDER

Autumn 1779. *On the outskirts of Savannah, Georgia, David George lay all alone, too sick to move. His family had left him, and now the enemy, a combined force of French and American soldiers, was approaching. George felt certain that the end was near: If the pox did not kill him, the Americans surely would.*

David George was a loyalist. He had been born a slave in Essex County, Virginia, around 1742, and his early recollections were of plantation discipline. He remembered his mother "on her knees, begging for mercy" before a beating, and he recalled seeing his sister whipped until her back was "all corruption, as though it would rot." Eventually, unable to tolerate his master's "rough and cruel usage," David George ran away.

His flight took him southward, out of Virginia, through the Carolinas, and into the central Georgia Piedmont. There a Creek Indian king named Blue Salt captured him and carried him to the village of Cussita, on the Chattahoochee River. Even in Cussita, among the Creeks, George found himself a slave. "The people were kind," he noted, but he nevertheless "worked hard." It was not long before his white master caught up with him. When Blue Salt agreed to return the fugitive in exchange for some "rum, linnen, and a gun," George took flight again. This time he sought refuge farther west, in a Natchez Indian village with a headman named King Jack.

King Jack sold David George back into slavery, brokering a deal that

*transferred the runaway from his Virginia owner to a South Carolina en-
trepreneur named George Galphin. For three years thereafter, David
George labored in the deerskin trade for his new master, living in the interior, mending skins, tending horses, and traveling some four hundred
miles east once a year to deliver the collected bounty to Galphin at his Silver Bluff, South Carolina, entrepôt. On George's third trip, the bondsman
asked his master if he could stay on at Silver Bluff. Galphin agreed.*

*For the next four years, David George lived what he termed "a bad
life," meaning a life of sin, at Galphin's estate. But then he got married,
and after the birth of his first child, he underwent a deeply felt religious
conversion. By the time the portentous shots sounded at Lexington and
Concord in 1775, George had become a preacher, and his Silver Bluff
congregation had become the first black Baptist church in America.*

*The Revolutionary War had great import for slaves, and black south-
erners followed its progress closely. In December 1778, British troops took
Savannah, the first of several prizes in their newly launched southern
campaign. Many patriots fled, George Galphin among them. "Being
afraid," David George recalled, his master "retired from home and left
the Slaves behind." The enslaved laborers saw opportunity in their
owner's departure. Along with more than fifty other Galphin slaves,
David George and his family ran to the British lines, taking refuge in a
stable in Savannah. When an American cannonball destroyed it, they
found shelter "under the floor of a house on the ground." Later, when the
siege lifted, they moved about a mile outside town.*

*It was here that George got smallpox, just as the American army at-
tempted to retake the city in October 1779. "I wished my wife to escape,
and to take care of herself and the children, and let me die," George said.
She did his bidding, but her husband did not die. Instead, he sustained
himself on a bit of rice and Indian corn while the Americans went down
to defeat. When the pox subsided, he made his way back to Savannah and
his family. For the next two years, David George managed a butcher stall
and his wife worked as a laundress for the British general Sir Henry
Clinton. They then took passage to the British-held city of Charleston, another safe haven.*

The Georges stayed in Charleston until the end of the war, when they joined other white and black loyalists sailing for the English colony of Nova Scotia. They lived in Nova Scotia for ten years. Here George's family grew, and here he continued his preaching, even addressing biracial audiences and baptizing white converts. "We had a little heaven together," he said. But it was not the kind of heaven envisioned by some in the white community. Offended by black enterprise and by interracial worship, angry whites destroyed George's home and the homes of many of his parishioners. The violence was part of an ongoing pattern of abuse inflicted on black Nova Scotians by their white neighbors.

With no peace to be found, David George accepted an offer to participate in the founding of Sierra Leone, on the west African coast. Intended as a moral counterbalance to the insidious slave trade, the abolitionist-inspired colony was to be settled by free blacks from throughout the British empire. In January 1792, George set sail with his wife and six children aboard a fleet carrying nearly twelve hundred black loyalists across the Atlantic. Tradition has it that in their first worship service on African soil, they lifted their voices in song: "The Year of Jubilee is come | Returned ye ransomed sinners home."

The early years in Sierra Leone were marked by tensions between the black colonists and their white governors. To the ex-slaves from America, the issues were familiar ones: British taxes and quitrents were exorbitant, and the colonists demanded relief. When the controversy exploded into armed rebellion in 1800, a man named Harry Washington, formerly the bondsman of George Washington, was among the rebels. David George's role is unclear, but he probably had a moderating influence on the doomed uprising, urging restraint upon his fellow settlers. George died in Sierra Leone in 1810.[1]

David George's story is emblematic of the age he lived in, an era of globalization in which warfare, politics, kinship, and commerce increasingly spanned oceans and continents. The Revolutionary War was a case in point. France's alliance with the Americans in 1778 instantly transformed the conflict from an internecine feud among Britons into an international struggle with worldwide repercussions. From this point forward, the fighting took place on a global stage. Troops gathered in the French cities of Le Havre and St. Malo for an invasion of England; naval battles were fought in the Mediterranean and in waters off of England, France, and India. In North America, still the main object of contention, the action turned southward, where new concerns and new opportunities drew British attention. The French sugar islands in the Caribbean Sea were now fair game, and the British colony of Jamaica required defense. In the Gulf of Mexico, Pensacola beckoned as a staging ground for a British attack on New Orleans. In Georgia, the Carolinas, and Virginia, where deep social divisions strengthened loyalist sentiment, King George III's advisors hoped that their army might meet with the success that had eluded it in the North.

It seems reasonable to expect that smallpox might have parted ways with the Revolution as the fighting moved south, given that patterns of immunity had changed. As landed "citizen-soldiers" grew disillusioned with military service, the Continental army increasingly filled its ranks with landless and jobless foreign immigrants. This alone helped boost the proportion of immune soldiers in the American line. Enlistments were now for the long term, moreover, significantly reducing the contagious threat presented by the constant turnover of men in the earlier campaigns. But the most important new variable was inoculation: The mass inoculations of 1777–78 had put the regular soldiers of the Continental army on a par with the regular soldiers of the British army.

Variola was not so easily thwarted, however. To succeed, the virus needed not soldiers but chaos, connections, and a steady supply of susceptible victims. The war in the South offered all these in abundance.

The events of 1775–76 had already shown how the turmoil of revolution could put civilians as well as soldiers in *Variola*'s path. The outbreak in Boston, which affected noncombatants above all others, was perhaps the most outstanding example, but not the only one. The disastrous epidemic that derailed the American invasion of Canada had also scattered the pox among civilians far and wide, despite General Schuyler's assurances "that Every Precaution will be taken to prevent their being infected by the small Pox." The primary vectors were veterans, drained and disillusioned, who brought home not just war stories but a virulent virus as well. During the winter of 1776–77, homeward-bound soldiers from the New York lakes launched smallpox epidemics in Pennsylvania as well as in Connecticut, where Governor Trumbull was so concerned that he addressed the problem in a special proclamation in February 1777. Veterans who had "taken the Infection" in the retreat from Canada had "been principally the means of spreading it in this State," he noted. To check the escalating contagion, he ordered "the Select Men in each Town" to "take the most effectual Care to have all suspected Soldiers and Travellers inspected." If they discovered individuals with signs of the pox, they were "to remove them to proper Places of Safety . . . where the best Care may be taken of them in their Sickness."[2]

Regular soldiers from the Continental army were not the only veterans who carried smallpox home with them. The Native American allies of the British did the same. Ottawa Indian warriors returning west transported the pestilence all the way to Michilimackinac, the famous military post and trading center located in what is now northern Michigan. Here, in the woodlands of the Great Lakes, the pox wintered among the natives. By February 1777, crown officials considered the survivors all the more valuable as allies thanks to the immunity they had acquired. Over the same winter, an unnamed epidemic, almost certainly smallpox from the Canadian conflict, ravaged the Onondaga Iroquois at their fortified "castle" in central New York, killing ninety people, including three "principal sachems." "Our council-fire is extinguished, and can no longer burn," the Onondagas told their Oneida confederates.[3]

As the circulation of people and microbes escalated, civilian outbreaks of smallpox flared like wildfires. Tidewater Virginians had to combat the disease after the routing of the Ethiopian Regiment in 1776, and Boston endured yet another epidemic in 1778. Residents of New York City suffered repeated episodes of the disease during the long British occupation of their strategically important town. In May 1777, the Englishman Nicholas Cresswell found New York in ruins, its residents crammed together "like herrings in a barrel, most of them very dirty and not a small number sick of some disease, the Itch, Pox, Fever, or Flux." The pox was still a problem and showed signs of spreading two years later, causing well-to-do New Yorkers to seek out inoculation for themselves and their children. In May 1779, the pestilence killed several people in the village of New Concord, located well to the north on the Hudson River. New Concord residents expressed "a universal Concern for Fear of the Spreading of that Contagious Distemper." *Variola* may also have been the "noisome pestilence" that swept western New York after the American general John Sullivan's vicious campaign against the Iroquois over the summer and fall of 1779. The virus again struck that region, and the Seneca Indians in particular, in the winter of 1781–82.[4]

The war made smallpox control difficult. In mere moments, simmering hostilities could release *Variola* from containment. When British raiders tried to burn the western Connecticut village of Danbury in April 1777, Whig forces from elsewhere in the state rushed to fend off the attack. In their defense of the town, one group of men unwittingly entered "a house where they found several of the family ill with the smallPox" and then carried the infection home to the central Connecticut town of Southington. From there the plague may well have spread farther; in nearby Middletown, several citizens died of smallpox in May 1777. Even such happy wartime events as prisoner releases could turn sour in the presence of *Variola*. Residents of coastal Connecticut complained that American captives discharged from New York

City often carried "the small pox, and other contagious disease, whereby the inhabitants of N. London and Groton" had "suffered greatly."[5]

As sporadic episodes of smallpox continued to remind civilians of their vulnerability in the Northeast, the main theater of the revolutionary struggle turned to warmer climes in 1779. In the South the conflict devolved into what scholars often describe as partisan warfare, a virtual civil war in which both sides struggled for the support of the populace and the Americans in particular relied upon "irregular" troops for their military strength. On the American side, these irregulars were most often militiamen and home guard volunteers. For the British, they were usually Indians and American loyalists. But whichever side they supported, these civilians and irregular combatants in the South had rarely had smallpox, and vulnerability ran high.

Residents of the Southeast had endured only two serious outbreaks of smallpox in the previous forty years. In 1738–39, a terrible epidemic had extended from Charleston to the Appalachian Mountains, and in 1759–60, another large outbreak had overrun the same region during the Cherokee Wars. The victims of these outbreaks included Native Americans as well as colonists of African and European descent; there can be no doubt that widespread immunity resulted.[6] But by the time the Revolution moved into the South, nearly a generation had passed since the last major epidemic, and the susceptible population had again grown large enough for the virus to take hold.

The disease seems to have converged on the region from several directions at once. It is possible that prisoners of war carried *Variola* into the area of Charleston, South Carolina, in 1778. On June 10 of that year, the American colonel Francis Marion, soon to be immortalized as the Swamp Fox, called for fourteen men to guard prisoners of war arriving shortly at Fort Moultrie on Sullivans Island. The men, Marion said, were to "be Chose from those who may have had the smallpox," almost certainly an indication that the disease had erupted among the unidentified captives.

Similar orders, equally ambiguous, came ten months later, on April 24, 1779, when immune guards were again needed for prisoners of war: "The Serg^t. and Party who has had the Small Pox to be for this Service."[7] Here too the record reveals nothing about the prisoners. But given the date, it is likely that they were local loyalists picked up in General Benjamin Lincoln's attempt to quash pro-British sentiment in the Carolina backcountry. The incidents themselves appear to have been mere warning signs; the pox made little headway in the Charleston area until the autumn of 1779.

This was not the case elsewhere. In April 1779, "raging" smallpox in the coastal North Carolina town of New Bern forced that state's general assembly to relocate its scheduled meeting to healthier surroundings. A few weeks later, as spring warmth gave way to summer heat across the Carolina Piedmont, the pox erupted farther inland at the Moravian community of Salem. However, the disease had come come not from New Bern but from soldiers headed south to thwart Britain's strengthening position in Georgia and South Carolina. On April 26, according to the official Salem record, a large contingent of troops "arrived unexpectedly" at the small but prosperous village.[8] It was a special legion of both cavalry and infantry under the leadership of General Casimir Pulaski, a highly regarded Polish volunteer in the Continental army. The unit's stay with the pacifist Moravians would prove deadly.

It is not clear whether all the legionnaires had escaped inoculation or whether one man among them had simply sidestepped the procedure.* Either way, the result was the same. "They had with them one man who was sick with small-pox," the Moravians noted, "and this brought the infection into our town." Most of the

---

*Pulaski began organizing the legion in March 1778, and his men may therefore have missed out on the mass immunizations at Valley Forge and elsewhere. It is also possible that they were exempted because of their "independent" status in the Continental army.

troops stayed at the village tavern, and the soldier with smallpox "lodged separately in a tent" close by. The men "behaved well," according to their hosts, who expressed satisfaction that "most" of the soldiers "came every day to preaching."[9]

After four days in Salem, Pulaski's Legion departed on April 30. But on May 13, the Moravians found that it had left the *Variola* virus behind. "Our only negro, Jacob, shows signs of small-pox," reads the Salem Diary, "and we suspect the same with Eva Schumacher who is helping Br. and Sr. Meyer in the tavern at present." Jacob, one of the first African American slaves held by the Moravians, had already established a reputation for financial acumen, arranging clandestine transactions and surreptitiously amassing substantial personal savings behind the backs of his owners. By 1779, he was in utter rebellion against the Moravians' efforts to curb his black-market brokering activities. Hence it is possible that Jacob came into contact with *Variola* through illicit dealings with the visiting troops or in the course of duties performed at the behest of his owners, duties they themselves may have shunned for fear of infection. Eva Schumacher's case is more straightforward than Jacob's. Her employment at the tavern put her at the hub of activity while the troops were in town, and she probably came into contact with the virus in the course of her work, perhaps even waiting upon the sick man in the tent nearby. She died of smallpox at 10:00 P.M. on May 20, 1779.[10]

As the pestilence spread through their community, the Moravians considered inoculating but decided against it when settlers nearby complained that the procedure might spread the sickness. "Our ignorant and malicious neighbors threatened to destroy the town if we inoculated," the Brethren complained, "so the small-pox stayed among us until October." Commerce came nearly to a halt. People who passed through town "were afraid," the Moravians noted, describing the measures some frightened travelers took to avoid the infection. "It was customary," they said, "for such people to have a leaf of tobacco which they smelled as a preventive, some stuck tobacco leaves in their nostrils, one even saw some passersby who had smeared tar on the forehead, under the nose, and elsewhere."[11]

Not everyone feared the virulent plague. For children naïve about the consequences and eager to be included in the activities of their peers, the pox could seem an enviable acquisition. Such was the case of "little Betsy Bagge," a Moravian child who had "often wept because she was the only little girl who did not have small-pox." The village diarist noted with some relief that Betsy finally came down with the pox on June 30, 1779. Like most of her friends, she appears to have survived. The town record indicates that in the end, only "a few adults and children" lost their lives.[12] Time would show, however, that many susceptible Moravians remained.

Pulaski's legionnaires had meanwhile continued southward after their fatal stop in Salem. It is likely that they carried the smallpox with them. On May 12, 1779, they helped turn back a British attempt to take Charleston led by General Augustine Prevost. But despite their admirable performance in battle at this time, Pulaski's men did not show up on the troop returns of the Continental army until late July, when they were cryptically listed in South Carolina at no specific location. Military recordkeeping disappoints us here; unlike most muster rolls, this one does not break down the broad category of "noneffective" men into subcategories that yield further insight. We do not learn how many of Pulaski's troops were sick, how many were wounded, how many were prisoners of war. The numbers are at once confounding and suggestive. Of 318 men in Pulaski's Legion, a staggering 40 percent, 126 men, were listed as "noneffective" in July 1779. The Southern Army as a whole reported only 22 percent of its troops noneffective at the same time. But we do not know if smallpox was to blame for the attrition among Pulaski's men.[13] They went on to fight in the American attempt to retake Savannah in September and October and in the American defense of Charleston in April and May 1780.

Even before Pulaski's Legion passed through Salem, *Variola* had found an entrée to the South from an entirely different direction. In the fall of 1778, a combined force of Maryland loyalists and German Waldeckers (mercenaries from the principality of Waldeck) sailed from New York with the intention of reinforcing the British post at Pensacola, on the Gulf Coast of Florida. Thanks to their years spent in Europe, the Waldeckers were largely immune to the *Variola* virus, but the Maryland contingent was not. On their voyage from New York, the ships stopped for supplies and repairs at the Caribbean island of Jamaica. The men were thoroughly smitten by what they saw there; the island, according to General John Campbell, was "a surprise to their eyes, a paradise on earth, which was that much more beautiful after the long and hazardous sea voyage." It was also deadly. The soldiers picked up smallpox, and when they departed, the first case broke out on shipboard as Jamaica receded from view.[14]

By the time the troops reached Pensacola Bay, the infection was general among the Maryland loyalists. They were so sick that although the Waldeckers disembarked and mustered on January 30, 1779, the Marylanders were unable to do so until February 22. By this time some units had suffered appalling mortality: Of thirty-two privates in Captain Isaac Costen's company, seventeen were dead; of thirty-nine in Captain Caleb Jones's company, thirteen were dead.[15] And the epidemic had not ended.

The Creek Indians who lived in what is now Georgia and Alabama traded regularly with British merchants at Pensacola. The Revolutionary War actually enhanced this trade because it disrupted merchant shipping to the Atlantic port cities of Charleston and Savannah. In the opinion of the West Florida General Assembly, "the whole of the southern Indian commerce" had shifted to the Gulf Coast colony by 1778. To complicate matters further, much of the Creek nation had endured successive years of famine in 1777 and 1778. The result, according to the British agent David Taitt, was that "great numbers" of both Creek and Cherokee Indians "came to Pensacola during the winter and spring" of 1779. For *Variola*, the timing could not have been better.[16]

It is not clear exactly when the Indians picked up the virus, but according to a newspaper report, the pox was raging "most violently among the Creek Indians" by September 1779. By this time, the British controlled Savannah, Augusta, and the rest of Georgia. They had also threatened Charleston, where American Whigs, unaware that they too would have to contend with *Variola*, took solace in the pestilence afflicting their enemies: "The small-pox, we are told, rages most violently among the Creek Indians at present, so that they will hardly be able to do any thing for their British brothers this campaign." On October 15, a report from the British Indian agent Alexander Cameron confirmed the Whig appraisal: Overcome by pestilence, the Creeks had little interest in armed conflict. "They seem to be tired of the War," he wrote, "and would much rather hunt the Bear who are very numerous about them at present than the Rebels, besides the Small Pox has reduced them much, and those Towns who have not had it as yet, have fled with their Families into the Woods."[17]

Cameron wrote from the Creek town of Little Tallassee, in central Alabama, near the ancient and well-traveled Trading Path that led from the Gulf Coast town of Mobile to the busy trading center of Augusta, Georgia. It was the very road that David George would have followed when he took each year's supply of deerskins to George Galphin at Silver Bluff. Inevitably, just as the road carried livestock, trade goods, and people across the South, so it also carried microbes. Despite the pox-induced disenchantment that prevailed among the Indians, several hundred Creek warriors followed the Trading Path to the Atlantic seaboard in 1779, participating in British actions in South Carolina and Georgia. If Pulaski's Legion had not already infected these regions, it may well have been the Creek Indians who did. As the fall of 1779 gave way to the winter of 1780, two port cities—Charleston in American hands and Savannah in British hands—struggled to keep *Variola* under wraps.[18]

David George was but one of many infected in this period. In March 1780, the mounting epidemic in Savannah (which George survived) prompted some 250 Chickamauga Cherokee visitors to hasten their departure from negotiations with the British commander Augustine Prevost. "The Indians have gone away to shun the Small Pox," Prevost wrote, "but have promised to take the Field whenever call'd upon." They might well have stayed where they were. Unbeknownst to the Chickamaugas in Savannah, their families in the mountains of Tennessee had just picked up smallpox in an attack on some settlers traveling on the Holston River.[19]

With smallpox simmering in the background, the military conflict in the South now came to a boil.

The British had already made two fruitless attempts to capture Charleston, South Carolina, by the spring of 1780. In June 1776, as smallpox peaked on the New York lakes and spiraled out of control in Boston, crown forces trying to capture Charleston had suffered a humiliating defeat that turned them away from the South for nearly three years. They had tried again in May 1779, marching overland from Savannah only to be repulsed by a patriot army strengthened by the last-minute arrival of Pulaski's Legion. Laden with plunder but denied a victory, the British had lumbered back to Georgia. There they spent the rest of the summer building the defenses that would withstand the Franco-American attack that came so near to pox-covered David George in the fall.

The British soon deepened their commitment to making Charleston their southern base of operations, and by the spring of 1780, the balance of power had tipped in their direction. With Savannah firmly under their control, the redcoats had a land base to draw upon, which they had missed sorely in their 1776 attempt. Moreover, with at least ten thousand troops assembled near Charleston, they had a numerical advantage they had lacked in their 1779 assault. The city's patriot defenders, by contrast, were now at a disadvantage: Their defenses were vulnerable, and their numbers were few; to make matters worse, smallpox had infected the city.

After a hiatus of nearly twenty years, the malady had taken hold with a vengeance in November 1779. "New discoveries are made every day of the small-pox; the persons are immediately removed to the pest-house," wrote General William Moultrie to Benjamin Lincoln, commander of the Americans' Southern Army. Repelling the British would have been hard enough without the pox; ensconced for another miserable winter at Morristown, the Continental army had few troops to spare. General Lincoln hoped that militia units might fill the void, but he soon learned they had a deep-seated aversion to the service. Because they were irregular soldiers, serving when called upon to fight close to home, these men had missed out on the mass inoculations that protected regular Continental troops. They were vulnerable to smallpox and terrified of it as well. Thus, when called upon to defend pox-plagued Charleston, they refused to respond. "Not one militia-man at this place on duty," wrote Moultrie to Lincoln in February 1780, as the British disembarked their men a few miles away. The militia were "much averse to going to town," he explained, the result of their apprehensions "of the small-pox breaking out." The pestilence, these men feared, "would be worse to them than the enemy."[20]

While Moultrie despaired, Lincoln raged. "[I] am much surprised to find the militia so unreasonable as to wish to avoid this town," he wrote, declaring there was "nothing to apprehend from the small-pox." Soldiers from as far away as Virginia disagreed, refusing to come to Charleston's aid for fear of catching the disease. While Clinton's British troops numbered ten thousand, the American forces defending Charleston came to a scant five thousand. Men from "the country round" had been "called in to defend the city," a newspaper report explained, "but they have excused themselves on account of the smallpox raging now there."[21]

The paltry American force held out for as long as it could. But after enduring a monthlong siege culminating in a "dreadful night" of "incessant" shelling on May 9–10, Lincoln's battle-worn little army gave up. Clinton claimed the town on May 12, 1780, and the city's defenders became prisoners of war. The militia, however, were lucky. The British general paroled most of them, permitting them to return to their homes so long as they set their arms aside.[22] It was an act intended to cultivate loyalist sympathies, and it may have succeeded. But it may have had another consequence as well: Between twelve hundred and two thousand paroled militiamen now scattered across the countryside, departing from a city held hostage not just by redcoats but also by *Variola*. A few of these men—perhaps more than a few—almost certainly carried the virus with them.

In Charleston itself, the epidemic took a turn for the worse with the British occupation. Always the most likely to be susceptible, children fell sick in growing numbers, and *Variola* appeared to undergo a simultaneous increase in virulence as summer set in. An eyewitness noted in July that the pox's symptoms were now "more unfavorable than they were three months ago." The British, as usual, paid little heed to the pestilence making headway around them; they had inoculated their susceptible regulars upon entering the pox-ridden city.[23] A far greater concern for these foreign soldiers would be the malaria that felled them in droves as the lowland swamps gave birth to millions of mosquitoes.

British columns had headed inland to "pacify" the Carolina backcountry within days of taking Charleston in May 1780. In the havoc that ensued, the epidemic extended itself among civilians, irregular troops, and partisans on both sides. As early as June 2, a plantation manager on the Cooper River noted the "great distress and Confusion" occasioned in part by "the Small pox spreading thro the Country." In August, a loyalist planter named Keating Simons sought to be exempted from British military service by General Charles Cornwallis, whom Clinton had left in charge of Britain's southern initiative. His family was in dire straits, Simons explained, "added to which the small pox is broke out among them." He therefore sought permission to remain at home, in order "to render that assistance to my family which nature & humanity requires." Although Simons was a loyalist, the pox played no favorites among susceptible South Carolinians. In November, the infamous British colonel Banastre Tarleton noted that in the area around Singleton Mills, all the Americans had taken up arms "except such as have the small Pox."[24]

Eager to keep Whiggish influences in check, the British deported many of South Carolina's most prominent patriots to St. Augustine, Florida. There the exiles learned of the progress of both the war and the pestilence from afar. The patriot Josiah Smith, manager of an enormous estate that had once belonged to his fellow merchant George Austin, received "a melancholy account" of "the Small Pox getting among the Negros" at his deceased client's Ashepoo River plantation. "We have lost with the small Pox several Negros," an overseer wrote to Smith on October 12, 1780. Among the dead were "one of the most principal hands" and the slave driver. The overseer was himself "just getting the better of it," and some sixty acres of rice lay "rotting in the fields." By December, to Smith's dismay, the pox had also "made no small havock amongst the Negro[s]" on Austin's Pee Dee River plantation, many miles away from the Ashepoo tract. Smith feared that the slaves there had suffered for lack of attendance while ill. Even the outcast patriot's own family was infected. In March 1781, Smith got word that his daughter and other relations had all "got safe over" the disease. "I may in truth say," he lamented, "the Sword, the Pestilence & fire hath ravaged our Land."[25]

From the American perspective, the fall of Charleston had demonstrated the essential problem with relying upon militia and other irregulars to defend the South. The militia, as General Lincoln had found, often did as they pleased: Frightened by the smallpox in Charleston, they had simply ignored his repeated orders to come to the city's defense. Eventually, men such as Thomas Sumter, Andrew Pickens, and Francis Marion would elevate irregular warfare to a high art, exploiting the particular advantages of fighting with motivated, if undisciplined, forces that were familiar with local terrain and demography. But for the American high command, an appreciation of the strengths and weaknesses of irregular troops came slowly. Nowhere was the cost greater than at Camden, South Carolina, on August 16, 1780.

It was at Camden that General Gates, mastermind of the American victory at Saratoga in 1777, met his denouement. In this unplanned showdown in central South Carolina, Gates and an American column of three thousand men stumbled into General Cornwallis and a British column of two thousand in the middle of the night. By daybreak, it was clear that a full-fledged battle would ensue. Despite their numerical advantage, the Americans performed terribly. Part of the problem was that Gates's men were exhausted from two weeks of near starvation and intolerably slow marching in the midsummer heat. But part of the problem was that while loyalist militia made up only one-third of Cornwallis's British army, patriot militia made up more than two-thirds of Gates's American force. When the battle got under way, the patriot militia units disintegrated. The Virginians ran at the first British volley and in doing so incited a similar panic in the North Carolinians beside them. The American line collapsed, carrying Gates and his officers with it. By the time the hero of Saratoga reached Hillsborough, North Carolina, and reassembled his army, he could muster only seven hundred of his three thousand men. Casualty reports were never compiled, but Cornwallis reported that when the smoke cleared, he had taken one thousand American prisoners.[26]

Militiamen had constituted the better part of Gates's army, and they appear to have constituted the vast majority of Cornwallis's captives. Where Clinton had believed in appeasement, paroling the militia he had captured earlier in the year, Cornwallis preferred punishment, marching the militiamen directly to Charleston and confining them aboard airless prison ships in the late-summer swelter. The change in attitude did not go unnoticed. "The unhappy men who belonged to the militia, and were taken prisoners on Gates's defeat, experienced the first effects of the cruelty of their new system," wrote one American eyewit-ness.[27]

In South Carolina, as elsewhere, British prison ships were no-toriously hellish. The most infamous of these floating islands of wretchedness was the *Jersey*, a rotting hulk moored in Wallabout Bay, off the coast of Long Island, New York. Even on approach, a former prisoner named Thomas Dring recalled of his 1782 incar-ceration, the smell of this vessel "produced a sensation of nausea far beyond my powers of description." The sensory assault inten-sified upon boarding. "The next disgusting object which met my sight," Dring said, "was a man suffering with the smallpox, and in a few minutes I found myself surrounded by many others laboring under the same disease, in every stage of its progress." Aware that his life was in danger, Dring took the initiative, inoculating him-self between the thumb and forefinger of one hand. More than forty years later, the sight of the scar could still transport the American privateer back in time. "I often look upon it when alone," he said, "and it brings fresh to my recollection the fearful scene in which I was then placed, the circumstances by which it was attended, and the feelings which I then experienced."[28]

The American militiamen captured at Camden very likely had similar memories—if they survived. According to the physician Peter Fayssoux, these men "were confined on board of prison-ships, in numbers by no means proportioned to the size of the ves-sels." The ships, Fayssoux observed, "were in general infected with the Small-Pox," and "very few of the prisoners had gone through that disorder." Infection was nearly inevitable. In desper-ation, the prisoners applied for permission to undergo inoculation at the hands of one of their own surgeons. This they received, Fayssoux said, but that was the extent of it: "The wretched ob-jects were still confined on board of the prison-ships, and fed on salt provisions, without the least medical aid, or any proper kind of nourishment." The result "was a Small-Pox with a fever of the pu-trid type," accompanied by "a putrid dysentery." From these causes alone, at least 150 died. Then, in October and November, yellow fever supplanted smallpox on board these harbor-bound death ships, inflicting still more suffering upon the men trapped within.[29]

After Camden, American partisans continued to fall into British hands as a result of the skirmishing in the Carolina interior. Many of these captives faced incarceration in Camden itself, some in the notorious prison pen, a fenced but unsheltered enclosure "like those for cows or pigs," and some in a crowded two-story jail in town. In both places, *Variola* found a steady supply of victims, for the prisoners tended to be armed locals and militiamen, rarely immune to the virus. Fourteen-year-old Andrew Jackson, later president of the United States, was typical. In the spring of 1781, the British picked up Andrew and his brother Robert in a fray near the Jackson home in the Waxhaws, a little pocket of land along the North Carolina–South Carolina border. A forty-five-mile forced march took them directly to Camden, where they joined other un-lucky captives in the pox-ridden jail. Eventually, Elizabeth Jackson managed to have her sons liberated in a prisoner exchange, but she failed to do so before they picked up smallpox. Both had symptoms of the disease at the time of their release, and Robert's condition was dire. His mother propped him up on a horse, and the trio made its way home in pouring rain, Andrew walking the distance in the full throes of the disease. Two days later, Robert was dead. Andrew's mother soon left to nurse other relatives and neighbors held aboard the prison ships in Charleston, where she caught a fever from the prisoners. She too died.[30]

In October 1780, the scales that had tipped so noticeably to-ward the British in the spring began to right themselves. Develop-ments came piecemeal. For one thing, it was now Cornwallis's army that reeled under the effects of disease, as soldier after sol-dier succumbed to yellow fever and malaria in the long southern mosquito season. Local Americans, for the most part inured to these infections by years of "seasoning," had a decisive advantage in fending off these plagues. Compounding the British losses to disease was an important loss in battle: On October 7, 1780, Major Patrick Ferguson and his loyalist militia went down in a surprising defeat at King's Mountain, a spur of the Blue Ridge near the North Carolina border. The battle was marked by ferocious fighting of the most unseemly kind, in which American frontiersmen refused to give quarter to their loyalist foes even after they had surrendered. By the time the encounter ended, the Americans had captured some seven hundred loyalists and killed or wounded hundreds more. Finally, to make matters worse for the British, October 1780 was the month in which the Continental Congress named a new man to head the Southern Department of the Continental Army. That man was Nathanael Greene.

Later nicknamed the fighting Quaker, Greene excelled in cultivating local leaders and in learning from his subordinates. He was flexible. He was open-minded. He appreciated the usefulness of militia units for guerrilla warfare, and in more conventional battles he learned to deploy them strategically to ensure both their safety and his own success. With Greene in charge, the Revolution now became a cat-and-mouse war that left the British entirely flummoxed. At Cowpens, South Carolina, in January 1781, the Americans scored a dramatic victory in which fast-moving irregulars under General Daniel Morgan's command were central. Afterward, Greene led Cornwallis on a wild pursuit through the North Carolina interior, forcing the British to abandon their wagons, tents, and provisions in their quest to keep up. After two hundred miles of maneuvering, Greene decided to risk a face-off at Guilford Courthouse, North Carolina. He deployed his militiamen effectively, but in the end, the enemy held the field. Cornwallis's victory was Pyrrhic: The Americans had suffered fewer than three hundred casualties, the British more than five hundred.

In the meantime, these fast-moving armies had set the North Carolina interior abuzz with activity, and *Variola* maximized its opportunities. On the Middle Fork of Muddy Creek, the once-quiet Moravian town of Salem again sat in the eye of the storm. In December 1780, fourteen months after the epidemic started by Pulaski's Legion had waned in the neatly planned village, the pox struck for a second time. While the Moravians had contained the 1779 outbreak to Salem and the nearby settlement of Friedberg, they had no such luck in 1780–81. Instead, *Variola* appears to have careered from one Moravian town to another, striking, departing, and returning, infecting not just Salem and Friedberg but also the neighboring settlements of Bethabara and Bethania.[31]

Day-to-day events in February 1781 show how the disruption of the war not only dispersed smallpox but also made its control impossible in this cluster of villages. On February 4, 1781, a group of American militiamen arrived in Bethania with two British deserters in tow. An unidentified young man with smallpox "breaking out on him" was "brought in" at the same time. The sick man left with the deserters. Five days later, on February 9, Cornwallis's army appeared, hot on the trail of Greene and the Americans. "The English really arrived here," wrote Bethania's diarist, impressed by the loss of thirty cattle and countless "sheep, geese and chickens" to the soldiers. The army marched on the next morning, leaving "as much as two wagon loads of meat" uneaten around smoldering campfires. Two weeks later, at nearby Salem, it was the American army that drew the Moravians' ire for making "unjust demands." Then, even as they were overwhelmed with Continentals and militiamen, the Moravians had a visit from a Baptist minister from Virginia with the pox "breaking out on him." The next day, in the Moravian settlement of Friedberg, a visitor reported the home of Peter Frey to be "a veritable lazaretto" with the smallpox. "The parents and eight children were all in bed," the visitor said. "The father had only a cold, and could be up part of the time, but all the others had small-pox." In such conditions, the epidemic dragged on for eight months. Not until August 1781 would the Moravians free themselves of the pestilence.[32]

With so many militiamen in the field, Greene's American army was particularly vulnerable. In January 1781, *Variola* began to spread at Salisbury, North Carolina, less than forty miles south of the Moravians at Salem. The pox appeared first "among the Prisoners of War Confined in this place," wrote Colonel James Phillips to Greene, and by January 10, it had "Seized some of the Militia" as well. Phillips feared the worst: "From the Apprehension of the disorder becoming generally Epidemic—I am humbly of opinion that general Inoculation is immediately necessary." The Quaker general demurred. Inoculation not only would immobilize the militia and consume hard-to-find resources but also might spread the disease to other susceptible troops. Greene was adamant about preserving the strength of his army. It was, in fact, his guiding principle, both on and off the battlefield. Hence, he believed, "it would be much better to dismiss" the militia than to "think of innoculating them."[33]

For the militia, avoidance was thus the order of the day. By April, the pox was so prevalent in Campbellton (now Fayetteville), North Carolina, that the American colonel James Emmet could not send any of his men into town. "This town, & indeed many parts of the County is much infested with the small pox," he told Greene, explaining that he could not "keep a single man" in the Cape Fear River community. So widespread was the infection that on April 28 Emmet reported that he could not even find a messenger to carry a letter to the general. "We have non[e] here but what are too bad with the small pox to undertake such a journey," he wrote. Similarly, on May 1, General Jethro Sumner learned "of the small pox raging very much in Hillsborough," the central North Carolina town where he had ordered new army drafts to rendezvous. Sumner quickly diverted as many men as possible to Halifax, but he soon received information "that the small pox" was "spreading itself in that neighbourhood" as well. In July, the Moravians at Bethania noted that Greene's troops heading northward from South Carolina avoided them for fear of contagion. "Because of small-pox in town they took the road outside," the village diarist reported.[34]

In March, in the aftermath of the Battle of Guilford Courthouse, Greene had feigned pursuit of Cornwallis toward Wilmington, the only true port city on North Carolina's treacherous coastline. Once it was clear that his opponent had committed himself, Greene broke away and sprinted south to wrest the South Carolina backcountry from British hands. By late summer his work was done. Cornwallis, in the meantime, had proceeded to Wilmington and then turned north toward Virginia on April 25, 1781. His plan, he wrote to Henry Clinton, was to make the Chesapeake "the seat of war."[35] It was a dramatic change of venue, a sign of Cornwallis's frustration. As the conflict followed him to Virginia, his frustration would only grow.

Throughout their campaign in the South, the British consciously exploited the deep cultural and social divisions that had undermined stability in the region for generations. The crown's alliance with the Creeks and Cherokees who succumbed to smallpox in 1779 and 1780 was one example of this. Concerned about American encroachments on their lands, the Indians made natural allies for His Majesty's forces. So too did thousands of Africans and African Americans enslaved throughout the South. With his famous proclamation of 1775, Lord Dunmore had been the first British official explicitly to solicit the support of black southerners. Four years later, in June 1779, Henry Clinton echoed him in a proclamation issued from Philipsburg, New York. It too offered security "to Every NEGROE who shall desert the Rebel Standard," and it too thrilled blacks far and wide.[36]

Slaves, however, did not need public proclamations to understand where their interests lay. In Virginia in 1775, many ran to Dunmore even before his November pronouncement. Likewise in 1778–79, African Americans near Savannah did the same, David George among them. In the short time between November 1778 and January 1779, some five thousand black Georgians—one-third of the province's slave population—sought liberty behind British lines. In neighboring South Carolina, the flight from slavery was even more dramatic. Here Africans and African Americans constituted 60 percent of the population. And here, in 1780, as Clinton took Charleston and Cornwallis moved inland, some twenty thousand black refugees escaped to the British.[37] The exodus continued in North Carolina and Virginia during the campaigns of 1780 and 1781.

Male and female, these fugitives performed a multitude of services in support of the king's army. Black boatmen ferried troops, black nurses looked after invalids, black herdsmen tended livestock, and black artisans repaired muskets, wagons, and other equipment. When heavy labor was needed, the British army often spared its white soldiers and instead set black workers to the tasks of building defenses and clearing roadways. Black women, like David George's wife, found employment as cooks or laundresses. However unfair, it was clearly a bargain that seemed worthwhile to both parties: The British undermined their enemies' cause and simultaneously got a vast and talented pool of labor; the runaways got their freedom—so long as the British held up their end of the deal.

As early as October 1779, *Variola* began to make inroads among the black loyalists gathering around the British army. David George, outside Savannah, was one of the first to fall ill.[38] George recovered, but as the war took its tortuous twists and turns for the next two years, the pox did not relent among his fellow black fugitives. The dynamics at work here were the same as those in the Chesapeake and in Canada in 1776. In each case, constant turmoil and a relentless influx of susceptibles ensured that epidemic smallpox would not subside. European-born troops had little to fear from *Variola*. But by the time the British surrendered at Yorktown in 1781, the virus had dashed the dreams of thousands of freedom-loving African Americans.

At Charleston alone, the toll was gruesome. "As the small pox was in the British camp thousands of Negroes dyed miserably with it," wrote Eliza Pinckney from the occupied city in September 1780. Camp fever—almost certainly typhus—added to the mortality. Among those infected in Charleston was a black South

Carolinian named Boston King, who discovered "the happiness of liberty" among the British not long after the city fell. "I was seized with the small-pox and suffered great hardships," King wrote in his memoirs. To check the contagion, the army implemented the cruelest sort of quarantine: "All the Blacks affected with that disease," including King himself, "were ordered to be carried a mile from the camp." There they were left by themselves, with no nurses in attendance. "This was a grievous circumstance to me and many others," the former slave recalled. "We lay sometimes a whole day without any thing to eat or drink." Unlike many, King was lucky, for a kindhearted British soldier took him under his care. "He brought me such things as I stood in need of," King remembered, "and by the blessing of the Lord I began to recover." Later, his gentle caretaker suffered a serious wound in the fighting at Camden, and King leaped at the chance to reciprocate. "As soon as I heard of his misfortune, I went to see him," he said, "and tarried with him in the hospital six weeks, till he recovered; rejoicing that it was in my power to return him the kindness he had shewed me." When the war ended, Boston King fled Charleston with David George and other black loyalists, sailing first to Nova Scotia and later to Sierra Leone.[39]

Not all black refugees stayed put in the port cities of Charleston and Savannah. Many followed Cornwallis's army into North Carolina and Virginia in 1780 and 1781, and others joined the redcoats while they were on the march. *Variola* trailed them everywhere. "The English according to custom, have left the small Pox behind them," a North Carolina observer wrote in the spring of 1781, as the British advanced down the Cape Fear River toward Wilmington. It was the army's black loyalist supporters, not the troops themselves, who usually spread the infection. During Cornwallis's stay in Wilmington, one prominent patriot, a signer of the Declaration of Independence named William Hooper, lost three slaves to the British and "five other negroes" to "the small-pox."[40]

In April 1781, the long line of British troops and refugees

turned north to Virginia. In the Old Dominion, as elsewhere, slaves undaunted by the pox welcomed the redcoats as liberators. According to one patriot observer, "vast numbers" of enslaved Virginians "flocked to the Enemy from all quarters" despite *Variola*'s ravages. "Your neighbors Col°. Taliaferro & Col°. Travis lost every slave they had in the world, and Mr. Paradise has lost all his but one," wrote Richard Henry Lee to his brother William. Slaves belonging to Virginia's governor, Thomas Nelson, also fled. Nelson "had 700 negroes *before the war*," wrote a visitor to his estate in 1782. "He has now only 80 or 100."[41]

It was in Virginia that the plight of African and African American refugees took its most tragic turn. Pursuing the British eastward from Richmond in the summer of 1781, American soldiers observed the bodies of black loyalists strewn along the roadsides. "Within these days past, I have marched by 18 or 20 Negroes that lay dead by the way-side, putrifying with the small pox," wrote a Connecticut soldier named Josiah Atkins on June 24, 1781. "These poor creatures, having no care taken of them, many crawl'd into the bushes about & died, where they lie infecting the air around with intolerable stench & great danger." The epidemic had exploded. So mortal was the smallpox and so sickly were the black loyalists that despite their great numbers, Cornwallis desperately sought more. As workers, he wrote in July, they were "constantly wanted" for a "variety of fatiguing Services" that white soldiers were unwilling to perform.[42]

It was not long before other expediencies took precedence. By October 1781, Cornwallis had barricaded himself behind the redoubts of Yorktown, and his position was faltering. Besieged by the French fleet offshore and by allied troops on land, the general felt the Franco-American noose drawing ever closer about him. His troops were precariously short of food, forage, and supplies, and pox-infected black refugees, in his estimation, were a drain on precious resources. He had complained of this as early as August. "Our consumption of provisions is considerably increased by a number of refugees lately come to us, and by negroes that are employed in different branches of the public service," he wrote. The British, despite promises of freedom, had already begun to abandon their black allies, finding them more burdensome than helpful. Both July and August were marked by ignominious moments in which British generals in Virginia left hundreds of "Wretched Negroes" behind to face whatever hand fate dealt them, be it death from disease or the wrath of their patriot masters.*[43]

At Yorktown in October, Cornwallis followed suit. "The British have sent from Yorktown a large number of negroes, sick with the small pox," wrote an American eyewitness on the scene. "During the siege," a Continental soldier recalled, "we saw in the woods herds of Negroes which Lord Cornwallis . . . in love and pity to them, had turned adrift, with no other recompense for their confidence in his humanity than the smallpox for their bounty and starvation and death for their wages." It was an act that disturbed even Cornwallis's most seasoned Hessian fighters. "I would just as soon forget to record a cruel happening," wrote Johann Ewald on October 14. "On the same day of the enemy assault, we drove back to the enemy all of our black friends, whom we had taken along to despoil the countryside. We had used them to good advantage and set them free, and now, with fear and trembling, they had to face the reward of their cruel masters." According to the Virginia patriot St. George Tucker, "An immense number of Negroes" met their end "in the most miserable Manner in York[town]."[44]

For all practical purposes, the British surrender on October 19 marked the end of the war. A Pennsylvania serviceman named

---

*One of Cornwallis's officers, General Charles O'Hara, was appalled at this action. It "ought not to be done," he wrote to Cornwallis, noting that the blacks "would inevitably perish" and that civilians were fearful of the contagion. Eventually, O'Hara ended up abandoning some four hundred blacks himself, but when he did so, he left them with sufficient provisions to get them through smallpox. O'Hara was clearly disturbed by what he was doing; he also took pains to leave the blacks in "the most friendly Quarter in our Neighbourhood" and "begg'd" local residents to be kind to the refugees he had once sheltered.

Ebenezer Denny recorded the events of that fateful day in his journal: the eerie British parade, the capitulation, the drunken riot of the defeated army. It was a day not just of triumph but of tragedy. "Glad to be relieved from this disagreeable station," he wrote. "Negroes lie about, sick and dying, in every stage of the small pox. Never was in so filthy a place." Thomas Jefferson later estimated that of the thirty thousand Virginia slaves he believed had joined the British "about 27,000 died of the small pox and camp fever."[45]

Many on the American side believed that the expulsion of the black loyalists was a deliberate British attempt to spread smallpox to the Continental forces, the militia, and the civilian population. Whig sympathizers had accused the British of utilizing biological warfare as early as the siege of Boston, and in Virginia it seemed that their fears were finally realized. On June 24, 1781, the Connecticut soldier Josiah Atkins stated his opinion that Cornwallis had "inoculated 4 or 500 [blacks] in order to spread *smallpox* thro' the country, & sent them out for that purpose." When a Pennsylvania regular found a "negro man with the small-pox lying on the road side" outside Williamsburg, the soldier assumed the sick man had been left by a British cavalry unit "to prevent the Virginia militia from pursuing them." The eviction of pox-covered black loyalists from Yorktown in October drew similar charges. James Thacher, a surgeon's mate in the Continental army, believed the terrified former slaves had "probably" been sent to the American lines "for the purpose of communicating the infection to our army."[46]

Regardless of their veracity, accusations of deliberate contagion served a valuable propaganda function for the American side. Patriots such as Robert Livingston of New York hoped that reports of such heinous conduct would sway Europeans to the American cause. "In Virginia," he wrote, the British "took the greatest pains to communicate the Small Pox to the Country; by exposing the dead bodies of those who had died with it, in the most frequented places." The *Pennsylvania Gazette* likewise believed the charge of biological warfare would have an international impact. "Lord Cornwallis's attempt to spread the smallpox among the inhabitants in the vicinity of York, has been reduced to a certainty," the paper reported, "and must render him contemptible in the eyes of every civilized nation." Benjamin Franklin reiterated the charge in his "Retort Courteous."[47]

It would be easy to dismiss these accusations as so much American hyperbole. But evidence indicates that in fact, the British did exactly what the Americans said they did. Three years before Yorktown, a book written by a British officer in New York had explicitly suggested that His Majesty's forces should propagate smallpox among the Americans. "Dip arrows in matter of smallpox," wrote Robert Donkin, "and twang them at the American rebels, in order to inoculate them; This would sooner disband these stubborn, ignorant, enthusiastic savages, than any other compulsive measures. Such is their dread and fear of that disorder!" At Portsmouth, Virginia, the British appear to have implemented one such scheme in the waning months of the war. On July 13, 1781, General Alexander Leslie outlined his plan in a letter to Cornwallis. "Above 700 Negroes are come down the River in the Small Pox," he wrote. "I shall distribute them about the Rebell Plantations."[48] Even if they pardoned their actions by saying they could no longer support so many camp followers, British officers were inevitably aware that sick African Americans might communicate smallpox to the enemy.

The American camp at Yorktown appears to have contained a fair number of susceptible troops: some militiamen and some regulars who had missed out on the army's inoculations. Immunity still ran high among the Continentals, however, and Washington was attentive to the danger the pestilence presented to the others. His general orders of September 29, 1781, reflected the lessons he had learned from the army's earlier encounters with the disease: "Our ungenerous Enemy having as usual propagated the small Pox in this part of the Country, the Commander in Chief forbids the Officers and soldiers of this Army having any connection with the Houses or Inhabitants in this neighbourhood or borrowing any utensils from them." Sentries, he announced a day later, were likewise to use "the most scrupulous attention" in preventing "any person infected with the small pox" from entering the allied camp.[49]

Not all these efforts were successful. In November 1781, soldiers from Yorktown carried *Variola* to Cumberland County, west of Richmond, where a serious outbreak erupted. Also, by early December, troops marching northward after the surrender had carried the pestilence all the way to West Point on New York's Hudson River. "The officers and soldiers, who had been in Virginia, were now returning to the army," wrote General Heath on December 8. "Some of the soldiers brought the small-pox with them." The disease spread among Heath's forces, prompting the inoculation of another two thousand men at West Point in January 1782.[50]

We can see, then, that the effect of smallpox in the southern campaign of the American Revolution was far more nuanced and varied than it had been in the war's opening episodes. The key distinction was the newly acquired immunity of the Continental army. *Variola* now had to find its victims not among regular soldiers but among civilians, irregular soldiers, and partisan allies of both armies. For the Creeks and the Cherokees (as for the Iroquois in New York), the pox and the war were disastrous: Having chosen the losing side, the Indians soon had to face an onslaught of Anglo-American expansion with much-depleted numbers. Similarly, the episode was tragic for many black loyalists. Some, like David George and Boston King, survived smallpox and made new lives for themselves in England, Nova Scotia, and Sierra Leone. But others saw their dreams of freedom dashed, if not by *Variola*, then by British duplicity and the Revolution's failure to address the fundamental issue of slavery.

For the Continental army, however, the southern campaign

ended with the greatest victory of the war, a victory that capital-
ized not just on hard fighting, clever generalship, and British blun-
ders, but also on the high level of immunity that had resulted from
inoculation. Despite *Variola*'s lurking presence and momentary incursions among militia and other irregulars, the virus never gained
a solid foothold among the American troops in the southern theater. The Quebec debacle did not repeat itself. Instead, even
when irregulars were infected, the invulnerability of the Continental regulars kept the virus in check. In view of this, Washington's unheralded and little-recognized resolution to inoculate the
Continental forces must surely rank among his most important de-
cisions of the war.[51] The general had outflanked his enemy.

But if Washington outflanked *Variola*, the virulent virus had
executed an even more stunning maneuver: It outflanked the war
itself. During the years of the southern campaign, as armies, militia, and partisans scrapped it out in Virginia and the Carolinas, an
unbroken chain of person-to-person connections introduced the
terrible pestilence to vast and vulnerable populations elsewhere
on the North American continent.

5

ENTIERROS

July 2, 1776. *Sitting astride a mule, the gray-robed Franciscan missionary rode east toward the Hopi pueblo of Oraibi. He still smarted from the rebuff of a young Indian man he had met on the trail just a few miles back. "I offered him tobacco but he refused it," he wrote in his journal. The man's hostility had been palpable. Now, drawing closer to Oraibi, the friar encountered two more Hopis. "I approached, as if to shake hands with them," he said, but the men "drew away making signs to me to go back." The thirty-eight-year-old missionary continued on despite his second rejection of the day.*

Francisco Tomás Hermenegildo Garcés was a man not easily daunted. In 1774, with Captain Juan Bautista de Anza, he had helped to pioneer an overland route from Sonora to Alta (upper) California. The expedition had been a trying one. Only after spending eleven parched days lost in the dunes of the Imperial Valley did the Spanish explorers find their way to San Gabriel, near what soon became Los Angeles. Garcés's present journey was similarly arduous. He had already spent more than eight months on the trail. While British and American troops had tested each other's mettle in Canada, Boston, and coastal Virginia, Fray Garcés had traveled across some of the most forbidding terrain on the North American continent: the Sonoran Desert, the Mojave Desert, and now the Painted Desert in north-central Arizona. The friar's quest was twofold: In the service of the Spanish crown, he wanted to open a road between the newly established missions of Alta California and the much older Spanish settlements of New Mexico, and in the service of the Catholic Church, he sought to cultivate friendship and Christian fervor among the Indian groups he encountered. With this in mind, Garcés carried a little painted canvas along with him. On one side was a picture of the Virgin Mary; on the other, a man destined for eternal damnation.

By a narrow path, Garcés ascended Black Mesa into Oraibi. Here, in a land of buttes and canyons, sandstone and adobe dwellings stacked up into flat-topped vertical heights that mimicked the surrounding cliffs. The missionary dismounted from his mule while Hopi women and children watched his every move from the rooftops above. "None would come close," he wrote in his journal. The Indians rejected the white shells he offered them. They refused to give him food. When Garcés tried to join a group on a rooftop, he received a harsh rebuke. "I was not to come [up], nor my things either," he wrote in his account of the day. "With the corncobs thrown in the street I built a fire and made a little gruel." The friar

Old Oraibi. Photograph by Stuart Malcolm Young, 1912, Stuart M. Young Collection, NAU.PH.643.3.35, Special Collections and Archives Department, Cline Library, Northern Arizona University

slept in the open air. The next day, he set out to visit the neighboring Hopi pueblos, but faced with universal hostility, he returned to Oraibi, reentering the town at nightfall as the Indians again watched from their roofs.

The following morning was July 4, 1776. As bells pealed in Philadelphia to celebrate the Declaration of Independence, Fray Garcés awoke to the sound of singing and the percussion of "small sticks on a shallow wooden basin." Dancers wearing feather headgear moved through the streets. "When the sun was up a great throng moved toward me and made me fear for my life," he wrote. "In the lead came four of the principal men, the tallest of whom demanded of me, with a smile: 'Why have you come here? Don't stay. Go back to your own land.' " Garcés responded with a homily on God, Jesus, and the crucifixion, delivered in a combination of hand signals and two Indian languages. "To this an old man, contorting his features, said in Spanish, 'No, no.' "

Fray Garcés could go no farther. Even if he made it to Santa Fe, Hopi hostility would make his return trip impossible. The tireless Franciscan fetched his mule, mounted, and left, returning southwestward across the desert to Yuma. There, on the banks of the lower Colorado River just seven months earlier, he had shown local Yuman Indians his painting of the damned man and the Virgin. "Did they wish the priests and Spaniards to come to live in their country?" he had asked. "They answered yes."[1]

By late 1779, as eager slaves flocked to the British standard in Georgia, *Variola* had begun to extend itself elsewhere in North America. The virus had appeared in Spanish New Orleans in the winter of 1778–79, and soon thereafter, it began making sinister inroads in Mexico City, the sprawling administrative center of Spain's New World empire. At first, there were no indications that the latter outbreak would be special. By the time the first victims succumbed to *Variola* there during the summer of 1779, the great Mexican metropolis had endured multiple encounters with the virus, beginning with Cortés's pox-assisted conquest of the Aztecs in 1521. But the epidemic that began so quietly in the summer of

1779 soon proved that it was indeed extraordinary, gathering momentum that would carry it thousands of miles. As human beings conveyed *Variola* over the maze of trails and waterways that tied far-flung regions of the continent together, the Mexico City outbreak generated a tidal wave of smallpox that reached as far north as Hudson Bay and as far west as Alaska.

The first signs of trouble appeared in August, when a few seemingly innocuous incidents of smallpox occurred in Mexico City. The source of the contagion remains unknown. Perhaps it came from New Orleans; acquired by Spain in 1763, Louisiana now had closer ties to Mexico City than ever before. Or perhaps it came from the Caribbean, where the sugar-producing islands of Puerto Rico, Cuba, and Santo Domingo were known for the brutality of both their labor systems and their disease environments.[2]

Whatever their source, the first cases of smallpox in Mexico City apparently drew little concern. Certainly there were no signs that this single outbreak would engulf much of the city and, in the end, much of the Western Hemisphere. But in retrospect, New Spain was a tinderbox waiting to ignite. *Variola* had not made an epidemic appearance in Mexico since the early 1760s, when it had taken thousands of lives before ebbing on the northern frontier in 1764.[3] The timing alone signaled trouble, for the greater part of a generation had gone through life without exposure to the virus. In Mexico City, as the first cases of smallpox made their quiet appearance in August 1779, virtually everyone under eighteen years of age was vulnerable.

It was not long before disquiet replaced nonchalance in the Mexican capital. On September 20, the ayuntamiento, or city council, officially declared an epidemic under way. Sick rolls filled, and mortality escalated. By mid-October, the ayuntamiento had received an appeal for assistance from the Hospital de San Juan de Dios, run by the Catholic Church. The outbreak, moreover, was only in its early stages. In late October, it took a dramatic turn for the worse. Burial records in city churches show a sharp increase in interments over the next month, as smallpox spiraled out of control. Pressed for funds, the ayuntamiento appealed to the city's wealthiest citizens for financial assistance. Many responded, and in the end, officials raised the enormous sum of 147,263 pesos, mostly from private citizens (a peso was roughly the equivalent of an American dollar at the time).[4]

The measures implemented to control the outbreak included regular street cleaning, bonfires lit throughout the city to cleanse the air, and a failed attempt at mass inoculation. The latter effort was particularly poignant, for it might have saved many lives. Despite relatively widespread use in the French- and English-speaking regions of North America, inoculation was a latecomer to Mexico. Dr. Esteban Morel ran the first trials of the procedure in Mexico City in October, while the epidemic was escalating in virulence. These may well have been the first inoculations ever carried out in New Spain. When the seven volunteers who underwent the operation emerged successfully, Morel quickly set up an inoculation hospital with the financial support of the ayuntamiento. But much to the doctor's chagrin, no patients appeared. The problem was not lack of publicity; the government had circulated a broadside announcing the hospital's opening and espousing the virtues of variolation. In Morel's opinion, the problem was public fear. "Everything was prepared and made ready," he wrote later, "but the innate repugnance of those who were naturally healthy to voluntarily contract a sickness by artificial means, as well as their hopeful expectations that they might avoid being among those who would be infected, all of this served to persuade the people they need not be inoculated."[5] Elsewhere, the operation met with more acceptance as the epidemic expanded.

Records indicate that 44,286 Mexico City residents had come down with smallpox by December 27, 1779. According to the viceroy, the streets were filled with corpses and the air was filled with the cries of the sick and bereaved. The epidemic had peaked, but it was far from over. Incidents of the disease continued into the early months of 1780. Even among contemporaries, appraisals of mortality in the city varied widely, ranging from a low estimate of "more than nine thousand" to a high estimate of twenty-two thousand. Donald B. Cooper, the only scholar who has examined the outbreak in detail, believes that the middling estimate of eighteen thousand deaths offered by the supreme court judge Cosme de Mier y Trespalacios may be the most accurate.[6] In any case, the daily reality of the epidemic was undeniable. "Every evening tumbrels passed through the streets to receive the corpses," wrote the Prussian explorer Alexander von Humboldt. "A great part of the Mexican youth was cut down that year."[7]

When the epidemic struck, Mexico City was the hub of an empire that ostensibly included all of what is now the southwestern United States. Spanish land claims even stretched as far north as Alaska. But the reality of Spanish control was much more limited. By 1776, the far northern frontier of New Spain consisted of a tenuous, disconnected series of missions and presidios (military posts) strung out across an enormous expanse of inhospitable terrain. At its western end, on the Alta California coast, the frontier extended as far north as the Golden Gate, where the Spanish had just established a brand-new colony called San Francisco. From there the frontier zigzagged vaguely southeastward to Santa Fe and then on to El Paso, San Antonio, Nacogdoches, and New Orleans. The acquisition of Louisiana from France in 1763 had also given Spain at least nominal control of posts on the west bank of the Mississippi River, including St. Louis, a site frequented by Indians and French fur traders for generations and permanently settled by Auguste Chouteau in 1764. Although these frontier installations established a Spanish presence in a few localized areas, the extent of Spanish control should not be exaggerated; the greater part of this vast and varied country remained the domain of Native Americans. To use one historian's apt description, the colonial outposts of the northern frontier were truly "islands" of Spanish control in a great sea of Indian territory.[8]

Between the frontier in the north and Mexico City in the south lay the great silver mines of central Mexico. Precious metals had driven Spanish enterprise in the Americas beginning with Hernán Cortés's theft of Aztec gold stores in 1520. But gold soon dwindled in importance as the extent of Mexico's silver lodes came to light, and silver, not gold, soon dominated the mining industry of New Spain. This was as true in the late eighteenth century as it had been in the late sixteenth. Despite more than two centuries of extraction, Mexican silver mines remained hugely profitable in the era of the American Revolution. They even quadrupled their output in the hundred years before 1810, much to the delight of Spain's revenue-hungry Bourbon crown.[9]

For infectious disease, the mines of Mexico presented an opportunity of spectacular proportions. They brought together thousands of people in conditions that both undermined human health and enhanced contagious transmission. By the 1790s, to cite just one example, the huge Valenciana mine of Guanajuato employed more than three thousand workers at arduous tasks in a maze of underground tunnels. Most of these laborers were Native Americans, and when smallpox struck, their genetic homogeneity may well have magnified its virulence. Moreover, the mines were far from isolated. Regular packtrains carried silver south to Mexico City and returned with textiles, wine, and other manufactured goods. Unavoidably, the packtrains carried microbes as well. For foodstuffs, the miners relied on the livestock and produce of outlying ranches and haciendas, which virtually guaranteed that any contagious pathogen that found its way into an urban mining center would also find its way into the countryside.[10]

Scattered across this countryside were not just haciendas, ranches, and little Indian settlements called rancherias but also Catholic missions. The missions were central to Spanish Indian policy, which called for the "reduction" of natives everywhere. The word "reduction" may seem odd to those more familiar with the language of British colonial conquest, but it is both revealing and appropriate. In essence, it meant complete submission to Spanish control. "Reduced" natives accepted Christianity and lived in towns organized around Catholic missions. They contributed labor to the maintenance of the parish and often paid an additional labor tribute to Spanish authorities, landholders, and mineowners. The missions thus served more than one master. As instruments of the church, they ostensibly introduced natives to the "benefits" of Christianity. But as instruments of industry and the state, they also produced profits, manpower, and compliance to authority.[11]

In their quest to reduce the Indians, the missionaries appear to have benefited from the great waves of pestilence that swept New Spain hand in hand with colonial conquest in the sixteenth and seventeeth centuries. The impact of these epidemics was stunning, particularly in the first century of European contact. From a pre-Columbian population that may have been as high as twenty-five million, the population of central Mexico plummeted to only two million by 1600, rebounding somewhat thereafter. Farther north, a similar pattern emerged, delayed by three-quarters of a century, but dramatic nonetheless. The Pueblo Indians of New Mexico saw their numbers drop from as many as one hundred thousand in 1600 to forty thousand in 1638 and only seventeen thousand in 1680. To the southwest, in the desert province of Sonora, one Jesuit missionary believed that the native population had declined more than 90 percent by 1706.[12]

These breathtaking numbers represent only the most quantifiable consequence of epidemic disease. Inevitably, the repercussions went far beyond simple statistical decline. Repeated bouts of pestilence shattered native tribal organization, disrupted kinship ties, undermined Indian belief systems, and called into question the skills of traditional medical practitioners. The chaos made many Indians more receptive to the alternative religious and social structures offered by Catholic evangelicals when they moved into disease-ravaged regions.[13]

From the perspective of *Variola*, arrival in Mexico City was the key to success. In the late eighteenth century, as for most of the second millennium, Mexico City was the most populous city in the Western Hemisphere. An epidemic that took hold there could generate centrifugal force that virtually guaranteed dispersion far and wide. If one carrier of *Variola* failed to transmit the virus to another susceptible individual, it hardly mattered. There were thousands of others who would, just as there were thousands of people who traveled to and from the city every day. An outbreak in a city as populous as Mexico City was destined to spread.

In most cases, the individuals who carried smallpox from place to place have gone undocumented in the historical record. Inevitably, they came from all walks of life and all segments of Mexico's stratified but diverse society. Cooks, soldiers, merchants, slaves, miners, ranchers, laborers, drivers, servants, neophytes, traders, housemaids, herdsmen, artisans, and farmers of all races and genders would have been among their number. They did their traveling, almost by necessity, during smallpox's twelve-day incubation period. Once they were afflicted with symptoms, it is doubtful that they could have continued in transit before recovery was well under way, by which time the damage was done. *Variola* had very likely taken hold in a new pool of unsuspecting carriers in which it could continue to travel and multiply.

In New Spain, as elsewhere, the great majority of deaths in the epidemic probably went unrecorded. But records of the Catholic Church nevertheless allow us to glimpse the devastation. Throughout the French and Spanish colonies, Catholic priests and missionaries dutifully noted in local parish registers every baptism, marriage, and burial they attended. Most entries include the age, gender, and ethnicity of the individuals named. For historians today, the end result is a rich and revealing demographic record. Burial registers—*libros de entierros*—are particularly useful for the study of epidemic disease. They reveal not just mortality but dates as well, showing clearly the movement of plagues across the historical landscape. Although burial registers are the only sacramental records used here, future scholars will no doubt use baptism and marriage registers as well to track not just mortality and transmission but also cultural responses and demographic recovery after epidemic episodes.[14]

While ecclesiastical burials were methodically recorded in the *libros de entierros*, cause of death was not. It was the rare priest or friar who noted cause of death diligently, and there is no indication that the church expected its recordkeepers to do so. This clearly presents a problem for the study of epidemic disease, but in the case of the smallpox spreading through Mexico in 1779, it is not insurmountable. In almost every case, the rise in mortality is so sudden and so huge that the epidemic cause is clear beyond any reasonable doubt. The Sanctuary of Santo Domingo Tehuantepec in the modern state of Oaxaca, for example, averaged 5.57 deaths per month from January 1775 to January 1780. The highest number recorded in any single month during this five-year period was 13. But in February 1780, smallpox, known in Spanish as *viruelas*, struck with a vengeance. Parish friars recorded 103 deaths in February and 296 in March. In this case, they noted the cause of death as well, beginning with the first death attributed to *viruelas* on February 4, 1780.[15] The enormous mortality in Tehuantepec is both typical and illustrative. Similarly dramatic mortality marked *Variola*'s arrival throughout New Spain, even where the priests and friars did not identify it by name. (In fact, it is the less dramatic increases that arouse suspicions of an agent other than *Variola* at work.) Timing adds an additional element of certainty; records in which cause of death is not listed can sometimes be correlated with records from nearby parishes that do specify smallpox as the cause of death.

It did not take long for smallpox to transcend the bounds of Mexico City. It spread south and east first, apparently following the road that led to the Gulf Coast port of Veracruz. By November 1779, when the epidemic was approaching its peak in the Mexican capital, the pox was appearing some sixty miles to the east in

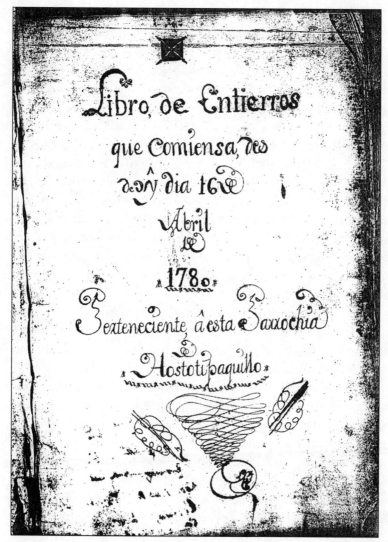

The *libro de entierros* containing the names of smallpox victims at Hostotipaquillo in the modern state of Jalisco. Nuestra Señora del Favor, Hostotipaquillo, Jalisco

Tlaxcala. Located in high, wheat-growing country near the route to the coast, Santa Cruz Tlaxcala and its outlying pueblos together averaged 6.5 burials per month from January 1775 to October 1779. Then, as smallpox spread outward from Mexico City, the number of interments shot up, escalating notably in November and cresting at 200 in December. Other towns near the Veracruz road were also among the first affected. Tlacotepec, now in the state of Puebla, probably saw its first smallpox deaths as early as October. A month later, in November, records show a full-blown epidemic under way. By January 1780, as the pox waned in Tlacotepec, it had begun raging closer to the coast in the region around Jalapa. There it intensified through December and January and climaxed in February 1780. Continuing south, the pox passed through Oaxaca, Chiapas, and Guatemala and extended itself into the South American continent at least as far as Colombia and Ecuador.[16]

The virus's northern spread was even more dramatic. The main artery of New Spain's internal transportation system was the camino real (royal road) of the interior, a long and difficult trail that tracked north from Mexico City through the great valley of central Mexico and beyond. Used primarily to serve the silver mines of Guanajuato, Zacatecas, and San Luis Potosí, the camino real also carried people and their goods all the way to its terminus at Santa Fe. It is no coincidence that the first signs of smallpox's spread northward occurred along this heavily traveled road. The fact that the epidemic erupted in Mexico City at the start of the dry winter season enhanced the likelihood that it would spread, for travelers and *Variola* alike preferred cool, dry conditions.[17]

By January 1780, burial records indicate that the disease had appeared in San Juan de los Lagos in the present-day state of Jalisco, some 250 miles north of Mexico City. It struck the nearby town of Asientos at about the same time.[18] Given *Variola*'s twelve-day incubation period and the fact that death is most likely to occur between ten and sixteen days after the appearance of symptoms, the mortality in these towns in January probably indicates that the virus itself had arrived at least a month earlier—and possibly as early as November.

The *libros de entierros* reveal a predictable pattern: The pox would strike first in the population centers clustered closest to the camino real; then, a month later, it would erupt in more remote towns along secondary travel routes. By March 1780, the widening epidemic from Mexico City had also begun to take a toll among people living along another "royal road," the camino real of the western coast. This trail also led northward from Mexico City, but instead of staying inland, it followed the Pacific seaboard to Arizpe, newly named the administrative headquarters of New Spain's Interior Provinces, the recently established unit comprising the northernmost sectors of the realm.[19]

Church records show the spread of smallpox along these travel routes to have been in most cases incremental and predictable. But in rare instances, surprises lie buried in the *libros de entierros*. One such surprise is the mortality that struck Canatlán, Durango, in late 1779 and early 1780. After averaging six to seven burials per month over the previous three years, the number of deaths in the Canatlán parish of San Diego de Alcalá began to climb as 1779 drew to a close, and mortality escalated dramatically at the start of the new year. November 1779 had brought only two burials; February 1780 brought one hundred.[20] While the burial records do not indicate the cause of the mortality, the pattern is typical of *Variola*. Yet the timing is not. Canatlán is located some five hundred miles north of Mexico City. If the rise in mortality does indeed represent the impact of smallpox, the epidemic somehow erupted in Canatlán well before it struck most of the other towns along the camino real en route from the capital.

Three logical explanations suggest themselves. The first is that some agent other than *Variola* lay behind this surprisingly early rise in monthly mortality. But if this were the case, mortality would leap upward again when smallpox did arrive—much as it did in nearby towns—and there is no subsequent wave of mortality that could represent smallpox in the Canatlán records. A second possibility is that the deaths do represent smallpox and that the gap in geographical continuity simply reflects a corresponding gap in the documentary record. Finally, perhaps *Variola* did indeed reach Canatlán before it infected other towns along the way. This is particularly plausible if infection occurred by means of a contaminated object, such as a blanket or an article of clothing. There is nothing far-fetched about either of these two possibilities: Mule trains would have covered the distance between Mexico City and Canatlán in five to seven weeks, plenty of time for a plague observed in the former city in August to reach the latter city by November or December.[21]

The epidemic engulfed most of central Mexico by April 1780. Overall population density was highest here, facilitating the transmission of *Variola* between susceptible contacts and allowing the virus to spread quickly. The close, unsanitary conditions found in labor camps at the region's many silver mines did the same. Residents of such mining centers as Guanajuato, Guadalajara, Bolaños, Sombrerete, and San Luis Potosí all succumbed in the epidemic. Ten thousand died in Guanajuato alone.[22]

By the late spring and summer of 1780, smallpox reached the southern edge of New Spain's vast Interior Provinces. The camino real of the interior blazed the way for the virus, carrying it incrementally northward. By April, the pox had reached Hidalgo del Parral, a mining center in Tarahumara Indian country, near the current boundary between Chihuahua and Durango. By July, it reached the city of Chihuahua itself, at the heart of the great mining district known by the same name. Chihuahua's mines had by this time gone into decline, but many Tarahumara Indians still labored in the silver industry alongside African slaves and Yaqui and Mayo natives from Mexico's Pacific coast. Inevitably, they were among those who filled the *libros de entierros* kept in churches throughout the region. Extant Chihuahuan burial records show 1,030 interments from July through December 1780, roughly 850 of these probably caused by smallpox. But this number represents only a portion of those who succumbed. In the Chihuahuan countryside, large numbers of Tarahumaras remained apostate or unconverted to Christianity, and the expulsion of the Jesuits from New Spain in 1767 had left countless others beyond the reach of the church. Unnoticed by priests and friars, these Indians died by the hundreds, if not thousands, in the arid heights of the Sierra Madre.[23]

Once it reached the northwestern provinces, smallpox lingered, spreading much more slowly in these less traveled, more thinly populated regions. At Temósachic, in what is now western Chihuahua, the first smallpox death occurred in July and the last in December 1780. Oddly, the disease then disappeared for eight months before striking again from August 1781 to May 1782. By this time much of the local population had acquired immunity, and friars at Temósachic recorded very few fatalities during the second wave of the epidemic.[24]

For months, moreover, the epidemic stayed on the east side of the Sierra Madre Occidental, the mountains that separate Mexico's Pacific coast from the interior. Despite smallpox's arrival in central Nueva Vizcaya (now Durango and Chihuahua) as early as March 1780, the first indications of the pestilence in the neighboring coastal province of Sinaloa y Sonora did not come until September of that year. Even then, it is not clear whether the pox moved westward over the mountains or northward along the coastal camino real. In March 1781, Fray Juan Agustín de Morfi bore witness to the devastation the contagion had wrought at San Miguel Culiacán, near the Sinaloan coast. Along with a plague called *dolores de costado* (side pains—very possibly a description of the early, prepustular stages of smallpox), *Variola* had taken many lives in the neatly planned little town. It took so many, according to Morfi, that the interments had overflowed the church cemetery, forcing local residents to create a new one nearby. Similar problems must have confronted communities throughout New Spain.[25]

On the Sonoran coastline, as on the eastern slope of the Sierra Madre, the pox spread slowly. This thinly populated region lacked both the economic machinery of the interior and the human traffic

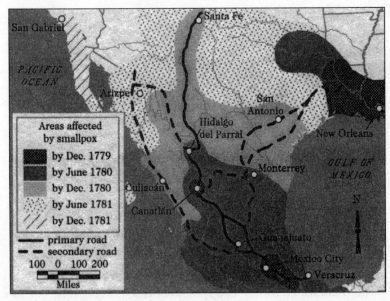

The northward spread of smallpox, 1779–82

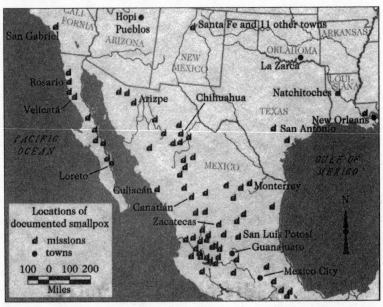

Missions and towns affected by smallpox

that came with it. Four months passed between the appearance of the pestilence at Culiacán in September 1780 and its appearance at Chínipas some two hundred miles farther north in January 1781. Another four months appear to have passed before the epidemic struck Arizpe, the colonial administrative center in Pima and Opata Indian country about seventy miles south of what is now the Arizona border. Thereafter, *Variola* remained in Sonora at least until November 1781, striking the Pimas, Opatas, and Yaquis who lived in mission settlements at Ati, San Ignacio, and Santa María Magdelena. These missions had declined since the Pima revolt against the Spaniards in 1751 and the expulsion of the Jesuits in 1767. Hence it is likely that here too the vast majority of smallpox victims suffered in the greasewood and saguaro backcountry, far from the eyes of the Franciscan friars who now served at the missions. A generation before, the Jesuit Fray Ignaz Pfefferkorn had witnessed the ravages of the epidemic of 1763–64 in Sonora. "Although many Spaniards die also," he noted, "smallpox kills incomparably more Indians. Few among the adults survive." If the disease itself did not prove fatal, starvation and lack of care would: "These pitiable people lie ill, without the necessary palliatives and remedies, often even without refreshment, and so die almost more from lack of care than from the sickness itself."[26]

The Sonoran epidemic of 1781 proved disastrous not just for the Pimas and their neighbors but also for the Guayacura, Cochimi, and Yuman natives who made their homes across the Sea of Cortés in Baja California. Beginning with the founding of Loreto on Baja's eastern strand in 1697, Jesuit, Franciscan, and finally Dominican missionaries had built a permanent chain of missions covering two-thirds of the length of the rugged peninsula, from San José del Cabo at its southern tip to San Vicente Ferrer in Baja California Norte. As elsewhere, the disruption caused by early episodes of Old World disease had assisted the Catholic friars in their enterprise. Mining had also taken hold in Baja, but it was inconsequential there by comparison to its role in the economy of central Mexico.[27] Unable to sustain themselves by their own agricultural endeavors, the missions of Baja relied on the regular arrival of supply ships from the mainland. In this way they too had a place in the vast web of commerce and communication that tied the Spanish empire together.

The epidemic's arrival in this far-flung realm of the empire is one of those rare episodes in which the documentary record actually describes the transmission of the disease. It was thanks to the attempt to colonize Alta California that *Variola* ravaged the Indians of the slender, mountainous Baja peninsula. In the late winter or spring of 1781, just as smallpox took a firm grip on Sonora, a company of settlers destined for Alta California gathered at the town of Alamos near the northwest coast of Mexico. The party's purpose was to establish the Pueblo de Nuestra Señora de los Angeles—modern-day Los Angeles—near San Gabriel Mission in the southern reaches of Alta California.

The little band of settlers eventually attained their objective, but they left havoc in their wake. Smallpox was only part of the problem.

Departing from Alamos, the aspiring colonists split into two groups. One, under the leadership of Captain Fernando Xavier de Rivera y Moncada, traveled overland, approaching San Gabriel by way of Tucson and Yuma. The route these settlers followed was close to the one pioneered by Juan Bautista de Anza and Fray Garcés in 1774, and in the end, the settlers' choice of this route had dire consequences for the unflappable Franciscan. The second group, led by Lieutenant José de Zúñiga, took a different course: It crossed the Gulf of California by boat and followed the Baja California peninsula north.

There is no evidence that the first group, Rivera's overland travelers, carried smallpox along with them on their journey. But nearly a thousand head of cattle did accompany them. By the time the party arrived at the lower Colorado River town of Yuma in the summer of 1781, the short history of Spanish relations with local Indians had already begun to sour. In a series of expeditions in the 1770s, the strategically placed Yumans had proved indispensable in assisting Spanish men, stock, and equipment in the difficult ford of the Colorado River at the Gila River junction. These were the Indians whose kind reception of Fray Garcés had contrasted so starkly with the hostility of the Hopis in 1776. One Yuman in particular, a leader who adopted the Spanish name Salvador Palma, repeatedly asked for Spanish missionaries and colonists to settle among his people. In 1779–80, Palma got what he wanted— or so he thought. First, late in 1779, Fray Garcés and another Franciscan arrived to proselytize among the Indians. The Yumans received the friars warmly despite the disappointing array of gifts they had brought with them. Then, a year later, an entourage of settlers and soldiers arrived. As Garcés supervised, they built two tiny colonies on the north side of the Colorado River.

The colonies at Yuma held little promise from the start. The settlements were poorly provisioned, and the surrounding desert was only marginally arable. Unwilling or unable to clear their own fields, some settlers appropriated Indian gardens as their own. Others allowed their livestock to graze among Indian plantings, where the animals trampled whatever crops they did not eat first. When the colonists ran short of food over the winter of 1780–81, their hunger pangs drew little sympathy from the Yumans. Even Salvador Palma was disgusted.[28]

Then, in June 1781, Rivera's Los Angeles–bound colonists passed through with their huge herd of livestock. As the expedition's free-ranging animals destroyed the local mesquite plants vital to Yuman subsistence, the captain actually had the gall to requisition food from the Indians. After ten days, most of the visiting party headed on to California, but Rivera and nineteen soldiers stayed on for a month to let the weakest livestock graze longer. For the Indians, this was the last straw. On July 17, they rose up in revolt, killing Fray Garcés, Rivera and his soldiers, and most of the adult males in the two new settlements. The California colonists who had departed for San Gabriel several weeks earlier, escaping unharmed, arrived safely at their destination on July 14, at the same time that on the other side of the continent,

Cornwallis's beleaguered British army was making its way to York-town.[29]

Meanwhile, the second party of Los Angeles settlers also pressed northward, leaving a different form of destruction in its wake. While Rivera's party traveled overland, Zúñiga's company crossed the Gulf of California to Loreto, on Baja California's eastern shore. They carried smallpox with them. In 1781, Fray Luis Sales recalled, "there entered the port of Loreto a bark which brought families from Sonora, infected with the small-pox." Showing a great "lack of precaution," Sales thought, the travelers "went into the town and immediately it spread like lightning through all the missions, not excepting the most distant ones, and caused havoc which only those who have seen it can believe." From Loreto the settlers hopscotched up the coastline in a series of mission shuttles, spreading smallpox wherever they landed. At the Bay of San Luis Gonzaga, not far from the mission of San Fernando de Velicatá, they disembarked and proceeded overland, finally arriving near San Gabriel Mission in Alta California on August 18. There, Governor Felipe de Neve immediately implemented a quarantine. "The recruits, colonists, and families," Neve explained, "camped one league distant because of arriving with some little children recently coming out of the smallpox." The effectiveness of the quarantine is not clear.[30]

What is clear is the devastation wrought in Baja California after the colonists passed through. The year 1781, according to Fray Sales, was a most "memorable year for [Baja] California because of the terribly violent smallpox which attacked the poor Indians." In Baja, as in Revolution-torn Virginia at the very same moment, smallpox casualties lay strewn across the countryside. "I can say from what I myself have experienced that many dead were to be seen in the fields. If one went into caves he saw the dying, and the missions were deserts for lack of people." From the mission of San Vicente Ferrer on Baja's northern frontier, Sales searched the rugged hills for victims. With the assistance of soldiers stationed at the adjoining pueblo, he cared for those who were sick or forsaken. "We would return loaded down with abandoned children," he wrote, "and we cared for them at the mission." At one location, Sales "found six dead adults in a cave and by their sides five boys and three girls dying, of hunger rather than of the smallpox, and they, once brought into the mission, were cured perfectly." Most deaths inevitably went unrecorded, as unconverted Indians died and spread the disease in the bush: "The heathen Indians crowded in the caves, when they noticed any infected with the disease, fled to another cave and abandoned those unfortunates, and the former, who were sometimes already infected, spread it to others, and all showed the same reactions."[31]

According to Sales, the Yuman and Cochimi Indians of Baja sought their own desperate cures for the plague. "As soon as they discover the pustules or ulcers some wash themselves with fresh water, some cast themselves into mudholes, others into fire, and still others set about burning the pustules with live coals," he observed. Some, terrified at their prospects, even threw "themselves into the sea at the onset of the disease." Sales believed that Indian responses combined with lack of food and care to create the appalling mortality that accompanied the epidemic.[32]

The missionaries applied their own medical knowledge to the problem. At three Baja California missions, Dominican friars implemented inoculation, the very procedure that had met with such a dismal reception in Mexico City during the early months of the epidemic. "A missionary father tried inoculating them for the small-pox, since he was going to be left without Indians, and he had such good success that hardly more than three or four died," wrote Sales. "This was at the mission of San Ignacio and I was present." The procedure also saw use at San Francisco de Borja and San Fernando de Velicatá. Although the population data are not complete enough to determine the case fatality rate, these missions did report fewer burials than others on the peninsula, very possibly a statistical reflection of the beneficial effect of inoculation.[33]

As elsewhere, the sacramental records kept by missionaries

give a view of the disease's transit. At San Fernando de Velicatá, nestled in Baja's northern sierra, Fray Pedro Gandiaga noted in July 1782 that the epidemic had begun "in the year of [17]81 and lasted until the middle of the present year." A short distance away, Fray Manuel Pérez recorded the arrival of *Variola* at the Rosario Mission on August 11, 1781. "This child was the first that died of the smallpox," he wrote next to his entry for a girl named Catarina, the daughter of two married Indians known by the Christian names Ignacio and Augustina. By October, and possibly as early as August, the virus had likewise begun to take lives forty miles north of Rosario at the Santo Domingo Mission, where ecclesiastical burials peaked in November with the deaths of twenty-one Christian Indians. Among those who succumbed were Gaspar and Domingo, husbands of Isabel and Felipa, two native women. The evidence makes it clear, moreover, that the Indians named in the *libros de entierros* were only the tip of the iceberg. The mendicant friars periodically received word of many *cimarrones*—apostate fugitives from the missions—who had died of smallpox among the non-Christian natives in the mountains, and hundreds, if not thousands, of deaths among these Indians inevitably went unrecorded.[34]

Far to the east, the arrival of the pox in New Mexico is a historical conundrum. A wave of mortality struck Santa Fe, Albuquerque, and many outlying pueblos in the spring of 1780, with a sudden surge in deaths cresting suddenly in May and tapering off over the next few months. Then smallpox struck with force in January 1781. Although the extant records do not appear to name it as such, some scholars have identified the pox as the cause of the earlier mortality as well. They may well be right; smallpox was known for waxing and waning seasonally, surging in the winter and subsiding in the summer, so it is possible that the virus struck in May 1780 and then faded quickly as summer set in.[35]

Even so, if this was indeed smallpox, Mexico City is not a

likely source. It took approximately nine months for packtrains that left Mexico City to travel the camino real to Santa Fe. For smallpox to have reached the New Mexican capital by May 1780, it would have had to begin its transit posthaste, at almost the very first moment it appeared in Mexico City in August 1779. Moreover, it would have had to outstrip the epidemic's known progress northward—progress methodically documented in the *libros de entierros* of parishes throughout the realm. These records show the epidemic inching through Nuevo Vizcaya, Coahuila, Nuevo León, and Nuevo Santander in May, taking victims five hundred or more miles *south* of Santa Fe. At times, *Variola* did seem to leap sizable distances, and this may well be what had already happened in Canatlán, Durango, in 1779. But such rapid transit from Mexico City to Santa Fe tests the limits of credulity. If the May 1780 mortality was indeed caused by smallpox, Louisiana may be a more plausible source; not only was *Variola* rampant in New Orleans almost a year earlier than in Mexico City, but the former French city was some three hundred miles closer to New Mexico.[36]

As 1780 drew to a close, a second, truly dramatic wave of mortality struck New Mexico. In December, it was barely perceptible. Then, as the new year dawned at Picuris Pueblo near Taos, Fray Francisco Xavier Davila Sabedra marked the start of his 1781 burial register with the following notation: "This year they expect mortality from epidemic smallpox." It was an ominous prediction, instantly fulfilled. In January 1781, mortality leaped skyward. It had taken more than a year, but the smallpox from Mexico City had finally arrived. After noting only 6 deaths in December, friars at the Santa Fe parish church recorded 39 in January and 181 in February. The mortality so overwhelmed Fray Juan Bermejo that he stopped making individual entries in the parish burial register, instead noting only a total at the end of each day, as he did on February 21: "On this day I gave ecclesiastical burial in this parish to fifteen souls, ten adults and five children."[37]

Among those affected were soldiers in the presidio of Santa Fe, where twelve men had taken sick by February 1, and nine more fell ill in the ensuing week. Soon twenty-seven were ailing, and one soldier was reportedly disconsolate because he had passed the infection to the presidio's housekeepers. In the register of the military chapel, friars logged 15 interments in January and 102 in February. Not until April was the garrison free of the pox.[38]

Outside the colonial centers of Albuquerque and Santa Fe, the victims were predominantly Native Americans. For centuries, villages of Tanoan- and Keresan-speaking Pueblo Indians had lined the upper Rio Grande from Taos in the north to Albuquerque, Isleta, Laguna, and Acoma in the south. Spain's early attempts at conversion and colonization of these communities, beginning in the sixteenth century, had ended with the successful Pueblo Revolt of 1680. But the Spaniards had returned twelve years later, and they had again established Catholic missions in these Indian towns by 1700. Not surprisingly, they brought smallpox with them. Outbreaks in 1719, 1733, and 1738 all can be documented in local burial records, as can numerous raids by "infidel" Indians.[39]

By 1781, though, two generations had passed since *Variola* had made its last appearance in New Mexico. The great majority of the province's native-born inhabitants had no immunity to the virus. When it struck, it took a terrible toll. Unfortunately, burial records do not survive for the northernmost pueblo of Taos, but they do survive from the nearby settlement of Picuris. Over the three years before the epidemic, friars at Picuris had recorded an average of 1.5 burials per month. Then *Variola* struck. In the first three months of 1781, some 27 residents of Picuris died, a seventeenfold increase in mortality.[40]

The pueblo closest to Picuris was San Juan, located south of Picuris with several others in a broad, fertile basin between the Jemez and Sangre de Cristo mountains. Here, after interring people at an average rate of 3 per month over the previous three years, the exhausted missionaries at the San Juan parish church interred more than 3 per *day* from January through March 1781. It appears that one-third of the Indian population died. At nearby Santa

Clara, situated at a high spot along the river in the same circular basin as San Juan, some 206 people died in the same three-month period. A Santa Clara cleric summed up the disaster by scrawling "Abundance of Smallpox" across the start of his 1781 burial register. So dramatic was the population loss that the Franciscans withdrew their full-time missionary and designated Santa Clara a mere *visita* (visiting outpost) of the San Ildefonso parish the next year. Though burial records are unavailable for San Ildefonso, it is inconceivable that it was spared. Between 1760 and 1790, a three-decade period in which smallpox struck twice, the population of the pueblo was halved. Inhabitants of the little settlements of Nambe and Pojoaque likewise succumbed to the virus. Among those who died in Pojoaque were "Joachin Martin, a widower, Indian servant of Francisco Martin," and "María Petra, Indian servant," who belonged to a man in Santa Fe.[41] Most Indian "servants" were in fact slaves, and these unlucky smallpox victims were often not Pueblos at all but Comanches, Apaches, or captives from some other "gentile" tribe.

Inevitably, the pestilence had arrived in these northern pueblos by way of their neighbors downstream on the Rio Grande. Here, in the shadow of their ancestral dwellings in the Jemez range, the Keresan-speaking Indians of Cochiti lost 142 people during the epidemic. At the great pueblo of Santo Domingo, just ten miles away, the pox took 266 lives and may well have interrupted surreptitious performances of the pueblo's hunting dance in February. At Sandia, beneath the towering Sandia Mountains still farther south, another 143 died.[42]

Elsewhere, burial records from many pueblos are incomplete or missing. This is the case for Pecos, situated on the eastern edge of New Mexico's mission frontier. Pecos was an important locus of trade and other interaction between the Pueblos and the Indians of the southern plains, particularly the Comanches and Apaches. The available demographic data indicate that the Pecos population plummeted from 235 in 1779 to 138 in 1789, a loss that probably reflects the impact of two separate smallpox outbreaks.[43]

By the time the 1781 epidemic was over, some 5,025 mission Indians had died throughout New Mexico.[44]

Mission Indians of course formed only a small portion of the native population. A Spanish visitor to New Mexico in 1766 had bemoaned "the disparity between the small number of our people and the infinite number of so many infidel nations."[45] Among these nations were the Hopis, perhaps the most resolute of the non-Christian tribes. The Hopis had resisted Spanish incursions for years. Unlike the Pueblo Indians of the Rio Grande, they had never readmitted Catholic missionaries to their towns after evicting them in the Pueblo Revolt of 1680. Fray Garcés was thus only one of many to be turned away.

Four months after he had mounted his mule and departed from Oraibi for Yuma, two more Franciscan missionaries approached the Hopi pueblo. Like Garcés, Francisco Atanasio Domínguez and Silvestre Vélez de Escalante had dreamed of opening a trail between New Mexico and California. But unlike Garcés, who had followed a southerly route from west to east, Domínguez and Escalante had tried to take a more northerly route from east to west. They had set out from Santa Fe in July 1776, just a few short weeks after the Hopis ejected their fellow Franciscan from Oraibi and the British colonies declared independence from Britain. By proceeding north into Colorado and then west across Utah, the explorers had hoped to find a passage to the Pacific that would avoid the hostile Hopis entirely.

But all did not go as planned. Months of hardship yielded little progress toward their goal, so Domínguez and Escalante gave up the venture and returned south and east through treacherous slickrock canyon country in the fall of that same year. For ten days they searched for a safe place to cross the Colorado River and its gorge. Finally, in desperation, they used axes to cut steps in the sandstone for their horses, and on November 7 they gratefully crossed to the river's eastern side.* The "great joy" they felt "in having overcome so great a problem" prompted them to fire their muskets in celebration.[46] The following month, on the eastern side of the continent, Washington's Continental army was to perform its own dramatic river crossing, fording the Delaware in a snowstorm to take Trenton.

Nine days after their jubilant success, the two Franciscans reached "the mesa of the pueblo of Oraybi," where the Hopis had so recently ousted Fray Garcés. Escalante had himself visited Oraibi from New Mexico the summer before, and the leader of the pueblo had told him then "that he did not want the Spaniards ever to live in his land." Now, less than eighteen months later, Domínguez and Escalante faced an initial reception that was predictably hostile. Oddly, however, relations soon warmed. Despite a language barrier, the Oraibi Hopis made it clear to the missionary-explorers "that they wanted to maintain friendship with the Spaniards."[47] The leader at Oraibi requested that other Hopi pueblos offer hospitality and sell provisions to the expedition as well.

Not until Domínguez and Escalante reached Walpi, another Hopi pueblo, did they find out the reason for this reluctant policy reversal on the part of the natives. They learned there that the Hopi and Pueblo Indians "were now at a fierce war" with the Navajos, who themselves may have suffered ongoing attacks from the Comanches farther east. The Hopis had in fact been "hoping that some fathers or Spaniards" would visit their towns "in order through them to beg from the Señor Governor some aid or defense against these enemies."[48]

For the Franciscan friars, the Hopis' plight represented an opportunity to preach the Christian Gospel. They called a meeting

---

*The steps they cut remained visible for nearly two centuries. But after the floodgates of Glen Canyon Dam closed in 1963, they were submerged beneath the waters of Lake Powell.

with other Hopi leaders for the next day, a gathering ironically held in a traditional ceremonial kiva at Walpi. When the Indians, as Escalante reported, "begged us to do everything possible in their behalf," the churchmen responded with religious exhortations. But Hopi resistance to Christianity did not waver. The Indians once again refused to submit, even if it meant forgoing assistance against their enemies. "They wished our friendship but by no means to become Christians," Escalante said.[49] The next day the Franciscans departed. Navajo attacks were to continue unabated over the next five years, and the resolute but ill-fated Hopis were to suffer enormously from other quarters as well.

By the summer of 1780, as smallpox caused havoc in the Carolinas and crept northward through central Mexico, the Hopis' situation had become truly desperate. Rains had failed for four years running, crops and livestock had died in the field, and Navajo raids had taken many lives. To make matters worse, the early unlabeled wave of mortality that had struck New Mexico now struck the Hopis as well. Again, smallpox was not named, but it might well have borne the blame.[50]

The net effect was devastating. Facing imminent starvation, many of the proud Hopis who had fended off Spanish incursions for so many years had second thoughts. In August 1780, they sent a message to Juan Bautista de Anza, now governor of New Mexico. Forty families were ready to depart for life in the mission towns, they told him, if only he would escort them safely through Navajo country. Like Domínguez and Escalante four years before, Anza saw opportunity in the Indians' suffering. He departed for Hopi country immediately, hoping he could finally bring about the "reduction" of the fiercely traditional tribe. At Zuni Pueblo, roughly midway on his journey, he noted signs of the ongoing drought. The condition of the Zunis was "deplorable," he wrote, thanks to "the failure of the rains for two years." Six days later, the expedition reached the Hopi community of Awatovi, where it had not rained for four.[51]

Despite their grave situation, the Hopis again frustrated the

Spanish colonizers. They told Anza that the forty refugee families were already gone. Fearing starvation, they had accepted a disingenuous offer of asylum from their Navajo enemies. The Navajos, according to the Hopis, had then broken their word, "killing all the men and making prisoners of the women and children." Two managed to flee and return home with their story. Anza sought out other volunteers for life on the Rio Grande but found very few. Hopi leaders explained that most of their people preferred to "finish out their lives" in their own pueblos. Already, very few remained. On a visit to the Hopis in 1775, Fray Escalante had counted a total of 7,494 people living in seven pueblos. Just five years later, after starvation, war, and pestilence, Anza found only 798 people left.[52]

It was in this state of attrition that the Hopis faced the rising tide of smallpox from Mexico City. Because these Indians so successfully repelled Spanish missionaries and colonizers, no substantial record of the epidemic's impact survives. The virus reached their pueblos the spring after the governor's visit, probably around June 1781. In November, Anza reported that the pox was still ravaging the Hopis. "For five months they have suffered a severe epidemic of small-pox," he wrote, "which as they inform me will almost result in the final extermination of this unhappy nation."[53] The Hopis, however, survived. Oraibi Pueblo, founded around 1150, is today the oldest continuously inhabited location in the United States. Thanks to the Hopis' steadfast refusal to accommodate Spanish and American values, their culture too remains alive and well.

While Hopi culture has survived to the present day, identifiable signs of the great epidemic have dissipated with time. Its primary legacy was emptiness. If emptiness is a quality hard to discern in the historical record, it is there, nevertheless, in the unremitting accumulation of souls in the *libros de entierros*. At first glance, these records appear to present little more than tedious lists of names. But when their vastness sinks in, when each death is considered

in its own right, the *libros* take on a meaning beyond the words
they contain:

> José Carlos, child of this pueblo, two months of age, the le-
> gitimate son of Fabian Nicolas and Isabel Rosa, Indians of
> this pueblo. (April 9, 1780, Santa Fe de la Laguna, Mi-
> choacán.)[54]

> María Gertrudis, little daughter of the Captain Don José
> Antonio Domíngues and Doña Mariana de Montenegro. . . .
> Died of smallpox. (July 6, 1780, Satevó, Chihuahua.)[55]

> An Indian man from Zuni, who died in the fields, given
> name Thomas. (February 4, 1781, Santo Domingo, New
> Mexico.)[56]

> María Petra, servant of Tomáz Sera, citizen of the villa of
> Santa Fe. (February 13, 1781, Pojoaque, New Mexico.)[57]

> Child Juan Manuel, of the Comanche nation, servant of
> Miguel Frugillo, Spaniard and citizen of this mission of
> Nuestra Señora de Guadalupe de Pojoaque. (February 17,
> 1781, Pojoaque, New Mexico.)[58]

> The little children that have died in this villa of Tehuante-
> pec in the epidemic of 1780, from February 6 until June 3
> in said year, are 284. (June 7, 1780, Santo Domingo
> Tehuantepec, Oaxaca.)[59]

> On February 15, 1781, I gave ecclesiastical burial to the
> following: to Lucas, widower of Theodora; to Ysidro
> Cuneque, single male; to María Rosa, wife of Ysidro; to
> Juachin Fzema, single male; to Mariano, husband of María
> of the Pueblo of Acoma. All died from the epidemic of
> smallpox. (Santo Domingo, New Mexico.)[60]

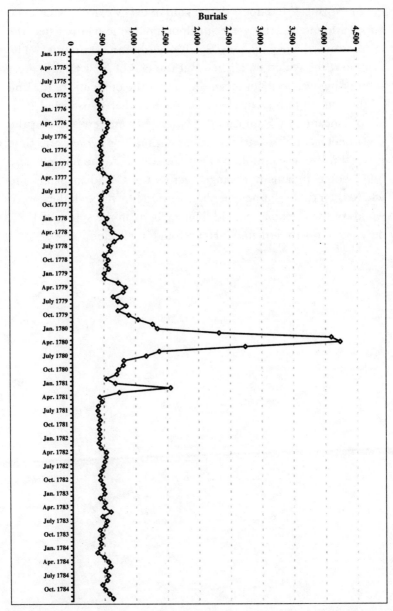

Burials in ninety-six parishes of New Spain. Statistics compiled in Elizabeth A. Fenn, "Pox Americana: The Great North American Smallpox Epidemic of 1776–1783" (Ph.D. diss., Yale University, 1999), 387–410

In Arizona's red rock desert and New Mexico's Sangre de Cristo Mountains, the great smallpox epidemic had reached the northernmost edge of New Spain's northernmost frontier. The camino real traveled no farther. But the end of New Spain's great interior highway did not mean the end of the epidemic or the end of the human-to-human chain of contacts that transmitted it. It simply meant that European eyewitnesses were few and that the documentary trail it left behind grew thin. For *Variola*, the time was right. Vast susceptible populations still lay to the north, where horse-borne Indians now ranged across the Canadian plains and where their canoe-borne neighbors carried furs through the spruce woods of the Canadian Shield. For smallpox in the spring of 1781, only one problem remained: How would it get there?

6

TRADERS

June 10, 1782. *The day dawned early and gray, muffled by a thick fog that eventually lifted to reveal a cloud-laden sky. The thermometer read forty-six degrees. It was a bit on the cool side, but still not unusual for a summer day at York Factory, a busy fur-trading post on the southwest shore of Hudson Bay.*

Sometime after the fog dissipated, sixteen canoes of Bungee Ojibwa Indians arrived at York Factory to trade. The canoes were "pretty well gooded," chief factor Matthew Cocking observed, pleased with the furs the Indians brought in. But what the Bungees told him was disturbing. "They inform me that a violent disorder has raged among their people which they describe as a violent eruption on the skin," he wrote in the post journal. The unnamed sickness, according to the Indians, had caused a great mortality even beyond Lake Winnipeg, "amongst the Swan River Red Deer River or Cowonitow [Cree] and Sahsahnew [Susuhana Cree] Indians who all border on their Country." It was an account that Cocking found "alarming indeed." Nevertheless, he hoped for the best. "The Natives most of them are such notorious Liars that great allowances ought to be made for exaggeration in the advices received from them," he noted; "this gives me some hopes that Events if not false, are not so bad as they have represented them."

Cocking clung to his hopes for nearly two weeks. Perhaps the Bungee Ojibwas had exaggerated. Perhaps their account of a great pestilence was not true. But on June 23, 1782, events confirmed his worst fears. It was a clear, windy Sunday. The chief factor read divine service to his men in the morning. Then, in the afternoon, a small party of "North River" Crees arrived on foot, forced by the gale to abandon their canoes a short distance away. "They consist only of three Women and three Boys," Cocking wrote. The women told him "their Husbands &.ᶜ died of a violent breaking out upon them all over their bodies and within the mouth and throat and which from their description of it must have been the small pox." Cocking's visitors had suffered from the disease themselves. One woman's "face, hands and body" were "all red spotted in the same manner as any persons is who has recently recovered from the Small Pox," and the others bore similar scars in lesser number. The Indians told Cocking that along with "another Woman and four Children," they were "all that remain of five Families the rest being dead." This depleted party of Crees had brought "268 made Beaver in good Furs, Beaver and Cats." Many additional furs remained inland with the dead. Their numbers reduced, the Indians had been unable to carry them to the post.

The mysterious disease now had a name, smallpox. But where had it come from, whom had it struck, and how far had it spread? The news from the North River survivors seemed to confirm what the Bungees had told Cocking two weeks earlier: The pestilence was widespread to the west, in the Canadian interior. One of the women explained that she and her husband, now dead, had visited Cumberland House before the smallpox struck them. Cumberland House was one of the Hudson's Bay Company's new inland posts, strategically located on the Saskatchewan River some five hundred miles southwest of York Factory. "The Indians that way died of the same complaint," she told Cocking. The couple had come down with the disease only after their visit to the interior post, the chief factor noted, which made him "suppose that She and her Husband caught the infection when there and communicated it to their Tribe when they fell ill after their return."

Cocking was anxious for details. It disturbed him that the Cumberland House trader William Tomison "did not send a Line" by an Indian to fill him in on "any particular events that might have happened." But news, he knew, would come shortly. Once a year, during the long days of

the northern summer, the annual brigade from Cumberland House ar-
rived at York Factory, ferrying furs to the coast for shipment to England.
Now, in the closing days of June, Cocking waited anxiously for Tomison
and his fleet of canoes to arrive.[1]

York Factory was the star performer in the Hudson Bay fur trade.
In 1782, the post was one of seven trading houses perched in a
seven-hundred-mile semicircle on the southern rim of Canada's
great saltwater bay. The first had been established more than a
century before, in 1668. All were owned by the Hudson's Bay
Company, which had been granted a monopoly by the British
crown in 1670 to trade in as much as one-third of modern-day
Canada. Location, for the Hudson's Bay Company, was everything. The company's posts lay in the very heart of the North
American continent, at the center of the vast Precambrian land-
mass known as the Canadian Shield. But despite their inland position, the posts remained accessible by sea. Ships loaded with
manufactured goods could sail from England directly to the rich-
est fur-bearing lands of the New World, deep in the Canadian interior.

York Factory itself had another advantage. Its location on the
southwestern edge of Hudson Bay's vast tidal flats marked the
point where two rivers, the Nelson and the Hayes, flowed into
the sea. The Hayes River drainage was relatively short and self-
contained. But the Nelson River watershed was enormous, extending west across the plains to the Canadian Rockies and south
beyond Lake Winnipeg to the Red River in what is now the
United States. These backcountry lakes and rivers were the highways of the fur trade, and most of them, it seemed, led to York
Factory.

The Hudson's Bay Company's partners in commerce were the
Cree Indians of the Canadian Shield and, to a lesser extent, their
Ojibwa, Chipewyan, and Assiniboine neighbors. These native
groups quickly took to European trade goods, especially firearms.

By 1716, after only a generation of trade on the bay, the Crees and
other trading Indians seem to have lost the use of the bow and arrow, instead relying entirely on the guns, powder, and shot they
received in exchange for furs at company posts.* Central to this
exchange was the beaver, prized for its unique barbed undercoat,
which, when pressed, formed a superior felt for making the hats
that had become so popular in the streets of seventeenth-century
Europe. So important was the beaver to the Hudson's Bay Company's business that like the "buck" in the Southeast, the "Made
Beaver" (MB) became the unit by which all other pelts, goods,
and services were valued. At York Factory in 1782, for example,
one wolf was valued at two MB, one black fox was valued at four
MB, and two prime martens were valued at one MB. Trade goods
were appraised in the same way.[2] At the trade's peak in 1730, the
company shipped 62,256 beaver skins from the bay in a single
year, 43,690 of these from York Factory alone.[3]

Even the most plentiful beaver country could not sustain such
a trade for long. In the 1730s, Indians began reporting shortages of
fur-bearing animals. "Itt's: y^c: Generall Complaint of all y^c: Indians
y^t: there is neither Beav^r: nor any other furs to be gott . . . wth: in
Several miles of y^c: factory," wrote James Isham at York Factory in
1738. The next year, after a lengthy trek to the post, fifty-eight
canoes of Indians from the Saskatchewan River echoed these

---

*The events of 1716 and 1717 highlighted the extent of Indian dependence upon
European goods and technologies. In the fall of 1716, the Hudson's Bay Company
ship bringing the annual supply of trade goods failed to arrive. This meant that
company employees had no merchandise—particularly guns, powder, and shot—
to exchange for furs the following summer. Unaware of this, the Indians made the
long spring journey to York Factory with their furs only to be disappointed. "The
Indians," wrote chief factor James Knight, "look upon themselves in as Manner
allmost Dead Men in Returning back into their own Country when they cannot
gett Powder and Shott to carry them back again." Starvation and mortality marked
the following winter. Some Indians had returned to the backcountry without the
arms they needed, while others waited through the summer for the next ship to
arrive. Unfortunately, the guns that were finally delivered were inferior, and few
remained in service through the winter.

Hudson's Bay Company ships in the Thames. Oil painting by Francis Holman, 1771. Courtesy Hudson's Bay Company Archives, Provincial Archives of Manitoba

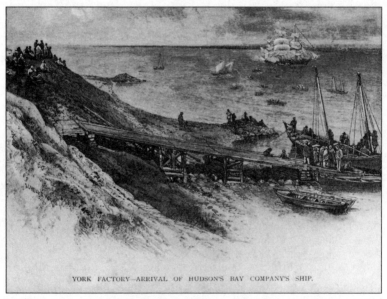

YORK FACTORY—ARRIVAL OF HUDSON'S BAY COMPANY'S SHIP.

York Factory—arrival of Hudson's Bay Company's ship. Print by Schell & Hogan

sentiments: "Itt'ˢ: yᵉ: Complaint amongst them all yᵗ: martins, &. other furs are so scarce they Can hardly gett waywithall to Live upon."[4]

The Hudson Bay trade soon dropped off. At York Factory, the take in beaver skins fell to 26,460 by 1735. The shortfall, however, was not entirely ecological in origin. Even before the Hudson's Bay Company had established itself on the bay, French fur traders, known commonly as coureurs de bois, had circulated among the Indians farther south, following the St. Lawrence and Ottawa rivers and eventually the Great Lakes to the continental interior. By 1684 the coureurs de bois had built trading houses as far inland as Lake Nipigon, and they soon added another one at Kaministiquia on Lake Superior. During the 1730s, Pierre Gaultier de Varennes, sieur de La Vérendrye, and his sons pushed the French trade still deeper into the Canadian heartland, building posts at Lake of the Woods and at the south end of Lake Winnipeg. Eventually, in the 1740s and early 1750s, these explorer-entrepreneurs established additional trading posts as far north as the Saskatchewan River, where they competed directly with the Hudson's Bay Company for the furs of the great Nelson River watershed.[5] After France ceded Canada to the English in 1763, Canadian "pedlars" working for the North West Company and other interests took over these French posts, but the competition continued much as before. Not until the 1770s did the Hudson's Bay Company respond with its own inland trading houses on the Saskatchewan River.

The Native Americans who frequented these rapidly multiplying trading posts made adjustments of their own. The fierce rivalry among European competitors gave Cree and Assiniboine traders room to dictate both the terms of trade and the quality of the goods they would accept. If their demands were not met, they carried their business elsewhere. Furthermore, as quality furs disappeared in the watery woodlands of the Canadian Shield, Indians from this region pushed westward into the parklands and prairies of modern-day Saskatchewan and Manitoba, not as hunters and trappers but as middlemen, carrying manufactured goods to the Blackfeet, Bloods, Atsinas, Mandans, and Hidatsas and ferrying furs back to European traders.[6]

By the time of the American Revolution, an immense trading network controlled largely by Cree middlemen sprawled far across Canada. From the foothills of the Canadian Rockies near what is now Edmonton, furs and people traveled the length of the Saskatchewan to Lake Winnipeg, which was like a great switchyard of sorts. From Lake Winnipeg, the options seemed limitless. At the north end of the lake, the Nelson and Hayes rivers flowed northeast to York Factory and Hudson Bay. At the south end, four significant rivers converged in close proximity: The Red River tied the vast fur-producing regions of the Canadian Shield to the Mississippi River and points south; the Souris River, dipping south into present North Dakota, connected these same regions to the agricultural Indian villages of the upper Missouri; the Assiniboine River tapped the windswept plains of southern Saskatchewan by way of the Qu'Appelle River; and the southeastward-flowing Winnipeg River linked the northern trade to the St. Lawrence and Montreal by way of Lake Superior. Lake Superior too was a hub, with connections not just to Montreal but also to Niagara, Detroit, James Bay, the Mississippi, and the western prairies.[7] Ultimately, these trade routes connected to still others, extending even across the Atlantic to the commercial and manufacturing concerns of the European powers. It was an intricate web of connections that could carry pox as well as pelts far and wide.

The Cumberland House brigade arrived at York Factory on July 2, 1782. Thirty-four days in passage, the brigade had descended to the sea by way of the Saskatchewan River, Lake Winnipeg, and then the Hayes River. Included in the entourage were twenty-two company employees "in 12 Canoes assisted by three Canoes only of Indians." William Tomison, the factor at Cumberland House,

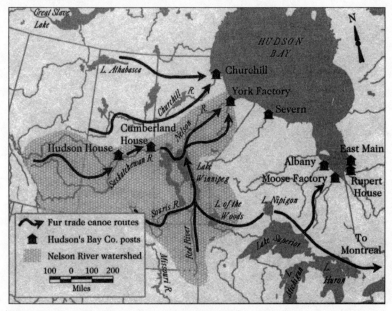

Hudson's Bay Company posts and major canoe routes

was in charge. After disembarking, Tomison apologized to Matthew Cocking for his failure to send news by way of the North River Indians who had stopped at York Factory less than ten days before. The lapse had upset the senior officer, but Tomison's explanation was simple: He knew the Indians were debtors at York Factory, and he feared that Cocking would be "vexed" upon learning he had allowed them to trade at his inland post. Had Tomison sent a written report, the story he related would have been bleak. Now he recounted it firsthand, sketching for his listeners the grim events of the preceding winter and spring.[8]

The inland traders had first gotten wind of trouble at Hudson House, a newly established post on the North Saskatchewan River nearly seven hundred miles from York Factory and the sea. Built in the parkland transition zone between spruce-aspen woods and wide-open prairies, Hudson House was even farther inland than Tomison's station at Cumberland House, staunchly situated in the evergreen monotony of the Canadian lake country. Hudson House therefore was closer to the plains than any other company post at the time.

On October 19, 1781, Dominican friars were watching the Yumans succumb to *Variola* in Baja California, and the British were surrendering at Yorktown. Three days later, the first sick Indian appeared at Hudson House. According to William Walker, the master of the trading post, the ailing man reported "that one of their Tents they was oblidged to leave standing in the Barren Ground with Seven Indians laying dead in the Inside that died of the Small pox." The man himself, Walker feared, was "taken so bad that I believe he never will recover." The man's fate, name, and nation all remain unknown. The next day, however, some of the companions he had left behind also came in to the post. Three were "very bad with the Small Pox," Walker reported, "and two they buried the night before they came here."[9] Many more afflicted Indians stumbled into Hudson House in the days and months that followed. Thanks to the continuous ebb and flow of people, the epidemic raged around the North Saskatchewan trading hub for a full seven months.

Because of their location at the edge of the prairie, the traders at Hudson House got a better glimpse than others of the epidemic's impact upon the tribes of the northern plains. No one got a closer view of the damage than a man named Mitchell Oman. Like many Hudson's Bay Company "servants," Oman was a native of the Orkney Islands, off the northern tip of Scotland. On October 15, 1781, William Walker had sent Oman and four other men out from Hudson House "to supply themselves in the Barren Ground" for the duration of the winter.[10] "The Barren Ground" was, ironically, the common term for the game-laden grasslands southwest of the trading post. It was Walker's hope that by having these men fend for themselves, he might alleviate the post's severe food shortage.

Oman later told the great Canadian explorer David Thompson what he and his companions encountered.

They proceeded "up the River to the Eagle Hills," he said,

where they came upon some Indians cooling themselves on the beach. "To our surprise they had marks of the small pox, were weak and just recovering," he told Thompson. As yet, however, Oman and his companions had no comprehension of the scope of the calamity. Surely the Indians would have some food to share with the hungry traders. "None of us had the least idea of the desolation this dreadful disease had done," Oman explained, "until we went up the bank to the camp and looked into the tents, in many of which they were all dead, and the stench was horrid." The survivors had tried to move but could get no farther than two hundred yards, where they had again pitched their tents. "They were in such a state of despair and despondence," Oman recalled, "that they could hardly converse with us." A few of the Indians "had gained strength to hunt which kept them alive." In his estimation, "three fifths had died under this disease."[11]

It is quite possible that these Indians were Assiniboines, like so many of the natives who traded at Hudson House a short distance downstream. Sometimes called Stone Indians, the Assiniboines had prospered as middlemen, carrying goods and furs between trading houses and distant tribes such as the Blackfeet and Atsinas. Now, however, the Assiniboines' prospects looked bleak. "As for the Stone Indians," Walker later wrote, there were "very few, if any left alive." Reports trickling into other trading posts also pointed to many deaths in this tribe.[12]

With no buffalo to be found and no provisions to be purchased from the Indians, Oman and his starving companions soon returned to Hudson House. They had expected "a crowd of Indians" to greet them upon their arrival. Instead, "all was solitary silence."[13] The epidemic had reached the trading post in their absence.

The return of Oman and his companions was not good news for William Walker, for their presence made the post's ongoing food shortage more acute. "There is very little provisions in the House and no likelihood of getting any more," Walker wrote. With Indians dying near and far, few, if any, hunters could supply the company servants with food. A métis (mixed race) trader named Charles Isham had fallen ill, and the rest of Walker's men were preoccupied caring for the sick and burying the dead. The chief factor had to act fast. The next day, therefore, he "fitted out Eight Men to go to Cumberland House," roughly two hundred miles downstream. Perhaps Tomison could feed his men.[14]

Tomison had troubles of his own. On December 11, 1781, while Walker's men were still making their way through the forest, the first smallpox case appeared at his Cumberland House post. "In the Evening," he wrote, "three Men & four Women arrived from the southward with Furs to trade," bringing "Disagreeable News of many Indians Dying." One of the four women in the party was herself not well, "troubled with a Violent pain in her back & much inclined to Vomitting." In the earliest stages of smallpox when she arrived, the woman died the next day, on "only the fourth Day of her ailment." It is doubtful that she ever developed the rash that would have made a diagnosis of smallpox possible, and Tomison, not surprisingly, does not name her disorder. Even if the fur trader could not identify her disease, it is clear that the woman's companions had already learned something of its contagious nature. "Those that came with Her would not touch her," wrote Tomison, "although some of them were very near Relations." Company employees buried her body.[15]

Tomison soon learned more details. On December 17, six days after the woman died, the Hudson House men arrived, bearing a letter from William Walker. "I am very Sorry that I should have such disagreeable News to send You," Walker began. "But the Small Pox is raging all round Us with great Violence, sparing very few that takes it." The letter briefly described the deadly plague, and Walker's men would surely have filled in the details.[16]

As Tomison took in this news, he must have realized its connection to the dead woman and the account of "many Indians Dying" he had heard only the week before. "God knowes what will be the End thereof," he wrote in the Cumberland House journal. The disease was closing in on the trading post, attacking one susceptible victim after another as it traveled north and east along the icebound riverine highways of the fur trade. On December 24, "five Indian Men & four Women arrived from the Southward" with "Melancholy News" of "the small pox rageing amongst them." One member of the party had turned back sick that very morning. Tomison feared what was to come. Smallpox was "now spreading over the Whole Country," he wrote. His melancholy entry for Christmas Eve predicted it would be as "shocking [an] Affair as ever was known."[17]

Soon there were signs that as a central gathering spot, Cumberland House might contribute to the spreading contagion. On December 20, Tomison had sent a young Indian "lad" and his family out to hunt for local provisions. It was nine days after the first sick Indian, the woman who died, had arrived. Because the incubation period of smallpox was almost always twelve days, anyone she had infected at Cumberland House would not yet have shown symptoms. This may well have been the case for the young Indian hunter, who appeared to set out for the woods in good health. But late at night on December 25, "two Indian Boys arrived" towing the hunter "on a Sledge." It was now fourteen days after the sick woman had come in, and if he had picked up the *Variola* virus from her, it would by now have run through its incubation period. The lad, Tomison wrote, had been "taken bad" the previous night "with a Violent pain in his breast & Belly," symptoms signaling the onset of smallpox. The next day, December 26, and Indian woman at the post also took ill. Despite nursing care from company employees, the hunter died on January 4, 1782.[18] The woman's fate is unknown.[19]

Tomison took these events to heart and tried to protect susceptible Indians from the contagion as they came to the post. On January 2, 1782, a band of Indians arrived from the Pasquia region, eastward and downstream from Cumberland House. They had "not heard of the disorder that is rageing amongst the Natives, Untill now," Tomison wrote. In an attempt to keep them clear of the infection, he implemented a quarantine of sorts. "I would not let them come into the House, but had a Tent pitched for them some Distance off," he explained. Two months later, as the epidemic continued its ravages, he would again turn to quarantine when "five Men and three Women arrived from the northward with Furs and provisions to Trade," informing him "that they have heard Nothing of the Disorder that is rageing in this Quarter."[20] Post records do not indicate the immediate success or failure of these efforts, in part because the disease's incubation period makes it hard to track the fate of the Indians who traded and then left the busy Hudson's Bay Company outpost. The Pasquia Indians picked up the infection eventually, although Cumberland House was not necessarily the source.

In those early days of the new year, ailing Indians inundated Cumberland House, bringing reports of additional sickness and rapid death elsewhere. The Indians, Tomison observed, "chiefly Die within the third or fourth Night" of the disease, even before a full-blown rash could develop. Such accelerated mortality is relatively rare in the records of twentieth-century medical observers, occurring in no more than 9 percent of cases, but it was apparently common among the natives of Canada in 1781–82.[21] "There is something very malignant, that we are not sensible of," wrote Tomison, "either in the Constitution of the Natives or in the Disorder, those that Die before the small pox breaks out is tormented with great pains and many of them Die within 48 Hours." Hudson's Bay Company traders could not have known about the unique genetic circumstances that made their Native American trading partners so vulnerable, but they recognized that something extraordinary was going on.[22]

Many of the afflicted sought refuge with the traders, most of whom appear to have possessed immunity to the disorder. The traders also provided at least a modicum of nursing care. On January 25, 1782, a cold, clear day with "a fresh gale," company employees at Cumberland House were largely preoccupied with tending the sick. "One man cutting firewood for the sick Natives," wrote Tomison in the post journal; "two men Digging a

Grave & burying a Woman that Died last Night"—no easy task in the frozen earth. At noon Tomison received word of another pox-ridden Indian nearby and "sent two men with Sledges to haul him to the House." Nine or ten ailing Indians were on the premises; four of them stayed "in the House," where they had "due attendance Night & Day." On January 30, while other company men cut firewood, buried the dead, and searched for incapacitated Indians, one man spent his whole day "attending the sick Natives." Months later, when the epidemic hit York Factory on Hudson Bay's swampy coastline, chief factor Matthew Cocking deployed his men similarly. "The Labourers employed one in attending upon the sick Indians, two more buried the one that died last night, and the remainder making the bank," he wrote on July 3, 1782.[23]

Repeatedly, Hudson's Bay Company employees went to the aid of ailing Indians in the bush, and although documentation does not exist, it is likely that traders at North West Company houses did the same. Walker and Tomison often sent men from their posts to search for Indians reported sick. On January 21, 1782, for example, Tomison "sent James Wass to assist a sick Indian & bring him to the House." The next day at noon Wass returned with "the Indian called Weeshenow" in tow, while William Flatt and George Ross retrieved the sick man's gun and "a small Bundle of Furs" from the tent in which the Indian's wife had died. In the course of their one day away, the men had performed other duties as well. They had buried three Indians "& found several more dead, which they could not bury for want of Provisions."[24]

The traders also made forays into the bush to retrieve furs from the tents of dead Native Americans. While this clearly added to the company's coffers, it is worth noting that the Indians themselves did not hesitate to retrieve "the furrs of their deceased relations," and they sometimes asked company men to help them with this task. At Hudson House, for example, the Indians were said to have told traders "that the Indians of the forest had beaver robes in their tents some of which were spread over the dead bod-

ies, which we might take, and replace them by a new blanket."
The furs of the dead bought supplies for the living. "By going to
the tents," the Indians reportedly told Mitchell Oman, "we would
render a service to those that were living by furnishing them with
tobacco, ammunition, and a few other necessaries."[25]

When company servants found beaver robes covering dead Indians, they replaced them with blankets or duffel. Often, however, they found little. When James Banks and James Saunderson
returned from one such outing in February 1782, they reported
"that they had found where four Indians had died, but nothing remain'd of three except the Hair of their Heads & a few scraps of
their Coats, all which had been eat up by the wild Animals."
Where the bodies remained intact, the men buried them in the
frozen earth or took other steps to prevent their desecration.
Oman described the traders' efforts awkwardly but graphically:
"The bodies lately dead, and not destroyed by the Wolves and
Dogs, for both devoured them, we laid logs over them to prevent
these animals."[26]

On May 30, 1782, when William Tomison and the Cumberland
House brigade left on their annual trek to the sea, their task was to
carry all the furs collected at the inland posts to York Factory and
then to return upriver with a year's supply of trade goods. In all,
the men would cover more than a thousand mosquito-plagued
miles on a round-trip journey that would give them a firsthand
look at the progress of the epidemic since it had first appeared at
Cumberland House in the winter. What they saw was a catastrophe in progress.

When the brigade left its inland post, smallpox still had not
reached York Factory's bayside location. But it was clear that the
disease had taken hold in much of the region between the two
posts, moving east from Cumberland House and north from the
Cree and Ojibwa country surrounding Lake Winnipeg. Two days
after setting out, the brigade camped near the mouth of the

Pasquia River, a site denoted today by the town of The Pas. It was a frequent rendezvous spot for trading Indians, and smallpox had made its appearance here by the end of January 1782 as it progressed down the Saskatchewan from Cumberland House. A little farther on, along the north shore of Lake Winnipeg, Tomison and his fellow travelers "came to two Tents of Indians, the most part of which are died of the Small pox." There were "but two Men, a Young Lad, two Women and a few Children" left alive, and three of these were very ill. Unable to proceed onward to York Factory, one of the men begged Tomison to take his furs, even though the trader lacked sufficient goods for payment. Tomison agreed to do so, and for once the tables were turned: Typically, it was the Indians who bought goods on credit from the Hudson's Bay Company, but now the company became the debtor as Tomison promised to deliver the man's furs and then repay him on the brigade's return trip.[27]

A week later, on June 22, the party met a canoe of Indians also headed to York Factory. They informed Tomison that in addition to killing many Indians, the pox had taken the life of a Canadian trader named William Bruce in southwest Manitoba, probably near Dauphin Lake.[28] The next day—June 23, when at York Factory chief factor Matthew Cocking finally identified the mysterious pestilence from the scars he saw on recently arrived Indians—Tomison and his companions ran into two canoes of Indians returning from Cocking's bayside post. They told him that some of those who had traded at York Factory had taken sick and died since their departure. "Several more Sick," they told him, had "gone up Shemataway River" (the present-day Gods River, which flows toward York Factory from the southeast).[29]

Nearly all the Indians the brigade encountered along the way were heading to or from York Factory, and nearly all were sick or recovering from smallpox. *Variola*, it seemed, had unwittingly become an article of trade. "At Noon passed by one Tent of Indians containing two Men, One woman and four Children," wrote Tomison at Knee Lake on June 24. They had "just now got over the Small Pox," he noted, and their situation was dire. They "neither had pitch to pitch their Canoes, not paddles to paddle her with nor even a Stick to make a fire." Tomison gave them pitch, paddles, and firewood and "also lent them a Gun and gave a little Tobacco and ammunition as encouragement for them to embark tomorrow for York Fort with their furrs."[30]

Two days later, in "squally weather with thunder and Rain," the brigade encountered some Bungee Ojibwas; they were the ones who had brought the first news of the plague to Matthew Cocking at York Factory a fortnight before. They had appeared healthy at the time. But since they had left the trading post and headed upstream, the pox had erupted among them. "At 2 in the Afternoon met two Canoes of Bungee Indians come from the fort," wrote Tomison on June 26; "three of these are bad with the Small pox and not likely to get over with it." The Bungees told him that several of their group had died since leaving York Factory. The timing of the outbreak indicates that they must have picked up *Variola* before they arrived at York Factory. Unaware that they incubated the smallpox, they traded there and left. The disease burst out among them shortly thereafter.[31]

Tomison and his party continued to encounter sick Indians as they proceeded downstream. Some may have been remnants of the Bungee Ojibwas, but Tomison does not identify them as such. On July 1, drawing close to the bay, the traders "found an Indian Man and Child laying at the River Side bad of the Small Pox." For eight days they had lain unattended, "without a fire and nothing to eat." The man had already traded his furs at York Factory, but when he took ill, he said, his companions "robb'd him of all his things and left him to perish." The Cumberland House traders "put him into a small Canoe with two Indians to paddle him to the fort." They assisted the child as well. That night the brigade camped on Woody Island just upstream from their destination. At 4:00 A.M. on July 2, they set out once more. Three hours later, they finally arrived at York Factory, just three weeks after the first rumors of the massive epidemic had reached the saltwater post.[32]

The inland fur traders, engulfed by the epidemic during the winter and spring, had finally caught up with the leading edge of the outbreak after paddling hard for more than a month. The sick man they transported appears to have been the first active case— hence the first infectious case—of smallpox to reach York Factory. In the preceding weeks, some Indians had visited the post while incubating the disease, and others had arrived bearing scars after weathering it. But until the Cumberland brigade arrived, no active cases had appeared at York Factory. Now it took only hours for more to come in. "Towards noon," wrote Cocking, "six Canoes arrived with Furs to trade, five of them are Sahsahnew [Cree] Indians, the sixth Lake [Bungee] Indians." Three of the latter were "ill of the Small Pox which seized them on the way down," and a fourth apparently fell sick soon after arriving. Cocking put them "immediately under the Surgeons care; one of them died in the evening, the others have spots coming out on them very thick . . . and their throats are excessive sore." Only one of these four survived. The sick man and child conveyed by the Cumberland House brigade in a starving condition may have fared better. On July 10, according to Tomison, they moved toward "recovery tho' slowly, the Man in particular is yet helpless, his feet are quite raw and he is much troubled with swellings which succeed each other in different parts of his Body and Limbs."[33]

For seven weeks after Tomison and his fellow travelers arrived, post records show smallpox coursing through the lowlands around York Factory. On July 11, Cocking traded with several Bungee Ojibwas, including a woman who "complained of a pain in the head" and a man whose brother "was taken ill with the Head ache last night." Headache was one of the first signs of smallpox. Three days later, "Five Men and three Boys of Lake Indians" came in to trade, having recently recovered from the disease. They "said they are all the Males that remain alive" from their band. Just seven miles up the Hayes River, traders found a desperate little Indian girl on July 22. She was "about seven Years of Age" and "almost Starved to Death for want of Food." Her father, she told the traders, "was left, about a month agoe up hayes river where he died of the Smallpox." She, however, had gotten over the disease.[34]

Since he had sick Indians at the post through much of July, Cocking tried to keep susceptible newcomers away from the premises, often providing supplies for them while they camped at a distance. On July 10, for example, nine canoes of deer hunters promised that upon their return they would "stop at the Sloops Creek and wait" until Cocking sent word for them to come in for trade. The next day, another party also agreed "not to attempt coming to the Fort until we think it safe." With smallpox all around the post, however, there was no assurance that these Indians would not pick up the infection elsewhere. Cocking urged them to notify him if they fell ill. "I desired them so to do," he explained, "hoping to prevent its being so fatal to them when under our care as when left to themselves."[35]

Cocking's efforts at controlling smallpox were successful in part. By July 25, 1782, the York Factory premises were clear of the smallpox, and company laborers spent several days cleaning, sweeping, and painting in order to eliminate residual contamination.[36] These measures apparently succeeded in keeping *Variola* from taking hold among local "home guard" Indians, primarily Swampy Crees, who were employed year-round in provisioning the post.[37] But the virus continued to rage in the countryside, and through most of August, Cocking and his men tended to sick Indians in the bush to avoid reinfecting the trading house.

Not surprisingly, the smallpox also struck Indians who frequented the Hudson's Bay Company's post at Churchill. Despite being only one hundred miles northwest of York Factory, Churchill sat in a markedly different landscape. Here, in the tundra beyond the permafrost line, trees were stunted and few, and polar bears regularly threatened travelers in the bush. Because the Churchill post journal does not survive, we know relatively little about the epidemic there. But we do know that some years before *Variola* struck, Churchill's chief factor, Samuel Hearne, had facilitated a peace between the traditionally hostile Cree Indians, who lived south of the post, and the Chipewyan Indians to the north. With the arrival of smallpox, this peace became deadly. "The Northern [Chipewyan] Indians," Hearne later explained, "contracted the small-pox" by "visiting their Southern friends, the Athapuscow [Cree] Indians." The disease "carried off nine-tenths of them, and particularly those people who composed the trade at Churchill Factory."[38]

Southeast of York Factory, the Hudson's Bay Company post at Severn seems to have dodged the epidemic. Given the fort's proximity to York Factory and the nature of its trading traffic, the escape seems astonishing, one more reminder that *Variola* could be elusive and mercurial. Severn tapped a very short drainage adjoining the massive Nelson-Hayes watershed entering the bay at York Factory. It is inconceivable that trading Indians did not cross the divides between these waterways. The Bungee Ojibwas, for example, frequented both York Factory and Severn. Yet on August 8, Matthew Cocking had a visit from two Severn traders who had not even heard of the epidemic. "Thank God," Cocking wrote, "the Small Pox had not yet reached any of their Pungee Indians as yet." Almost immediately, a message was sent to the man left in charge at Severn, warning him to be on the lookout for the illness and to prevent contact between home guard Indians and any arriving Bungees. Whether the result of sheer luck, a limited watershed, or preventive measures, Severn escaped the plague. The following year, in the spring of 1783, smallpox-scarred Indians told traders there that the Indians were "all dead Inland" but that they themselves had recovered from the illness many months before.[39]

As in Quebec and Baja California, starvation and lack of care added to the suffering of these many smallpox victims in the Canadian interior. Traditionally, the Indians of the region shared their resources when the hunt failed or sickness took hold. As the explorer David Thompson explained, "Especially in provisions is great attention [paid] to those that are unfortunate in the chace, and the tent of a sick man is well supplied." Now, however, ailing

Indians were too weak even to help themselves. According to
Matthew Cocking, "there was none left in many Tribes able to
hunt for or administer to the wants of each other." Hence, in the
words of another York Factory eyewitness, "hundreds lay expiring
together without assistance, without courage, or the least glim-
mering hopes of recovery."[40]

Smallpox undermined traditions of mutual support in other
ways as well. As Indians began to recognize the plague's contagious nature, friends and relations fled in terror, sometimes
spreading the pestilence as they went. Those they left behind
faced the malady without assistance. "They are frightened of going nigh one to another as soon as they take bad," observed
William Walker at Hudson House. "So the one half for want of indulgencies is starved before they can gather Strength to help
themselves." The escalating mortality reinforced this behavior;
some apparently believed that anyone who caught the pox was
doomed. "If any of their Relations should be bad with this disorder," Walker explained, "they think they need not look for any
Recovery, they just throw them away, and so the poor Soul per-
ishes."[41]

Many would probably have suffered from famine regardless of
the epidemic. As we have seen, a great shortage of provisions afflicted both traders and Indians in the winter of 1781–82. At Hudson House in January 1782, three Indian men arrived with no furs.
They were "all starving," Walker noted, and they had "not had
the Small Pox yet." The first Indians to report the epidemic to
William Tomison at Cumberland House had likewise complained
"much for want of Food." According to Churchill chief factor
Samuel Hearne, those Indians "not carried off by the small pox"
were "greatly reduced by famine." The encroaching famine may
well have helped to spread *Variola* across the woods and plains as
people moved about in search of scarce food resources.[42]

Nutritional depletion did not bode well for Canadian First
Peoples as they battled the pox. Not only did malnourished patients fare worse under the disease, but they suffered more com-

plications as well. Modern medical practitioners have noted that in malnourished children with smallpox, eye infections (and hence blindness) "were far more common" than in well-nourished children with the same disease. The year after the epidemic reached Hudson Bay, a fur trader at the company's Severn post recorded the arrival of two Indian men and their families, all "very deeply marked with the small Pox." One of them, the trader observed, "has lost all his Children by it except one poor Boy, which is both blind and Lame, and they have been obliged to haul him all the Winter." Arthritis, bone deformity, and joint inflammation are all side effects of smallpox that are particularly common in children.[43]

Two factors worsened the famine. First, the Indians who provisioned Hudson's Bay Company posts often set fire to nearby hunting grounds in order to keep English hunters from provisioning themselves. Fires of unknown origin had destroyed woodlands around York Factory in the summers of 1780 and 1781, but elsewhere the cause was apparent. "The Ground is all Burnt & no Buffaloe," wrote Hudson House's Robert Longmoore in January 1781. "The Natives burnt it," he added, "on purpose that they might get a great price for provisions, but great part of them has payed for it since by Hunger." The same conditions prevailed in October when smallpox struck. "The Barren Ground is all burnt," wrote Walker at Hudson House, "so that their is no Beasts resting nigh hand, Which I believe we shall be very hard put to it for provisions."[44]

The other factor aggravating the famine is more mysterious. It may or may not have been related to fire damage. Many observers noted that a strange reduction of the animal population accompanied the arrival of *Variola* in western Canada. The first Indians who described the epidemic to Cocking told him "that the Moose, Buffalo and other Animals died" as well. "It might be almost concluded," wrote the trader-explorer Alexander Mackenzie, "that some fatal circumstance had destroyed the game, as war and small pox had diminished the inhabitants." Mitchell Oman also noted the loss. "With the death of the Indians a circumstance took place which never has, and in all probability, never will be accounted for," he told David Thompson. "It was noted by the Traders and Natives, that at the death of the latter, and there being thus reduced to a small number, the numerous herds of Bison and Deer also disappeared both in the Woods and in the Plains."[45]

The consistency of these accounts makes them hard to dismiss, especially when combined with the scarcity of provisions reported in 1781–82. It is possible that fires had caused some of the game shortage. It is also possible that the physical and emotional consequences of smallpox made game seem harder to find than it had formerly been. Finally, it is possible that unusual weather, ecological upheaval, or an unknown pathogen was responsible for the decline. There is no animal reservoir for smallpox; indeed, other primates are the only nonhuman species known to be susceptible to *Variola*.[46] Yet the documentary evidence seems to indicate that as the virus ran riot among the human inhabitants of the north woods, an equivalent calamity struck animal populations in the same area.

On August 20, 1782, the American Revolution arrived at York Factory. It came on a sudden, without warning, even as the epidemic continued its grim work among the Crees and Ojibwas near the post. The annual Hudson's Bay Company ship had arrived a few days before to pick up the year's furs and deliver a year's supply of manufactured goods for trade. It had also brought a new chief factor, Humphrey Marten, who took over the administration of York Factory from Matthew Cocking on August 15. But while the reins of leadership changed, little else did. The surgeon continued his rounds among the sick Indians, and the pestilence showed no signs of abating. "The Surgeon visited the Sick," wrote Marten on August 19; "another Boy dead: A few out of danger some dubious."[47]

August 20, however, brought a stunning development. "Three masted Ships were seen in the Offing," the new chief factor reported. They could only be hostile. Ships rarely ventured into Hudson Bay's frigid, tide-driven waters; the huge inland sea was simply too remote and too dangerous to attract idle visitors. Besides, the company ship already lay at anchor nearby. Marten and other York Factory hands did not know that the threatening sail, a little French war fleet in the charge of Jean-François de Galaup, comte de la Pérouse, had already visited the more northerly post of Churchill and burned it to the ground.* But they knew full well that as long as the American Revolution continued, the British Hudson's Bay Company could be subject to hostile action on the part of American forces and their French allies. "Loaded our Guns to make the best defence we can," wrote Marten in the post journal. The crewmen on the company ship also made ready to fight.[48]

Information gathered the next day confirmed the chief factor's fears: "The ships were of force and an Enemy." Marten recruited ten Indians to assist in the fort's defense, and he watched as a launch from the company ship scuttled a shallow-water warning beacon in an attempt to lure the hostile vessels aground. With its cargo of furs, the ship itself soon slipped away for England undetected by the enemy. Meanwhile, in the early-morning hours of August 22, a telltale whistling in the woods warned the men inside the York Factory fort that French troops had landed nearby. "We are now assured the French are landed in great force," Marten wrote the next day. Finally, on August 24, Marten "observed the French Troops in motion." They consisted of "about 700 Men" who "came to the Fort and demanded Entrance." The Hudson's Bay Company's servants and their Indian allies were poorly situated for combat against such a force. The chief factor demanded a parley, and the French responded: "They deliver'd a Letter sign'd La Perouse & Rostaing offering us our Lives & private property but threatning the utmost fury should we resist." Marten soon capitulated.[49]

---

*The destruction of Churchill resulted in the loss of the post journal. It is for this reason that the epidemic at Churchill is so poorly documented.

The surrender was a cordial one. La Pérouse let the chief factor and his officers take with them "any thing in the Fort that would be of service." Perhaps at Marten's request, the French commander also ordered the erection of "a kind of Tent" onshore "to put provisions and stores in for the distressed Indians to prevent them from starving." Then, on Sunday, September 1, 1782, the French razed York Factory. "This day the Factory was burnt," Marten wrote, "& all the remaining of the Company's Servants & the French Troops embarked . . . for the French Fleet."[50]

For more than a year, the charred remains of the York Factory trading post lay abandoned. The smallpox epidemic inevitably continued until it ran short of susceptible victims, but without a written record of its course, it is difficult to fill in the missing details. York Factory and Churchill were the only English posts to fall in the late-season French campaign, and records from the surviving trading houses yield clues but little more.

At the inland posts of Cumberland House and Hudson House, active smallpox cases had begun to dwindle even as William Tomison and the brigade made their voyage down to York Factory in the spring of 1782. But over the summer, while Tomison was gone, Indians continued to arrive with reports of the destruction it had left behind. At Gloucester House, an inland post in Ojibwa country on the Albany River, stories of the epidemic's destruction came in for many more months, indeed through the spring of 1783. A few accounts came into Severn as well.[51]

In the fall of 1783, a year after the French destruction of Churchill and York Factory, Hudson's Bay Company traders reoccupied and rebuilt the two abandoned forts. Trading Indians were still staggering under the impact of the epidemic, and now they poured their hearts out to the newly returned fur traders. On October 2, three canoes of them came into York Factory. "These Indians," Marten wrote, "give a Melancholy account of the havock, Deaths hath made amongst the Northern tribes, most of whom are no more." Hearne found the situation no better at Churchill: "Sickness and famine has made such havock amongst my home

Indians dureing my absence that, out of 69 that I left all well on[ly] 32 is arrived here safe, amongst whome there is but 6 Men & Boys that can lift a gun, the Remainder being all women and Children." Among the many dead were "the famous Northern [Chipewyan] Indian leader called Matonabbee and most of the prinsaple Northern Indians."[52]

The traders' long absence had made matters worse. Not only did the Indians of central Canada have to contend with personal loss, social upheaval, and famine, but many did so without the manufactured goods, particularly firearms and ammunition, on which they had come to depend. At Cumberland and Hudson houses, the effects of this were most severe in the winter of 1783–84, for the men who reoccupied York Factory in the fall of 1783 had arrived too close to winter to carry supplies upriver to the inland posts. A Bungee Ojibwa Indian came into Cumberland House in March 1784, complaining "much for want of food, not having had any Ammunition for some time Past." Eight days later, another Bungee arrived who had traveled to York Factory the previous summer. Finding the post in ashes, "they throwed all their Furs away, not thinking to outlive the Winter for want of Ammunition."[53]

Firsthand accounts make it clear that at the time the epidemic struck, the population of western Canada consisted almost entirely of individuals susceptible to smallpox. A few elderly Crees west of the Great Lakes may have garnered immunity in a limited outbreak of smallpox in that area in 1738. Some Ojibwas may have been exposed to *Variola* during the outbreaks of the Seven Years' War, but there is no evidence of either immunity or earlier outbreaks in the records of the Hudson's Bay Company. This very likely indicates that the 1781–82 epidemic was a virgin soil outbreak among many northern groups. One eyewitness said so directly. "The small-pox had never before been among them," wrote Edward Umfreville, "and they were utter strangers to the malignity of its infectious property." The trader Mitchell Oman concurred: "They had no idea of the disease and its dreadful nature," he wrote, after witnessing the epidemic's ravages on the prairies along the North Saskatchewan River.[54]

Accounts of mortality confirm the impression that the epidemic had indeed been a virgin soil episode in the western interior of Canada. The North West Company trader John Macdonnell believed that the outbreak carried off three-fourths of the natives near Portage La Prairie. He also stated that thanks to "wars with their neighbours, the small Pox of 1780/81 and other misfortunes," the Cree population had dropped by two-thirds. An Indian told David Thompson that the epidemic "swept away more than half of us." Of the Atsina Indians who inhabited the Saskatchewan River country, Alexander Henry said simply, "The Small Pox carried off the major part of them." In the same region, the sick Indians encountered by Mitchell Oman in the autumn of 1781 "allowed that far more than one half had died." Oman himself was more precise: "From the number of tents which remained, it appeared that about [th]ree fifths had perished." Farther north, among the Chipewyans, Samuel Hearne pushed the estimates still higher, suggesting that smallpox had "carried off nine-tenths of them." Tomison likewise informed Cocking at York Factory "that of the several Tribes of Assinnee Poet [Assiniboine] Pegogomew and others bordering on Saskachiwan River he realy believed not one in fifty have survived." Umfreville, who may well have overheard Tomison's statement, echoed his estimate: "It was computed that scarce one in fifty survived it." Of the plains Indians, he guessed "that at least one half of the inhabitants were swept off."[55]

Some of these numbers are no doubt exaggerations in the face of overwhelming devastation. But in the few instances in which actual numbers or ratios exist, small glimpses reveal a loss of life that was indeed staggering. "We have buried Upwards of 30 for Which Number there is only two recovered," wrote Tomison on February 19, 1782. His figures point to a case fatality rate exceeding 93 percent. At Hudson House in April, Walker recorded the burial of the last Indian man from a party of fourteen that had arrived a month earlier. "Not one of them recover'd," he observed. Of the fourteen canoes of Bungee Ojibwas that left York Factory on June 14, 1782, only two canoes plus one man and a child lived through the disease: a case fatality rate of 80 to 83 percent. Similarly, of the four sick Ojibwas who arrived at York Factory on July 2, 1782, only one lived through the disease.[56]

Ironically, the epidemic that the fur trade helped spread nearly brought the very same commerce to its knees. Tomison reported that his competition, the North West Company, had collected more than 330 packs of furs in the 1780–81 trading year, before the epidemic arrived in the Canadian interior, but in 1781–82, as the epidemic raged, only 84 packs. Hudson's Bay Company account books reveal similar shortfalls. In fiscal year 1781 (August 1, 1780–July 31, 1781), traders had shipped some 25,901 Made Beaver in furs from York Factory to England. In fiscal year 1782, however, the epidemic cut this trade in half: Only 12,837 MB from York Factory made the journey across the Atlantic. After the French attack and the abandonment of the destroyed fort for a year, trading resumed; but in 1784—only six weeks short of a complete fiscal year—the post took in only 2,832 MB. Even if growing competition from the North West Company and decline among the animals share the blame for this precipitous drop, the drastic decrease in the harvesting of furs makes it clear that the Native American population of the Canadian heartland was still reeling from the epidemic.[57]

For more than a hundred years, the fur trade had brought prosperity not just to the Hudson's Bay Company but also to the firm's Ojibwa, Cree, and Assiniboine trading partners on the Canadian Shield. But in 1781–82, prosperity turned to poison, as commerce became deadly. The Cree-Assiniboine alliance that had adapted so well to the fur trade was helpless in the face of smallpox. So devastating was the epidemic that years later, canoe travelers reported passing "a point covered with human bones, the relics of the small pox."[58] Control of the inland trade soon slipped from the Indians' hands to those of Hudson's Bay Company employees who established direct connections to the tribes of the plains, for the once-prosperous middlemen never recovered their central brokering role after the smallpox. Here the irony ran deep for the Crees and Assiniboines: Their own connections to the Indians of the plains had been the source of the epidemic that had brought them down.

It is on the wide-open prairies of the West that the story of the epidemic becomes elusive indeed.

7

CONNECTIONS

♋♋ May 1784. *London-born David Thompson was only fourteen years old when he set out for Hudson Bay.* "In the month of May 1784 at the Port of London," *he wrote at the start of his memoir,* "I embarked in the ship Prince Rupert belonging to the Hudson's Bay Company, as apprentice and clerk to the said company, bound for Churchill Factory, on the west side of the bay." *This pivotal moment changed his life forever. Four months later, after dodging the ice floes that littered Hudson Strait, the* Prince Rupert *delivered the boy to his destination. Now, with experienced company men as his teachers, Thompson learned the rudiments of life on the bay. He learned how to walk wearing snowshoes, how to kill a beluga whale, and how to stay warm through the subarctic winter.*

After a year, Thompson received orders transferring him to York Factory, one hundred miles to the south. The fifteen-year-old clerk made the journey on foot, crossing treacherous, boulder-strewn tidal flats in the company of two Indian guides. At York Factory, he continued his fur trade education, a far cry from his earlier formal schooling at a charity institution in London. He salted geese, snared rabbits, set traps for wolves, and chopped down scores of trees for winter fuel. He learned to keep a wary eye out for polar bears as well.

Then, in the summer of 1786, the Hudson's Bay Company sent Thompson upstream with a party assigned to build a new trading house on the South Saskatchewan River. The journey inland was difficult, but it was typical for the fur trade: With fully laden canoes weighing eight hundred pounds apiece, the men paddled, poled, pulled, and portaged their way upstream at a rate of two miles per hour. Their labors were "rendered almost dreadful by the heat and torment of the Musketoes," Thompson wrote. West of Lake Winnipeg, they stopped briefly at Cumberland House and then continued on, soon emerging from the evergreen tedium onto the parklands that adjoined the prairies. The change delighted him. "Every hour appeared to bring us to a better country," he said; "instead of dark pine forests the woods were of well grown Poplar, Aspen and white Birch and for the first time saplings of Ash." In what is now central Saskatchewan, the men built a post they named South Branch House, and the teenager from London immersed himself in plains life.

The year 1787 expanded the young fur trader's horizons. In early October, the bay company sent seventeen-year-old Thompson and five other men westward to pursue trade with the Piegan Indians at the foot of the Canadian Rockies. Crossing the prairies and fording the Bow River within view of the mountains, the party proceeded only a few miles more before encountering "about a dozen Peeagans" near modern-day Calgary. The Piegans, along with the Bloods and the Blackfeet proper, made up the great Blackfoot nation, a bison-hunting plains tribe that ranged from the North Saskatchewan River valley south almost to the Missouri. Thompson and his companions wintered among these Indians, separating themselves in twos among the "three different tents where the most respectable men lived."

Thompson's host for the winter was an old man named Saukamappee. Born a "Nahathaway," or Cree, Saukamappee had nevertheless spent most of his life among the Piegan Blackfeet. He was, by Thompson's estimate, at least seventy-five years old. The old Indian and the English teenager spent hours together, conversing in the Cree language that Thompson had mastered in his first three years on the bay. "Almost every evening for the time of four months I sat and listened to the old man without being in the least tired," wrote Thompson. From his Indian teacher, he acquired a knowledge of plains protocol that was to serve him well in the years to come. He learned the symbolic significance of gifts, and he learned the

proper way to shake hands. "If one of our people offers you his left hand,
give him your left hand," Saukamappee said. While the left hand embod-
ied truth and friendship, the right was "the hand of death," which wielded
the spear, the bow, and the gun.

Saukamappee held forth on history as well as protocol. He had seen a
world of change within his lifetime. He told his rapt companion story af-
ter story about the upheavals that had altered native life forever. Many
years later, when Thompson himself was an old man with failing eyesight
and feet forever sore from frostbite, he recorded Saukamappee's stories in
his masterful Narrative. *The progression was simple, but the changes*
were breathtaking: First had come the gun, next had come the horse, and
then had come the smallpox.[1]

Witnesses to the pestilence in the Hudson Bay hinterlands could
not help speculating as to its origins. Various sources suggested
themselves, and conflicting stories circulated among the traders of
the north woods. York Factory's Matthew Cocking was initially inclined to blame his North West Company competition: Before
William Tomison and the brigade arrived bearing the year's furs
from Cumberland House in July 1782, Cocking guessed that the
Pasquia Indians had picked up the disease "from some of the
Canadian Pedlers who may have brought the disorder up with
them from Canada." The trader Mitchell Oman, who had seen Indians enduring smallpox in the Eagle Hills of western Saskatchewan, reported that it had arrived by way of unspecified white
settlers: "From the best information this disease was caught by
the Chipaway (the forest Indians) and the Sieux (of the Plains)
about the same time, in the year 1780, by attacking some families
of the white people, who had it, and wearing their clothes."[2]

Most reports did not point to European settlers or traders, but
rather to the Indians of the plains. Inevitably, these accounts came
second and third hand to the men who recorded them. European
familiarity with the great northern grasslands was limited, and in

most cases, the traders simply reiterated what knowledgeable Indians had told them. The surviving stories of the epidemic's origins are often vague, and they frequently deviate in details. In the end, however, the assembled evidence points squarely to the people known as Shoshones, whose eighteenth-century range extended out of the mountains of Idaho and Wyoming and onto the plains as far north as Saskatchewan.[3] Beyond the Shoshones, the smallpox trail veers south, dwindling to a trace in the thin air of the Colorado high country. Faint though it is, it clearly leads back to the northern frontier of New Spain.

At the time of the American Revolution, Europeans had barely begun to probe the vast prairies that stretched from the Saskatchewan River in the north to the Texas plateau country in the south. But their presence along the fringes of this region—in the eastern woodlands and in the northernmost outposts of New Spain—had nevertheless prompted important alterations in plains Indian life. The changes were in large part due to two new arrivals on the North American grasslands, arrivals that came simultaneously but from different directions. One was the gun; the other, the horse. Unlikely though it may seem, the stories of the gun and the horse are inseparable from the story of *Variola*'s transit to the Canadian interior.

Colonial policy dictated the route by which firearms appeared on the plains. In New Spain, where Native Americans were to be "reduced" into submission to church and state authority, Spanish officials believed that selling guns to Indians was tantamount to arming the enemy. Restrictions on the sale of weapons to New World natives were in place as early as 1501, when the crown made it illegal "to sell arms to the Indians, or for them to have them." Colonial authorities enforced these restrictions for the next three hundred years. By contrast, English and French colonists, including traders in Canada and the Hudson Bay country, readily exchanged muskets for furs. Firearms, which the Indians highly coveted, thus arrived on the plains from the northeast and east.[4]

Among the first to carry guns onto the prairies were the Sioux. Formerly the inhabitants of the spruce-poplar forests around the western Great Lakes, the Sioux began to move toward the plains in the late 1600s, responding to new pressures and opportunities arising from trade, warfare, and shifting political coalitions. Already, by this time, an alliance of Cree and Assiniboine Indians armed with Hudson's Bay Company muskets had driven the Lakota (Teton) and Nakota (Yanktonai) Sioux from their homelands in the northern Minnesota lake country. Other nations were in motion as well. In response to the relentless attacks of the Iroquois of New York, a mélange of refugee peoples—Hurons, Potawatomis, Mascoutens, Kickapoos, Miamis, Ottawas, and others—took up residence on the wedge of land known to the French as the *pays d'en haut*, south of Lake Superior. If these nations sometimes came into conflict with the Sioux, they also brought new opportunities, for French coureurs de bois from Montreal followed them westward, building posts at St. Ignace and Sault Ste. Marie in 1668. In the 1680s, these French traders pushed beyond the refugee tribes and made direct contact with the Sioux, whom they soon provided with a steady and reliable supply of firearms.[5] Well armed but still on foot, the Lakota and Nakota Sioux now began moving onto the western prairies, where teeming bison and beaver populations promised ample food, numerous pelts, and a prosperous commerce with French traders.

The Sioux were known for their fierceness in battle even before they acquired guns. Then, in the early eighteenth century, easy access to firearms through traders to the east gave them a distinct advantage over such established plains tribes as the Omahas, Pawnees, Arikaras, Mandans, and Hidatsas. "Winter counts"— pictorial Sioux chronologies that mark each passing year with a notable incident—refer often to military encounters with other plains peoples in this period. As early as 1685, according to a winter count kept by a Sioux man named John K. Bear, the Lakotas had engaged in a major battle with the Omahas, perhaps contesting the latter tribe's claim to the Big Sioux River valley, in what is now eastern South Dakota. The same count notes a battle with either the Arikaras or the Pawnees, two related tribes, in 1694. By 1732, according to another chronology, the Sicangu (Brulé) Lakotas has clashed with the Hidatsas and Arikaras of the upper Missouri River and the Pawnees and Omahas farther south.[6]

By the time of the American Revolution, the Sioux had firm control of the plains east of the Missouri River, but here their advance halted. The Arikaras, Mandans, and Hidatsas of the upper Missouri presented a formidable obstacle. These sedentary agriculturalists lived in large villages surrounded by impenetrable stockades. They had adopted horses from tribes to the south and west. More important, they had begun to acquire guns of their own through Cree and Assiniboine middlemen ferrying manufactured goods from Hudson Bay. To the south, on the lower Missouri, the Pawnees and Omahas also got a limited supply of firearms from traders now ascending the river from St. Louis.[7]

So well armed were the Missouri River tribes that by 1767–68, the Sioux themselves lived in constant fear of attack. It was an unsettling winter far and wide, remembered for varied reasons across the continent. Among the English colonists of the North Atlantic seaboard, the winter of 1767–68 was marked by Britain's burdensome Townshend Acts and the nonimportation agreements they fostered. Among the apprehensive Lakotas, it was remembered for the constant menace of the Missouri River tribes. Hence it bore the label "Went-out-to-ease-themselves-with-their-bows-on winter," designated in the winter count of Battiste Good by a figure relieving himself near a tepee, holding a bow and arrow at the ready.[8] It took the arrival of smallpox to break the military deadlock between the Sioux and their enemies. The crowded Missouri River villages that fared so well in the face of Sioux incursions were to prove highly vulnerable when *Variola* attacked.

North of the Missouri River, in the grasslands of western

"1706–'07.—'Killed-the-Gros-Ventre [Hidatsa]-with-snowshoes-on winter.' " Sicangu Lakota winter count of Battiste Good, in Garrick Mallery, *Picture-Writing of the American Indians*, Tenth Annual Report of the Bureau of Ethnology to the Secretary of the Smithsonian Institution, 1888–'89 (1893; rpt., New York: Dover, n.d.), 1:295

"1767–'68.—'Went-out-to-ease-themselves-with-their-bows-on winter.' " Sicangu Lakota winter count of Battiste Good, in Garrick Mallery, *Picture-Writing of the American Indians*, Tenth Annual Report of the Bureau of Ethnology to the Secretary of the Smithsonian Institution, 1888–'89 (1893; rpt., New York: Dover, n.d.), 1:306

Canada, similar power dynamics came to bear. Here it was the Blackfeet who benefited from access to firearms, which they acquired in limited numbers through Cree and Assiniboine go-betweens. Thanks to David Thompson's friendship with Saukamappee, we know the story firsthand.

Saukamappee's stories went back to his boyhood, in the early 1700s, when the eastern branch of the Shoshone (Snake) tribe had briefly dominated the northern Great Plains along the foothills of the Rockies. This had not always been the case. At one time, the Shoshones all had lived in the vast, semiarid Great Basin region west of the mountains. But shortly before Columbus sailed, bands of eastern Shoshones began wandering into the Rockies, which they eventually crossed entirely, emerging onto the northwestern fringes of the Great Plains. Here, in the grasslands abutting the Bighorn, Wind River, and Absaroka mountains, the eastern Shoshones adopted the rudiments of plains life. They learned to live in hide tepees instead of traditional grass huts and to subsist off plains bison rather than fish and bighorn sheep.[9]

By 1700, another change had occurred. Toward the end of the seventeenth century, drawn at least in part by the availability of horses in the Spanish settlements of Texas and New Mexico, a branch of proto-Comanche Shoshones split off from their northerly kin and migrated southward. Soon thereafter, they emerged onto the plains of New Mexico and Texas as full-fledged Comanches.[10]

Ties between the Comanches and the Shoshones remained strong despite the geographical separation. In the first half of the eighteenth century, the Shoshones gained access to a steady supply of horses through their Comanche relations, who now ranged across the plains of Texas and New Mexico. Just as horses had given Hernán Cortés an advantage over the Aztecs two hundred years earlier, so they now gave the Shoshones a temporary advantage over the other peoples of the northern plains. For a short period, while their enemies remained unmounted and while firearms remained inaccessible to all parties, horse-borne Shoshones overpowered their neighbors—the Assiniboines, the Plains Crees, and especially the Blackfeet. Saukamappee told David Thompson about years of fierce warfare between the Shoshones and the Piegan Blackfeet. "The Peeagans were always the frontier Tribe," the elderly Indian explained, "upon whom the Snake [Shoshone] Indians made their attacks." The battles could be impressively large, involving more than seven hundred warriors.[11]

For a generation, mounted Shoshone warriors instilled terror in nearby tribes on the northern plains. But around 1730, the balance of power began to shift. By this time, the Piegans and other Blackfeet had begun to acquire firearms through Cree and Assiniboine middlemen. Saukamappee recalled the telling encounter: a battle in 1730. Unbeknownst to their Shoshone enemies, the Piegans and their Assiniboine allies had acquired ten muskets and "about thirty balls, and powder" through trade. When the action started, the first rounds fired "either killed, or severely wounded, every one we aimed at," and within moments, "the greater part of the enemy took to flight." In the decades that followed, the Shoshones' domination waned. Their years of aggressive raiding had earned them the universal enmity of other plains tribes, which were now acquiring secondhand guns from Indian middlemen engaged in the Canadian fur trade. "While we have these weapons," Saukamappee told Thompson, "the Snake [Shoshone] Indians have none, but what few they sometimes take from one of our small camps." Although the Shoshones obtained an occasional musket through war and trade, nearby tribes imposed a firearms quarantine on their much-hated neighbors for the duration of the eighteenth century. In 1805, according to one fur trader's report, the Shoshones had "as yet no guns."[12]

The Shoshones may have suffered for want of guns, but they did have horses. Spanish mustangs had arrived on the southern plains with the expansion of Spanish missions and settlements from Mexico in the sixteenth and seventeenth centuries. Governor

Juan de Oñate's establishment of a permanent Spanish colony in New Mexico in 1598 put the Pueblo Indians in regular contact with the animals, but for more than a generation thereafter, the Rio Grande colony remained an isolated pocket of horse culture in the otherwise horseless Southwest. As the seventeenth century progressed, silver bonanzas drew Spanish settlers and ponies northward. By 1675, horses were widespread among Indians south of the Rio Grande, and some tribes on the plains of New Mexico, Texas, Kansas, and Colorado had acquired mounts as well. Farther north, the animals remained rare.[13]

Events in 1680 changed all this. In that year, driven by the accumulated insults of nearly a century of Spanish occupation, the Pueblo Indians revolted, expelling their colonizers from New Mexico for twelve years. It was the most successful Indian rebellion in American history. Among its many consequences was the rapid dispersal of Spanish horse herds among the southwestern tribes, which over the next hundred years revolutionized life on the plains. It was the horse, for example, that appears to have drawn the Comanches away from their Shoshone relatives to the southern prairies. Proto-Comanche Shoshones probably got their first mounts from the Utes who bordered on Spanish settlements in New Mexico. The Comanches first appear in the colonial records there in 1706, when residents of Taos Pueblo feared an attack from a combined force of Ute and Comanche warriors. If this attack did not materialize, others did. Comanche horsemen soon struck fear into the hearts not just of Spanish colonists but of neighboring Native American peoples as well.[14]

For the next half century, the Comanches forced their way onto the southern plains, pushing the Apaches south and the Wichitas east. A visitor to New Mexico in 1726–27 reported that the Comanches always traveled "in battle formation, for they make war on all the Nations." These belligerent new arrivals, mounted on their Spanish ponies, ruled the southern shortgrass prairies for years, alternately trading and raiding in the European settlements of New Mexico and Texas. In their quest for the

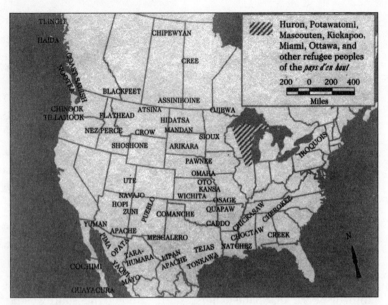

Tribes of Native Americans mentioned in text

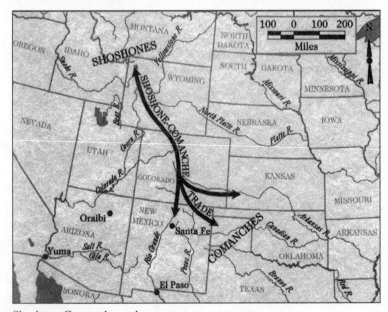

Shoshone-Comanche trade

horses they so desired, the Comanches quickly learned that what the Spaniards coveted most was Indian slaves. The demand was nearly insatiable, and the Comanches' relentless raids on the Apaches were as much for captives to be sold in New Mexican markets as they were for horses or territory.

While Comanche horses arrived by way of New Mexico, Spanish restrictions on the sale of firearms forced the Indians to look elsewhere for guns. The few guns the Comanches got their hands on therefore came from the east, most consistently from Wichita Indian villages on the Arkansas and Red rivers, in territory claimed by France. At these heavily fortified towns, Indian, French, and Anglo-American traders bartered a limited supply of European wares. After 1763, when Spain acquired Louisiana from France in the first Treaty of Paris, these traders ostensibly came under Spanish control, but a contraband musket trade apparently continued.[15]

Even as they pushed southward and eastward, the Comanches continued to trade actively with their Shoshone kin in the northern plains and mountains. It was a commerce that briefly turned the Shoshones into the titans of their realm, giving them a near monopoly on access to Spanish goods, horses, and accoutrements. "These horses come from New Mexico and are of the Spanish race," wrote Gabriel Franchère during his stay among the Shoshones in 1814. "We even saw some which had been marked with a hot iron by Spaniards." At the mouth of the Yellowstone River in 1805, the Canadian fur trader François-Antoine Larocque met a Shoshone man who "had been absent since the spring and had seen part of his nation who trade with the Spaniards; he brought a Spanish B[r]idle and Battle ax, a large thick blanket, striped white and black and a few other articles." The Shoshones themselves, in Larocque's opinion, had "no direct trade with the Spaniard[s]." Instead, the transactions were "carried on at a second or thir[d] hand." In return for horses, the Shoshones gave the Comanches peltries and Indian captives taken in war for exchange in the New Mexico slave trade.[16] This commerce did little to endear the

Shoshones to their neighbors. But early in the eighteenth century, it allowed mounted Shoshones to dominate the northwestern Great Plains before their unmounted enemies gained access to firearms. Here they introduced the horse to the Piegan Blackfeet, and here the horse frontier and the gun frontier collided.

Our source of knowledge is once again David Thompson's elderly friend Saukamappee, who lived among the Piegans. In 1730, after Saukamappee and his companions had routed the Shoshones in their first gun battle, they collected scalps and then set out in large bands for the edge of Shoshone territory. Their purpose was twofold: to hunt buffalo and elk, "which were numerous," and "to see a horse of which we had heard so much." The Piegans hoped that by encroaching on Shoshone territory, they might view the mysterious beast. Finally, "as the leaves were falling," they got their chance when "one was killed by an arrow shot through his belly." The Shoshone rider escaped, but the Piegan Blackfeet gathered around the dead animal. "He put us in mind of a Stag that had lost his horns," said Saukamappee, "and we did not know what name to give him. But as he was a slave to Man, like the dog, which carried our things, he was named the Big Dog."[17]

At this transitional moment, Saukamappee and his Piegan companions had just seen their first horse and, using firearms in battle for the first time, had just routed their fearsome Shoshone enemies. Already, as they stared in wonder at the "Big Dog," the tide was turning. For muskets, even in limited supply, gave the Blackfeet a significant advantage in their raids on the Shoshones. Success in raiding meant that the Blackfeet acquired ponies, and like other tribes of the plains, they eagerly adopted life on horseback. By 1754, when the Hudson's Bay Company servant Anthony Hendey followed the Saskatchewan River west to the Rockies, the Blackfeet were both warlike and mounted. And when the trader Matthew Cocking followed a similar route inland from Hudson Bay in 1772, he described them simply as "Equestrians."[18]

Farther south, the Mandans and Hidatsas, the agricultural nations on the upper Missouri River that were fending off the Sioux, had also acquired horses by 1750. Crow Indians along the Yellowstone River shuttled horses between Comanche and Shoshone nomads in the west and Mandan and Hidatsa farmers in the east. As early as 1739, two Frenchmen among the Mandans reported that "several tribes which use horses" came annually to trade in the Missouri River towns. One Indian wore a cross around his neck and gave the Frenchmen a detailed account of his experiences among the Spaniards. Before long, the Mandan and Hidatsa villages became hubs of commerce on the plains, where guns from the east and horses from the southwest changed hands. "It seems that these Mandans also hold communication with the Spaniards, or with nations neighboring to them," wrote the lieutenant governor of Spanish Illinois in 1792, "for they have Mexican type saddles and bridles for horses, as well as other utensils."[19] In the end, however, the very acquisitions that made the upper Missouri settlements trading centers also made them a target for the Sioux and other raiders. Moreover, in both capacities—as a commercial hub and as an object of attack—this area was a likely dispersal point for contagion when it struck.

Hundreds of difficult miles separated the Mandans, Hidatsas, Blackfeet, and Sioux from the settlements of Texas and New Mexico, where Spanish friars and officials reported rampant smallpox in late 1780 and early 1781. Surviving records do not indicate conclusively the course of *Variola*'s transit. Nor do they indicate precisely who carried the pestilence from the northern frontier of New Spain to the north-central Rockies and plains. But it was very likely Indians on horseback, for no one else could have spanned such distances at such speeds.

Our understanding of the Comanche encounter with smallpox is at once tantalizing in its possibilities and exasperating in its incompleteness. The story hangs upon a single shred of substantial evidence and the concurrence of a number of widely varying circumstances. The circumstances were as follows. By the late 1750s, mounted Comanche raiders had extended their domain deep into Texas, where they repeatedly battled both the Apaches and the Spanish; they destroyed a newly established mission and presidio in 1757. Despite several peace pacts with the Spaniards, hostilities inevitably resurfaced. In one four-month period in 1774, while the British Parliament imposed the Coercive Acts on the rebellious citizens of Boston far to the east, the Comanches launched no fewer than five raids on Spanish settlements in New Mexico. In 1778, the Comanches again "swept over the province," wrote Teodoro de Croix, commander general of the Interior Provinces of New Spain. Scattered about in widely dispersed missions and towns, the settlers "were unable to resist," and New Mexico's Spanish outposts lost "127 persons dead and captured" in the raids.[20]

Then, in August 1779, New Mexico's governor, the indomitable Indian-fighter Juan Bautista de Anza, determined to rein in the warlike horsemen of the plains. With six hundred men, he set out from Santa Fe on a punitive expedition to the north. (A year later, on a more conciliatory mission, Anza was to witness the great drought in Hopi country.) On August 31, in the Rocky Mountain foothills above what is now Colorado Springs, the governor's forces spied a party of more than a thousand Yamparica Comanches to the east. A running battle ensued, in which the Comanches fled, and Anza took thirty-four women and children captive. From these, the governor learned that he had come upon the band of Cuerno Verde, or Green Horn, the single Comanche leader most feared by the Spanish. Anza's heart quickened, and he decided "to see if fortune would grant me an encounter" with the great Comanche war chief.[21]

For three days, Anza's men pursued the Indians until Cuerno Verde deliberately engaged the Spaniards so his people could escape, leading fifty warriors into battle against a Spanish force of six hundred. In an action that even Anza admitted was "as brave as it was glorious," Cuerno Verde made his stand alongside his son and fifteen others in a boggy ravine. The Comanche headman died in the clash, but his people got away as their chieftain went down. "Nothing was seen but the dust and smoke of their retreat," wrote the New Mexico governor, "which was made out for a distance of twelve leagues." Two months later, when Anza sent his diary of the campaign to the commander general, he accompanied it with the distinctive horned headdress of the fallen Comanche leader.[22]

The 1779 battle, marked by Cuerno Verde's demise, was a notable disaster for the Comanches. In its aftermath, their raids on New Mexico waned, but their attacks on Spanish settlers in Texas did not. Ranches, missions, and presidios from Rosario to Nacogdoches bore the brunt of Comanche assaults for another two years. "Every day," Governor Domingo Cabello wrote from San Antonio, "I receive news of people in these environs finding signs of the hostiles." Then, in late 1781, the Comanches disappeared altogether from the view of the Texas colonists. "There was no direct contact for almost eighteen months," writes the historian Thomas Kavanagh, speculating that the cause might have been smallpox. Contact was also very limited in 1783 and 1784.[23]

But was smallpox indeed the reason? Very possibly. In the spring of 1780, smallpox traveling northward from Mexico City began to erupt in the northeastern provinces of New Spain known today as the states of Tamaulipas, Nuevo León, and Coahuila. The pestilence appeared at Santander Jiménez, Tamaulipas, less than 150 miles south of the Rio Grande, in March 1780. Parish priests at Jiménez identified the first smallpox death on March 14 and the last on July 20, 1780. In April, the pox also appeared in the parched but rugged hills of what is now southern Coahuila, in the parishes of Parras and Saltillo, occupied by some 15,674 inhabitants. In the three months from April through June, about 4 percent of the region's population died: 288 in Parras, and 284 in Saltillo.[24]

As the pox crept closer to the great river, mortality leaped upward in Monterrey, the capital of Nuevo León, from June through

August 1780. The plague probably struck Monclova next and then the little cluster of missions on the south bank of the Rio Grande upstream from Laredo. "These four missions of the Rio Grande at one time were well populated with Indians," a visitor wrote six years later, noting a dramatic decline. "The cause of their depopulation (in my opinion) cannot be other than the contagious diseases to which they are subject by their natural constitution."[25] The impact of the epidemic on the Apache and Coahuiltecan hunter-gatherers who inhabited the surrounding countryside appears to be completely undocumented.

Documented or not, *Variola* kept moving. By October 1780, the pestilence had reached the Lipan Apaches around the presidio of La Bahia del Espíritu Santo, near the Texas coast and Matagorda Bay. In the eyes of Texas Governor Cabello, it was a most welcome arrival. During the previous year, the Spaniards had done their best to incite other tribes—including the Mescaleros, Tejas, and Tonkawas—against the Lipans. But now *Variola* did this dirty work for them. "The smallpox epidemic that has so afflicted the outlying provinces of this kingdom has now spread to this province," Cabello wrote to Commander General Croix from San Antonio, informing him that the epidemic had erupted near Matagorda Bay. "And without offending decency," he added, "one might hope that not a single Lipan-Apache lives through it, for these Indians are pernicious—despite their apparent peacefulness and friendliness."[26]

The governor soon had reason to regret his words, as the plague struck closer to home. A month after he had taken pleasure in the pox's ravages among the Lipan Apaches, a distraught Cabello told Croix that the presidio of San Antonio was "so infected with the said contagion" that he was "reduced to the greatest consternation." The villa had no medicine and no doctor, and the number who had fallen ill was "uncountable." The sixty-two-year-old settlement had taken on a most doleful air. "One does not hear or see anything day or night except the tolling of bells and the sight of burials," Cabello reported. In the surrounding countryside, countless Lipan Apaches succumbed to *Variola* and an ailment the governor labeled "garrotillos," or throat distemper—possibly early-stage smallpox. "These Indians," he said, "are being decimated to a degree inexpressible." The devastation left them "utterly distracted and confused," he reported. Seeking aid, Native Americans poured into the San Antonio missions. So many bodies littered the surrounding countryside that Cabello feared some new infection would erupt. In December, as the epidemic entered its third month, the Lipans told the governor that "more than four hundred" of their number had died in the plague. But the pestilence was not over. Not until January 31, 1781, could Cabello report that at least at San Antonio the epidemic was, "by God's grace, totally mitigated." Burial records confirm his report. The Indian population of the San Antonio missions dropped from roughly 800 in 1777 to 543 in 1783.[27]

The epidemic's next move is unclear. Did *Variola* pass from the Lipan Apaches to their Comanche enemy-neighbors, who had pushed them relentlessly southward for three-quarters of a century? Given the unceasing hostilities between the two tribes, it seems almost inevitable. Comanche raids on both the Spanish settlements and the Lipan Apaches were ongoing during the period of the epidemic. In December 1780, Cabello discussed both smallpox and Comanche raids in a single letter.[28] But if the Comanches did catch the pox from the Apaches south and west of them, they very probably picked it up elsewhere as well.

In the summer of 1785, Governor Cabello sent two emissaries, Pedro Vial and Francisco Chaves, into Comanche country to probe the Indians' mood and invite them to peace negotiations. The two men traveled with Taovaya and Wichita escorts to the "first" rancheria of the Comanches, on the Little Wichita River. Before negotiations began, the Comanches expressed trepidation: "They asked us if we had brought some illness that would bring death to their nation, since smallpox had struck them as a result of some Frenchmen having entered their *rancheria* from La Zarca." La Zarca was the designation of a newly formed group of Wichita villages on Oklahoma's Blue River, some thirty miles north of its confluence with the Red River.[29] Vial and Chaves did not indicate when the smallpox epidemic had occurred, but the level of concern on the part of the Indians seems to indicate it was recent. Even more significant, the Comanches' identification of La Zarca as the source of the infection almost certainly indicates that it came from the east, *not* from the southwest (Apache country) or west (New Mexico).

This seemingly unlikely scenario is in fact quite plausible. A terrible pestilence had swept much of eastern Texas and western Louisiana in late 1777 and early 1778. Despite repeated references to the "epidemic" in firsthand reports, the plague is neither named nor described. In the parish records of Natchitoches, the decimation it caused is very apparent in the burial records for November and December 1777. The mortality subsided in January 1778, but the epidemic appears to have kept moving, following the Red River to the Mississippi. In May, the New Orleans City Council expressed concern because it was "coming down this way swiftly." The pestilence reached New Orleans by November, at which time it appears in the records as smallpox. Despite the construction of the city's first smallpox hospital in an attempt to quarantine the outbreak, *Variola* raged in New Orleans through the winter of 1779. While the full extent of the epidemic's spread is not clear, upriver from New Orleans, it struck Galveztown, where newly recruited colonists from the Canary Islands succumbed to the pestilence en masse after establishing a precarious little settlement in early 1779. By January 17, 1780, some 141 of the 404 original Galveztown colonists had died; by March, the number of deaths had reached 161.[30]

So it was probably this Louisiana outbreak, spreading northwestward from Natchitoches along the Red River, that was the source of the contagion that reached the Comanches by way of La Zarca. The smallpox, according to Vial and Chaves, had "devastated" the Indians—probably soon after they had lost the great Cuerno Verde. It is possible and even likely that after picking up

Variola from the Frenchmen from La Zarca, the Comanches carried it to the west, where it collided with the epidemic arriving on the northern frontier from Mexico City. Far removed from the eyes of European observers, the Comanches may thus have found themselves caught in a maelstrom of smallpox on the southern plains, a maelstrom they appear to have transported to their Shoshone relatives a thousand miles to the north.

In the summer of 1782, smallpox converged on the Hudson's Bay Company's York Factory outpost from both the south and the west. The first to bring word of the epidemic to the trading post were those who brought it from the south, the Bungee Ojibwas who lived in the woods north of Lake Superior. If they told chief factor Matthew Cocking where the infection came from, he did not record it. But other evidence indicates they may have picked up the pestilence among the Mandans and Hidatsas of the upper Missouri River.

An old tradition among the Canadian Ojibwas holds that in 1781, a war party of Crees, Assiniboines, and Ojibwas set out southwestward for the Missouri from a large village south of Manitoba's Lake Winnipeg. When they arrived, they attacked a Hidatsa town. Resistance was feeble. Then, as the warriors closed in "to secure their scalps," they "discovered the lodges filled with dead bodies, and they could not withstand the stench arising therefrom." They took their trophies anyway, and among them was one scalp "giant in size," supposedly "as large as a beaver skin." On successive nights, as they returned homeward, the warriors planted a short stick in the ground with the great scalp attached. Each morning they found it leaning ominously to the west. Finally, one man died unexpectedly, and the frightened war party discarded the mysterious scalp. Day by day, more fell sick and died, until only four survived to make their way home. These brought the smallpox with them, the tradition says, and it was this episode that infected the Ojibwas, Crees, and Assiniboines of the surrounding region—and perhaps nearby Canadian trader William Bruce as well. Today, the river on which their village was located is known as Riviere aux Morts (River of the Dead).[31]

The Ojibwa story designates the Hidatsas as the source of the infection, and other information tends to confirm the substance of the account. "It was never satisfactorily ascertained by what means this malignant disorder was introduced," wrote the North West Company's Alexander Mackenzie, "but it was generally supposed to be from Missouri, by a war party."[32]

South of the Hidatsas, the Mandans also suffered. St. Louis fur traders were among the first non-Indians to witness the devastation. According to a 1796 writer who based his report on the observations of the fur trader Jean-Baptiste Truteau, the Mandans "were formerly very numerous, but were attacked several times by the nations lying to the north of the Missouri, and were depopulated by the small-pox." As the explorers Meriwether Lewis and William Clark mapped the Missouri in 1805, they plotted the locations of numerous abandoned Mandan villages near the mouth of the Heart River. It had been "about 25 years" since anyone had lived in the villages, Clark wrote. The adventurers learned the details through an interpreter. "Maney years ago they lived in Several Villages on the Missourie low down," Clark reported, but "the Smallpox destroyed the greater part of the nation and reduced them to one large Village and Some Small ones."[33]

Before the pox struck, the fortified Mandan and Hidatsa villages had kept expansionist Sioux marauders confined to the prairies on the east side of the river. But the Sioux and other nations that feared the Mandans before the epidemic no longer did so in its aftermath, when they "waged war, and killed a great maney." Lewis and Clark's map of the Mandan region is littered with abandoned villages, "destroyed by the Sous & Small Pox." The Hidatsas appear to have fared better against the raiders than their neighbors did. "These people have also suffered considerably by the small-pox," wrote Clark, "but have successfully re-

sisted the attacks of the Sioux." Many surviving Mandans therefore sought refuge among them. The densely populated agrarian
towns of the Mandans and Hidatsas had made both nations extremely vulnerable to *Variola*, enhancing its ability to spread from
person to person. Half a century later, in the epidemic of 1837,
smallpox was to destroy the Mandans entirely.[34]

To the south of the Mandans, farther down the Missouri River,
the Arikaras and their Pawnee kin suffered similar losses for similar reasons. They too were agriculturalists living in large, crowded
towns. Later travelers on the Missouri (including Lewis and
Clark) noted that like the Mandans, they abandoned many villages in the years following the epidemic. According to Jean-
Baptiste Truteau, successive smallpox outbreaks reduced the
Arikaras from "thirty-two populous villages" to only two or three
by the 1790s, and these included not just Arikaras but many
Pawnees as well. The former tribe, Truteau said, could once "turn
out four thousand warriors," but was "now reduced to about five
hundred fighting men." These Indians all found it difficult to
ward off Sioux assaults in the epidemic's aftermath. At least one
band of Arikaras sought refuge among the Mandans and Hidatsas
upriver.[35]

The Sioux aggressors did not escape unscathed. The available
evidence does not indicate where they picked up *Variola*, but
given their raiding patterns, it most likely came from one of the
infected Missouri River tribes. Warfare with the Pawnees,
Arikaras, Mandans, and Hidatsas was ongoing through the closing
decades of the eighteenth century. In the early 1770s, Sioux attackers in all likelihood destroyed a South Dakota Arikara village,
leaving behind the skeletal remains of seventy-one victims for archaeologists to unearth two centuries later. The Sicangu Lakota
winter count of High Hawk refers to "Two *Palani* [Arikaras]
killed" in 1779. A Yanktonai chronology recalls 1780 as "OKI-
CIZE TANKA . . . . A big battle took place"—probably a reference to the destruction of a Mandan village in what is now North

"Many died of smallpox,"
1780–81. American Horse winter count,
in Garrick Mallery, *Picture-Writing of the
American Indians*, Tenth Annual Report of
the Bureau of Ethnology to the Secretary
of the Smithsonian Institution, 1888–'89
(1893; rpt., New York: Dover, n.d.), 2:589

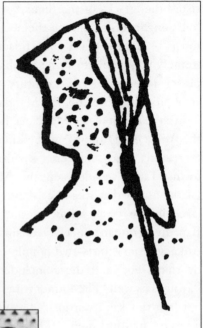

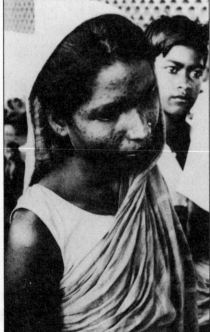

Smallpox scars. World Health
Organization photograph by L. Dale,
National Library of Medicine, Bethesda,
Maryland, A014038

Dakota. In this battle the Yanktonais took many prisoners.[36] Similar encounters may well have communicated *Variola* to the Sioux in 1781.

A winter count kept by an Oglala Lakota man named American Horse captured the essence of the epidemic, designating the year 1780–81 by the simple phrase "Many died of smallpox" and indicating that the sickness continued the next year as well. In all, the epidemic appears in thirteen different plains winter counts covering the years 1779–83. Most of the entries label the plague smallpox, although three describe it simply as a "rash," and four call it measles. The likelihood that it was anything other than smallpox is very slim. Winter count images were subject to interpretation by those who kept them, and smallpox, measles, and other rashes all bore a single designation in the Sioux language. Six of the counts (namely, those of Hardin, Battiste Good, American Horse, White Bull, Steamboat, and Cloud Shield) indicate that it lasted for two successive winters. While they do associate diverging dates with the epidemic, the differences may not be significant. Because counts usually marked the winter season by the dates of the first and last snows, variations of one year could emerge when they were correlated with the Western calendar.[37]

If it is possible that the Sioux picked up *Variola* from the Missouri River tribes, where, in turn, did these corn- and squash-growing farmers pick up the virus? In the absence of illuminating evidence, all we can do is speculate. Given the presence of smallpox in New Orleans and the southern regions of Spanish Louisiana, it is tempting to think that the pox might have followed the Mississippi River to St. Louis and then the Missouri River to the Mandans. But despite the raging pestilence both upstream and down, St. Louis escaped the epidemic entirely.[38] Hence the Mississippi proper was not a likely source. It seems probable that the Wichitas picked up the infection at La Zarca, and it is conceivable that central plains tribes, such as the Otos, Omahas, Kansas, Osages, Quapaws, and Caddos, contracted smallpox from neighboring nations and carried it north. But if the pestilence struck these peoples, it seems to have gone undocumented.

A more likely source for the Missouri River pestilence was the Crows. The Crows were close relations of the Hidatsas who made their home on the Yellowstone River of Wyoming and Montana. Two knowledgeable writers, François-Antoine Larocque and James MacKay, implied that the Crows succumbed to *Variola* during the great epidemic. The "small Pox," Larocque wrote in 1805, "raged among them for many years successively & as late as three years ago." On the basis of his own observations in the 1790s, MacKay counted the Crows among those tribes bordering on the Missouri for which smallpox was a "most Terrible" affliction, resulting in "a Mortality as frightful as Universal." To the west, Crow territory abutted that of the Shoshones, and the Crows actively traded Shoshone horses eastward to the Missouri River tribes. According to Larocque, the Crows got horses from the Shoshones "in great numbers and very cheap" and then sold them to the Mandans and Hidatas "at duble the price they purchase them." The Crows, he noted in 1805, "had as yet given no Guns or Amunition" to the Shoshones."[39] Guns or not, contact with the Shoshones could have been deadly in 1781.

As he wintered with young David Thompson in 1787, Saukamappee recalled what had happened when the Blackfeet encountered the Shoshones during that fateful summer of smallpox six years before. Armed with guns from the Hudson's Bay and North West companies, men from Saukamappee's Piegan Blackfoot band had spotted a large Shoshone camp near the Red Deer River of Alberta. There was something odd about it, the scouts reported; the camp was strangely still. The Piegans suspected a trap. Their scouts had been spotted, however, and they decided to take the offensive. "Next morning at the dawn of day," Saukamappee said, "we attacked the Tents, and with our sharp flat daggers and knives, cut through the tents and entered for the fight; but our war whoop instantly stopt, our eyes were appalled with terror; there was no one to fight with but the dead and the dying, each a mass of corruption. We did not touch them, but left the tents, and held a council on what was to be done." The evil spirit was "master of the camp," the Piegans decided, and they "agreed to take some of the best of the tents, and any other plunder that was clean and good, which we did."[40]

Soon thereafter, smallpox broke out among them. In Saukamappee's words, it "spread from one tent to another as if the Bad Spirit carried it. We had no belief that one Man could give it to another, any more than a wounded Man could give his wound to another." Those near lakes and rivers suffered most. Overwhelmed with the pox's fever, they rushed into the cooling water and drowned. One-third of Saukamappee's camp was lost. But among other bands "there were tents in which every one died."[41]

Saukamappee described vividly the devastation, and the interpretation, of the pestilence among the Indians. "We believed the Good Spirit had forsaken us, and allowed the Bad Spirit to become our Master," he told David Thompson. "What little we could spare we offered to the Bad Spirit to let us alone and go to our enemies. To the Good Spirit we offered feathers, branches of trees, and sweet smelling grass." All across Canada, others did the same. In the spruce woods surrounding Cumberland House, two fur traders "found 19 made Beaver in Cats" that Indians now dead had "thrown away to the good Spirrit, that they might live." When the survivors recovered, Saukamappee recalled, "we moved about to find our people, it was no longer with the song and the dance; but with tears, shrieks, and howlings of despair for those who would never return to us."[42]

Years before Saukamappee told his detailed version of the story to David Thompson, other Indians had recited its outlines to Hudson's Bay Company traders. "This plaguey disorder by what I can hear was brought from the Snake [Shoshone] Indians last Summer, by the Different Tribes that trades about this River," wrote William Walker on the North Saskatchewan in October 1781. As the epidemic raged at Cumberland House during the winter that followed, William Tomison too was "of Opinion that it has come from the snake [Shoshone] Indians." By July 2, 1782, when Tomison and his men arrived at York Factory with the year's furs, the inland trader had learned many of the details later corroborated by Saukamappee. Some of the company's trading Indians had "met with a Tent of Snake [Shoshone] Indians who were ill of the Small Pox," he told Matthew Cocking; "they killed & Skalped them, by this means they recieved the disorder themselves, and most of them died on their return, the few that reached their own Parts communicated the Disorder to their Countrymen."[43]

Tomison, moreover, had learned an important piece of the puzzle that was missing from Saukamappee's account. The Shoshones with the smallpox, he told Cocking, "were supposed to have recieved it from the Spaniards whom tis said thse people trade with." Farther north on Hudson Bay, at the company's subarctic Churchill post, an anonymous writer confirmed Tomison's report. The smallpox, it was said, had "been brought by the Equestrian natives from Mexico, who trade with the Spaniards."[44]

Variola had arrived from the southwest on horseback, dispersed first and foremost by the Shoshones, who most probably acquired the virus from their Comanche friends and relations. If the documentary evidence regarding the Comanches as vectors is weak, the evidence regarding the Shoshones is overwhelming. Known Shoshone trading patterns make it all the more likely that the pestilence came from the great equestrians of the southern plains. The conclusion may not be inescapable, but it borders upon it as closely as the Comanches bordered upon their Shoshone kinfolk.

While fast-moving horse riders carried *Variola* northward, warfare helped disperse it farther. Three days after Cornwallis's surrender, as the pox raged at once in Virginia and the Canadian heartland, the trader William Tomison lamented the catastrophe caused by the fateful Blackfoot attack on that silent Shoshone camp the previous summer. "I can remember the time," he wrote, when the Indians "did not go to War above Once in three" years. But now they had "such great supplies of ammunition &c. that they dont know what to do with it, [and] they go every Year."[45] The availability of firearms had changed not just the nature of plains military encounters but also their frequency; as a result, smallpox may well have been the gun's most lethal legacy. On the plains of the late eighteenth century, a new means of transportation and a novel weapon of war had combined to swell the great smallpox epidemic to continental proportions.

8

PASSAGES

June 15, 1811. *The Astoria traders were baffled. Two strange Indians—"one of them a man and the other a woman"—had just arrived at the Pacific Fur Company's three-month-old post at the mouth of the Columbia River. The newcomers wore "long buckskin jackets," and their dress was in general quite different from that of the nearby Chinook and Clatsop natives. Communication was difficult; it took place only in the language of the Cree Indians who lived near Hudson Bay, a great distance indeed from the Columbia River's Pacific Ocean terminus. Even more perplexing was the letter that the visitors carried with them, written by a known North West Company trader but addressed to a man at a trading post that simply did not exist. In spite of all this, the peculiar Indian couple that conveyed the bizarre missive impressed the Americans. "The husband," according to the trader Alexander Ross, was "a very shrewd and intelligent Indian" who provided "much information respecting the interior of the country."*

The local Chinooks and Clatsops found the pair much less likable than the traders did. The Indians directed their ire at the husband in particular, and they had good reason to be displeased. A few days after arriving at Astoria, the strange man had "incurred the enmity of the Tchinouks" by boasting that he had the ability to give them smallpox. A generation had passed since Variola's first appearance among these Indians, and nearly a decade since its second. But neither the Chinooks nor the

Clatsops had forgotten its ravages. Their reaction to the newcomer's threat was so fierce that he sought refuge among the Pacific Fur Company men. Thereafter, one trader wrote, "the chiefs of the Tchinouks and the Clatsops frequently came begging that we surrender him to them, as well as his squaw, for the purpose of making them slaves, or that we ourselves keep them as such. We pretended to consent to this latter part, well knowing that, if these unfortunates were once in their power, their death was inevitable."

For a month, the Indian couple lived under the protection of the Astorians. Then, on July 15, a large canoe appeared off Tongue Point, just upstream from the trading post. To the traders' astonishment, when the canoe landed, a "well-dressed" European stepped ashore. It was David Thompson, the same David Thompson who had wintered with Saukamappee among the Piegan Blackfeet in 1787, now in the employ of the North West Company. The Astorians greeted their rival warmly, and the intrepid explorer-surveyor stayed with them for a week. Much to the surprise of the men at the post, Thompson recognized the Indian couple sheltered among them. The latter were not what they appeared to be, he said. In fact, they were not a man and a woman at all, but two women. Thompson explained more fully in his Narrative: *"In the Man I recognised the Woman who three years ago was the wife of Boisverd, a canadian and my servant." The marriage had not gone well. The woman's conduct had been "so loose" that at Thompson's request, Boisverd had sent her back to her people, the Kutenais. Soon thereafter, "she became a prophetess, declared her sex changed, that she was now a Man, dressed, and armed herself as such." She had become a berdache, living and dressing not as a woman but as a man. She also, Thompson explained, "took a young woman to Wife."*

Although homosexuality and cross-dressing berdaches were widely accepted among Native Americans, the Kutenai woman seemed to have a uniquely irksome personality. She had annoyed Thompson in their earlier encounters, and by his account, "the Kootanaes were also displeased with her." In fact, Kutenai informants interviewed in the 1930s still talked of this contentious berdache. Her name was Qánqon, and she was both violent and temperamental, known for gambling and for beating her wife.

Certainly the Chinooks and Clatsops at the mouth of the Columbia had little patience for her. They found her claims about smallpox so troubling that they threatened her life.

On July 22, Thompson and his crew left Astoria and went back up the Columbia River. Qánqon and her wife departed at nearly the same time, hoping to find safety among the nations of the interior. But as they traveled upstream, they met with ongoing hostility, for rumors of smallpox had preceded them. On July 28, the women appeared in Thompson's camp and asked for protection, which he gave them. Soon thereafter, when four Indian men asked him if the members of his party had "brought with them the Small Pox to destroy us," Thompson did his best to dispel their fears. Even so, he said, "if the man woman had not been sitting behind us they would have plunged a dagger in her."

The Kutenai berdache and her wife survived their voyage upstream. Qánqon continued to claim supernatural powers until her death in 1837 at the hands of Blackfeet, whose hostilities with the Shoshones and their Kutenai allies had continued unabated. It was said that in her final battle, all of Qánqon's wounds healed themselves until an attacker cut open her chest and cut out a piece of her heart. Only then did her magic fail. A generation earlier, Qánqon's mystical claims had aroused potent memories of the first smallpox epidemics among the Chinooks, Clatsops, and other nations of the Columbia River. Ironically, the year of her death was marked by yet another terrible outbreak of the pox among the Indians of the American West.[1]

Although there is ample documentation for many other parts of the great pestilence of 1775–82, the pox's arrival in the Pacific Northwest remains an enigma, for firsthand descriptions do not survive in written form. But accounts collected in later years indicate that the Native Americans who made their homes in this vast and varied region were not spared *Variola*'s ravages. At some point in the late 1770s or early 1780s, the virus attacked them just as it attacked other peoples across the continent. The question is how and when it did so. Several possibilities exist. Each is plausible, and each is intriguing in its own right. But the great preponderance of evidence points up the Columbia River toward the Shoshones, the very same people who infected Saukamappee's Piegan Blackfoot band in the summer of 1781.[2]

Smallpox made its first known appearance in the historical record of the Pacific Northwest only in 1787, when an English expedition under Captains Nathaniel Portlock and George Dixon touched on the southeast coast of Alaska at Goulding Harbor, just north of modern-day Sitka. On the morning of August 12, Captain Portlock set out in a whaleboat to visit a Tlingit town a few miles from the ship. A crewman and a local Indian guide accompanied him. Around noon they approached the village. Portlock noted several boats on the beach, one big enough to hold thirty people and three others big enough for ten. "From this circumstance," he wrote, "I expected to have seen a numerous tribe, and was quite surprised when I found that it consisted only of three men, three women, the same number of girls, two boys about twelve years old, and two infants." He soon found out why: "I observed the oldest of the men to be very much marked with the small-pox, as was a girl who appeared to be about fourteen years old." Moreover, he added, "I did not observe any of the children under ten or twelve years of age that were marked; therefore I have great reason to suppose that the disorder raged a little more than that number of years ago." An old man gave an animated description of "the excessive torments he endured whilst afflicted with the disorder that had marked his face" and left the English seafarer with the understanding "that it happened some years ago." Portlock learned "that the distemper carried off great numbers of the inhabitants" and that the man "himself had lost ten children by it." To commemorate the loss, "he had ten strokes tattooed on one of his arms."[3]

Portlock's account is not only the earliest known reference to smallpox in the region but the westernmost reference as well. "A number of the Indians who visited us from the Eastward were marked with the small-pox, and one man who had lost an eye gave me to understand that he lost it by that disorder," the captain wrote, "but none of the natives from the Westward had the least traces of it." The intricate coastline runs in a northwesterly direction, and other accounts of the epidemic all come from sites south and east of Portlock and Dixon's location. It seems possible, then, that even as the Tlingits suffered under *Variola*'s impact, the virus itself expired among them, finally ending its inexorable spread through North America. Years later, a Tlingit man told a Russian administrator at New Arkhangel (now Sitka) that the pestilence "spread from Stakhin (Stikine) to Sitka, but did not go further north."[4]

Oddly, Captain Dixon gave a starkly contrasting account of the region's disease history. On August 15, 1787, he wrote, "The people are totally free from that long catalog of disease, which luxury and intemperance have introduced amongst more civilized nations." The statement is baffling. For aside from the observations already made by Captain Portlock, two adventurous crewmen had returned that very day from explorations near Cape Edgecumbe, and they too had found "many" people "marked with the smallpox."[5] Perhaps Dixon was unaware of these reports or ignored them. Or perhaps his own observations simply differed from those of the others. Within a year, in any case, the findings of other explorers indicated that Dixon was wrong and the others were right: Smallpox had indeed visited the Northwest Coast in the very recent past.

In August 1788, one year later, two American vessels—the *Columbia Rediviva* and the *Lady Washington*—cruised the coast of Oregon, a thousand miles to the south. Funded by a consortium of New England merchants and commanded by Captains John Kendrick and Robert Gray, the ships signaled a blossoming American interest in a region already contested by the governments of Russia, England, and Spain. *Variola* had outflanked the American traders, however. Near Oregon's Yaquina Bay on August 10, the *Lady Washington* received two canoes of Tillamook Indian visitors, who had set aside their annual harvest of huckleberries, strawberries, and chinook salmon to call upon the American ship. "Two or three of our visitors were much pitted with the small pox," noted a crewman, Robert Haswell, in his journal entry for the day.[6]

Three years later, in the summer of 1791, the *Columbia* again cruised the coastline, plying the sea otter trade. In the Strait of Juan de Fuca, which now marks the watery boundary between Canada and the United States, Captain Gray and his crew bartered with Wakashan-speaking Indians at the village of Nitinaht, where "several very valuable skins were purchased for copper and cloathing; also a few fine hallibut for trifles." The scars of smallpox were everywhere. " 'Twas evident that these Natives had been visited by that scourge of mankind the Smallpox," wrote another crewman, John Boit. Nor had it spared the village chief, a man named Cassacan, whose face bore the "evident marks" of "the small pox." The epidemic had come and gone, but its visible ravages nevertheless elicited a rhetorical outburst from the sailor John Hoskins: "Infamous Europeans, a scandal to the Christian name; is it you, who bring and leave in a country with people you deem savages the most loathsome diseases?"[7]

By the time Hoskins arrived, the Northwest Coast was abuzz with activity as a variety of private and national interests sought a piece of the China trade. At Baranof Island's Sitka Sound, barely south of the site where Nathaniel Portlock had first noted smallpox scars in 1787, a French trader named Étienne Marchand pursued commerce anew with the Tlingits in 1791. Among Marchand's crew was a man named Charles Pierre Claret de Fleurieu, who had read Portlock's account and now confirmed it. "It cannot be doubted that the small-pox has been introduced into the countries which border on TCHINKITANAY Bay," Fleurieu wrote, referring to Sitka Sound by its contemporary name, "for several individuals of both sexes bear unequivocal marks of it." The Tlingits had "explained very clearly" to the ship's surgeon, "who questioned them concerning the cause of these marks, that they proceeded from a disorder which made the face swell, and covered the body with virulent pustules that occasioned violent itchings." The Indians "even remarked that the French must be well acquainted" with the smallpox, "since some of them also bore the Marks of it." From Baranof Island, the French expedition sailed south to the Queen Charlotte archipelago, where it arrived in late August. Here too, among the plank houses and carved totem poles of the Haidas, the crew found signs that *Variola* had visited the Indians in the not-so-distant past. "Several among them," Fleurieu wrote, "have the face deeply marked with the small-pox."[8]

The famous British voyage of Captain George Vancouver followed only a year later. Its intent was twofold: Vancouver was to secure British claims to the region in the aftermath of the Nootka Sound controversy, a nasty spat between sea captains that had escalated into an international dispute between Britain and Spain in 1790, and he was to determine for posterity whether the Northwest Passage was reality or fantasy. In pursuit of the latter charge, Vancouver's men explored the coastline and mapped it in extraordinary detail, dashing all remaining hopes that a Northwest Passage existed. In so doing, they also encountered the empty villages and signs of smallpox that caused the great navigator to ponder, in his journal of the expedition, "the present apparent depopulation" of the coastline.[9]

For Vancouver, the depopulation was most notable among the Coast Salish peoples who lived on the shores of Puget Sound, the Strait of Juan de Fuca, and the Strait of Georgia, adjoining waterways that bound the interior shoreline of Vancouver Island. Deserted villages, now "over-run with weeds," dotted the banks of these channels. "I frequently met with human bones during my rambles," the crewman Thomas Manby noted after reconnoitering the southern shore of the Strait of Juan de Fuca. Farther north, he encountered an "uninhabited Village near half a Mile long," constructed "with a good deal of regularity, and ornamented with a prodigious number of carved logs." He estimated that it "once gave lodging to many hundred." Captain Vancouver made similar observations. In his estimation, the capacity of the empty villages far exceeded the number of Indians now in the area: "Each of the deserted villages was nearly, if not quite, equal to contain all the scattered inhabitants we saw." A report from a Spanish expedition in the area at the same time confirms the English accounts. "In these inlets there are various abandoned villages," wrote an unnamed Spanish diarist near the present site of Vancouver, British Columbia, on June 15, 1792. It is possible of course that these ruins showed the effects of a nondisease disaster, such as famine or war, but given the evidence, *Variola* is the likelier culprit.[10]

The Indians encountered by the explorers frequently bore the pitted scars that marked them as smallpox survivors. The naturalist Archibald Menzies and a small survey party met a group of southern Coast Salish Indians engaged in the "collecting & drying of fish" on a beach in Hood Canal on May 12. "Several of them were pock markd," Menzies noted, and "a number of them had lost an eye." Nine days later, in the nearby sound that bears his name today, the pilot Peter Puget approached a canoe carrying three Indians. "Two of the three in the Canoe had lost the Right Eye & were much pitted with the Small Pox," he wrote, "which Disorder in all probability is the Cause of that Defect." In general, Vancouver wrote of the surviving natives in the region, "their skins were mostly unblemished by scars, excepting such as the small pox seemed to have occasioned." The disease, he believed, was "very fatal amongst them."[11]

These accumulated after-the-fact accounts of smallpox are widely dispersed along the rugged northwestern coastline. They reveal only one certainty: that smallpox had struck the region by 1787, when Nathaniel Portlock and his crew first noted telltale scars and depopulation among the Tlingits. Given the age clusters of the victims and the sudden appearance of references to smallpox in the documentary record, it seems likely that the accounts refer to a single epidemic episode, not to separate, unrelated outbreaks. But this, like so much else, is not certain. The records do not indicate precisely how or when smallpox came to the Pacific Northwest. In the last quarter of the eighteenth century, ties between that coast and the world at large were multiplying rapidly.

This fact alone points to several possible routes by which *Variola* may have arrived in the region. In the final analysis, however, one possibility, the mighty Columbia River, stands out from the rest.

David Thompson's transcontinental journey to the mouth of the Columbia River in 1811 came less than six years after Meriwether Lewis and William Clark's more famous expedition had brought them down the same waterway. Lewis and Clark had attained the Columbia drainage by ascending the Missouri River from St. Louis, but Thompson and his men had taken a more northerly route: In January 1811, using snowshoes and dogsleds, they had crossed the Canadian Rockies at Athabasca Pass. "Ther[mometer] −30° A fine tho' very cold day," Thompson noted on January 5.[12] They then followed the upper reaches of the Columbia south for two hundred miles before portaging to the Kootenay River and descending Clark Fork to the lower Columbia and the Pacific. The route was circuitous not just because of the current state of non-Indian geographical knowledge but also because of Thompson's ties to the Canadian fur trade and to his North West Company employers.

Strange though it seems, the men in Thompson's party were actually disappointed when they emerged from the Cascade Mountains and caught their first glimpse of the sea on July 15. As seasoned canoemen, their leader explained, they had become "accustomed to the boundless horizon of the great Lakes of Canada," and at the Pacific Ocean "they expected a more boundless view, a something beyond the power of their senses which they could not describe." Thompson the geographer, however, felt no such disappointment, for he saw invisible connections beyond the horizon. Describing them, he tried unsuccessfully to fire the imaginations of his men. "My informing them, that directly opposite to us, at the distance of five thousand miles was the Empire of Japan added nothing to their Ideas," he wrote.[13] Scorned by Thompson's unreflective companions, the ocean view perhaps has symbolic significance only in retrospect. For during the four decades that preceded Thompson's arrival at the mouth of the Columbia, sail after sail had appeared on the blue-gray horizon, carrying people and trade goods from around the world and incrementally drawing the inhabitants of the Pacific Northwest into the expanding global economy.

The first nonnatives to have a noticeable effect on the Northwest Coast were not the French, Spanish, or British seafarers so commonly associated with the exploration and exploitation of the New World and its resources. Rather they were Russians, sailing east from the ports of Okhotsk, on the Asian mainland, and Petropavlovsk, on the Kamchatka Peninsula. Over the course of the seventeenth century, the Russian frontier had advanced eastward through the swamps and piney woods of central Siberia, crossing the great Lena River basin, and eventually pausing at the Pacific Ocean. In 1728, Vitus Bering made the first seaborne probe toward North America. Under orders to discover where Kamchatka was "joined to America," Bering sailed northeast through the sea and the strait that now bear his name, but he failed to sight the American mainland—present-day Alaska—through the fog.[14]

Despite the near miss, the Russian explorer established that water did indeed separate the two continents. Others pursued similar explorations, and Bering himself launched another expedition from Petropavlovsk in 1741. His two ships separated early in the voyage, and the undertaking lost many men, including its leader, to shipwrecks and scurvy. But both ships touched on the Alaskan coastline, and survivors returned to the west with accounts of a land teeming with fur-bearing animals, especially the highly prized and glossy-coated sea otter.[15]

Thereafter it was furs that drove Russian enterprise. The Russian fur trade to the northwestern coast of America was in many ways an extension of the brutal commerce already imposed upon the hapless natives of Siberia. In truth it can hardly be called trade. It was a taxation system that required indigenous Siberians to pay *iasak*—fur tributes—to the Russian crown. To assure

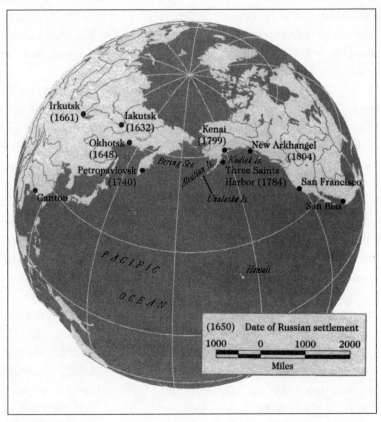

The North Pacific

compliance, Russian officials took hostages from among the natives, holding them until they collected the required furs. "If they did not give hostages, they would never come back to pay their iasak," one eyewitness explained of the Siberian natives. Landing at Petropavlovsk on Kamchatka in 1779, an English surgeon who sailed with Captain James Cook described the system in the plainest of terms. "As to the Kamtschadales," he wrote, "they are totally enslaved by the Russians."[16]

It was this system that Russian promyshlenniki (hunters and traders) transplanted to American soil. The promyshlenniki made eighty fur-trading voyages to the Alaskan coastline from 1744 to 1789, concentrating first on the westernmost Aleutian Islands and then, by 1780, engaging with inhabitants of the Alaskan Peninsula and mainland as well. The first permanent Russian settlement came only in 1784, when Grigorii Ivanovich Shelikhov set up a trading house on Kodiak Island, at Three Saints Harbor. Here too, the coercive trading tactics apparently continued. In encounters that would have been astonishing to witness, the promyshlenniki simply landed among the natives, told them they were Russian subjects, and demanded that they pay *iasak* and more. A 1771 account by two Russian officers described the method used in Alaska's Aleutian Islands: "They beach their vessels and try to take hostages, children from that island or nearby islands. If they cannot do this peacefully they will use force." At times the traders gave traps and trinkets to the indigenous Aleuts. But, the officers said, "no matter where the natives hunt, on shore or at sea, they must give everything to the promyshlenniks." For entertainment, according to another report, the traders would line up native men one behind the other and fire a gun at the first man to see "through how many the ball of their rifle-barrelled musket would pass."[17]

Could the promyshlenniki have carried *Variola* eastward across the Pacific from Siberia? The Russian conquest of Siberia, like the European conquest of America, inflicted wave after wave of smallpox upon native peoples. The energetic American explorer John

John Webber, *A Woman of
Kamschatka* [Kamchatka].
Courtesy National Library of
Australia

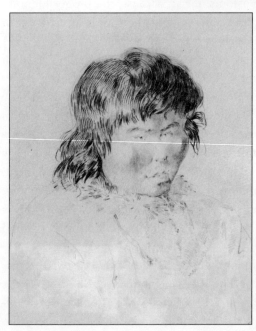

John Webber, *A Man of
Kamchatka.* By permission
of the British Library, ADD.
15514 f35

Ledyard, who had sailed with Captain Cook on his final voyage in 1776–80, pursued an overland journey eastward across Siberia as far as Iakutsk on the Lena River in 1787 and 1788. His account of the ravages of disease among indigenous Siberians might well have described North America. "Contact with the Russians brought new diseases, especially smallpox and venereal disease, and the mortality rate among many tribes increased by leaps and bounds," he wrote from Irkutsk on Lake Baikal, near the Russia-China border. Another eyewitness added details. "When they are stricken with smallpox they die like flies," wrote Heinrich von Füch, a political exile who observed the devastating effects of Russian contact farther east. Years of isolation had made native Siberians (like Native Americans) particularly vulnerable when European diseases struck. "Nine years ago I saw one nomadic settlement where only two out of ten men survived," Füch recalled. Survivors of smallpox, he noted, nevertheless had to pay the *iasak* of "all those who had died."[18]

From the perspective of America's northwestern coast, the most noteworthy Russian smallpox epidemic was probably the one that reached Kamchatka in 1768. It was in fact part of a vast pandemic, extending east from St. Petersburg (where it prompted the inoculation of Catherine the Great) to the Pacific Ocean. According to one account, the Alaskan fur trade bore the blame for bringing the virulent virus to Kamchatka: The disease was "brought into the country," wrote the French traveler Jean Lesseps, "by a Russian vessel bound to the Eastern islands, for the purpose of hunting otters, foxes, and other animals." The vessel had departed from the Siberian port of Okhotsk, Lesseps explained, with a man on board who still showed the "recent marks" of smallpox. When he landed at Petropavlovsk, "he communicated this cruel malady to the poor Kamtchadales," and it "carried off three fourths of them." Local officials could not keep track of fatalities during the epidemic since so many people fled to the mountains to avoid the pestilence, but later accounts of mortality were universally high. A report published in 1780 asserted that Kamchatka had lost "five thousand three hundred and sixty-eight persons" in the epidemic. When Captain Cook's men stopped at Petropavlovsk in 1779, the Russians there told them "that in the Year 1769 above 10,000 of them were destroyed by the small Pox."[19]

Russian traders could clearly have carried smallpox to America in the mid- to late eighteenth century, but both geography and timing suggest that they probably did not. The promyshlenniki in this period operated primarily in western regions of Alaska that appear to have escaped the epidemic. While the pestilence described here extended up the coastline to the Tlingits around Sitka, regions farther north and west appear to have remained smallpox-free until the 1790s. These were the lands frequented by the Russians in the early days of the fur trade. Grigorii Shelikhov, who commanded the Russian post at Kodiak Island from 1783 to 1786, noted explicitly that smallpox had not yet afflicted the local Koniag natives. "They do not appear to have communicable diseases, with the exception of venereal disease," he wrote; "they know nothing of smallpox and it has never occurred there."[20]

Timing, moreover, makes transmission still more unlikely. The Kamchatkan outbreaks occurred in 1768 and 1769, and any ensuing outbreaks in the American Northwest would have occurred concurrently or very close on the heels of these eruptions. Yet the disease does not turn up in the available written accounts of the Northwest until 1787, nearly two decades later. It is hard to imagine that the effects of such an epidemic could have eluded the literary record for so long, failing to appear in any of the known journals kept by visitors to the northwestern coast in the 1770s. In fairness it should be noted that there is an isolated report of smallpox on Kamchatka in 1774, closer to the time it seems to have appeared in America. But this account is uncorroborated, and it may well be in error.[21]

A second possibility is that smallpox arrived on board one of the other European vessels that touched on the Northwest Coast in the years 1774–86. Several accounts laid the blame on shipborne visitors, the Spanish in particular. "As the Spaniards were on this part of the coast in 1775," wrote Nathaniel Portlock in southeastern Alaska, "it is very probable that from them these poor wretches caught this fatal infection." In 1791, among the pockmarked Indians of the Strait of Juan de Fuca, the sailor John Boit reiterated the accusation: "The Spaniards as the natives say brought it among them."[22] The possibility of contagion from a European ship, Spanish or not, was a real one. For the 1770s and 1780s brought a great many outsiders to the bountiful northwestern coast.

Whereas Russians were interested almost exclusively in furs, it was exploration and territorial claims first, and trade only second, that drew other Europeans to America's northern Pacific shores in the late 1700s. Despite centuries of exploration in the Western Hemisphere, the northwest coastline remained little known to Europeans even by the time of the American Revolution. Seaborne adventurers—British, French, and Spanish alike—continued to be captivated by hopes of discovering the Northwest Passage, the same mythical lure that had drawn the Italian navigator Giovanni da Verrazano to the New World centuries earlier. None believed, as Verrazano did, that the Pacific Ocean and thence Asia lay just over the barrier islands of the North Carolina coast. But many thought they might find a watery connection of some sort extending from the interior of the continent to the Pacific. While adventurers with ties to the inland fur trade probed westward by land with the assistance of Native American guides, others made their explorations by sea. In the last quarter of the eighteenth century, a plethora of newcomers, including sailors under Spanish, British, French, and American flags, flocked to the Northwest Coast, drawing the previously remote region of the continent into unprecedented contact with the outside world.

Of the European contenders, none had stronger imperial interests in the area than Spain. The end of the Seven Years' War in 1763 had brought huge territorial gains to the Iberian power as

France turned over all of Louisiana to the Spanish crown. But with these gains came a problem: Spain's New World holdings had become too big to defend and administer. Anxious about Russian expansion and concerned about encroachments by other European powers, Spanish missionaries and soldiers had established posts on the California coast as far north as San Francisco by 1776.[23] But farther north, the empire's Pacific seaboard remained undefended by Spain and barely explored by Europeans. From 1774 until 1779, as anti-British sentiments coalesced and exploded on the eastern coast of North America, Spain tried to assert its claim to the Northwest, sending three different expeditions to the spectacular shoreline. The task would prove difficult, however, for Spanish officials faced competition not just from Russian traders but from British explorers as well.

All three Spanish voyages set out from the unheralded port of San Blas, a small, swampy anchorage on Mexico's Pacific coast just north of Puerto Vallarta, in what is now the state of Nayarit. In 1774, an expedition under Juan José Pérez Hernández sailed as far north as the Queen Charlotte Islands, in the southern reaches of Alaska, where for two days in July crew members engaged in a spirited trade with two hundred Haida Indians. The Haidas approached the Spanish vessels in canoes that carried as many as twenty-one people apiece. Eager to trade, the Indians offered mats, skins, hats, feathers, and elaborately embroidered woolens to the newcomers. "It was apparent," wrote a Catholic friar who sailed on the mission, "that what they liked most were things made of iron." The expedition soon returned southward. At Vancouver Island, which he assumed was a part of the mainland, Pérez dropped anchor near the mouth of Nootka Sound on August 9, 1774. Again, the crew did not land, but local natives paddled out to visit the alien vessel in their waters, and trade ensued. In exchange for pelts and native handicrafts, the sailors handed over "old clothes, shells which they had brought from Monterey and some knives." Several Nootkans even came aboard the *Santiago*, filching two silver spoons from Pérez's second officer.[24]

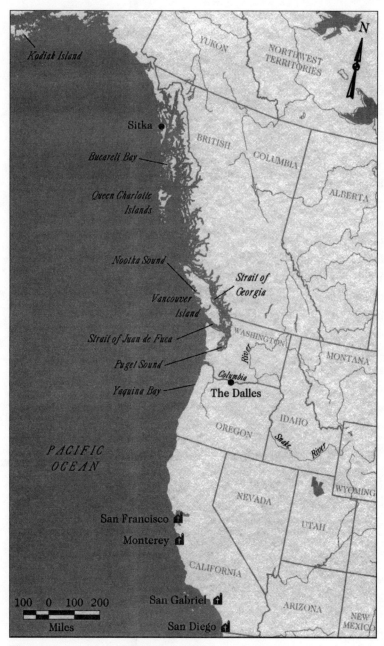

The northwest coast of North America

Had any of the men on the ship carried the *Variola* virus, they certainly could have transmitted it in these exchanges, either directly or in clothing traded to the Indians. The problem is that there is no indication of active smallpox aboard the *Santiago* although the expedition did struggle with several health problems. The vessel's boatswain died of an unnamed but virulent "fever" during the expedition's stopover in Monterey, California, in June 1774. On July 19, the expedition navigator had a tooth pulled to alleviate an inflammation of his face. Trade with the Haidas commenced the next day. Six days later, after the men had traded with the Haidas but before they had traded with the Nootkans, a Mexican sailor named Salvador Antonio died of an unidentified ailment.[25] Was it smallpox? Probably not. The *Santiago* had departed from San Blas in January 1774, but Antonio did not die until July. Even if *Variola* had boarded the frigate at San Blas—and there is no evidence that it did—any resulting epidemic should have burned itself out in the seven months that passed before Antonio died. The expedition did stop at San Diego and Monterey on its way northward, but there is no evidence of smallpox at these locations either.[26] Moreover, if Antonio had succumbed to an ailment so recognizable and so feared as smallpox, it is unlikely that it would have gone unnamed, especially given the possibility that other susceptibles on the *Santiago* could have acquired the infection.

What is named in the journals of the voyage is the "*mal de Loanda*, or scurvy," the ailment characterized by loose teeth and bleeding sores that plagued vitamin C–deficient sailors for centuries. Scurvy, according to Fray Tomás de la Peña, afflicted the crew of the *Santiago* through most of the voyage, and not surprisingly, it got worse with time. By August 19, 1774, Peña said, the disorder had left "more than twenty men unfit for duty, in addition to which many others, though able to go about, have sores in the mouth and on the legs." Two days later, another Catholic priest on the voyage found the "greater part of the crew . . . unfit for duty on account of scurvy." His own mouth was so sore that he could not celebrate mass.[27] It is extremely unlikely that these eye-witnesses, who themselves fell ill on the voyage, misidentified smallpox as scurvy. Finally, it is conceivable in the abstract that a piece of clothing or some other item given to the Indians carried the virus from a source unknown. But given the apparent absence of epidemic smallpox in Mexico, San Diego, and Monterey at this time, the possibility is dubious at best.

A year after the Pérez expedition, the Mexican viceroy Antonio María de Bucareli sent the frigate *Santiago* northward again, this time accompanied by a schooner named the *Sonora*, only thirty-three feet long with a beam of less than nine feet.[28] The expedition commander, sailing aboard the *Santiago*, was Bruno de Hezeta. Departing from San Blas on March 16, 1775, barely a month before the battles of Lexington and Concord brought the conflict between Britain and its colonists to a head in Massachusetts, the Hezeta expedition reached the coast of present Washington State on July 13, by which time the siege of Boston was well under way. Trade with local Indians, probably southwestern Coast Salish, occurred almost immediately upon the vessels' arrival, as nine canoes paddled out to greet the newcomers.

The following morning, Hezeta and a party of armed men from the *Santiago* erected a cross onshore in an official act of possession. They soon returned to their ship. A little later, Juan Francisco de la Bodega y Quadra, captain of the *Sonora*, sent seven men ashore to collect water and firewood. To the dismay of Bodega, who watched them land through his telescope, the unsuspecting foraging party stumbled into an Indian ambush. All members of the party were lost. Until that moment, relations with the Indians had been genial, and trade had taken place from the *Sonora* that very day.[29]

If smallpox afflicted the men aboard either the *Santiago* or the *Sonora*, they clearly could have transmitted it to the Indians in any of these encounters. In fact, the crews of both vessels were in poor health. By April 14, 1775, an unnamed illness had appeared aboard the *Sonora*, and a mysterious "fever" had taken hold on the

Santiago. Three months later, the adventurers remained unwell. "The whole crew of the frigate [*Santiago*] had been sick for the two last days, whilst the commander himself was far from well," wrote the young pilot Francisco Antonio Mourelle de la Rúa on July 13. Conditions quickly spiraled downhill. "Those sick with scurvy and other illnesses continue to increase daily until now they number fourteen," observed Fray Miguel Campa a few days later. By July 19, the men were so ill that Commander Hezeta called Bodega and his officers to a meeting on the *Santiago* to propose abandoning the expedition. Incredibly, the Peruvian captain of the tiny, unseaworthy schooner wanted to continue, while the expedition commander aboard the well-equipped frigate wanted to turn back.[30]

In the days that followed, the frigate *Santiago* did turn back, while the little *Sonora* continued north with its sickly but intrepid crew. The schooner ventured as far north as Alaska, performing an act of possession very close to the site where Nathaniel Portlock was to land twelve years later. The act itself was brief: The five men sent ashore erected a cross and a flag, and they etched another cross in a rock close by. The next day, when another party landed to gather water and firewood, a few Tlingits emerged from the woods, apparently demanding payment for the resources the Spaniards were taking. Both sides kept their distance, and contact was minimal. The sailors withdrew to their ship and soon sailed south to Bucareli Bay at Prince of Wales Island. Here too, a few men performed an act of possession for Spain. After nearly seven months at sea, the *Sonora* returned safely to Monterey on October 7, 1775. "On the 8th we landed our sick," wrote the pilot, "and amongst the rest our captain and myself, who had suffered more from scurvy than any of them. Not one of the whole crew indeed was free from his complaint."[31]

At least one scholar believes that the Hezeta expedition was the likeliest source of the smallpox epidemic that erupted among the nations of the northwestern coast near this time. Captain Portlock, who visited among the smallpox-scarred Tlingits in 1787, pointed to the *Sonora* in particular. Yet the little schooner was not a probable culprit. It carried fewer than seventeen men, and the available evidence does not indicate that any of them suffered from smallpox. Even if they did, it would have been quite unusual if it was communicated in the limited contact the crew had with the northwestern natives.[32] Eyewitness accounts make it clear that it was scurvy that caused most of the suffering among the crews of both the *Sonora* and the *Santiago*.[33]

But what were the "fever" and the "other illnesses" identified aboard the *Santiago* in April and July? The answer is most probably typhus, the lice-borne contagion commonly known as camp fever. Typhus regularly plagued eighteenth-century armies and expeditions of exploration, and it appears to have plagued the *Santiago* as well. On November 2, 1775, as the frigate made its way back to San Blas, the second captain, Don Juan Pérez, "died at six in the morning of typhus."[34] Yet the presence of typhus does not exclude smallpox, and it is tempting to speculate that *Variola* may also have been aboard one of the ships. This is not likely for one simple reason: Smallpox comes from where smallpox was. There is no evidence of smallpox in San Blas near the date of the expedition's departure in March 1775. There is likewise no evidence of the virus at Alta California's Humboldt Bay, where the expedition stopped on its way north.

It was to be four years before Juan Francisco de la Bodega y Quadra and Francisco Antonio Mourelle de la Rúa, two of the most daring and competent San Blas–based officers, once again probed the Pacific Northwest. When they did, it was in response to a direct challenge from the great English navigator James Cook, who had embarked on his third and last voyage of discovery in the summer of 1776. Chief among Cook's goals was the discovery of a Northwest Passage, his interest piqued and his knowledge primed by reading a copy of Mourelle's 1775 journal that had found its way into British hands.[35]

In the ships *Resolution* and *Discovery*, Cook's well-equipped and well-funded expedition reached the Oregon coast in March

1778. Sailing north, the explorers found no Northwest Passage and somehow missed the Columbia River and the Strait of Juan de Fuca. They did stop at Nootka Sound on Vancouver Island, where Cook found signs of the Spanish visitors who had preceded them in the form of "two small silver table Spoons which one of my people purchased of a man who had them hung round his neck as an ornament." These were the very spoons the Nootkans had lifted from the *Santiago* in 1774. Cook and his men spent nearly a month among the Wakashan-speaking Indians of Nootka Sound. The sailors traded extensively. They visited the Nootkans' village, with its plank houses and extraordinary woodwork. Everywhere they documented what they saw, leaving modern historians with a remarkable ethnography of visual images and written descriptions of northwestern life at the time of European contact.

Could Cook's men have given smallpox to the Nootkans? The answer is almost certainly not. The navigator's expeditions were probably the healthiest of the eighteenth century. They were also the best documented. No fewer than eight accounts of the voyage saw publication upon its conclusion. So abundant were the onboard writers, in fact, that the *Resolution* and *Discovery* each produced a newspaper of sorts, exchanged weekly between the vessels. The only mention of smallpox amid the crew came while the *Resolution*, in the charge of Captain Charles Clerke, remained in port at Plymouth, England, making preparations to sail in August 1776. One of the sailors had taken ill "with the Small Pox," reported Clerke, who deemed it "an unfortunate precedent." He addressed the problem directly, exchanging two marines who had not had the smallpox for two who had. In the end, only two sailors remained who had not had the disease, and Clerke held them to be "very good men very desirous of going the Voyage." The pox, he believed, would spread "no farther."[36] Indeed, among the ship's crewmen, it is not mentioned again. The incident took place a full year and a half before the expedition was to reach Vancouver Island. Cook's boats could not have been the source of the contagion.

John Webber, *A View in Ship Cove* [Nootka Sound], April 1778. By permission of the British Library, ADD. 15514 f10

John Webber, *Habitations in Nootka Sound*, April 1778. By permission of the British Library, ADD. 15514 f7

Just as significantly, Cook and his fellow diarists fail to mention any signs of smallpox among the Wakashan-speaking Nootkans with whom they spent so much time in 1778. In the many published accounts of this expedition, there is no mention of empty villages, and there is no mention of smallpox scars among northwestern natives. Moreover, there are no pockmarks to be found in the published Indian portraits produced by the artists on the voyage. Could indications of the disease have gone unnoticed by so many eager observers? Possibly, but not likely. Accounts of smallpox elsewhere earned a place in these annals, as did the incident Clerke reported in Plymouth. Venereal diseases turn up frequently in the diarists' accounts of both North America and the South Pacific. Surely, had there been indications of smallpox among the natives Cook encountered, some mention would have been made.[37]

It is in fact possible that the epidemic somehow skipped the Nootka Indians with whom Cook visited. Later callers at the harbor also fail to mention signs of the disease, but many of these visitors were caught up in the intrigues of the Nootka Sound controversy of 1790, and their writing about local Indians is sometimes less detailed than that of their predecessors. Smallpox did strike other Wakashan speakers on Vancouver Island (notably the village of Nitinaht) and it struck the island's Coast Salish residents as well. It would be surprising indeed if the Nootkans escaped it. The absence of references in the records of Cook's voyage suggests (but by no means proves) that *Variola* reached the Northwest Coast some time *after* 1778, when the navigator stopped at Nootka, and *before* 1787, when Portlock gave the first written description of its impact.[38]

Unaware that Cook had already come and gone, Spain set out to intercept the British intruders in its tenuously held northwestern territory. In February 1779, as King George's forces entrenched themselves in Savannah, Georgia, and prepared for their southern campaign, two armed frigates, the *Favorita* and the *Princesa*, sailed north from San Blas. In command was Ignacio de Arteaga, accompanied by an officer corps well traveled in northwestern waters. After a storm separated the vessels for two weeks, they rendezvoused at Bucareli Bay in the first week of May. There, on the windward side of what is now Alaska's Prince of Wales Island, local Tlingit Indians greeted them with great ceremony, sprinkling feathers gently into the water. Interpreted by the Spanish sailors as a "sign of peace," the ritual actually marked the moment of meeting between two important people. Trade began very shortly, and the Indians retired to their village "demonstrating great joy."[39]

The Arteaga expedition, with its roughly two hundred men, remained at Bucareli Bay for almost two months. Among the most important reasons for staying so long was the outbreak of an epidemic amidst the crew of the *Princesa*. Eyewitness accounts from the voyage fail to identify the plague.[40] One scholar has speculated that it might have been smallpox, and another that whatever it was, the sick sailors may have passed the malady on to local Tlingits. Both suggestions seem plausible. The presence of virulent smallpox in central Mexico in 1779, the year the expedition sailed, makes the latter possibility all the more intriguing. Though records have not yet been found to show that the Mexican epidemic struck San Blas, it is nearly inconceivable that it missed this much-maligned anchorage. However, Arteaga sailed in February 1779, and the great Mexican smallpox epidemic did not erupt until August, some six months later. It does not seem to have appeared anywhere near San Blas until February 1780, a full year *after* he had sailed.[41]

All this does not mean that the expedition did not communicate disease to the Tlingits at Bucareli Bay; it simply makes it less likely that it was smallpox. The Tlingits helped provision and care for the sick sailors in their temporary quarters onshore. The captain of the *Favorita* observed that the "gentle behavior of the Indians" greatly aided the convalescence of his men.[42] If the affliction they suffered under was smallpox, the Tlingits would almost certainly have picked it up. Yet there is no indication that Indians began falling ill during the fifty-eight days the expedition remained at Bucareli Bay. Given *Variola*'s twelve-day incubation period, at least some Indians would have shown symptoms before the sailors left. Moreover, one would once again expect that a disease as terrifying and as identifiable as smallpox would be named if it were present.

Of all the European voyages to the Northwest Coast in this period, the Arteaga expedition seems the likeliest candidate for transmitting smallpox to the region's vulnerable native population. For political, financial, and military reasons, Spanish explorations came to a temporary halt after Arteaga's return. In the years 1780–84, no European vessels are known to have visited the northwestern coast of America. By 1785, however, word of the profits to be reaped trading sea otter skins to China had spread among British merchants and financiers. A flurry of activity resulted: One English ship visited the Northwest Coast in 1785; in 1786, two French vessels and at least seven British vessels pursued trade in the region. One of these seafarers noted "a ruined Village" consisting of "twenty or thirty Houses" on the shores of Prince William Sound, Alaska, in 1785. He also observed that the fur trade had brought "every species of wretchedness, and new diseases" to the natives of the area, but he did not name smallpox. The location, moreover, was well to the north of the areas known to be affected by *Variola*. If any of these lucrative trading voyages infected northwestern natives with the virus, the evidence remains to be discovered.[43]

Could smallpox possibly have afflicted the Northwest Coast during the 1780–84 period, when no European visitors were present to observe it? The evidence is less than definitive, but this scenario appears more plausible than any other. While the voyages of 1774–79 promoted tentative links between indigenous northwesterners and an expanding world economy, the men who sailed on them noted that the natives of the region already had extensive trade networks of their own. At Nootka Sound with Pérez in 1774,

John Webber, *A Woman of Nootka Sound*, April 1778

Fray Tomás de la Peña noticed that local Wakashan Indians possessed "some implements of iron and copper." The Catholic friar and his companions were the first known European visitors to the area, yet metal goods had preceded them. The copper may well have come from inland Athapaskans, who had for centuries exchanged locally mined metal for coastal goods such as seashells. But iron was not produced by natives. It might have come from a shipwreck, yet more likely came from other tribes with access to Russian or other European wares. Sailors with Pérez also noted iron harpoon heads among the Haidas farther north.[44]

Later visitors commented more explicitly about the extent of native commerce. In 1778, when Captain Cook noticed iron chisels and knives among the Wakashans at Nootka Sound, he attributed it to a vast trade network with remote ties to Europeans. "Indeed one cannot be surprised at finding iron with all the Nations in America sence they have been so many years in a manner surrounded by Europeans and other Nations who make use of iron," he wrote, "and who knows how far these Indian Nations may extend their traffick one with a nother."[45]

Those who followed Cook shared his opinion. The contentious Spanish commander Estéban José Martínez sailed with Pérez to the Northwest in 1774, and in 1789 he returned to Nootka to protect the region from British incursions. His diary of the mission included a description of the elaborate web of native commerce: "I am of the opinion that the iron that they use they have acquired from village to village to village." The commerce was not limited to the seacoast. Martínez believed that an inland trade between "coastal residents and the villages of the interior" also flourished. He speculated that in return for fish and skins sent to the interior, seaside natives received metal goods passed person to person from establishments as far away as the "Mississippi, if not Hudson Bay and the land of Labrador." At Nootka with Vancouver in 1793, seaman Thomas Manby also thought that coastal natives participated in a trade network that extended all the way to Hudson Bay. "As neither Land, or Water, stops the car[r]ier of commerce," he wrote, "I dare say, many of our articles have by this time, nearly approached, the opposite side of the Continent, as a continual chain of barter, exists between Tribe and Tribe, through this amazing track of Country, which in time, will no doubt, find their way, to our factories in Canada, or the back settlements of Hudsons bay."[46]

It was indeed a remarkable "chain of barter," and nowhere did it penetrate the continental interior more readily than along the Columbia River, a veritable highway of the eighteenth century. The headwaters of this great river lie in the snowcapped peaks of the Rocky Mountains, far beyond the rugged Cascades and the rolling Palouse. In the Canadian Rockies, the Columbia River flows circuitously southwestward from the continental divide near Banff, where its watershed adjoins the great Nelson River drainage that flows into Hudson Bay. Farther south, as Lewis and Clark suspected before setting out on their famous journey of

1804–06, the Columbia drainage abuts that of the Missouri in the mountains of Montana and Idaho. In the late eighteenth century, this great interior country remained completely unknown to Europeans. But evidence indicates that an indigenous chain of barter already linked it to the Pacific coast. Archaeologists have unearthed numerous shell artifacts from the Pacific at the very origins of the Columbia River: along Idaho's Snake and Salmon rivers and in the Beaverhead Mountains on the continental divide.[47] These lands lay in the heart of Shoshone Indian territory. It was no accident that Sacagawea, the Indian interpreter who led Lewis and Clark from the drainage of the Mississippi to that of the Columbia, was a Shoshone.

The Shoshones cast their net broadly. They had in all likelihood picked up *Variola* through trade with their Comanche kin to the south. Once infected, they passed it on to the Blackfeet and other northern plains tribes in the summer of 1781. But the virus also took a toll west of the Shoshones, among their Flathead and Nez Perce neighbors. Were the Shoshones again the source? The evidence is belated and does not name them specifically, but they probably were. At a post near what is now the Idaho-Montana border, a Jesuit missionary named Gregory Mengarini noted in 1847 that smallpox had struck local Flathead Indians "about seventy years ago." The timing is such that the account could only describe the great outbreak of 1781. "The disease," the Indians told Mengarini, "caused the growth of large red and black pustules over the entire body, particularly on the chest. Those developing red pustules died within a few days, but those who were plagued by the black pustules died almost instantly." The reference to black pustules may well describe the hemorrhagic form of smallpox, characterized in some cases by a "dark-purple velvet" appearance and in others by black-colored pustules. Such cases were fatal in 97 to 100 percent of victims. Before the epidemic struck, according to Mengarini, the Flatheads had numbered "at least eight hundred families or about four thousand people." By 1847, after at least three additional smallpox outbreaks and untold encounters with other diseases, they numbered "little more than five hundred souls."[48]

Corroboration for Mengarini's report of smallpox among the Flatheads can be found in comments by Asa Bowen Smith, another mid-nineteenth-century visitor to the Rocky Mountain West. In a letter written from north-central Idaho, Smith placed the epidemic not just among the Flatheads but among their Nez Perce neighbors to the north and west. The Nez Perces, Smith said, had by their own account dwindled greatly in number. "Twice during the remembrance of the most aged among this people has the small pox been among them," he wrote in July 1840. "The first time it visited them must have been 60 or perhaps 70 years ago," as only "very old people" could recall the plague.[49] The epidemic described was almost certainly the plague of 1781–82, so amply documented in Hudson's Bay Company records and the winter counts of the Sioux Indians.

According to Smith, "some very old people, I should think 70 or 80 years old & perhaps more, relate that when they were children a large number of people both of the Nez Perces & Flatheads wintered in the buffalo country." This placed them on the plains east of their usual territory—very likely in Shoshone country—at just the wrong time. In the spring, the rest of the tribe went to join them for the hunt. But "instead of finding their people as they expected they found their lodges standing in order, & the people almost to an individual dead. Only here & there one survived the disease." The plague was evidently "the most virulent form of the small pox." From the plains, according to Smith, the Nez Perces and Flatheads had carried smallpox westward to the Snake River, on the Columbia drainage. There it "swept through the whole country, very few surviving the attack of the disease." If these seasonal migrations seem exaggerated, documentary evidence bears them out: The "natives of the upper Columbia," noted a fur trader in 1814, "penetrate even to the Missouri to kill buffaloes."[50]

There is no reason to suspect the authenticity of Asa Smith's account. Despite its late date, it is extremely important, for it places the great smallpox epidemic conclusively on the Columbia River watershed, west of the continental divide. The Nez Perces, furthermore, ranged into the treeless grasslands of what is now western Washington State, where the waters of the Columbia and Snake rivers join and wind their way 250 miles west to the Pacific Ocean. Here the evidence regarding smallpox dwindles to nothing. But given *Variola*'s transit thus far, it takes no great leap of faith to imagine the disease traveling so short a distance, circulating among Indians gathered at the now-submerged Dalles trading center, passing from person to person down the river, and then reappearing in the documentary record when it reached the lower Chinook Indians near the site of today's Portland, Oregon. The lower Chinooks, according to the fur trader Alexander Ross, migrated "towards the interior sometimes for months together; war and traffic in slaves often call them to a distance."[51]

It was among these Indians that Lewis and Clark, having already seen remnants of the epidemic's impact on the Missouri River tribes, picked up its trail once again. The evidence from the explorers' journals is often ambiguous. A second smallpox epidemic swept through many parts of the West, including sections of the Missouri and Columbia rivers, in 1800–02, and it is often hard to distinguish in their writings between the later and earlier epidemics. In some places where the two explorers mention smallpox, they make no attempt to date their discussions. But in other instances, surrounding evidence makes the time frame clear. Such was the case at the Ne-cha-co-lee Chinook village, near the modern site of Portland. By the time Lewis and Clark passed through the little settlement on their upstream journey in 1806, very few people remained. The village consisted of only one house in good repair, behind which stood "the wreck of 5 houses remaining of a very large Village." Curious about the decay, William Clark asked the remaining inhabitants "the Situation of their nation, if scattered or what had become of the nativs who must have peopled this great town." The Indians "brought forward a woman who was badly marked with the Small Pox and made Signs that they all died with the disorder which marked her face." The woman herself had come "verry near dieing" from the pox as a girl. "From the age of this woman," Clark added, "this Distructive disorder I judge must have been about 28 or 30 years past." This places the epidemic squarely in the 1780s.[52]

Lewis, Clark, and their Corps of Discovery were now on their return trip, having wintered among the Clatsops at the Columbia's Pacific Ocean terminus. The Clatsops, the explorers noted, had also dwindled under smallpox, as recently as 1802. "The small pox has distroyed a great number of the natives in this quarter," wrote Meriwether Lewis. But the 1802 epidemic was only partially to blame. The Clatsops also had apparently borne the brunt of the earlier outbreak. When he learned that the Ne-cha-co-lee Chinooks had endured smallpox "about 28 or 30 years past," Clark noted that this was "about the time the Clatsops inform us that this disorder raged in their towns and distroyed their nation." If the smallpox did indeed follow the Columbia River to the Pacific, it may well have then spread from the Clatsops and other Chinookan Indians along the coast, scarring survivors and causing the depopulation noted by seafarers in its aftermath. Among Indians in Puget Sound, tradition has long maintained that the first smallpox epidemic "came from the south," as well it would have if the Columbia River was its source.[53]

The evidence does not show conclusively that this is what occurred, but given the other possibilities, it stands out as the most plausible scenario. Again, the guiding principle is simple: Smallpox comes from where smallpox was. For several fur trader–adventurers, the case needed no argument. David Thompson, who knew the Northwest as well as anyone, stated simply that the epidemic had "crossed the Rocky Mountains" from the plains. Ross Cox, who served at John Jacob Astor's ill-fated fur-trading post at the Columbia River's mouth in 1812, believed "the disease first proceeded from the banks of the Missouri . . . crossed the Rocky Mountains at the sources of the Missouri, and having fastened its deadly venom on the Snake [Shoshone] Indians, spread its devastating course to the northward and westward, until its frightful progress was arrested by the Pacific Ocean." Cox himself ascended the Columbia and crossed the continent from west to east in 1812–13. Robert Stuart, along with several other "Astorians," accompanied him on the journey. Stuart's appraisal was the same as Cox's. The Indians of the lower Columbia, he wrote, "are never troubled with epidemic, or contagious diseases, except the small-pox, which, from nation to nation, has found its way across the rocky mountains, and sometimes its effects are so calamitous as to carry off three fourths of those who have the misfortune to be attacked therewith."[54]

In 1811, ten months after David Thompson and Qánqon had headed back up the Columbia River from Astoria, the traders at the isolated Pacific Fur Company post received unsettling news. On June 5, the ship *Tonquin* had departed from Astoria to ply the fur trade along the northern coastline. In the weeks and months that followed, the Astorians heard nothing from the *Tonquin* itself, but they did hear rumors about the ship's fate from local Indians. On May 12, 1812, these rumors were confirmed: At Clayoquot Sound on Vancouver Island, Nootkan Indians had boarded the ship, killed its crew, and commenced plundering its stores. Then, with four or five hundred Indians aboard, an unexplained explosion blew the ship to smithereens, taking the lives of nearly two hundred natives. At the time this news arrived, the traders at Astoria feared that an attack on their own post was imminent. To defend themselves, they strengthened their fortifications and posted around-the-clock sentinels. One trader, Duncan McDougall, reportedly took another step as well. Assembling "several of the chieftains, and showing them a small bottle," he "declared that it contained the small-pox." The bottle, he said, would remain corked only "if the white people were not attacked or robbed." The Indians were terrified. They promised to remain peaceful, protesting that if released, the pestilence "would run like fire among the good people as well as among the bad." From then on, they viewed McDougall with dread, designating him "the great small-pox chief."[55]

A generation after the first epidemic and a decade after the second, *Variola* continued to instill terror in the Indians of the Northwest Coast. But fear was not the only legacy the virus left behind. Were records of Native American life more complete, they might well show significant cultural voids, the loss of generations of unrecoverable knowledge. They would show other changes as well: households combined, kinship alliances annihilated, religious convictions altered or abandoned. As smallpox squeezed the life from thousands of victims, it extinguished the accumulated wisdom of generations, leaving those who survived without the familiar markers by which they organized their worlds and leaving the generations that followed with a mere shell of their former heritage.

Both the arrival and the expiration of the great smallpox pestilence on the northwestern coast of America went undocumented. But on this rugged shoreline, *Variola* finally ran out of the human connections it needed to thrive. While vulnerable populations still existed in Alaska, the virus, for the moment, was unable to get there. Records do not indicate the precise date on which the epidemic expired, but the great smallpox pestilence had finally come to a close.

EPILOGUE

When Lewis and Clark returned east from their Voyage of Discovery in 1806, they melded the disparate regions of North America into one in the collective Jeffersonian consciousness. But the world the explorers described to the American people was one that had already undergone momentous change. As their own journals indicated, *Variola*'s transit of the continent had preceded them by a full generation. In the years of the American Revolution, long before the two explorers forged a unified continent in the American psyche, converging military, political, social, environmental, and economic upheavals had unwittingly united North Americans far and wide in a common, if horrific, experience. That experience was epidemic smallpox, passed from one human being to another in a chain of connections as terrible as it was stunning. Yet connections are only what gave birth to the pestilence. They do not explain what followed. The great epidemic was a tremendous upheaval in its own right, and just as it arose out of the turmoil that preceded it, so it created repercussions of its own.

The consequences of the pox were as diverse as the places and peoples it afflicted. On the eastern seaboard of the continent, where the initial outbreaks occurred, the lessons taken from early episodes, particularly the Canadian calamity of 1775–76, prompted George Washington and his medical staff to address the all-important issue of smallpox control in the Continental army. Had they not done so, it is likely that the Quebec debacle would have repeated itself, possibly many times, in later campaigns. Immunization liberated Washington's army from almost certain infection, especially given the broad circulation of people and microbes that went with the war. The army inoculations of 1777–78 represent the first large-scale, state-sponsored immunization campaign in American history. Afterward, in the brief period between the end of the war and Edward Jenner's development of cowpox vaccination in 1796, variolation gained wider acceptance than it had had previously, as local governments throughout the United States eased long-standing restrictions on the practice.

Inoculation liberated the Continental troops from fear of contagion, but *Variola* still dashed the hopes of many African Americans who sought a more momentous sort of freedom than that envisioned by the American patriots. For the Ethiopian Regiment and for the thousands of black loyalists who joined the British during the southern campaign of the war, smallpox was the deadliest of enemies. Despite the slaves' exclusion from the limited notions of liberty that inspired the Revolution, their experience with smallpox showed how very American they had become. Born and raised on New World soil, they shared a common vulnerability to smallpox with their country-born neighbors—unlike Europeans, who usually encountered *Variola* and acquired immunity in childhood.

For the Indian groups whose lands bordered the western fringes of Anglo-American settlement, the pestilence compounded a catastrophic pattern of population decline that had begun centuries earlier. The Creeks, Cherokees, and Iroquois had endured repeated bouts of Old World disease by the time of the Revolutionary War, and the smallpox then ensured that demographic recovery would not come soon. As land-hungry Anglo-Americans looked westward after the Treaty of Paris, many of these Indians reeled from the triple disaster of smallpox, war, and abandonment by their British allies. "You are a subdued people," American treaty commissioners told the one group of Indians in 1784. "We are at peace with all but *you; you* now stand out *alone* against our *whole* force." The force was overwhelming, and the years that followed were marked by Indian resistance, defeat, and removal to lands west of the Mississippi River.[1]

Far west of the Mississippi, in the mountains and deserts of northern New Spain, the demographic impact of the smallpox epidemic was so severe that even in the Hispanic population, the mean age of marriage dropped visibly over the next decade, a phenomenon that one scholar has labeled a "reproductive strategy" for "recovering lost numbers." Confronted with severe losses among the Christian Indians of New Mexico, Governor Juan Bautista de Anza ordered a contraction of the province's mission system. The move was approved by Viceroy Teodoro de Croix, but it raised the ire of local Franciscans, locked in an unending battle with governmental authority. At the same time, the pox itself may have pushed traditionalist Pueblos to conversion: As their time-honored healing practices failed and desperation set in, they apparently sought a cure for smallpox in baptism.[2] By correlating baptism and burial records, scholars in the future may well be able to appraise the statistical significance of these deathbed conversions.

In the colonial settlements of Texas and New Mexico, fierce Comanche raids had marked the years before the great smallpox outbreak.[3] But in the mid-1780s, after nearly three-quarters of a century of relentless hostilities with the Spaniards, these warlike people of the plains made peace on both flanks: They concluded treaties with Texas Governor Domingo Cabello in October 1785 and with New Mexico Governor Anza in April 1787. What brought about this shift in affairs? The impulse toward peace inevitably stemmed from a convergence of needs and events: Anza's defeat of Cuerno Verde in 1779 was a devastating blow to the Indians.

Moreover, a Spanish-Comanche alliance against the Apaches held obvious appeal for both parties. But from the Comanches' perspective, it may well have been losses from smallpox that made such an alliance appealing or necessary.

The epidemic's impact was likewise dramatic farther north. On the upper Missouri River, horrific mortality among the agricultural Mandans, Hidatsas, and Arikaras left these tribes ill equipped to fend off the Sioux marauders who threatened them from the east. Reeling from their losses, the sedentary tribes sought safety in numbers, combining villages and moving when necessary. The trader-explorer Jean-Baptiste Truteau visited the Arikaras in June 1795, in central South Dakota near the junction of the Cheyenne and Missouri rivers. The Indians had been "almost entirely destroyed by the smallpox," he wrote, "which broke out among them at three different times." The few survivors had merged the remains of thirty-two villages into only two. Moreover, in the quest for security, some Arikaras chose to depart entirely, taking refuge among other tribes. Two chiefs "seceded last spring with their bands," Truteau wrote. "One is gone to make his residence with the Pani-Mahas [Omahas], the other with the Mandans."[4]

The Mandans and Hidatsas engaged in a similar consolidation even as they welcomed the Arikaras as neighbors. Meriwether Lewis and William Clark stayed among the Mandans at the Knife River's confluence with the Missouri in 1804–05. The Mandans, according to the explorers, were comparative newcomers to the neighborhood, having migrated north from the Heart River to join forces with their Hidatsa friends. "Maney years ago they lived in Several Villages on the Missourie low down," wrote Clark, but "the Smallpox destroyed the greater part of the nation and reduced them to one large Village and Some Small ones." When the adventurers revisited the Indians on their return trip, Clark reiterated the point: "Small pox killed the greater part of them and made them So weak that all that were left only made two Small villages when Collected."[5]

On the maps they drew of their travels, Lewis and Clark noted the locations of ruined Mandan towns that pointed to the ultimate triumph of the Sioux in the aftermath of the epidemic. At the Heart River, they noted many such sites, including one "Old Mandan Village destroyed by the Sioux and Small Pox" and another that they marked with the legend "killed by the Soux." Until *Variola* struck, the contest between the Sioux and the Mandans had stood at a draw. But the plague took a greater toll on densely populated towns than it did on nomadic bands, and afterward, the balance tipped in favor of the Sioux raiders. Life for the Mandans had changed forever: "All <the> nations before this maladey [smallpox] was affrd. [afraid] of them," wrote Clark in 1804, but "after they were reduced the Sioux and other Indians waged war, and killed a great maney." By this time, according to the historian Richard White, the Sioux "dominated the upper Missouri nearly to the Yellowstone River." In 1837, another virulent wave of smallpox struck the Mandans, leaving only a handful of survivors and ending their existence as an autonomous nation.[6] The Sioux soon became undisputed lords of the plains.

The Blackfeet too turned the epidemic to their advantage, launching their own hegemonic reign farther north. With so many Crees and Assiniboines dead, the Blackfeet managed to establish direct contact with the traders of the Hudson's Bay and North West companies, circumventing the Indian middlemen who had controlled their access to guns and goods for so long. Well armed and ascendant, the Blackfeet now pushed the Shoshones back into the mountains from which the latter Indians had briefly emerged with their acquisition of horses earlier in the century. The Blackfeet, according to the fur trader Alexander Henry, were by 1811 "the most independent and happy people of all the tribes E. of the Rocky mountains. War, women, horses and buffalo are their delights, and all these they have at their command."[7]

While the records of the late eighteenth century give us enough detail to trace *Variola*'s movement across most of the continent, they fall short when it comes to demographic data. Only rarely do they yield the kind of specific statistical information necessary to ascertain morbidity and mortality with precision. In a word, the documentation is spotty. To complicate matters further, the demography of North America is itself unclear at the time of the great pestilence. While rough population estimates exist for both the British and Spanish colonies near the time of the Revolutionary War, similar figures do not exist for many of the vast expanses of North America peopled almost exclusively by Native Americans.[8] We simply do not know how many people were living in the Midwest, in the Great Plains, in the Canadian interior, and in the greater Northwest in 1775. In addition, even where population statistics do exist, the task of extrapolating mortality is a treacherous one. In many communities, the presence of individuals with acquired immunity to *Variola* makes it nearly impossible to reach sound conclusions about transmission rates, morbidity, or overall mortality. An accurate appraisal would have to consider in- and out-migration, birthrates, death rates, and the impact of other plagues and events on populations known to have some level of acquired immunity to *Variola*.

Yet some attempt must nevertheless be made to assess the effects of the great pestilence on North American demography. The statistical appraisal that follows represents a baseline from which future scholarship can and should evolve. It is a representation solely of those deaths that can be documented in the historical record. The resulting estimate should therefore be considered a *minimum*. Inevitably, the actual number of fatalities was higher— probably much higher.

Let us start where we started our story: in Boston and outlying areas as the crisis with Britain came to a head in 1775. Here, as early as January 25, an anecdotal report indicated that thanks to epidemic smallpox, "there has been three buried every day for this month past," yielding a total of 90 deaths even before events at Lexington and Concord launched the siege of Boston and the Revolutionary War. Although mortality must have continued in

February and March, statistical data remain elusive. By contrast, we do have some evidence from Boston once the siege was under way. According to a secondhand account from a "gentleman" who escaped on July 10, the city was "very sickly: from ten to thirty funerals a day." If we accept an average of 20 fatalities per day, a single week of such mortality would yield 140 deaths. It is true that the Boston outbreak lasted for much longer than a week. But because some of these deaths must have stemmed from causes other than smallpox, and because we have no clear picture of the time span referred to, a higher estimate does not seem warranted without additional supporting evidence. No numbers exist for besieged Boston in the second half of 1775. But Boston records for the following year show only 57 deaths from inoculated and natural smallpox combined. Although this number seems quite low, it may not be: Some 4,988 of the 5,292 total cases of the disease appear to have stemmed from inoculation.[9] In the Boston area, then, it appears that at least 287 individuals died of smallpox in the 1775–76 outbreak.

Documentable fatalities were much more numerous in the Continental army's ill-fated Canadian campaign. Henry Caldwell, a British officer, estimated that the besieging Americans lost a minimum of 500 men to *Variola* while they remained in their camp before Quebec. Moreover, roughly 400 Continental soldiers passed the winter imprisoned within the city after their failed attack of December 31, 1775. By one estimate, "about one-twelfth of the prisoners died that Winter with the small-pox." By another, "about one ninth part of the prisoners died" from "this mortal disease."[10] A simple average of these estimates points to approximately 38 deaths among the prisoners of war, for a total of 538 deaths from smallpox among the Americans at Quebec. Mortality among local residents must also have occurred, but it remains unknown and uncounted.

In the spring of 1776, the chaos of the American retreat made accurate troop returns nearly impossible to obtain for the Northern Army. Enlistments expired, men deserted, and smallpox victims died while reinforcements poured in. Even eyewitnesses could only guess at the size of the army at any given time, and the resulting appraisals varied wildly. Anecdotal evidence, however, gives a graphic picture of the smallpox-induced mortality that accompanied the withdrawal. On June 22, John Lacey estimated that 30 to 40 men died daily. Four days later he said 8 to 10 died each day in his detachment alone. "Death visits us almost every hour," wrote the physician Lewis Beebe, commenting on June 30 that it took several men all day to bury the dead. At Crown Point on July 10, Charles Cushing observed that on some days 15 or 20 died in his regiment. Lewis Beebe commented on July 11 that more than 100 had died in eight days, and General Gates informed Washington a few days later that since the start of the retreat, "the Losses sustain'd by the Enemy, Death & Desertion, amounts to more than Five Thousand Men, and to this must be added, three Thousand that are now Sick." In mid-August, Ebenezer David observed 20 to 30 deaths per day at Fort George. And on August 28, physician Beebe noted that more than 300 men had been buried over a five-week period at Fort George alone.[11] By this time, however, yellow fever and dysentery had probably supplanted smallpox as the leading cause of death. In the end, it seems reasonable to suggest that very conservatively, some 100 soldiers per week died of smallpox over the seven-week period from early June until the end of July 1776, yielding a total of 700.

These grim statistics present only a partial picture of the pox's impact. Military hostilities spread *Variola* far and wide. Untold numbers may have died in Pennsylvania and Connecticut when returning soldiers launched epidemics there. In Nova Scotia, 144 died of smallpox in 1775 alone, and at least 7 more died in 1776. We have no indication of how many Indians succumbed after picking up the virus at the Cedars in May 1776, nor do we know how many expired at Michilimackinac, also infected by returning combatants. In addition, if the pestilence that swept the Iroquois castles of New York in 1776–77 was smallpox—and it probably was—this mortality would augment the total by 90 or more. The Oneidas and Senecas suffered again from the pox in 1780, 1781, and 1782, although the only known account of mortality relates solely to the death of 80 Senecas at Conewago, Pennsylvania. It therefore seems clear that at least 170 Iroquois succumbed to *Variola* over the course of the war. In all probability, the number was much higher. Moreover, when soldiers returning from Yorktown spread smallpox to troops on the Hudson River in 1781–82, some 58 Continentals died from both the "natural" and inoculated forms of the disease.[12]

For other northeastern outbreaks, meaningful statistics still need to be unearthed. An unknown number of people lost their lives to the pestilence in Pennsylvania's Wyoming Valley in 1778, and likewise, the number of fatalities along the Hudson River in the 1779 outbreak around New Concord remains a mystery. Residents of British-held New York City also contended with *Variola* in 1779–80, but even vague numbers have not yet been compiled. Similarly inaccessible are the smallpox fatalities among prisoners of war held aboard ships such as the notorious *Jersey*, anchored off Long Island. By the accounting of one inmate in October 1780, more than 10 a day had died over the previous three months.[13] But since these deaths resulted from a plethora of ailments including smallpox, the number attributable to *Variola* is impossible to ascertain.

In the Southeast in 1775–76, Lord Dunmore's Ethiopian Regiment left "nearly three hundred graves" behind at Tucker's Point near Norfolk. At Gwynn's Island, their next stopping point, they lost "near five hundred souls." In both locations, however, camp fever appears to have augmented the toll from smallpox. Even if *Variola* was responsible for only 60 percent of the fatalities—again, a conservative estimate—the toll would approach 480. Mortality among the unlucky Virginia soldiers and civilians who caught smallpox in the aftermath of the affair still needs to be appraised, so once more, the total numbers inevitably fall short. Among soldiers who underwent inoculation at the army's Virginia immunization sites in 1777–78, the known documentation reveals only 20 deaths at Alexandria.[14]

Elsewhere in the South, specific records of fatalities are likewise hard to come by. In late 1777 and early 1778, the pox appears to have taken the lives of 58 victims in Natchitoches. It arrived in New Orleans by November 1778, but the historical record has yet to reveal the resultant mortality. Records do indicate that in nearby Galveztown, a settlement of 404, some 161 people died between March 1779 and March 1780. Not all these deaths were from smallpox, but apparently "a large number" of them were. It thus seems safe to say that at least 80 Galveztown deaths resulted from *Variola*. To the east, the virus ravaged loyalist troops at Pensacola in the same period. There troop returns reveal that 40 soldiers lost their lives to the virus. The pox also raged "most violently" among nearby Creek Indians and "reduced them much." But because the available documents do not address morbidity or mortality, no estimate can be made in a population that almost certainly had some level of acquired immunity. In North Carolina, only 3 died when Pulaski's Legion left smallpox among the Moravians at Salem in the spring of 1779, but two years later the pestilence returned and took 10 lives.[15]

Statistics for the great tides of pox that swept Georgia, South Carolina, North Carolina, and Virginia with the southern campaign of the Revolutionary War are tantalizing but slim. George Abbott Hall stated vaguely that white South Carolinians lost more than 20,000 slaves to smallpox, camp fevers, and the British. Eliza Pinckney was likewise vague. "As the small pox was in the British camp," she wrote, "thousands of Negroes dyed miserably with it."[16] To judge by Pinckney's use of the plural "thousands," it seems safe to hazard that at a minimum, some 2,000 South Carolina blacks perished from the virus. Here too, the actual number may have been much higher.

Aboard the prison ships in Charleston Harbor in the summer and fall of 1780, smallpox, yellow fever, and "a putrid dysentery" combined to take more than 150 lives. Again, it is impossible to discern *Variola*'s portion of the blame. The pox also infected the jail and prison yard at Camden, South Carolina, where Andrew Jackson and his brother Robert picked it up in the spring of 1781. Certainly Robert cannot have been alone in losing his life to the contagion, but additional statistics remain to be compiled. In Wilmington, North Carolina, the Declaration of Independence signer William Hooper lost 5 slaves to smallpox when the war (and the virus) passed through in 1781.[17] Additional data would no doubt reveal losses in neighboring households as well.

In the summer and fall of 1781, the pox also spread through Virginia as the British army and its supporting column of refugees marched through the Tidewater's piney woods to Yorktown. At Portsmouth on July 13, General Alexander Leslie reported that smallpox currently afflicted more than 700 former slaves attached to his forces. Almost four weeks later, General Charles O'Hara reported "the Sick Negroes" at Portsmouth to be "above 1,000 in number." It is certainly possible that some of these loyalist freedom fighters had acquired the infection by inoculation. But records do not indicate if this was the case. During the siege of Yorktown, American soldiers such as Joseph Plumb Martin reported desperate former slaves "scattered about in every direction, dead and dying." St. George Tucker stated simply that the number of dead African Americans at Yorktown was "immense." In 1788, Thomas Jefferson gave his own retrospective appraisal of the damage: "I supposed the state of Virginia lost under Ld. Cornwallis's hands that year [1781] about 30,000 slaves, and that of these about 27,000 died of the small pox and camp fever."[18] Even if we cut this number in half to allow for exaggeration and for deaths from camp fever, the toll would be 13,500.

By the time of Yorktown, smallpox had also erupted in Mexico, migrated northward, and wreaked havoc across much of the American West. In Mexico City, estimates of fatalities ranged from "more than nine thousand" to "more than 18,000" to 22,000. The 18,000 estimate is probably the most accurate. When the pestilence moved southward into the Chuchumatán highlands of Guatemala, a region beyond the purview of this study, it took another 4,396 lives. North of Mexico City, 10,000 died in the mining center of Guanajuato.[19] The burial records of the Catholic Church point to a minimum of 18,053 more fatalities in Mexico alone. In New Mexico, another 5,025 mission Indians died.[20] These seemingly solid statistics in fact reveal only the tip of the pestilential iceberg. For one thing, *libros de entierros* do not survive for every parish. But more important, church records denoted only the demise of baptized Christians. Among non-Christian Native Americans, thousands of deaths inevitably went unrecorded.

In Texas, the Lipan Apaches near San Antonio told Domingo Cabello in December 1780 that they had lost "more than four hundred" in the pestilence. But beyond the northern frontier of New Spain, numerical accounts are more tenuous. Of the Apaches' Comanche enemies, we know only what Pedro Vial and Francisco Chaves reported of the Cuchanec (eastern) Comanches in 1785: "Two-thirds of them had died, from which had followed the total destruction of their nation." Despite the losses, Vial and Chaves said that the Cuchanecs still had "nearly two thousand men at arms" plus "many women and children." If these numbers are accurate, they indicate that 4,000 fighting men alone had died in the outbreak. Surely the number would more than double if women, children, and the elderly were taken into account. It is possible, of course, that the estimate of two-thirds mortality is an overstatement. But even if it is too high by half, at least 4,000 Comanches died. In addition to the Comanches, neighboring tribes—such as the Wichitas, Caddos, and Taovayas—may well have been afflicted, but the losses they sustained are thus far undetermined. Similarly, mortality data for the Comanches' Shoshone kinfolk are nonexistent despite the seminal role these Indians appear to have played in the epidemic's spread.[21]

Statistics are somewhat better, although still sparse, for other plains peoples. Using a variety of sources, the archaeologist Donald Lehmer estimated that the Mandans, Hidatsas, and Arikaras combined lost some 13,000 tribal members in the epidemic, reflecting an overall mortality rate of 68 percent among these groups. It may well have been the Crow Indians, also known as the Absarokas, who carried *Variola* to the Hidatsas and Mandans from the Shoshones to the west. Writing in 1805, after the Crows had suffered under another smallpox outbreak in 1801–02, François-Antoine Larocque put the tribe's numbers at 2,400. They "were reduced to their present number," he wrote, "by the ravage of the small Pox, which raged among them for many years successively & as late as three years ago. They told me they counted 2000 Lodges or tents in their Camp when all together before the small Pox had infected them." Larocque counted 8 persons per tent. Thus, by his accounting, the Crows had numbered approximately 16,000 before smallpox struck. Documentary evidence does not reveal the rate of morbidity (infectivity) for the 1781–82 outbreak among the Crows. But even if only half were infected and these suffered a 43 percent case fatality rate (as reported in Madras, India, in the 1960s), the tribe would have endured the loss of 3,440 people in the epidemic.[22] The losses among these Indians by 1805 indicate that both morbidity and mortality may have been much, much higher.

To the east, the Sioux enemy-neighbors of the Mandans and Hidatsas also suffered, although morbidity was probably lower thanks to their nomadic way of life. According to one estimate, these westward-pushing nomads numbered approximately 25,000 in 1780, the year before the epidemic struck. Some individuals almost certainly benefited from immunity acquired in the epidemic of 1734–35, so overall mortality rates would have been lower than among many other peoples, but even if the epidemic infected only one-third of all Sioux, some 8,333 Indians would have become ill. Moreover, if it had a case fatality rate of 43 percent, some 3,583 would have lost their lives.[23]

Northeast of the Sioux, the Ojibwa Indians probably had a higher level of acquired immunity than that found among most plains tribes, since many of them would have been survivors of the outbreak of 1757. William W. Warren, the nineteenth-century linguist-historian who recorded the story of the Ojibwas' infection in their attack on the Hidatsas in 1781, also appraised their mortality rate. Growing up among the Ojibwas, Warren clearly heard his numbers from survivors. "As near as can be computed from their accounts at the present day," he wrote in 1852–53, their losses "amounted to not less than fifteen hundred, or two thousand."[24]

The Ojibwas' neighbors on the northern grasslands were not so lucky. Fur trade writings indicate that across the Canadian plains, the death toll was ghastly. As we have seen, estimates of overall mortality among the Atsinas, Crees, Assiniboines, Chipewyans, and Blackfeet ranged from 50 to 98 percent. But for the northern plains and western Canadian Shield, as for the Comanches in the south, the dearth of pre-epidemic demographic data hinders any attempt at a precise appraisal of fatalities in 1781–82. The geographer Jody Decker has put the Canadian plains Indian population at 16,500 in 1800. Obviously, by this time, some recovery—even dramatic recovery—may have occurred, even if (as Decker suggests) it never exceeded 1 percent per year. (At a 1 percent growth rate, a population that has suffered 40 percent mortality can recover its numbers in full after forty years; after thirty years, a 94 percent recovery.) "The Small Pox some years ago made great havock among these people, and destroyed entire Camps," wrote Alexander Henry of the plains Crees in 1809. "They are however again increasing very fast in numbers." The Blackfeet too were "increasing very fast every day." John Ewers has speculated that the Piegan Blackfeet actually managed to double their postsmallpox population by 1809.[25]

If Decker's estimate of 16,500 plains natives in 1800 reflects an optimistic 1 percent growth rate over the previous 18 years, it indicates a population of 13,794 immediately following the smallpox outbreak. Moreover, if this number reflects a 43 percent loss (a figure that is actually lower than that reported in many firsthand accounts), it points to a pre-epidemic population of 24,200 and the loss of some 10,406 lives in the great pestilence. It should be stressed that this number is speculative. It assumes an infection rate of 100 percent, surely not the case. But because the fur traders themselves so often suggested that mortality actually exceeded 43 percent of the population, the 10,406 figure seems a fair starting point. The overall mortality may well have been closer to the 50 to 75 percent reported by many eyewitnesses.[26] Furthermore, nonplains Indians such as the Swampy Crees and the Chipewyans are not included here, although they certainly incurred losses during the epidemic.

For the late eighteenth century, sound numbers are nowhere more elusive than in the greater Northwest. Among the Flatheads, we have only an improbable report collected by the missionary Gregory Mengarini in 1847, which said that of 4,000 Flatheads, the only survivors of the epidemic were 15 children and a hunting party that escaped infection. Clearly, this appraisal is beyond the limits of credulity. For the Nez Perces, no useful statistics have yet surfaced, although we know the tribe did not escape the pestilence. Farther west, Robert Boyd has recently placed the precontact population of the Northwest Coast at 188,344. No outbreaks of Old World disease are known to have afflicted these Indians prior to smallpox in the late eighteenth century, and Boyd estimates (conservatively) that the first epidemic had a mortality rate of 30 percent among groups afflicted. These groups appear to have included the Tlingits, the Haidas, the Nitinahts (Nootkans), the upper Chinookans, the Tillamooks, and most of the Coast Salish. As a whole, these nations had an estimated precontact population of 83,832.[27] If they did indeed experience 30 percent mortality, 25,149 died in the epidemic. This estimate, moreover, may well be too low. Mortality could certainly have been higher than 30 percent, and other afflicted groups of Northwest Coast natives may have escaped documentation.

None of the numbers offered here should be considered precise or irrefutable. They are rough estimates at best, and they are intended to be a starting point. But rough or not, they indicate that more than 130,000 North Americans died in the great small-

PLACE/PEOPLE	BASELINE (MINIMAL) MORTALITY ESTIMATE
Boston	287
Quebec	538
Retreat from Canada (American troops)	700
Nova Scotia	153
Iroquois	170
Hudson River/Highlands	58
Ethiopian Regiment	480
Alexandria	20
Natchitoches	58
Galveztown	80
Pensacola	40
N.C. Moravians	13
S.C. black loyalists	2,000
Wilmington, N.C.	5
Va. black loyalists	3,500
Mexico City	18,000
Guanajuato (city only)	10,000
Mexico (excluding Mexico City and Guanajuato)	18,053
New Mexico	5,025
Comanches	4,000
Mandans, Hidatsas, and Arikaras	13,000
Lipan Apaches	400
Crows	3,440
Sioux	3,583
Ojibwas	1,500
Northern Plains Indians	10,406
Northwest Coast Indians	25,149
TOTAL	130,658

Baseline (minimal) mortality from smallpox, 1775–82

pox pestilence of 1775–82. In roughly the same years, just over 25,000 soldiers died in the service of the Continental army, and these included some who succumbed to the pox.[28] The disparity between these numbers should give us pause, especially since it would almost certainly be even greater if better documentation existed for *Variola*'s ravages. But even the baseline figure of 130,658 directs our attention away from the standard historical narrative. While the American Revolution may have defined the era for history, epidemic smallpox nevertheless defined it for many of the Americans who lived and died in that time.

The American Revolution, the seminal event of the era, was not excluded from *Variola*'s maelstrom. Nor did events stop elsewhere while the revolutionary conflict was waged. The very breadth of *Variola*'s movement redirects our attention to turmoils occurring in places far removed from the well-known fields of battle. The pestilence can teach us the ways in which other upheavals—native warfare, missionization, the fur trade, and the acquisition of horses and guns, all of which enabled *Variola* to be transmitted—had already reshaped human life on the North American continent. The movement of the virus from one human being to another shows us how people actually lived in the late eighteenth century. For despite the political, social, and racial boundaries of the day, people rubbed elbows: They lived side by side, they talked, they fought, they traveled, they traded, and in these daily transactions, they passed *Variola* on to one another.

Smallpox moved incrementally through incidental encounters, yet it also seemed to move with a purpose. In a New World environment where acquired immunity was rare, *Variola* was a virus of empire. It made winners and losers, at once serving the conquerors and determining whom they would be. Smallpox reshaped political and military relations across the continent, even as the Revolution reshaped such relations around the world. In the short term, even such Native American groups as the Sioux and the Blackfeet could benefit from the devastation smallpox left behind, but in the long run, the pestilence seemed invariably to favor the great imperial powers of Europe and the United States. Over the course of the nineteenth century, both the Sioux and the Blackfeet suffered dramatic losses not just to Anglo-American interlopers and the whiskey they brought with them but also to recurring bouts of smallpox and other Old World diseases.[29] An unwitting instrument of empire, the pestilence of 1775–82 constitutes another piece in the larger puzzle of Native American population decline as European settlements expanded. It clearly shows that the enormous losses of the early postcontact era were followed by continued losses at a lesser level. Nearly three centuries after Columbus sailed, indigenous depopulation remained far-reaching and ongoing.

The most fundamental outcome of the pestilence of 1775–82, though, was massive human suffering and mortality. All other consequences stemmed from this. Many years after smallpox struck, the physical manifestations of this human toll were still visible not just in the scars borne by survivors but also in a landscape littered with empty villages, human remains, and the graveyards of the dead. In 1801, the Arctic explorer Alexander Mackenzie described a point on Saskatchewan's Churchill River called Portage des Morts. "On the left side," he explained, "is a point covered with human bones, the relics of the small pox." An adjoining body of water still bears the designation "Dead Lake." A year earlier, Alexander Henry had camped at the confluence of the Assiniboine and Red rivers, once the site of a village decimated by *Variola* when a returning war party carried the virus home. He found "an uncommon number" of old graves in the empty town, which had "been a place of great resort for the Nations many Years ago in 1781 & 2" when "the small pox made such havock." According to Henry, "many hundreds of men, women and children died and was buried here." Hundreds of miles to the west, at an old camp on the South Saskatchewan River, Peter Fidler likewise found the remains of seven adults and a child in September 1800. "These people have either been killed by an Enemy," he wrote, "or else cut off by the small pox in the fall [of] 1781."[30]

All these scenes were of a piece with the reports from elsewhere. The mass graves at Île-aux-Noix, the deserted Indian towns on the upper Missouri River, the crowded cemeteries of Culiacán, and the desolate, bone-littered villages along the Pacific Northwest Coast were emblems of a common experience that spanned the continent from 1775 to 1782. "This was the small pox," wrote Alexander Mackenzie, "which spread its destructive and desolating power, as the fire consumes the dry grass of the field."[31]

NOTES

ABBREVIATIONS

Online Computer Library Center (OCLC) designations are used wherever possible.

AASF   Archives of the Archdiocese of Santa Fe, Santa Fe, New Mexico

Am. Arch.   Peter Force, ed., *American Archives*, 6 volumes (Washington, D.C.: n.p., 1837–53)

CLU (WAC)   William Andrews Clark Memorial Library, University of California, Los Angeles, California

DLC   Library of Congress, Washington, D.C.

FHL   Family History Library of the Church of Jesus Christ of Latter-day Saints, Salt Lake City, Utah

HUV   Henry E. Huntington Library, San Marino, California

IXA (CAH)   Center for American History, University of Texas at Austin

March to Quebec   Kenneth Roberts, ed., *March to Quebec: Journals of the Members of Arnold's Expedition* (3d ed., New York: Doubleday, Doran & Co., 1940)

Med. in Va.   Wyndham B. Blanton, *Medicine in Virginia in the Eighteenth Century* (Richmond: Garrett and Massie, 1931)

MLC   William L. Clements Library, University of Michigan, Ann Arbor, Michigan

NAC   National Archives of Canada, Ottawa, Ontario

NAC (HBC)   Hudson's Bay Company Archives (microfilm copy), National Archives of Canada, Ottawa, Ontario

NAR	National Archives, Washington, D.C.
NAR (PCC)	Papers of the Continental Congress, National Archives, Washington, D.C.
Nav. Docs.	William Bell Clark, William James Morgan, and Michael J. Crawford, eds., *Naval Documents of the American Revolution*, 10 volumes (Washington, D.C.: Naval Historical Center, Department of the Navy, 1964–96)
NL4	New Hampshire Historical Society, Concord, New Hampshire
Pa. Gaz.	*Pennsylvania Gazette*
Papers of G. W.	W. W. Abbot and Dorothy Twohig, eds., *The Papers of George Washington*, 39 volumes (Charlottesville: University Press of Virginia, 1983–)
Papers of T. J.	Julian P. Boyd, ed., *The Papers of Thomas Jefferson*, 28 volumes (Princeton: Princeton University Press, 1950–)
DV6 (SANM)	Spanish Archives of New Mexico, 1621–1821, State of New Mexico Records Center, Santa Fe, New Mexico
Smallpox and Its Eradication	F. Fenner, D. A. Henderson, I. Arita, Z. Ježek, and I. D. Ladnyi, *Smallpox and Its Eradication* (Geneva: World Health Organization, 1988)
RQE	Bancroft Library, University of California, Berkeley, California
VIC	Library of Virginia, Richmond, Virginia
Writings of G. W.	John C. Fitzpatrick, ed., *The Writings of George Washington*, 39 volumes (Washington, D.C.: U.S. Government Printing Office, 1931–44)
WMQ	*William and Mary Quarterly*
YUS (B)	Beinecke Rare Book and Manuscript Library, Yale University, New Haven, Connecticut

INTRODUCTION

1. F. Fenner et al., *Smallpox and Its Eradication* (Geneva: World Health Organization, 1988), 467 (hereafter cited as *Smallpox and Its Eradication*).
2. George Vancouver, *A Voyage of Discovery to the North Pacific Ocean and round the World, 1791–1795*, ed. William Kaye Lamb (London: Hakluyt Society, 1984), 2:516–17.
3. Ibid., 2:520, 536, 538.
4. While he acknowledges the possible impact of disease on northwestern cultures, editor William Kaye Lamb nevertheless suggests that Vancou-

ver was obsessed with depopulation "not only here but elsewhere." Ibid., 2:540 n. 1.

5. Ibid., 2:538; Peter Puget, "The Vancouver Expedition: Peter Puget's Journal of the Exploration of Puget Sound, May 7–June 11, 1792," *Pacific Northwest Quarterly* 30 (April 1939): 215; and Thomas Manby, "Voyage of H.M.S. Discovery and Chatham to the Northwest Coast of America," Beinecke Rare Book and Manuscript Library, Yale University, New Haven, Connecticut, 2d part, 18, 26–27 (hereafter cited as YUS [B]).

6. Vancouver, *Voyage of Discovery*, 2:528.

7. On Jenner turning down Cook, see Donald R. Hopkins, *Princes and Peasants: Smallpox in History* (Chicago: University of Chicago Press, 1983), 77. For Menzies' account, see Archibald Menzies, *Menzies' Journal of Vancouver's Voyage, April to October 1792*, ed. C. F. Newcombe, Archives of British Columbia, memoir 5 (Victoria, B.C., 1923), 29, 35.

8. Vancouver, *Voyage of Discovery*, 2:540.

1. VARIOLA

1. For the diary entries used in this sketch and for an explanation of dating difficulties, see George Washington, *The Diaries of George Washington*, ed. Donald Jackson and Dorothy Twohig (Charlottesville: University Press of Virginia, 1976), 1:33–35, 73, 82–83.

2. Washington, *Diaries*, 1:73; and *Smallpox and Its Eradication*, 117–18, 1333.

3. *Smallpox and Its Eradication*, 6, 41, 188.

4. Cyril William Dixon, *Smallpox* (London: J. & A. Churchill, 1962), chap. 2; *Smallpox and Its Eradication*, chap. 1; and A. Ramachandra Rao, *Smallpox* (Bombay: Kothari Book Depot, 1972), 17–18. For an example of deadly "early hemorrhagic" or "fulminating" smallpox among American Indians, see E. E. Rich, ed., *Cumberland House Journals and Inland Journals*, 2d ser., 1779–82 (London: Hudson's Bay Record Society, 1952), 231, 234.

5. *Smallpox and Its Eradication*, 5; Douglass to Colden, May 1, 1722, in Jared Sparks, ed., "Letters from Dr. William Douglass to Dr. Cadwallader Colden of New York," *Collections of the Massachusetts Historical Society*, 4th ser., 2 (1854): 168; António Blásques to Diego Mirón, Bahia, May 31, 1563, in *Monumenta Brasilae*, ed. Serafim Soares Leite (Rome, 1956–60), 4:55, quoted in John Hemming, *Red Gold: The Conquest of the Brazilian Indians* (Cambridge: Harvard University Press, 1978), 142.

6. William Bradford, *Bradford's History of Plymouth Plantation, 1606–1646*, ed. William T. Davis (1908; rpt., New York: Barnes & Noble, 1971), 313; and Simão de Vasconcellos, *Das cousas do Brasil*, and *Chronica da Compa-*

nhia de Jesus do Estado do Brasil e do que obrarão seus filhos nesta parte do Novo Mundo (Lisbon, 1663; Lisbon, 1865), bk. 3:283, quoted in Hemming, *Red Gold*, 142.

7. James Thomas Flexner, *George Washington* (Boston: Little, Brown, 1965), 1:50.

8. The statistics cited are drawn from the following sources: Anne Hardy, "Smallpox in London: Factors in the Decline of the Disease in the Nineteenth Century," *Medical History* 27 (April 1983): 111–13; Ann G. Carmichael and Arthur M. Silverstein, "Smallpox in Europe before the Seventeenth Century: Virulent Killer or Benign Disease?," *Journal of the History of Medicine* 42 (April 1987): 147–68; John B. Blake, *Public Health in the Town of Boston, 1630–1822* (Cambridge: Harvard University Press, 1959), 244; Deborah Brunton, "Smallpox Inoculation and Demographic Trends in Eighteenth Century Scotland," *Medical History* 36 (October 1992): 410; *Smallpox and Its Eradication*, 227; and Rao, *Smallpox*, 37.

9. *Smallpox and Its Eradication*, 176.

10. Rao, *Smallpox*, 121–26; and *Smallpox and Its Eradication*, 5.

11. *Smallpox and Its Eradication*, 50, 164; David Arnold, "Social Crisis and Epidemic Disease in the Famines of 19th-Century India," *Social History of Medicine* 6 (December 1993): 385–404; and Linea Sundstrom, "Smallpox Used Them Up: References to Epidemic Disease in Plains Winter Counts," *Ethnohistory* 44 (Spring 1997): 317–20.

12. The friar is quoted in Robert McCaa, "Spanish and Nahuatl Views on Smallpox and Demographic Catastrophe in Mexico," *Journal of Interdisciplinary History* 25 (Winter 1995): 399. Bradford's account is in his *History of Plymouth Plantation*, 312. See also John Winthrop, *Winthrop's Journal: "History of New England," 1630–1649*, ed. James Kendall Hosmer (1908; rpt., New York: Barnes & Noble, 1966), 111, 119.

13. Samuel Hearne, *A Journey from Prince of Wales's Fort in Hudson's Bay to the Northern Ocean in the Years 1769, 1770, 1771, and 1772*, ed. J. B. Tyrell (Toronto: Champlain Society, 1911), 200–01; "The Red River, by John McDonnell of the North-West Company," in W. Raymond Wood and Thomas D. Thiessen, eds., *Early Fur Trade on the Northern Plains: Canadian Traders among the Mandan and Hidatsa Indians, 1738–1818* (Norman: University of Oklahoma Press, 1985), 82; David Zeisberger, *Diary of David Zeisberger, a Moravian Missionary among the Indians of Ohio*, ed. Eugene F. Bliss (Cincinnati: Robert Clarke, 1885), 1:362; and Charles Larpenteur, *Forty Years a Fur Trader on the Upper Missouri: The Personal Narrative of Charles Larpenteur, 1833–1872*, ed. Elliot Coues (rpt., Minneapolis: Ross & Haines, 1962), 134.

14. Ignaz Pfefferkorn, *Sonora: A Description of the Province*, trans. Theodore E.

Treutlein (Albuquerque: University of New Mexico Press, 1949), 219; and Antoine Simon Le Page du Pratz, *The History of Louisiana, or of the Western Parts of Virginia and Carolina* (1774; rpt., New Orleans: J.S.W. Harmanson, 1947), 305.

15. William Walker, "Hudson House Journal, 1781–82," in Rich, *Cumberland and Hudson House Journals*, 265; Luis Sales, *Observations on California, 1772–1790*, ed. Charles N. Rudkin (Los Angeles: Glen Dawson, 1956), 60–61; and Rao, *Smallpox*, 55.

16. John Ferdinand Dalziel Smyth, *A Tour in the United States of America* (Dublin: G. Perrin, 1784), 119–20; Daniel Williams Harmon, "A General Account of the Indians on the East Side of the Rocky Mountain," in *A Journal of Voyages and Travels in the Interior of North America* (New York: A. S. Barnes, 1903), 271; and Nicholas Cresswell, *The Journal of Nicholas Cresswell, 1774–1777* (1924; rpt., Port Washington, N.Y.: Kennikat Press, 1968), 113.

17. Smyth, *Tour*, 119–20; Mourning Dove, *Mourning Dove: A Salishan Autobiography*, ed. Jay Miller (Lincoln: University of Nebraska Press, 1990), 15–16; Ross Cox, *The Columbia River: Or Scenes and Adventures during a Residence of Six Years on the Western Side of the Rocky Mountains* (Norman: University of Oklahoma Press, 1957), 169–70. For other accounts of drownings, see Joseph Ioor Waring, *A History of Medicine in South Carolina 1670–1825* (Columbia: South Carolina Medical Assoc., 1964), 74; Emmanuel Henri Dieudonné Domenech, *Seven Years Residence in the Great Deserts of North America* (London: Longman, Green, Longman and Roberts, 1860), 1:431; Henry R. Schoolcraft, *Historical and Statistical Information Respecting the History, Condition, and Prospects of the Indian Tribes of the United States* (Philadelphia: Lippincott, Grambo, 1857), 1:234; and Sales, *Observations*, 60–61.

18. J. D. Schöpf, *Travels in the Confederation, 1783–1784*, trans. and ed. Alfred J. Morrison (1911; rpt., New York: Bergman, 1968), 1:286. For one British physician's prescribed treatment for smallpox, see Thomas Dickson Reide, *A View of the Diseases of the Army in Great Britain, America, the West Indies, and on Board of King's Ships and Transports* (London: J. Johnson, 1793), 274–75. Additional descriptions of treatments can be found in John Duffy, *Epidemics in Colonial America* (Baton Rouge: Louisiana State University Press, 1953), 8–9; and Ola Elizabeth Winslow, *A Destroying Angel: The Conquest of Smallpox in Colonial Boston* (Boston: Houghton Mifflin, 1974), 7.

19. Alfred W. Crosby, Jr., "Virgin Soil Epidemics as a Factor in the Aboriginal Depopulation in America," *William and Mary Quarterly* 33 (1976): 291–92 (hereafter cited as *WMQ*).

20. The study of innate immunity is developing rapidly today. The current state of the field is elegantly summarized in Ruslan Medzhitov and Charles Janeway, Jr., "Innate Immunity," *New England Journal of Medicine* 343 (August 2000): 338–44. For a short but seminal overview of human immune response, see Peter J. Delves and Ivan M. Roitt, "The Immune System," *New England Journal of Medicine* 343 (July 2000): 37–49, 108–17.

21. Francis L. Black, "An Explanation of High Death Rates among New World Peoples When in Contact with Old World Diseases," *Perspectives in Biology and Medicine* 37 (Winter 1994): 295.

22. Ibid., 296–99, 305–06.

23. Ibid., 299–300; and Francis L. Black, "Why Did They Die?," *Science* 258 (December 1992): 1739.

24. Black, "Explanation," 300; and Black, "Why Did They Die?," 1740.

25. S. R. Duncan, Susan Scott, and C. J. Duncan, "The Dynamics of Small-pox Epidemics in Britain, 1550–1800," *Demography* 30 (August 1993): 409–12; and S. R. Duncan, S. Scott, and C. J. Duncan, "An Hypothesis for the Periodicity of Smallpox Epidemics as Revealed by Time Series Analysis," *Journal of Theoretical Biology* 160 (January 1993): 233–39.

26. Henry F. Dobyns, with the assistance of William R. Swagerty, *Their Number Become Thinned: Native Population Dynamics in Eastern North America* (Knoxville: University of Tennessee Press, 1983), 15 (table 1); and Ann F. Ramenofsky, *Vectors of Death: The Archaeology of European Contact* (Albuquerque: University of New Mexico Press, 1987), passim.

27. On the Seven Years' War, see D. Peter MacLeod, "Microbes and Muskets: Smallpox and the Participation of the Amerindian Allies of New France in the Seven Years' War," *Ethnohistory* 39 (Winter 1992): 42–64. On Pontiac's Revolt, see Elizabeth A. Fenn, "Biological Warfare in Eighteenth-Century America: Beyond Jeffery Amherst," *Journal of American History* 86 (March 2000): 1552–58. On the Georgia and South Carolina epidemic, see Suzanne Krebsbach, "The Great Charlestown Smallpox Epidemic of 1760," *South Carolina Historical Magazine* 97 (January 1996): 30–37. On Mexico and northern New Spain, see Donald B. Cooper, *Epidemic Disease in Mexico City, 1761–1813: An Administrative, Social, and Medical Study* (Austin: University of Texas Press, 1965), 56; Robert H. Jackson, "Causes of Indian Population Decline in the Pimería Alta Missions of Northern Sonora," *Journal of Arizona History* 24 (1983): 409, 412–13; Robert H. Jackson, "Epidemic Disease and Population Decline in the Baja California Missions, 1697–1834," *Southern California Quarterly* 63 (Winter 1981): 316, 321; and Jacob Baegert, *Observations in Lower California*, trans. M. M. Brandenberg (Berkeley: University of California Press, 1952), 77. On Texas and the lower Mississippi, see Curtis

D. Tunnell and W. W. Newcomb, *A Lipan Apache Mission: San Lorenzo de la Santa Cruz, 1762–1771*, Texas Memorial Museum Bulletin 14 (July 1969): 171; and John Duffy, "Smallpox and the Indians in the American Colonies," *Bulletin of the History of Medicine* 25 (1951): 340. On Philadelphia and Boston, see Francis R. Packard, *History of Medicine in the United States* (New York: Paul B. Hoeber, 1931), 1:88; and Blake, *Public Health*, 244.

28. François-Alexandre-Frédéric duc de La Rochefoucauld-Liancourt, *Travels through the United States of North America, the Country of the Iroquois, and Upper Canada in the Years 1795, 1796, and 1797* (London: T. Davison, 1799), 1:40–42; Winthrop, *Winthrop's Journal*, 2:329; *South Carolina Provincial Statutes*, 1738, chap. 651, cited in Elizabeth C. Tandy, "Local Quarantine and Inoculation for Smallpox in the American Colonies, 1620–1775," *American Journal of Public Health* 13 (March 1923): 205; Wyndham B. Blanton, *Medicine in Virginia in the Eighteenth Century* (Richmond: Garrett and Massie, 1931), 287 (hereafter cited as *Med. in Va.*); Johann Conrad Döhla, *A Hessian Diary of the American Revolution*, ed. and trans. Bruce E. Burgoyne (Norman: University of Oklahoma Press, 1990), 97; Tandy, "Local Quarantine," 205; and Blake, *Public Health*, 109.

29. *Pennsylvania Gazette* (hereafter cited as *Pa. Gaz.*), no. 1654, September 4, 1760, quoted in Duffy, "Smallpox and the Indians," 338.

30. Letter of Mrs. Affra Coming to her sister, MSS. letters in possession of Mr. Isaac Ball, quoted in Edward McCrady, *The History of South Carolina under the Proprietary Government, 1670–1719* (New York: Macmillan, 1897), 308; Duffy, *Epidemics*, 23; Blake, *Public Health*, 109; and *Pa. Gaz.*, no. 1654, September 4, 1760, quoted in Duffy, "Smallpox and the Indians," 338.

31. *Pa. Gaz.*, no. 1654, September 4, 1760, quoted in Duffy, "Smallpox and the Indians," 338. The same thing had probably occurred during the 1721 epidemic, when smallpox very likely spread from Boston to Cambridge, Roxbury, Brookline, Medford, and later Marblehead. Duffy, *Epidemics*, 52, 60.

32. George Lyman Kittredge, ed., "Lost Works of Cotton Mather," *Proceedings of the Massachusetts Historical Society* 45 (1912): 422. The history of inoculation in Africa is obscure at best. The practice was not common on the west coast, but it was used more frequently inland. As a Coromantee, Onesimus may well have come from the central Sudan, and that might explain his familiarity with the practice. Eugenia Herbert, "Smallpox Inoculation in Africa," *Journal of African History* 16 (1975): 543. See also Richard Pankhurst, "The History and Traditional Treatment of Smallpox in Ethiopia," *Medical History* 9 (October 1965): 343–55; and Larry Stew-

art, "The Edge of Utility: Slaves and Smallpox in the Early Eighteenth Century," *Medical History* 29 (January 1985): 54–70. Montagu is quoted in Donald R. Hopkins, *Princes and Peasants: Smallpox in History* (Chicago: University of Chicago Press, 1983), 47.

33. Edward J. Edwardes, *A Concise History of Small-Pox and Vaccination in Europe* (London: H. K. Lewis, 1902), quoted in *Smallpox and Its Eradication*, 261.

34. Duffy, *Epidemics*, 35–37; Winslow, *Destroying Angel*, 57–58 and passim; Blake, *Public Health*, 244.

35. William Douglass, *A Dissertation Concerning Inoculation of the Smallpox* (London, 1730), 63, quoted in Winslow, *Destroying Angel*, 86–87.

36. John Adams, *Diary and Autobiography of John Adams*, ed. L. H. Butterfield (Cambridge: Belknap Press of Harvard University Press, 1961), 3:280; and Adams to Smith, April 8, 1764, in L. H. Butterfield et al., eds., *The Book of Abigail and John: Selected Letters of the Adams Family 1762–1784* (Cambridge: Harvard University Press, 1975), 24.

37. Adams, *Diary*, 3:280. I am indebted to Dr. Walter Rogan of the National Institutes of Health for diagnosing Adams's symptoms as mercury poisoning. Adams to Smith, April 4, 1764, and Adams to Smith, April 11, 1764, in Butterfield et al., *Book of Abigail and John*, 24, 26.

38. Adams to Smith, April 13, 1764, in Butterfield et al., *Book of Abigail and John*, 30–31.

39. Adams to Smith, April 17, 1764, ibid., 34.

40. Adams to Smith, April 26, 1764, ibid., 38–39.

41. Adams to Smith, April 26, 1764, ibid., 39–40.

42. Blake, *Public Health*, 129; and Joseph Ioor Waring, "James Killpatrick and Smallpox Inoculation in Charleston," *Annals of Medical History* 10 (July 1938): 304–05.

43. Abigail Adams to John Adams, July 13, 1776, in Butterfield et al., *Book of Abigail and John*, 144.

44. Edmund Massey, *A Sermon against the Dangerous and Sinful Practice of Inoculation* (London, 1722), 24, quoted in Duffy, *Epidemics*, 31; Douglass to Colden, Boston, May 1, 1722, in Sparks, "Letters from Douglass to Colden," 170; and Cotton Mather, *The Diary of Cotton Mather*, ed. Worthington Chauncey Ford, *Collections of the Massachusetts Historical Society* 68 (Boston, 1912): 658.

45. Abigail Adams to John Adams, July 21, 1776, in Butterfield et al., *Book of Abigail and John*, 148.

46. Abigail Adams to John Adams, July 21, 1776, and Abigail Adams to John Adams, August 5, 1776, ibid., 148, 151.

47. Abigail Adams to John Adams, March 31, 1776, ibid., 120.

48. Henry Newman, "The Way of Proceeding in the Small Pox Inoculation in New England," *Philosophical Transactions* 32 (1722): 33–34, quoted in Duffy, *Epidemics*, 37–38; and James Thacher, *Military Journal of the American Revolution* (1862; rpt., New York: New York Times, 1969), 44.

49. William Nelson to John Norton, August 14, 1767, and February 27, 1768, in Frances Norton Mason, ed., *John Norton & Sons, Merchants of London and Virginia* (Richmond: Dietz Press, 1937), 31–32, 38, See also *Med. in Va.*, 285.

50. On the links between crowd violence against smallpox hospitals and crowd action against the British crown, see Pauline Maier, *From Resistance to Revolution: Colonial Radicals and the Development of American Opposition to Britain, 1765–1776* (New York: Vintage Books, 1972), 4–5, 13. The Norfolk incident is described in *Med. in Va.*, 285. For more on the Massachusetts episodes, see George A. Billias, "Pox and Politics in Marblehead 1773–1774," *Essex Institute Historical Collections* 92 (1956): 43–58; Gerard H. Clarfield, "Salem's Great Inoculation Controversy, 1773–1774," *Essex Institute Historical Collections* 106 (1970): 277–96; and Richard W. Searle, "History of Catta Island off Marblehead," *Essex Institute Historical Collections* 83 (1947): 323.

51. The Virginia petitions and regulations can be found in John P. Kennedy, ed., *Journals of the House of Burgesses of Virginia, 1766–1769* (Richmond: [Library Board, Virginia State Library], 1906), 203, 246, 269. See also Hening, *Statutes at Large*, 8:371–73, cited in *Med. in Va.*, 285. For the South Carolina law, see Duffy, *Epidemics*, 38; and *South Carolina Provincial Statutes*, 1738, chap. 551, cited in Tandy, "Local Quarantine," 206. On New York, see Proclamation of Governor George Clinton of New York, June 6, 1747, quoted in Packard, *History of Medicine*, 1:82, in turn quoted in Duffy, *Epidemics*, 38.

52. Benjamin Waterhouse, *A Prospect of Exterminating the Small Pox Part II . . .* (Cambridge, 1802), 6, quoted in Blake, *Public Health*, 108–09.

53. Blake, *Public Health*, 109; Rind's *Virginia Gazette*, April 13, 1769, quoted in *Med. in Va.*, 286; and Purdie and Dixon's *Virginia Gazette*, 1772, 1773, and March 17, 1774, quoted in *Med. in Va.*, 285–86.

54. Searle, "History of Catta Island," 328–29; and unattributed quotations in Carl Bridenbaugh, *Cities in Revolt: Urban Life in America, 1743–1776* (New York: Oxford University Press, 1955), 328–30.

55. José G. Rigau-Pérez, "Smallpox Epidemics in Puerto Rico during the Prevaccine Era (1518–1803)," *Journal of the History of Medicine and Allied Sciences* 37 (October 1982): 423–38; and Genevieve Miller, *The Adoption of Inoculation for Smallpox in England and France* (Philadelphia: University of Pennsylvania Press, 1957), 195–240.

56. Blake, *Public Health*, 113n, 114; Hopkins, *Princes and Peasants*, 256; and Bridenbaugh, *Cities in Revolt*, 129.
57. Benjamin Franklin and Heberden, *Some Account of the Success of Inoculation*, 5–6, quoted in Blake, *Public Health*, 113; and unattributed quotation in Bridenbaugh, *Cities in Revolt*, 329.
58. Hopkins, *Princes and Peasants*, 256; Blake, *Public Health*, 108; and Bridenbaugh, *Cities in Revolt*, 329.
59. Hopkins, *Princes and Peasants*, 76; and Bridenbaugh, *Cities in Revolt*, 326–27, 329. On the success of the institution, see *Pa. Gaz.*, May 29, 1776.

2. VIGILANCE

1. For the diary entries used in this sketch, see Matthew Patten, *The Diary of Matthew Patten of Bedford, N.H.: From Seventeen Hundred Fifty-four to Seventeen Hundred Eighty-eight* (Concord, N.H.: Rumford Printing, 1903), 342–43, 345, 348–49, 352, 356, 358.
2. John Adams, *Diary and Autobiography of John Adams*, ed. L. H. Butterfield (Cambridge: Belknap Press of Harvard University Press, 1961), 2:93. On liberty as contagion, see Bernard Bailyn, *The Ideological Origins of the American Revolution* (Cambridge: Belknap Press of Harvard University Press, 1967), chap. 6.
3. John Duffy, *Epidemics in Colonial America* (Baton Rouge: Louisiana State University Press, 1953), 68–69; Manasseh Cutler, *The Life, Journals, and Correspondence of Manasseh Cutler, LL.D.*, ed. William P. Cutler and Julia L. Cutler (Cincinnati: R. Clarke, 1888), 1:45; Duffy, *Epidemics*, 68–69; Philip Cash, *Medical Men at the Siege of Boston* (Philadelphia: American Philosophical Society, 1973), 37n, 38–39; and Ezekiel Price, "Diary," *Proceedings of the Massachusetts Historical Society*, 1st ser., 7 (November 1863): 185. On smallpox in Boston, see *Pa. Gaz.*, February 15, 1775, and February 22, 1775.
4. Christopher Marshall, *Passages from the Remembrancer of Christopher Marshall*, ed. William Duane, Jr. (Philadelphia: James Crissy, 1839), 38.
5. On early efforts at prevention and quarantine, see Cash, *Medical Men*, 38. On the army's smallpox hospital, see GW, General Orders, July 4, 1775, in John C. Fitzpatrick, ed., *The Writings of George Washington* (Washington, D.C.: U.S. Government Printing Office, 1931), 3:310 (hereafter cited as *Writings of G. W.*); and GW, General Orders, July 27, 1775, in *Writings of G. W.*, 3:369. There are two versions of the Hancock letter. The first is quoted here: GW to the President of Congress, Cambridge, July 21, 1775, Papers of the Continental Congress, National Archives, Washington,

D.C., M247, r166, i152, v1, p35 (hereafter cited as NAR [PCC]). Cf. GW to the President of Congress, July 20, 1775, in *Writings of G. W.*, 3:350–51.

6. Richard Frothingham, *History of the Siege of Boston* (3d ed., Boston: Little, Brown, 1872), 237. The petition of July 21 is included with the Resolve on the Petition of the Select Men of Boston, July 27, 1775, Thomas Gage Papers, 1754–83, Amer. Ser., 132, William L. Clements Library, University of Michigan, Ann Arbor, Michigan (hereafter cited as MLC).

7. Resolve on the Petition of the Select Men of Boston, July 27, 1775, Thomas Gage Papers, 1754–83, Amer. Ser., 132, MLC. The resolution (but not the petition) can also be found in Peter Force, ed., *American Archives*, 4th ser. (Washington, D.C.: n.p, 1840), 3:279–80 (hereafter cited as *Am. Arch.*).

8. Resolution of the Mass. House of Representatives, October 5, 1775, in *Am. Arch.*, 4th ser., 3:1454. Cf. Reports of Captain Dodge, December 16, 1775, ibid., 4:298–99.

9. Benjamin F. Stevens, ed., *General Sir William Howe's Orderly Book at Charlestown, Boston, and Halifax, June 17, 1775 to May 26, 1776* (1890; rpt., Port Washington, N.Y.: Kennikat Press, 1970), 148, 156 (also reproduced in Stephen Kemble, "General Orders of Gen. Sir William Howe, 1775–1778," *Collections of the New-York Historical Society* 16 [1883]: 266–67).

10. Expenses incurred on his Majesty's Service in the Engineers Department, December 25, 1774–March 24, 1775, Thomas Gage Papers, 1754–83, Amer. Ser., 127, MLC; and Cash, *Medical Men*, 113, 156, appendix 2.

11. On permission to inoculate as of November 24, 1775, see William Cheever, "William Cheever's Diary, 1775–1776," *Proceedings of the Massachusetts Historical Society*, 3d ser., 60 (January 1927): 91–97. Washington's letter to Congress is quoted in James E. Gibson, *Dr. Bodo Otto and the Medical Background of the American Revolution* (Springfield, Mass.: Charles C. Thomas, 1937), 88.

12. GW to the President of Congress, November 28, 1775, in *Writings of G. W.*, 4:122; GW to Hancock, Cambridge, December 4, 1775, in W. W. Abbot and Dorothy Twohig, eds., *The Papers of George Washington*, War Ser. (Charlottesville: University Press of Virginia, 1987), 2:447 (hereafter cited as *Papers of G. W.*); GW to Hancock, Cambridge, December 4, 1775, in *Papers of G. W.*, War Ser., 2:486; Robert H. Harrison to Council of Massachusetts, December 3, 1775, in *Am. Arch.*, 4th ser., 4:168, and 4:1321–22; Samuel Bixby, "Diary of Samuel Bixby," *Proceedings of the Massachusetts Historical Society*, 1st ser., 14 (March 1876): 297; and *Am. Arch.*, 4th ser., 4:1325.

13. Frederick Ridgely, Certification re John Morgan, Philadelphia, December 11, 1778, NAR (PCC), M247, r77, i63, p301; and Ebenezer Huntington to Jabez Huntington, Roxbury Camp, February 22, 1776, in *Letters Written by Ebenezer Huntington during the American Revolution*, ed. Charles Frederick Heartman (New York, 1914), 29.

14. On the smallpox outbreak in Nova Scotia, see Allan E. Marble, "Epidemics and Mortality in Nova Scotia, 1749–1799," *Nova Scotia Historical Review* 8 (1988): 83–88; and Allan E. Marble, *Surgeons, Smallpox and the Poor: A History of Medicine and Social Conditions in Nova Scotia, 1749–1799* (Montreal: McGill-Queen's Press, 1993), 103–04. On smallpox in Liverpool, N.S., see Simeon Perkins, *The Diary of Simeon Perkins, 1766–1780*, ed. Harold Innis (Toronto: Champlain Society, 1948), 111–12, 115–16.

15. GW to the President of Congress, March 19, 1776, in *Writings of G. W.*, 4:403; Pension Application of Richard Wallace, in John C. Dann, ed., *The Revolution Remembered: Eyewitness Accounts of the War for Independence* (Chicago: University of Chicago Press, 1980), 96; and GW to the Massachusetts Legislature, March 21, 1776, in *Writings of G. W.*, 4:416–17.

16. Patten, *Diary*, 356; and William Health, *Memoirs of Major-General Heath* (1798; rpt., New York: A. Wessels, 1904), 52–53.

17. Isaac Smith, Sr., to John Adams, Salem, April 6, 1776, in William Bell Clark, William James Morgan, and Michael J. Crawford, eds., *Naval Documents of the American Revolution* (Washington, D.C.: Naval Historical Center, Dept. of the Navy, 1969), 4:676 (hereafter cited as *Nav. Docs.*); Acts and Resolves of the Massachusetts General Court, April 5, 1776, in *Nav. Docs.*, 4:668; Winthrop Sargent to GW, April 7, 1776, in *Papers of G. W.*, War Ser., 4:47 (for a slightly different version, see *Nav. Docs.*, 4:694); and *Am. Arch.*, 4th ser., 5:1246.

18. Arthur Gilman, ed., *The Cambridge of 1776* (1876; rpt., Port Washington, N.Y.: Kennikat Press, 1970), 60–61; Abigail Adams to John Adams, March 31, 1776, in L. H. Butterfield et al., eds., *The Book of Abigail and John: Selected Letters of the Adams Family 1762–1784* (Cambridge: Harvard University Press, 1975), 120; John B. Blake, *Public Health in the Town of Boston, 1630–1822* (Cambridge: Harvard University Press, 1959), 126–27; and Price, "Diary," 259.

19. James Thacher, *A Military Journal of the American Revolution* (Boston: Richardson and Lord, 1823), 53; and Whitfield J. Bell, Jr., *John Morgan, Continental Doctor* (Philadelphia: University of Pennsylvania Press, 1965), 188.

20. Price's account of the lifting of the ban and the inoculation of his family is in Price, "Diary," 259, 260. On the American troops, see Artemas Ward to GW, July 4, 1776, GW to Hancock, July 11, 1776, GW to Ward, July 11,

1776, and Ward to GW, July 15, 1776, in *Papers of G. W.*, War Ser., 5:210, 267–68, 277, 332; Council of Massachusetts to Ward, July 9, 1776, and Ward to Council of Massachusetts, July 9, 1776, in *Am. Arch.*, 5th ser., 1:146. On Harvard College, see Benj[amin] Guild to Daniel Newcomb, Wrentham [Massachusetts], July 28, 1776, Newcomb-Johnson Collection, Box 1, Henry E. Huntington Library, San Marino, California (hereafter cited as HUV). On Adams and her children, see Abigail Adams to John Adams, July 13, 1776, in Butterfield et al., *Book of Abigail and John*, 144–45. On Manasseh Cutler, see Cutler, *Life, Journals, and Correspondence*, 1:56. The Hannah Winthrop quotation is from a letter to Mercy Otis Warren in Alice Brown, *Life of Mercy Warren*, quoted in Francis R. Packard, *History of Medicine in the United States* (New York: Paul B. Hoeber, 1931), 1:83. The five thousand figure comes from Blake, *Public Health*, 127. Morse's account is in his letter to the Commanding Officer at Crown-Point, July 9, 1776, in *Am. Arch.*, 5th ser., 1:145.

21. Proceedings of the Selectmen of Boston, August 26, 1776, ibid., 1:1172; Orders of the Selectmen of the Town of Boston, September 11, 1776, ibid., 2:297; and Selectmen of Boston—Smallpox, September 14, 1776, ibid., 2:339.

22. GW to Joseph Reed, Cambridge, December 15, 1775, in *Papers of G. W.*, War Ser., 2:553; and Graham Russell Hodges, ed., *The Black Loyalist Directory: African Americans in Exile after the American Revolution* (New York: Garland Publishing in association with the New England Historic Genealogical Society, 1996), 172–73.

23. Lund Washington to GW, Mount Vernon, September 29, 1775, in *Papers of G. W.*, War Ser., 2:64, 66n. Washington may also have lost a slave named Harry to Dunmore in 1775. See "Inspection Roll of Negroes, Book No. 1," in Hodges, *Black Loyalist Directory*, 111–12. "Liberty is sweet" comes from Lund Washington to GW, Mount Vernon, December 3, 1775, in *Papers of G. W.*, War Ser., 2:480.

24. Dunmore's comments on social divisions and military vulnerability are quoted in Gerald W. Mullin, *Flight and Rebellion: Slave Resistance in Eighteenth-Century Virginia* (1972; rpt., New York: Oxford University Press, 1975), 131. On class tensions among whites, see Landon Carter to GW, Sabine Hall, May 9, 1776, in *Papers of G. W.*, War Ser., 4:236–37; and John P. Kennedy, ed., *Journals of the House of Burgesses of Virginia, 1773–1776* (Richmond: [Library Board, Virginia State Library], 1905), 231. On the clandestine offer, see ibid., 231, 232.

25. GW to Richard Henry Lee, Cambridge, December 26, 1775, in *Papers of G. W.*, War Ser., 2:611; Andrew Lewis to GW, Williamsburg, January 18, 1776, ibid., 3:136; Lee to [Samuel Adams], Williamsburg, July 6, 1776, in

James Curtis Ballagh, ed., *The Letters of Richard Henry Lee* (New York: Macmillan, 1912), 1:208; Richard Henry Lee to Jefferson, Chantilly, July 21, 1776, in Julian P. Boyd, ed., *The Papers of Thomas Jefferson* (Princeton: Princeton University Press, 1950), 1:471 (hereafter cited as *Papers of T. J.*); and Landon Carter, "Diary," *WMQ*, 1st ser., 16 (January 1908): 149–50.

26. Peter H. Wood, "The Changing Population of the Colonial South: An Overview by Race and Region, 1685–1790," in *Powhatan's Mantle: Indians in the Colonial Southeast*, ed. Peter H. Wood, Gregory A. Waselkov, and M. Thomas Hatley (Lincoln: University of Nebraska Press, 1989), 38; Benjamin Quarles, *The Negro in the American Revolution* (Chapel Hill: University of North Carolina Press, 1961), 31; Mullin, *Flight and Rebellion*, 132; and George Washington Papers, Library of Congress, Washington, D.C., quoted in *Papers of G. W.*, War Ser., 2:501n. See also John Page to Jefferson, Williamsburg, November 24, 1775, in *Papers of T. J.*, 1:265.

27. "Extract of a Letter from the Midshipman on Board His Majesty's Ship Otter," in H. S. Parsons, comp., "Contemporary English Accounts of the Destruction of Norfolk in 1776," *WMQ*, 2d ser., 13 (October 1933): 220.

28. In April 1775, there appears to have been a smallpox outbreak in the Danville, Virginia, area. But connections to the outbreak among Dunmore's men ten months later remain elusive. "Diary of Salem Congregation, 1775," in Adelaide L. Fries, ed., *Records of the Moravians in North Carolina* (rpt., Raleigh: State Department of Archives and History, 1968), 2:871, 872. For evidence that smallpox had broken out by the time the *Roebuck* arrived, see Account of A. S. Hamond's part in the American Revolution (1775–77), February 12, 1776–February 27, 1776, A. S. Hamond Naval Papers, 1766–1825, roll I, Alderman Lib., microfilm, Foundation Lib., cited in John E. Selby, *The Revolution in Virginia 1775–1783* (Williamsburg: Colonial Williamsburg Foundation, 1988), 86, 349n.

29. Narrative of Captain Andrew Snape Hamond, [HMS *Roebuck*, May 16 to May 31], in *Nav. Docs.*, 5:321; and Selby, *Revolution in Virginia*, 126.

30. Edmund Pendleton to Thomas Jefferson, Williamsburg, May 25, 1776, in *Nav. Docs.*, 5:240; and Narrative of Captain Hamond, in *Nav. Docs.*, 5:321. The number 650 comes from [James] Cunningham's Examination, ibid., 5:1135–37; and Purdie's *Virginia Gazette*, July 19, 1776, ibid., 5:1147–50. Cf. Selby, *Revolution in Virginia*, 105. On the assistance of the marines and the influx of new arrivals, see Narrative of Captain Hamond, in *Nav. Docs.*, 5:840; and Dunmore to the Secretary of State, Virginia, June 26, 1776, cited in George W. Williams, *History of the Negro Race in America from 1619–1800* (New York, 1885), 342, in turn cited in Mullin, *Flight and Rebellion*, 132, 197n.

31. Quarles, *Negro in the American Revolution*, 30n; Narrative of Captain Hamond, in *Nav. Docs.*, 5:840, 321; Dixon and Hunter's *Virginia Gazette*, June 15, 1776, in ibid., 5:554; [James] Cunningham's Examination, ibid., 5:1136; and Ellen Gibson Wilson, *The Loyal Blacks* (New York: G. P. Putnam's Sons, 1976), 27.

32. Diary of Miguel Antonio Eduardo, in *Nav. Docs.*, 5:1344 (Appendix B); Richard Henry Lee to [General Charles Lee], Williamsburg, July 6, 1776, in Ballagh, *Letters of Richard Henry Lee*, 1:206; Narrative of Captain Hamond, in *Nav. Docs.*, 5:1078; John Page to Jefferson, Williamsburg, July 16, 1776, in *Papers of T. J.*, 1:462; and Purdie's *Virginia Gazette*, July 19, 1776, in *Nav. Docs.*, 5:1147.

33. Thomas Price to the Maryland Council of Safety, Upper Camp, St. George's Island, July 23, 1776, in *Nav. Docs.*, 5:1193; and Bracco to Maryland Council of Safety, Port-Tobacco, July 26, 1776, in *Am. Arch.*, 5th ser., 1:592. Bracco's request for permission to inoculate is odd, for his unit had apparently undergone inoculation in late June and early July 1776. See Maryland Council of Safety to Bracco, June 29, 1776, ibid., 4th ser., 6:1130–31; and Bracco to Gabriel Duvall, Port-Tobacco, July 2, 1776, ibid., 4th ser., 6:1201–02. On St. Inigoes, see Richard Barnes to the Maryland Council of Safety, St. Inigoes, July 13, 1776, in *Nav. Docs.*, 5:1066.

34. Particular Account of the Attack and Rout of Lord Dunmore, in *Am. Arch.*, 5th ser., 1:151 (also reproduced in Purdie's *Virginia Gazette*, Friday, July 19, 1776, in *Nav. Docs.*, 5:1147–50); and [James] Cunningham's Examination, in *Nav. Docs.*, 5:1135.

35. Extract of a Letter Dated Williamsburgh, Virginia, July 13, 1776, in *Am. Arch.*, 5th ser., 1:152; George Johnstone to Leven Powell, August 6, 1776, in *Biographical Sketch*, 37–38, quoted in Michael McDonnell, "The Politics of Mobilization in Revolutionary Virginia: Military Culture and Political and Social Relations, 1775–1783" (Ph.D. diss., Oxford University, 1996), 177–79; and Honyman, Diary, October 10, 1776, f. 75, quoted in McDonnell, "Politics of Mobilization," 177–79.

36. Westmoreland County Court Order Books, 1776–86, reel 61:6, 8, Library of Virginia, Richmond (hereafter cited as VIC). (I am grateful to Michael McDonnell for sharing this reference with me.) Inoculation petitions can be found in John P. Kennedy, ed., *Journals of the House of Burgesses, 1766–1769* (Richmond, Va.: [Colonial Press], 1906), 203, 246, 269.

37. Edmund Pendleton to R. H. Lee, February 8, 1777, in *The Lee Family Papers, 1742–1795*, ed. Paul P. Hoffman (Charlottesville: Microfilm Publications, University of Virginia Library, 1966); and Westmoreland County Court Order Books, 1776–86, reel 61:17–18, 40, VIC. (I would like to thank Michael McDonnell for both these references.) On Leesburg, see

Nicholas Cresswell, *The Journal of Nicholas Cresswell, 1774–1777* (1924; rpt., Port Washington, N.Y.: Kennikat Press, 1968), 192. On Mount Vernon, see GW to William Shippen, May 3, 1777, in *Writings of G. W.*, 37:539. On Martha Washington's inoculation, see the following: GW to John Augustine Washington, New York, April 29, 1776; Hancock to GW, Philadelphia, May 16, 1776; Hancock to GW, Philadelphia, May 21, 1776; GW to John Augustine Washington, Philadelphia, May 31, 1776; GW to Burwell Bassett, Philadelphia, June 4, 1776; and John Parke Custis to GW, Mount Airy, June 10, 1776, all in *Papers of G. W.*, War Ser., 4:173, 313, 352, 353n, 413, 435, 484–85. The request for medicine is in GW to Shippen, May 3, 1777, in *Writings of G. W.*, 37:539.

38. The best firsthand accounts of Arnold's march can be found in Kenneth Roberts, ed., *March to Quebec: Journals of the Members of Arnold's Expedition* (3d ed., New York: Doubleday, Doran, 1940) (hereafter cited as *March to Quebec*); and Jeremiah Greenman, *Diary of a Common Soldier in the American Revolution, 1775–1783*, ed. Robert C. Bray and Paul E. Bushnell (DeKalb: Northern Illinois University Press, 1978).

39. Caleb Haskell, "Diary at the Siege of Boston and on the March to Quebec," in *March to Quebec*, 482; Thomas Ainslie, *Canada Preserved: The Journal of Captain Thomas Ainslie*, ed. Sheldon S. Cohen (New York: New York University Press, 1968), 27; and Jacob Danford, "Journal of the Most Remarkable Occurrences in Quebec, by an Officer of the Garrison," *New-York Historical Society Collections* 13 (1880): 181.

40. Greenman, *Diary*, 22–23; Haskell, "Diary," in *March to Quebec*, 484; and Isaac Senter, "Dr. Senter's Journal," in *March to Quebec*, 230. On "breaf," see *Oxford English Dictionary*, 1965 ed., s.v. "brief." Greenman, *Diary*, 23. The quotation about Maynard and Brigham is from John Pierce, "Journal by the Advance Surveyor," in *March to Quebec*, 701. (Note that Pierce's journal cannot be found in earlier editions of this book.) The multiplication of cases is described in Greenman, *Diary*, 23.

41. John Joseph Henry, "Campaign against Quebec," in *March to Quebec*, 363; Haskell, "Diary," ibid., 485; Pierce, "Journal," ibid., 701, 698–99.

42. Henry, "Campaign," ibid., 374; Pierce, "Journal," ibid., 703.

43. James Melvin, "Journal of an Expedition to Quebec," ibid., 443; and Simon Fobes, "Narrative of Arnold's Expedition to Quebec," ibid., 592–94.

44. Greenman, *Diary*, 24–25; Fobes, "Narrative," in *March to Quebec*, 592; and Henry, "Campaign," ibid., 396.

45. Greenman, *Diary*, 24; Fobes, "Narrative," in *March to Quebec*, 592.

46. Francis Nichols, "Diary," *Pennsylvania Magazine of History and Biography* 20 (1896): 506; Henry Dearborn, "Journal of the Quebec Expedition," in

March to Quebec, 156; and Simeon Thayer, "Journal of His March through the Wilderness to Quebec," ibid., 279; and Pierce, "Journal," ibid., 706. Of the sixteen inoculees, three had apparently picked up the *Variola* virus before the inoculation and thus came down with more severe cases. One, probably Lieutenant Abijah Savage of Connecticut, died from the disease. Dearborn, "Journal," ibid., 157; and Thayer, "Journal," ibid., 279.

47. *Am. Arch.*, 4th ser., 4:751–53; and Pierce, "Journal," in *March to Quebec*, 705.

48. General Orders before Quebeck, February 11, 1776, in *Am. Arch.*, 4th ser., 5:550.

49. On Arnold's efforts to control smallpox, see General Orders, March 26, 1776, in Doyen Salsig, ed., *Parole: Quebec; Countersign: Ticonderoga: Second New Jersey Regimental Orderly Book 1776* (Cranbury, N.J.: Associated University Presses, 1980), 55–56. For Arnold's communications with Washington, see General Orders before Quebeck, February 15, 1776, in *Am. Arch.*, 4th ser., 5:551; and Arnold to GW, February 27, 1776, ibid., 4th ser., 4:1513–14. The two hundred figure is from M. Sanguinet, *L'Invasion du Canada par les Bastonnois*, ed. Richard Oullet and Jean-Pierre Therrien (Quebec: Éditeur Officiel du Québec, 1975), 81.

50. Arnold to Hancock, February 12, 1776, in *March to Quebec*, 121; Sanguinet, *L'Invasion*, 84–85; and A Return of the Troops before Quebeck, March 30, 1776, in *Am. Arch.*, 4th ser., 5:550.

51. Thomas to GW, May 8, 1776, in *Papers of G. W.*, War Ser., 4:231, 232, 233; and Senter, "Journal," in *March to Quebec*, 238–41.

52. Senter, "Journal," in *March to Quebec*, 238.

53. Ibid.; Elisha Porter, "Diary," ed. Appleton Morgan, *Magazine of American History* 30 (July–August 1893): 194; and Danford, "Journal," 236.

54. Carleton's orders are in Andrew Parke, *An Authentic Narrative of Facts Relating to the Exchange of Prisoners Taken at the Cedars* (London: T. Cadell, 1777), 4–5. Reports of the number of "prisoners" (mostly men sick with the smallpox) taken by the British varied. See Jeduthan Baldwin, *The Revolutionary Journal of Col. Jeduthan Baldwin*, ed. Thomas Williams Baldwin (1906; rpt., New York: Arno, 1971), 42–43; and Robert McConnell Hatch, *Thrust for Canada: The American Attempt on Quebec in 1775–1776* (Boston: Houghton Mifflin, 1979), 129.

55. Lemuel Roberts, *Memoirs of Captain Lemuel Roberts* (Bennington, Vt.: Anthony Haswell, 1809), 32–34; and Senter, "Journal," *March to Quebec*, 239.

56. Carroll and Chase to Schuyler, May 11, 1776, George Washington Papers, Library of Congress, quoted in *Papers of G. W.*, War Ser., 4:319n; and

Commissioners in Canada to Hancock, May 1, 1776, in William B. Willcox, ed., *The Papers of Benjamin Franklin* (New Haven: Yale University Press, 1982), 22:415.

57. Carroll and Chase to Schuyler, May 11, 1776, George Washington Papers, Library of Congress, quoted in *Papers of G. W.*, War Ser., 4:319n; Commissioners in Canada to President of Congress, May 27, 1776, in *Am. Arch.*, 4th ser., 6:590 (see also Senter, "Journal," *March to Quebec*, 238–41); and Schuyler to GW, June 11–12, 1776, in *Papers of G. W.*, War Ser., 4:505.

58. General Orders before Quebeck, February 15, 1776, in *Am. Arch.*, 4th ser., 5:551; General Orders, March 26, 1776, in Salsig, *Parole: Quebec*, 56; and General Orders, May 3, 1776, ibid., 96.

59. On illicit inoculations, see Senter, "Journal," in *March to Quebec*, 230; and Pierce, "Journal," ibid., 706. On fingernail inoculations, see Henry, "Campaign," ibid., 375. On fear of "natural" smallpox, see Senter, "Journal," ibid., 238; and Charles Cushing to his brother, July 8, 1776, in *Am. Arch.*, 5th ser., 1:130.

60. On Seth Warner, see Israel Warner to Henry Stephens, January 15, 1846, "Papers of Seth Warner," *Proceedings of the Vermont Historical Society* 11 (June 1943): 111–12; and Pension Application of Josiah Sabin, in Dann, *Revolution Remembered*, 19–21. More detail on illegal inoculations can be found in Jefferson, Notes of Witnesses' Testimony, in *Papers of T. J.*, 1:435; Arnold to Silas Deane, March 30, 1776, in *Am. Arch.*, 4th ser., 5:549; and Senter, "Journal," in *March to Quebec*, 238.

61. On Arnold's suspension of the inoculation ban, see Salsig, *Parole: Quebec*, 96; Senter, "Journal," in *March to Quebec*, 239–40; Arnold to Commissioners in Canada, May 17, 1776, in *Am. Arch.*, 4th ser., 6:593; Lewis Beebe, "Journal of a Physician on the Expedition against Canada, 1776," *Pennsylvania Magazine of History and Biography* 59 (October 1935): 328; and Baldwin, *Revolutionary Journal*, 43–44. For Thomas's reinstatement of the ban, see Beebe, "Journal," 328.

62. Frye Bayley, "Reminiscences of Colonel Frye Bayley of Newbury and Peacham, Vermont, 1763–1778," in *The Upper Connecticut: Narratives of Its Settlement and Its Part in the American Revolution*, vol. 4, *Collections of the Vermont Historical Society* (Montpelier: Vermont Historical Society, 1943), 2:33.

63. Ibid., 2:32.

64. On Iroquois neutrality, see Barbara Graymont, *The Iroquois in the American Revolution* (Syracuse: Syracuse University Press, 1972), 86–103. The account of Bedel's influence over the Indians is from Bayley, "Reminiscences," 2:38. For more on this topic, see Schuyler to Bedel, January 6, 1777, "The Trial of Major General Schuyler, October, 1778," *Collections of*

the New-York Historical Society 12 (1880): 4–211. Bedel described his sense of duty in Copy Colo: Bedels Defence, Crown Point, July 9, 1776, Timothy Bedel Papers, New Hampshire Historical Society, Concord, N.H. (hereafter cited as NL4), box 1, folder 1B.

65. On Bedel's inoculation, see Bayley, "Reminiscences," 2:32. On his negotiations with the Indians, see Colin G. Calloway, *The Western Abenakis of Vermont, 1600–1800: War, Migration, and the Survival of an Indian People* (Norman: University of Oklahoma Press, 1990), 209–10. The account of meeting with the Indians while sick is from Copy Colo: Bedels Defence, Crown Point, July 9, 1776, Timothy Bedel Papers, NL4, box 1, folder 1B. On the contagiousness of oral secretions, see *Smallpox and Its Eradication*, 183–86, 188. Twelve funerals were held at Kahnawake in 1771; fifteen in 1772; nineteen in 1773; seventeen in 1774; thirty-one in 1775; forty-five in 1776; and thirty-one in 1777. John Demos, letter to the author, March 13, 1996.

66. Bayley, "Reminiscences," 2:33, 34, 38; Copy Colo: Bedels Defence, Crown Point, July 9, 1776, Timothy Bedel Papers, NL4, box 1, folder 1B.

67. Bayze Wells, "Journal," *Collections of the Connecticut Historical Society* 7 (1899): 265–66. For the composition of Forster's force, see Parke, *Authentic Narrative*, 21.

68. Extract of a Letter from Major Henry Sherburne, June 18, 1776, in *Am. Arch.*, 4th ser., 6:598–99; and Bayley, "Reminiscences," 2:35.

69. Parke, *Authentic Narrative*, 27–29; *Am. Arch.*, 4th ser., 6:598–99n; and Extract of a Letter from Major Henry Sherburne, June 18, 1776, ibid., 6:598–99. The "stark naked" quotation is from John Greenwood, *The Revolutionary Services of John Greenwood of Boston and New York 1775–1783* (New York: De Vinne, 1922), 26–33. For Adams's letter, see John Adams to Abigail Adams, June 26, 1776, in Butterfield et al., *Book of Abigail and John*, 137–38. On men from Detroit, see Baldwin, *Revolutionary Journal*, 44. On the pox at Michilimackinac, see Extracts from Letters from the Upper Posts, Ar. S. De Peyster [to Carleton], Michilimackinac, February 1777, *Michigan Pioneer and Historical Collections* (Lansing, 1888), 10:271.

70. Beebe, "Journal," 328–32 (date confirmed in Baldwin, *Revolutionary Journal*, 44); and Schuyler to GW, May 31, 1776, in *Papers of G. W.*, War Ser., 4:410. The account of Thomas's interment is in Porter, "Diary," 196.

71. The account of Montreal is from Greenwood, *Revolutionary Services*, 34. The twenty-nine hundred figure comes from Baldwin, *Revolutionary Journal*, 54. The descriptions of St. Jean are from Beebe, "Journal," 330, 333; and Bayley, "Reminiscences," 2:38.

72. On British inoculations, see James M. Hadden, *Hadden's Journal and Orderly Books: A Journal Kept in Canada and upon Burgoyne's Campaign in*

1776 and 1777, ed. Horatio Rogers (1884; rpt., Boston: Gregg, 1972), 193; and Thomas Dickson Reide, *A View of the Diseases of the Army in Great Britain, America, the West Indies, and on Board of King's Ships and Transports* (London: J. Johnson, 1793), 5–6. For Baldwin's description, see his *Revolutionary Journal*, 55.

73. Wells, "Journal," 267; Beebe, "Journal," 336; and John Lacey, "Memoirs," *Pennsylvania Magazine of History and Biography* 25 (1901): 203–04.

74. Patten, *Diary*, 360–61.

75. Sullivan to GW, June 24, 1776, George Washington Papers, Library of Congress, quoted in *Papers of G. W.*, War Ser., 5:92–93. On orders to evacuate, see Beebe, "Journal," 336. Trumbull's account is in *The Autobiography of Colonel John Trumbull, Patriot-Artist, 1756–1843*, ed. Theodore Sizer (New Haven: Yale University Press, 1953), 27–28. On drowning, see Beebe, "Journal," 344.

76. Schuyler to Jeremiah Powell, July 13, 1776, in *Am. Arch.*, 5th ser., 1:260; and Minutes of Council of War, July 7, 1776, quoted in *Papers of G. W.*, War Ser., 5:288n; U.S. Army (Continental), General Orders, Crown Point, July 7, 1776, 4th Pennsylvania Battalion Orderly Book, March 31, 1776–September 1, 1776, HM 605, v. 1, HUV; Gates to GW, July 29, 1776, in *Papers of G. W.*, War Ser., 5:499 (see also Gates to Hancock, July 16, 1776, George Washington Papers, Library of Congress, quoted in *Papers of G. W.*, War Ser., 5:338–39n); and U.S. Army (Continental), General Orders, Ticonderoga, August 19, 1776, 4th Pennsylvania Battalion Orderly Book, March 31, 1776–September 1, 1776, HM 605, v. 1, HUV.

77. Ira Allen to New Hampshire Committee of Safety, July 10, 1776, in *Am. Arch.*, 5th ser., 1:177; Beebe, "Journal," 342–43; Potts to JM, August 10, 1776, quoted in Bell, *John Morgan*, 190; Gates to Trumbull, August 19, 1776, in *Am. Arch.*, 5th ser., 1:1073; Gates to GW, August 28, 1776, in *Papers of G. W.*, War Ser., 6:146; and Beebe, "Journal," 345.

78. GW to Trumbull, July 7, 1776, in *Am. Arch.*, 5th ser., 1:106–07; and John Adams to Abigail Adams, June 26, 1776, in Butterfield et al., *Book of Abigail and John*, 137–38.

3. CONTROL

1. The sources for this sketch are as follows, listed in the order in which they are utilized: Hardy Murfree, Affidavit re William Rickman, Valley Forge, February 1778, NAR (PCC), M247, r101, i78, v19, p127; Hugh F. Rankin, *The North Carolina Continentals* (Chapel Hill: University of North Carolina Press, 1971), 128; John Crittenden, Affidavit re William Rick-

man, York County, Virginia, February 26, 1778, NAR (PCC), M247, r101, i78, v19, p119; and John Williams and John Crittenden, Declarations re a hospital at Alexandria, undated, NAR (PCC), M247, r73, i59, v3, p189; and Hardy Murfree, Affidavit re William Rickman, Valley Forge, February 1778, NAR (PCC), M247, r101, i78, v19, p127.

2. On smallpox in Philadelphia during the French and Indian War, see Francis R. Packard, *History of Medicine in the United States* (New York: Paul B. Hoeber, 1931), 1:88; John Duffy, "Smallpox and the Indians in the American Colonies," *Bulletin of the History of Medicine* 25 (1951): 337; and John Duffy, *Epidemics in Colonial America* (Baton Rouge: Louisiana State University Press, 1953), 88, 91, 97. On the disease's continuing presence in Philadelphia between the French and Indian War and the American Revolution, see Duffy, *Epidemics*, 100. Implying that it was endemic, John Blake suggests that cyclic smallpox existed in Philadelphia throughout the period after 1730. John B. Blake, *Public Health in the Town of Boston, 1630–1822* (Cambridge: Harvard University Press, 1959), 112. On the cyclical nature of smallpox even where it is endemic, see S. R. Duncan, Susan Scott, and C. J. Duncan, "The Dynamics of Smallpox Epidemics in Britain, 1550–1800," *Demography* 30 (August 1993): 417.

3. On the absence of quarantine in Philadelphia, see Blake, *Public Health*, 109; and Elizabeth C. Tandy, "Local Quarantine and Inoculation for Smallpox in the American Colonies, 1620–1775," *American Journal of Public Health* 13 (March 1923): 205. On Jefferson, see George Gilmer to John Morgan, May 11, 1766, in *Papers of T. J.*, 1:18, 18n, 20. On Martha Washington, see Hancock to GW, Philadelphia, May 16, 1776, in *Papers of G. W.*, War Ser., 4:313; Hancock to GW, Philadelphia, May 21, 1776, ibid., 4:352, 353n; GW to John Augustine Washington, Philadelphia, May 31, 1776, ibid., 4:413; and GW to Burwell Bassett, Philadelphia, June 4, 1776, ibid., 4:435. On Rush's role in popularizing Suttonian inoculation in Philadelphia in 1769, see Benjamin Rush, *The Autobiography of Benjamin Rush*, ed. George W. Corner (Princeton: Princeton University Press, 1948), 80.

4. On mortality among poor children, see Carl Bridenbaugh and Jessica Bridenbaugh, *Rebels and Gentlemen: Philadelphia in the Age of Franklin* (1942; rpt., New York: Oxford University Press, 1968), 248. On Francis Franklin, see Benjamin Franklin, *The Autobiography and Other Writings*, ed. L. Jesse Lemisch (New York: New American Library, 1961), 112, 284. On the founding of the inoculation society, see Christopher Marshall, *Passages from the Remembrancer of Christopher Marshall*, ed. William Duane, Jr. (Philadelphia: James Crissy, 1839), 5. The society is discussed further in Bridenbaugh and Bridenbaugh, *Rebels and Gentlemen*, 248–49. The 1776

account is from "GENERAL STATE of the ACCOUNTS of the CON-
TRIBUTORS for the Relief and Employment of the POOR in the City
of Philadelphia, &c. from May 8, 1775, to May 13, 1776," in *Pa. Gaz.*,
May 29, 1776.

5. Adams to James Warren, Philadelphia, July 24, 1776, quoted in Packard,
History of Medicine, 1:84.

6. The comments on the suspension of inoculation come from an unattrib-
uted quotation in Packard, *History of Medicine*, 1:89. On the Secret Com-
mittee, see Edmund C. Burnett, *The Continental Congress* (New York:
Macmillan, 1941), 118–19. The bare outlines of Ward's illness and death
are documented in Marshall, *Passages*, 71; and *Pa. Gaz.*, March 27, 1776.
(See also *Pa. Gaz.*, May 22, 1776.) On Thomas Burke, see William
Hooper to Joseph Hewes, February 15, 1777, in Edmund C. Burnett, ed.,
Letters of Members of the Continental Congress (Washington, D.C.: Carnegie
Institution, 1923), 2:256.

7. Josiah to Mary Bartlett, Philadelphia, September 16, 1775, in Frank C.
Mevers, ed., *The Papers of Josiah Bartlett* (Hanover: University Press of
New England for the New Hampshire Historical Society, 1979), 18–19;
Josiah to Mary Bartlett, Philadelphia, October 25, 1775, ibid., 25; and
Josiah Bartlett, Expense Account with New Hampshire, ca. March 30,
1776, ibid., 54.

8. On Patrick Henry, see Rush, *Autobiography*, 110. For the Matthew Thornton quotation, see Thornton to Meshech Weare, Philadelphia, November 12, 1776, in *Am. Arch.*, 5th ser., 3:652. More on Thornton's inoculation
can be found in William Whipple to Bartlett, Philadelphia, November 16,
1776, in Mevers, *Papers of Josiah Bartlett*, 133; and Whippel [Whipple] to
Meshech Weare, November 28, 1776, in *Am. Arch.*, 5th ser., 3:890. For the
unnamed New Hampshire delegate, see Ezra L'Hommedieu to the Governor of New York (George Clinton), February 22, 1780, in Burnett,
Letters of Members, 5:45. On Huntington, see Oliver Ellsworth to the Governor of Connecticut (John Trumbull), June 23, 1780, ibid., 5:234.

9. Smallpox in the fleet is described in Esek Hopkins to Hancock, On the
ALFRED, New London Harbor, April 9, 1776, NAR (PCC), M247, r96,
i78, v11, p33. On avoiding the American coastline, see *Connecticut Gazette*,
Friday, April 12, 1776, in *Nav. Docs.*, 4:784. The departure from Philadel-
phia and the events at Nassau are described in Samuel Eliot Morison,
John Paul Jones: A Sailor's Biography (1959; special paperback ed., New
York: Time, Inc., 1964), 42–45. On pox from Philadelphia arriving in
South Carolina, see Proceedings of the South Carolina Assembly, Sep-
tember 19, 1776, and September 20, 1776, in *Am. Arch.*, 5th ser., 3:5, 6.

10. Hancock's orders are in Hancock to unknown, Philadelphia, August 28,

1776, NAR (PCC), M247, r23, i12A, v2, p24. (For a published rendition of this document, see President of Congress [John Hancock] to Commanding Officer of Virginia Battalion, August 28, 1776, in *Am. Arch.*, 5th ser., 1:1191.) The February 1777 orders are in Medical Committee to GW, Baltimore, February 13, 1777, in Burnett, *Letters of Members*, 2:249–50. (See also Richard Peters to the Committee of Congress, War Office, February 14, 1777, NAR [PCC], M247, r157, i147, v1, p67.) For Washington's frustration, see GW to William Shippen, Jr., Morristown, January 28, 1777, in *Writings of G. W.*, 7:75–76.

11. For the Trumbull quotations, see Jonathan Trumbull, Sr., to GW, July 4, 1776, in *Papers of G. W.*, 5:208 (cf. Trumbull to the President of Congress, July 5, 1776, in *Am. Arch.*, 5th ser., 1:29–30); and Trumbull to GW, Lebanon, Connecticut, July 6, 1776, in *Papers of G. W.*, War Ser., 5:226–27). Washington did make efforts to send immune men to the Northern Army. See GW to Artemas Ward, July 19, 1776, ibid., 5:395; Ward to GW, July 22, 1776, ibid., 5:427; and GW to Ward, July 29, 1776, ibid., 5:506. Schuyler refers to the New Englanders as "Militia from the Eastern Colonies." Schuyler to GW, Albany, July 12, 1776, ibid., 5:28. New Hampshire soldiers had the same fears. See Nathaniel Folsom to Josiah Bartlett, Exeter, August 14, 1776, in Mevers, *Papers of Josiah Bartlett*, 104.

12. Pendleton to R. H. Lee, February 28, 1777, in *The Lee Family Papers, 1742–1795*, ed. Paul P. Hoffman (Charlottesville: Microfilm Publications, University of Virginia Library, 1966). I would like to thank Michael McDonnell for sharing this reference with me. (See also the Medical Committee to GW, February 13, 1777, in Burnett, *Letters of Members*, 2:249–50.) For Henry's account, see his letter to Adam Stephen, March 31, 1777, in H. R. McIlwaine, ed., *Official Letters of the Governors of the State of Virginia* (Richmond: Virginia State Library, 1926–29), 1:133, quoted in Michael McDonnell, "The Politics of Mobilization in Revolutionary Virginia: Military Culture and Political and Social Relations, 1775–1783" (Ph.D. diss., Oxford University, 1996), 177–79. For continued slow enlistments, see John Augustine Washington to R. H. Lee, May 20, 1777, in Hoffman, *Lee Family Papers*. I am grateful to Michael McDonnell for sharing this reference with me. Washington's admission is in GW to Patrick Henry, April 13, 1777, in *Writings of G. W.*, 7:409.

13. The inoculations of Thomas Jefferson, Martha Washington, and Patrick Henry are mentioned above. For the inoculations of John Custis, James Wormeley, and the family of John Walker, see James Wilkinson, *Memoirs of My Own Times* (Philadelphia: A. Small, 1816), 1:10–11; Walker to Jefferson, Philadelphia, June 13, 1780, in *Papers of T. J.*, 3:441; and Walker to

Jefferson, Philadelphia, June 12, 1780, ibid., 3:455. Lee's comments are from R. H. Lee to Jefferson, May 1, 1777, in Hoffman, *Lee Family Papers*, quoted in McDonnell, "Politics of Mobilization," 177–79. On resentment of the draft, see ibid., chap. 3. John Augustine's account is from John Augustine Washington to R. H. Lee, Mount Clear, June 20, 1778, in Hoffman, *Lee Family Papers*. I am grateful to Michael McDonnell for sharing this reference with me.

14. Williams to Trumbull, November 6, 1776, in Burnett, *Letters of Members*, 2:142.

15. William Trent, "William Trent's Journal at Fort Pitt, 1763," ed. A. T. Volwiler, *Mississippi Valley Historical Review* 11 (December 1924): 400. For Gage's approval of reimbursements, see Levy, Trent and Company: Account against the Crown, August 13, 1763, in *The Papers of Col. Henry Bouquet*, ed. Sylvester Kirby Stevens and Donald H. Kent, ser. 21654 (Harrisburg: Department of Public Instruction, Pennsylvania Historical Commission, 1941), 218–19. For more on the Fort Pitt affair, see Elizabeth A. Fenn, "Biological Warfare in Eighteenth-Century America: Beyond Jeffery Amherst," *Journal of American History* 86 (March 2000): 1552–58. Pomeroy's warning is in Seth Pomeroy to Asahel Pomeroy, Cambridge, May 13, 1775, in Louis Effingham de Forest, ed., *The Journals and Papers of Seth Pomeroy* (New Haven: Society of Colonial Wars in the State of New York, 1926), 167. For the March 1775 accusations, see Extract of a letter from Boston, author unknown, *London Evening Post*, March 25–March 28, 1775, in Margaret W. Willard, ed., *Letters on the American Revolution, 1774–1776* (Boston and New York: Houghton Mifflin, 1925), 57–58.

16. Robert H. Harrison to Council of Massachusetts, December 3, 1775, in *Am. Arch.*, 4th ser., 4:168; and GW to Hancock, Cambridge, December 4, 1775, in *Papers of G. W.*, War Ser., 2:486.

17. Thomas Crafts, Jr., to William Cooper, December 10, 1775, in *Am. Arch.*, 4th ser., 4:1229n; GW to James Otis, Sr. [Massachusetts General Court], Cambridge, December 10, 1775, *Papers of G. W.*, War Ser., 2:526; GW to Hancock, December 11, 1775, ibid., 2:533; and Deposition of Thomas Francis, *Boston Gazette and Country Journal* (Boston, Massachusetts: February 12, 1776), 4. For another account of foul play, see Ezekiel Price, "Diary of Ezekiel Price, 1775–1776," *Proceedings of the Massachusetts Historical Society*, 1st ser., 7 (November 1863): 220.

18. GW to the President of Congress, December 14, 1775, in *Papers of G. W.*, War Ser., 2:548; and GW to Joseph Reed, December 15, 1775, ibid., 2:553.

19. GW, General Orders, March 13, 1776, ibid., 3:458; and GW, General Orders, March 14, 1776, ibid., 3:466.

20. John Joseph Henry, "Campaign against Quebec," in *March to Quebec*, 374–75; Jefferson, Notes of Witnesses' Testimony, July 1–27, 1776, in *Papers of T. J.*, 1:435, 437, 448; and Jefferson, "Comments on Soulés' *Histoire*," August 8, 1786, ibid., 10:373, 377n.

21. Dixon and Hunter's *Virginia Gazette*, Saturday, June 15, 1776, in *Nav. Docs.*, 5:554; and "[James] Cunningham's Examination 18th July 1776," ibid., 5:1136.

22. Bartlett to Whipple, Kingston, New Hampshire, April 21, 1777, in Mevers, *Papers of Josiah Bartlett*, 157–58.

23. On outbreaks in New Hampshire and the New Hampshire grants, see Schuyler to Hancock, Albany, February 24, 1777, NAR (PCC), M247, r173, i153, v3, p100; and Mary to Josiah Bartlett, May 28, 1778, in Mevers, *Papers of Josiah Bartlett*, 421. For the Ethan Allen quotation, see Ethan to Heman Allen, June 4, 1777, Ethan Allen Papers, Henry Stevens Collection, Vermont State Archives, Montpelier, quoted in Michael A. Bellesiles, *Revolutionary Outlaws: Ethan Allen and the Struggle for Independence on the Early American Frontier* (Charlottesville: University Press of Virginia, 1993), 129.

24. GW to William Shippen, January 6, 1777, in *Writings of G. W.*, 6:473–74.

25. Thomas Dickson Reide, *A View of the Diseases of the Army in Great Britain, America, the West Indies, and on Board of King's Ships and Transports* (London: J. Johnson, 1793), 5–6. For another account of these inoculations, see James M. Hadden, *Hadden's Journal and Orderly Books: A Journal Kept in Canada and upon Burgoyne's Campaign in 1776 and 1777*, ed. Horatio Rogers (1884; rpt., Boston: Gregg, 1972), 193.

26. The 23 percent figure is derived from numbers in Pendleton to Richard Henry Lee, Caroline, May 11, 1777, in David John Mays, ed., *The Letters and Papers of Edmund Pendleton, 1734–1803* (Charlottesville: University Press of Virginia for the Virginia Historical Society, 1967), 1:208, 210. For Washington's orders, see GW to William Shippen, Morristown, January 28, 1777, in *Writings of G. W.*, 7:75–76. Cf. GW to Horatio Gates, January 28, 1777, ibid., 7:72–73.

27. GW to Hancock, Morristown, February 5, 1777, NAR (PCC), M247, r167, i152, v3, p517 (see also GW to Nicholas Cooke, Morristown, February 10, 1777, Schoff Revolutionary War Collection, MLC); Medical Committee to GW, Baltimore, February 13, 1777, in Burnett, *Letters of Members*, 2:249–50. On the Newtown outbreak, see GW to Robert Hanson Harrison, Morristown, January 20, 1777, in *Writings of G. W.*, 7:38; GW to John

Cochran, January 20, 1777, ibid., 7:44–45; and Morris H. Saffron, *Surgeon to Washington: Dr. John Cochran, 1730–1807* (New York: Columbia University Press, 1977), 32–33.

28. On Virginia, see Pendleton to R. H. Lee, Caroline, February 28, 1777, in Mays, *Letters and Papers of Pendleton*, 1:205; GW to William Shippen, May 3, 1777, in *Writings of G. W.*, 37:539; John Augustine Washington to R. H. Lee, May 20, 1777, in Hoffman, *Lee Family Papers*. (I am grateful to Michael McDonnell for sharing the last reference with me.) On Ticonderoga, see Schuyler to Hancock, Albany, February 15, 1777, NAR (PCC), M247, r173, i153, v3, p88.

29. GW to Nicholas Cooke, Morristown, February 10, 1777, Schoff Revolutionary War Collection, MLC. For more discussion of "keeping the matter as secret as possible," see GW to William Shippen, Morristown, January 6, 1777, in *Writings of G. W.*, 6:473–74. Edmund Pendleton also addressed the issue: "I wish the enemy were locked up somewhere, at least for so long time as would admit a General innoculation of our Troops." Pendleton to R. H. Lee, Caroline, February 8, 1777, in Mays, *Letters and Papers of Pendleton*, 1:205.

30. The Virginia and Hudson Highlands, New York, operations are examined in more detail below. On Georgetown, see GW to Lachlan McIntosh, April 3, 1778, in *Writings of G. W.*, 11:202–03. On Morristown, see GW to William Shippen, Morristown, January 6, 1777, ibid., 6:473–74; Packard, *History of Medicine*, 1:577; GW to Hancock, Morristown, February 5, 1777, NAR (PCC), Washington, D.C., M247, r167, i152, v3, p517; Saffron, *Surgeon*, 31–33; and Jeremiah Greenman, *Diary of a Common Soldier in the American Revolution, 1775–1783*, ed. Robert C. Bray and Paul E. Bushnell (DeKalb: Northern Illinois University Press, 1978), 73. On Ticonderoga, see GW to Nicholas Cooke, Morristown, February 10, 1777, Schoff Revolutionary War Collection, MLC; and Philip Schuyler to Hancock, Albany, May 2, 1777, NAR (PCC), M247, r173, i153, v3, p110. On Newtown and Bethlehem, see GW to Robert Hanson Harrison, Morristown, January 20, 1777, in *Writings of G. W.*, 7:38; GW to John Cochran, January 20, 1777, ibid., 7:44–45; and Packard, *History of Medicine*, 1:581–82. More on the Pennsylvania outbreaks can be found in John Smith Hanna, *A History of the Life and Services of Captain Samuel Dewees, a Native of Pennsylvania* (Baltimore: R. Neilson, 1844), 138–39; and Lembke to Graff, Nazareth Hall, June 6, 1777, in Adelaide L. Fries, ed., *Records of the Moravians in North Carolina* (Raleigh: State Department of Archives and History, 1922–69), 3:1411.

31. Virginia Historical Register, v. 2, p. 144, quoted in *Med. in Va.*, 259–60 (see also GW to Hancock, Morristown, February 5, 1777, NAR [PCC],

M247, r167, i152, v3, p517); and GW to Nicholas Cooke, Morristown, February 10, 1777, Schoff Revolutionary War Collection, MLC.

32. While under inoculation, Martin and his companions came down with "the itch," probably the parasitic disorder caused by the mite *Sarcoptes scabiei*. Joseph Plumb Martin, *Private Yankee Doodle: Being a Narrative of Some of the Adventures, Dangers and Sufferings of a Revolutionary Soldier*, ed. George F. Scheer (Boston: Little, Brown, 1962), 66, 110. For a physician's account of the West Point inoculations, see Nicholas Noel, *Nicholas à ses concitoyens* (Rheims: Imprimerie de Regnier, 1826), 14n.

33. In April 1777 the Medical Committee apparently sent Dr. James Tilton of Delaware to Dumfries to supervise the Virginia inoculations. Erna Risch, *Supplying Washington's Army* (Washington, D.C.: Center of Military History, U.S. Army, 1981), 379–80. Later, Dr. William Shippen seems to have taken charge, and in August or September, William Rickman took over. Shippen to Hancock, Philadelphia, August 16, 1777, NAR (PCC), M247, r102, i78, v20, p147. On the North Carolina troops, see Pendleton to Richard Henry Lee, Caroline, May 11, 1777, in Mays, *Letters and Papers of Pendleton*, 1:208, 210. For slightly different estimates regarding these troops, see Alexander Martin to Hancock, near Fredericksburg, May 10, 1777, NAR (PCC), M247, r99, i78, v15, p189. The "pock-eyed" quotation is from Nicholas Cresswell, *The Journal of Nicholas Cresswell, 1774–1777* (1924; rpt., Port Washington, N.Y.: Kennikat Press, 1968), 203.

34. Jacob Walker, Affidavit re William Rickman, York County, Virginia, January 20, 1778, NAR (PCC), M247, r101, i78, v19, p107; Richard Randolph et al., Affidavit re William Rickman, Henrico County, January 29, 1778, NAR (PCC), M247, r101, i78, v19, p123; Anthony T. Dixon, Affidavit re William Rickman, Alexandria, February 7, 1778, NAR (PCC), M247, r101, i78, v19, p113; and William Rickman, List of sick who died between September 22 and November 30, 1777, Alexandria, NAR (PCC), M247, r101, i78, v19, p139.

35. John Williams and John Crittenden, Declarations re a hospital at Alexandria, undated, NAR (PCC), M247, r73, i59, v3, p189; William T. Coles et al., Depositions re William Rickman, 1776, NAR (PCC), M247, r71, i58, v1, p483. Although the doctor is labeled "Rickham," his suspension is mentioned in Rankin, *North Carolina Continentals*, 91.

36. GW to Jonathan Trumbull, March 31, 1778, *Writings of G. W.*, 11:181–83. On the Valley Forge inoculations, see Albigence Waldo, "Diary of Surgeon Albigence Waldo, of the Connecticut Line, Valley Forge, 1777–1778," *Pennsylvania Magazine of History and Biography* 21 (1897): 321, 322. Inoculations also continued among recruits in New York and Virginia in the winter of 1777–78. See Israel Putnam to Henry Laurens,

Camp, West Point, February 10, 1778, in David R. Chesnutt, ed., *The Papers of Henry Laurens* (Columbia: University of South Carolina Press, 1990), 12:440; and R. H. Lee to George Weedon, March 14, 1778, in Hoffman, *Lee Family Papers*. (I am grateful to Michael McDonnell for sharing the last reference with me.)

37. The March 25 quotation is from GW to the Board of War, March 25, 1778, *Writings of G. W.*, 11:143. For another account of the impact of inoculation on the number of available men, see John Laurens to Henry Laurens, March 9, 1778, in Chesnutt, *Papers of Henry Laurens*, 12:531. March 1778 was the month in which the highest proportion (32 percent) of sick and inoculated soldiers was reported. Charles H. Lesser, ed., *The Sinews of Independence: Monthly Strength Reports of the Continental Army* (Chicago: University of Chicago Press, 1976), xxx–xxxi, 54–70. The comments on secrecy are from Henry Lee, *Memoirs of the War in the Southern Department of the United States*, ed. Robert E. Lee (new ed.; New York: University Publishing, 1870), 107.

38. Lesser, *Sinews of Independence*, 55, 58, 61.

39. GW to Alexander McDougall, Valley Forge, March 25, 1778, in *Writings of G. W.*, 11:146. The general expresses the same sentiment in GW to William Heath, Valley Forge, March 25, 1778, ibid., 11:145. R. H. Lee to George Weedon, March 14, 1778, in Hoffman, *Lee Family Papers*. (I am grateful to Michael McDonnell for sharing this reference with me.)

40. GW to the Officer Commanding at Alexandria, Virginia, Valley Forge, March 20, 1778, in *Writings of G. W.*, 11:116.

41. GW to William Heath, Valley Forge, March 25, 1778, ibid., 11:145; GW to Trumbull, Valley Forge, March 31, 1778, ibid., 11:181–83; GW to Alexander McDougall, Valley Forge, March 25, 1778, ibid., 11:146; and Francis Lightfoot Lee to George Weedon, York, March 31, 1778, in Burnett, *Letters of Members*, 3:147.

42. GW to William Heath, Valley Forge, March 25, 1778, in *Writings of G. W.*, 11:145; GW to Alexander McDougall, Valley Forge, March 25, 1778, ibid., 11:146; and GW to James Bowdoin, March 31, 1778, ibid., 11:181.

43. GW, General Orders, March 18, 1778, ibid., 11:107; and GW to the Officer Commanding at Alexandria, Virginia, Valley Forge, March 20, 1778, ibid., 11:116.

44. Lesser, *Sinews of Independence*, 69.

45. Ibid.; and GW, General Orders, May 31, 1778, in *Writings of G. W.*, 11:497.

46. Linda Grant DePauw, "Women in Combat: The Revolutionary War Experience," *Armed Forces and Society* 7 (1981): 210; and GW, General Orders, May 31, 1778, in *Writings of G. W.*, 11:497–98.

47. Lesser, *Sinews of Independence*, 73.

4. SURRENDER

1. The sources for this sketch are as follows, listed in the order in which they are utilized: David George, "An Account of the Life of David George, from Sierra Leone in Africa," *Baptist Annual Register for 1790, 1791, 1792, and Part of 1793* ([1793?]): 474–77; Jack Salzman, David Lionel Smith, and Cornel West, *Encyclopedia of African-American Culture and History* (New York: Simon & Schuster, 1996), 2:1099; George, "Account of the Life," 476–79, 482–83; James W. St. G. Walker, *The Black Loyalists: The Search for a Promised Land in Nova Scotia and Sierra Leone 1783–1870* (New York: Africana Publishing, 1976), 145–46; Sylvia R. Frey, *Water from the Rock: Black Resistance in a Revolutionary Age* (Princeton: Princeton University Press, 1991), 195. On George's moderating influence in earlier protests, see Walker, *Black Loyalists*, 178, 199, 208–09; and Ellen Gibson Wilson, *The Loyal Blacks* (New York: G. P. Putnam's Sons, 1976), 273, 314, 329.

2. Philip Schuyler to GW, July 2, 1776, *Papers of G. W.*, War Ser., 5:185. On Pennsylvania, see Charles Royster, *A Revolutionary People at War: The Continental Army and the American Character, 1775–1783* (Chapel Hill: University of North Carolina Press for the Institute of Early American History and Culture, 1979), 132. On Connecticut, see Jonathan Trumbull, *A Proclamation*, February 1, 1777 (broadside at MLC).

3. On the Ottawa Indians, see Carleton to de Peyster, Montreal, June 25, 1776, [Carleton] to Hamilton, Montreal, July 19, 1776 [two letters], and Extracts from Letters from the Upper Posts, de Peyster [to Carleton], Michilimackinac, February 1777, *Michigan Pioneer and Historical Collections* (Lansing: The Society, 1888), 10:261–63, 271. The Onondaga quotations are in an Oneida speech reprinted in William L. Stone, *Life of Joseph Brant—Thayendanegea, Including the Indian Wars of the Revolution* (New York, 1838), 1:175–77. For indications that the Onondaga outbreak was smallpox, see Anthony F. C. Wallace, *The Death and Rebirth of the Seneca* (New York: Alfred A. Knopf, 1970), 195; and Colin G. Calloway, *The American Revolution in Indian Country: Crisis and Diversity in Native American Communities* (New York: Cambridge University Press, 1995), 58. (Cf. Barbara Graymont, *The Iroquois in the American Revolution* [Syracuse: Syracuse University Press, 1972], 113.) In August 1776, Philip Schuyler had tried to keep the smallpox in Albany from infecting the Iroquois by moving treaty negotiations to German Flatts. See [Philip John Schuyler], "German Flatts Treaty Speech to the Six Nations, [August 5, 1776]," HM 14186, HUV; and Six Nations in Council, "[A Reply to General Schuyler's Speech to the Six Nations], August 9, 1776," HM 14187, HUV.

4. John Duffy, *Epidemics in Colonial America* (Baton Rouge: Louisiana State University Press, 1953), 35–37; Nicholas Cresswell, *The Journal of Nicholas Cresswell, 1774–1777* (1924; rpt., Port Washington, N.Y.: Kennikat Press, 1968), 243–44 (see also 233); Simeon Perkins, *The Diary of Simeon Perkins, 1766–1780*, ed. Harold Innis (Toronto: Champlain Society, 1948), 253–54; Friederike Charlotte Luise Riedesel, *Letters and Memoirs Relating to the War of American Independence, and the Capture of the German Troops at Saratoga* (New York: G. & C. Carvill, 1827), 233–34, 235–37; John Beebe, Jr., "Excerpts from a Diary of John Beebe, Jr. (1727–1786)," Columbia County Historical Society, Kinderhook, New York, 2 (typescript of original in the New York State Archives; photocopy kindly furnished by John L. Brooke of Tufts University); *Notices of Sullivan's Campaign* (1842; rpt., Port Washington, N.Y.: Kennikat Press, 1970), 118–19; and George H. Harris, "The Life of Horatio Jones: The True Story of Hoc-Sa-Go-Wah, Prisoner, Pioneer, and Interpreter," *Publications of the Buffalo Historical Society* 6 (1903): 433–34.

5. Pension Application of Samuel Woodruff, in John C. Dann, ed., *The Revolution Remembered: Eyewitness Accounts of the War for Independence* (Chicago: University of Chicago Press, 1980), 101; John Summer to S. Huntington, Valley Forge, May 14, 1778, NAR (PCC), M247, r56, i42, v8, p165. *Variola* may have taken hold in the old Puritan settlement of Lyme as well. See Vine Utley, "Observations on Old People 80 Years of Age with a Brief Account of the State of the Body and Mind, Their Disease, &c., September 9, 1809," Box 2, Diedrich Collection, MLC. For the complaints about prisoner releases, see Trumbull to Samuel Huntington, Lebanon, May 1, 1780, NAR (PCC), M247, r80, i66, v2, p37.

6. On the 1738–39 epidemic, see James Mooney, *Myths of the Cherokee and Sacred Formulas of the Cherokees* (1891/1900; rpt., Nashville, Tenn.: Charles Elder, 1972), 36; James Adair, *Adair's History of the American Indians*, ed. Samuel Cole Williams (1930; rpt., New York: Argonaut Press for University Microfilms, 1966), 244n, 245–46; Russell Thornton, *The Cherokees: A Population History* (Lincoln: University of Nebraska Press, 1990), 29–30; and Joseph Ioor Waring, "James Killpatrick and Smallpox Inoculation in Charleston," *Annals of Medical History* 10 (July 1938): 301–08. On the 1759–60 epidemic, see Thornton, *Cherokees*, 33; Tom Hatley, *The Dividing Paths: Cherokees and South Carolinians through the Era of the Revolution* (New York: Oxford University Press, 1993), 123, 123n, 125, 141; Pierre G. Jenkins, "Alexander Garden, M.D., F.R.S. (1728–1791): Colonial Physician and Naturalist," *Annals of Medical History* 10 (June 1928): 154; George Fenwick Jones, ed., *Detailed Reports on the Salzburger Emigrants*

Who Settled in America (Athens: University of Georgia Press, 1993), 17:141, 158–61, 200–01, 203, 233, 264, 268, 274; Joseph Ioor Waring, *A History of Medicine in South Carolina 1670–1825* (Columbia: South Carolina Medical Association, 1964), 74–75; and Suzanne Krebsbach, "The Great Charlestown Smallpox Epidemic of 1760," *South Carolina Historical Magazine* 97 (January 1996): 30–37. Georgia suffered another significant outbreak in 1764. Harold E. Davis, *The Fledgling Province: Social and Cultural Life in Colonial Georgia, 1733–1776* (Chapel Hill: University of North Carolina Press for the Institute of Early American History and Culture, 1976), 91.

7. Orders for June 10, 1778, Fort Moultrie, Francis Marion Orderly Books, vol. 1, pt. 2 (HM 623) U8B2, HUV. The second set of orders appears in Marion's orderly book but was issued by Captain Motte. Orders for April 24, 1779, Fort Moultrie, Francis Marion Orderly Books, vol. 1, pt. 2 (HM 623) U8B2, HUV.

8. "Salem Diary, 1779," in Adelaide L. Fries, ed., *Records of the Moravians in North Carolina* (Raleigh: State Department of Archives and History, 1922–69), 3:1300; and "From the Bagge MS. 1779," ibid., 3:1283.

9. "Salem Diary, 1779," ibid., 3:1300; and "Salem Memorabilia, 1779," ibid., 3:1286.

10. "Salem Diary, 1779," ibid., 3:1303. Jacob's changing status in the Moravian community is described in Jon F. Sensbach, *A Separate Canaan: The Making of an Afro-Moravian World in North Carolina, 1763–1840* (Chapel Hill: University of North Carolina Press for the Omohundro Institute of Early American History and Culture, 1998), 95–101. On Schumacher, see "Salem Diary, 1779," in Fries, *Records of the Moravians*, 3:1304.

11. "From the Bagge MS. 1779," ibid., 1283.

12. "Salem Diary, 1779," ibid., 3:1308; and "From the Bagge MS. 1779," ibid., 3:1283.

13. Charles H. Lesser, ed., *The Sinews of Independence: Monthly Strength Reports of the Continental Army* (Chicago: University of Chicago Press, 1976), 126.

14. On the departure from New York, see [Clinton] to Prevost, New York, October 20, 1778, Sir Guy Carleton Papers [Headquarters Papers of the British Army in America] (microfilm), Library of Congress, Washington, D.C. (hereafter cited as DLC), P.R.O. 30/55, reel 4, item 1461. On the delights of Jamaica, see Ontario Bureau of Archives, Second Report, 1904, 2:1164–66, quoted in J. Barton Starr, *Tories, Dons, and Rebels: The American Revolution in British West Florida* (Gainesville: University Presses of Florida, 1976), 130–31. On smallpox breaking out, see Campbell to Clinton, Pensacola, February 10, 1779, Carleton Papers, DLC, P.R.O.

30/55, reel 5, item 1737. (This document can also be found in K. G. Davies, ed., *Documents of the American Revolution, 1770–1783*, Colonial Office Ser. [Shannon: Irish University Press, 1972–82], 17:54–65.)

15. Hugh Mackay Gordon to Winslow, Pensacola, March 20, 1779, Edward Winslow Papers, MG23 D 2, reel M-145 (first filming), microfilm copy of originals at the Harriet Irving Library, University of New Brunswick, Fredericton, New Brunswick, National Archives of Canada, Ottawa, Ontario (hereafter cited as NAC); Muster Roll of Capt. Isaac Costen's Company of Maryland Loyalists, Pensacola, February 22, 1779, British Military and Naval Records, "C" Ser. (microfilm copy of originals no longer in circulation), RG 8 I, v. 1904 (reel C-4223), NAC; and Muster Roll of Captain Caleb Jones's Company of the Maryland Loyalists, Pensacola, February 22, 1779, British Military and Naval Records, "C" Ser., RG 8 I, v. 1904 (reel C-4223), NAC.

16. Minutes of the Upper House of the West Florida Assembly, October 1, 1778, *The Minutes, Journals, and Acts of the General Assembly of British West Florida*, comp. Robert R. Rea (University of Alabama Press, 1979), 291, quoted in J. Russell Snapp, *John Stuart and the Struggle for Empire on the Southern Frontier* (Baton Rouge: Louisiana University Press, 1996), 199; David Taitt to Germain, Savannah, August 6, 1779, in CO 5/80/235–38, quoted in Snapp, *John Stuart*, 201. On the close connection between famine and the spread of disease, see David Arnold, "Social Crisis and Epidemic Disease in the Famines of 19th-Century India," *Social History of Medicine* 6 (December 1993): 385–404.

17. *Pa. Gaz.*, October 27, 1779; Cameron to Prevost, Little Tallassie, Creek Nation, October 15, 1779, Carleton Papers, DLC, P.R.O. 30/55, reel 7, item 2372. (I am grateful to Claudio Saunt for directing me to the last document.)

18. David H. Corkran, *The Creek Frontier, 1540–1783* (Norman: University of Oklahoma Press, 1967), 319–21. On epidemic smallpox in Savannah in the fall of 1779, see George, "Account of the Life," 476–77; and Allen D. Candler, comp., *The Colonial Records of the State of Georgia* (Atlanta: Franklin-Turner Co., 1907), 12:453. On Charleston, see Moultrie to Lincoln, November 17, 1779, in William Moultrie, *Memoirs of the American Revolution* (New York: Longworth, 1802), 2:43–44.

19. Prevost to Clinton [?], Savannah, March 19, 1780, Carleton Papers, DLC, P.R.O. 30/55, reel 8, item 2647. See also Prevost to Clinton, Savannah, March 2, 1780, Carleton Papers, DLC, P.R.O. 30/55, reel 7, item 2605. James O'Donnell claims that these events took place in March 1779, but this is an error. James M. O'Donnell III, *Southern Indians in the American Revolution* (Knoxville: University of Tennessee Press, 1973), 97. On the

Chickamaugas, see John Donelson, "Donelson's Journal," in *Three Pioneer Tennessee Documents: Donelson's Journal, Cumberland Compact, Minutes of Cumberland Court* (Nashville: Tennessee Historical Commission, 1964), 3–5.

20. Moultrie to Lincoln, November 17, 1779, in Moultrie, *Memoirs*, 2:43; and Moultrie to Rutledge, February 22, 1780, ibid., 2:48–49 (see also 2:44). See also David Ramsay, *The History of the Revolution of South Carolina* (Trenton: Collins, 1785), 2:46.

21. Lincoln to Moultrie, Charlestown, February 29, 1780, in Moultrie, *Memoirs*, 2:55–56. On the reluctance of the Virginia militia, see Michael McDonnell, "The Politics of Mobilization in Revolutionary Virginia: Military Culture and Political and Social Relations, 1775–1783" (Ph.D. diss., Oxford University, 1996), 179–80. The newspaper report is in *Pa. Gaz.*, April 5, 1780.

22. John S. Pancake, *This Destructive War: The British Campaign in the Carolinas, 1780–1782* (University: University of Alabama Press, 1985), 66.

23. Simpson to Clinton, Charleston, July 16, 1780, Carleton Papers, DLC, P.R.O. 30/55, reel 8, item 2915; and Waring, *History of Medicine*, 100.

24. Extract of a Letter from Mr. William Ancrum of Charles town South Carolina to Messrs. Greenwood &c., June 2, 1780, in Harold Easterby, ed., *Wadboo Barony: Its Fate as Told in Colleton Family Papers, 1773–1793* (Columbia: University of South Carolina Press, 1952), 6. (I am grateful to Max Edelson of the College of Charleston for directing me to this source.) On Simons, see Request of Mr. Keatg: Simons to remain on his Plantation, August 11, 1780, Cornwallis Papers (microfilm), DLC, reel 44, P.R.O. 30/11/63, items 36–37. On Singleton Mills, see Tarleton to Turnbull, Cross Roads near Singleton Mills, November 15, 1780, Cornwallis Papers (microfilm), DLC, reel 2, P.R.O. 30/11/4, items 63–64.

25. Josiah Smith, "Diary, 1780–1781," *South Carolina Historical and Genealogical Magazine* 33 (1932): 21. Smith quotes the overseer and discusses the Pee Dee plantation in his letter to George Appleby, St. Augustine, December 2, 1780, in "Josiah Smith Letter Book, 1771–1784," 405–06, Southern Historical Collection, University of North Carolina at Chapel Hill. On the infection in Smith's family, see Smith, "Diary, 1780–1781," 113. The "Sword, the Pestilence & fire" quotation is from Smith to James Poyas (London), St. Augustine, December 5, 1780, in "Josiah Smith Letter Book, 1771–1784," 411.

26. Pancake, *This Destructive War*, 99–107.

27. Peter Fayssoux to David Ramsay, March 26, 1785, in Robert Wilson Gibbes, ed., *Documentary History of the American Revolution* (1853–57; rpt., 3 vols. in 1, New York, 1971), 117–18, also quoted in Ramsay, *History of the Revolution*, 2:527–35.

28. Thomas Dring, *Recollections of the Jersey Prison-Ship* (Providence, 1829), chap. 3, quoted in Richard M. Dorson, ed., *America Rebels: Narratives of the Patriots* (New York: Pantheon, 1953), 65, 68.

29. Fayssoux to Ramsay, March 26, 1785, in Gibbes, *Documentary History*, 117–21. See also Chalmers Davidson, *Friend of the People: The Life of Dr. Peter Fayssoux* (Columbia: Medical Association of South Carolina,1950), 42–46.

30. Thomas J. Kirkland and Robert M. Kennedy, *Historic Camden* (Columbia, S.C.: State Co., 1905), 1:207–08, 275; Robert V. Remini, *Andrew Jackson and the Course of American Empire, 1767–1821* (New York: Harper & Row, 1977), 23.

31. On the December outbreak, see "Friedberg Diary, 1780," in Fries, *Records of the Moravians*, 4:1652. Cf. 4:1657–1777, 1884.

32. "Bethania Diary, 1781," ibid., 4:1764–66; "Diary of the Congregation in Salem, 1781," ibid., 4:1682; and "Friedberg Diary, 1781," ibid., 4:1776, 1778.

33. Ja[me]s Phillips to [Nathanael] Green[e], Camp at Salisbury, January 10, 1781, Nathanael Greene Papers, MLC. A summary of this letter can be found in Richard K. Showman et al., eds., *Papers of General Nathanael Greene* (Chapel Hill: University of North Carolina Press, 1994), 7:93. The general's response is in Greene to Phillips, Camp on the Peedee, January 15, 1781, in Showman, *Papers of General Nathanael Greene*, 7:124.

34. Emmet to Green[e], Campbleton, April 4, 1781, Nathanael Greene Papers, MLC; Emmet to Greene, Campbelltown April 28, 1781, letter summarized with brief excerpts in Showman, *Papers of General Nathanael Greene*, 8:170; Emmet to Green[e], Campbleton, April 29, 1781, Nathanael Greene Papers, MLC; Sumner to Greene, Warren, North Carolina, May 1, 1781, Nathanael Greene Papers, MLC; and "Bethania Diary, 1781," in Fries, *Records of the Moravians*, 4:1771.

35. Charles Ross, ed., *The Correspondence of Charles, First Marquis Cornwallis* (London: John Murray, 1859), 1:86.

36. The Philipsburg proclamation is reprinted in Philip S. Foner, *Blacks in the Revolution* (Westport, Conn.: Greenwood, 1975), 193.

37. The Georgia numbers are from Frey, *Water from the Rock*, 86–87. South Carolina population statistics can be found in Peter H. Wood, "The Changing Population of the Colonial South: An Overview by Race and Region, 1685–1790," in *Powhatan's Mantle: Indians in the Colonial Southeast*, ed. Peter H. Wood, Gregory A. Waselkov, and M. Thomas Hatley (Lincoln: University of Nebraska Press, 1989), 38. On refugees from slavery in South Carolina, see From Ralph Izard, June 10, 1785, in *Papers of T. J.*, 8:199, cited in Frey, *Water from the Rock*, 211n.

38. Smallpox appeared on a plantation outside Savannah at this time as well. Candler, *Colonial Records*, 12:453.

39. Eliza Pinckney [?] to [?], Charleston, September 25, 1780, Charles Cotesworth Pinckney Family Papers, DLC, 1st ser., box 5; and Simpson to Clinton, Charleston, July 16, 1780, Carleton Papers, DLC, P.R.O. 30/55, reel 8, item 2915. For King's account, see Boston King, "Memoirs of the Life of Boston King, a Black Preacher," *Methodist Magazine* 21 (March–June 1798): 107, passim. The quarantine King describes appears to have been put into effect on July 7, 1780. See the entry for July 7, 1780, Orderly Book, May 16, 1780–March 3, 1781, George Wray Papers, MLC.

40. James Emmet to Green[e], Campbleton, April 4, 1781, Nathanael Greene Papers, MLC; and Hooper to James Iredell, Wilmington, February 17, 1782, Don Higginbotham, ed., *The Papers of James Iredell* (Raleigh: Division of Archives and History, Department of Cultural Resources, 1976), 2:327–28.

41. Robert Honyman, "News of the Yorktown Campaign: The Journal of Dr. Robert Honyman, April 17–November 25, 1781," ed. Richard K. Mac-Master, *Virginia Magazine of History and Biography* 79 (1971): 394; Richard Henry Lee to William Lee, Virginia, July 15, 1781, in James Curtis Ballagh, ed., *The Letters of Richard Henry Lee* (New York: Macmillan, 1911–14), 2:242–43. William Lee himself lost sixty-five enslaved individuals to the British. Among the runaways were "45 valuable grown slaves and useful Artisans." Richard Henry Lee to [GW], Epping Forest, September 17, 1781, in Ballagh, *Letters of Richard Henry Lee*, 2:256. The account of Nelson's losses is in Ludwig von Closen, *The Revolutionary Journal of Baron Ludwig von Closen*, ed. Evelyn M. Acomb (Chapel Hill: University of North Carolina Press, 1958), 180.

42. Josiah Atkins, *The Diary of Josiah Atkins*, ed. Steven E. Kagle (New York: Arno, 1975), 32; Cornwallis to Clinton, Suffolk, July 17, 1781, Henry Clinton Papers, 1730–95, MLC; and Cornwallis to O'Hara, Yorktown, August 4, 1781, in Ross, *Correspondence of Cornwallis*, 1:113.

43. Cornwallis to Clinton, Yorktown, August 22, 1781, ibid., 1:117; Leslie to Cornwallis, Portsmouth, July 13, 1781, Cornwallis Papers (microfilm), DLC, reel 4, P.R.O. 30/11/6, items 280–81; and O'Hara to Cornwallis, Portsmouth, August 17, 1781, Cornwallis Papers (microfilm), DLC, reel 45, P.R.O. 30/11/70, items 22–23. See also O'Hara's correspondence with Cornwallis in Cornwallis Papers (microfilm), DLC, reel 45, P.R.O. 30/11/70, items 16–17, 18–19, 20.

44. James Thacher, *A Military Journal of the American Revolution* (Boston: Richardson and Lord, 1823), 337; Joseph Plumb Martin, *Private Yankee*

Doodle, ed. George F. Scheer (Boston: Little, Brown, 1962), 241; Johann Ewald, *Diary of the American War: A Hessian Journal*, ed. and trans. Joseph P. Tustin (New Haven: Yale University Press, 1979), 335; and St. George Tucker, "St. George Tucker's Journal of the Siege of Yorktown, 1781," *WMQ*, 3d ser., 5 (July 1948): 387.

45. Ebenezer Denny, "Military Journal of Major Ebenezer Denny," ed. William H. Denny, *Publications of the Historical Society of Pennsylvania* 7 (1860): 249; and Jefferson to William Gordon, July 16, 1788, in *Papers of T. J.*, 13:363–64.

46. Atkins, *Diary*, 32–33; William Feltman, *The Journal of Lt. William Feltman 1781–82* (1853; rpt., New York: Arno, 1969), 6; and Thacher, *Military Journal*, 337.

47. Livingston to Francis Dana, Philadelphia, October 22, 1781 (reel 102, i78, v21, p99), NAR (PCC); *Pa. Gaz.*, November 14, 1781; and Benjamin Franklin, "The Retort Courteous," in *Writings* (New York: Literary Classics of the United States, 1987), 1127.

48. The footnote containing this text has been excised from most extant copies of the book. See the insert in the William L. Clements Library copy of Robert Donkin, *Military Collections and Remarks* (New York: H. Gaine, 1777), 189–90n. Leslie's remarks are in Leslie to Cornwallis, Portsmouth, July 13, 1781, Cornwallis Papers (microfilm), reel 4, DLC, P.R.O. 30/11/6, items 280–81.

49. Although they may not have been carried out in all the enlistment centers, inoculations were ongoing in the Continental army. See Martin, *Private Yankee Doodle*, 213; John Cochran to Thomas Bond, Jr., New Windsor, March 25, 1781, in Morris H. Saffron, *Surgeon to Washington: Dr. John Cochran, 1730–1807* (New York: Columbia University Press, 1977), 100, 165; Thacher, *Military Journal*, 308–10; William Heath, *Memoirs of Major-General Heath* (1798; rpt., New York, 1904), 295–96; and Richard Call to Theodorick Bland, Jr., Winchester, Virginia, February 14, 1779, in Charles Campbell, ed., *The Bland Papers: Being a Selection from the Manuscripts of Colonel Theodorick Bland, Jr.* (Petersburg, Va.: E. & J. C. Ruffin, 1840–43), 1:114. (I am grateful to John Nelson of the University of North Carolina at Chapel Hill for directing me to the last reference.) For Washington's orders, see GW, General Orders, September 29, 1781, in *Writings of G. W.*, 23:152; GW, General Orders, September 30, 1781, ibid., 23:154–55; and GW, General Orders, August 2, 1781, ibid., 23:168.

50. On the Cumberland County outbreak, see Christian Febiger to Davies, November 16, 1781, Executive Papers, Box 18, VIC; and Christian Febiger to Governor Nelson, November 16, 1781, Executive Papers, Box 18 (November 1–November 22, 1781), folder 3, VIC. (I am grateful to

Michael McDonnell of the University of Wales Swansea for sharing these references with me.) On West Point, see Heath, *Memoirs*, 340, 341–42, 343; GW to Heath, December 24, 1781, in *Writings of G. W.*, 23:405; GW to Heath, January 12, 1782, ibid., 23:441; GW to Heath, Philadelphia, March 4, 1782, ibid., 24:39; and Saffron, *Surgeon*, 191.

51. Two medical scholars have made this point, but mainstream scholars rarely mention it. See Hugh Thursfield, "Smallpox in the American War for Independence," *Annals of Medical History*, 3d ser., 2 (1940): 312–18; and Richard B. Stark, "Immunization Saves Washington's Army," *Surgery, Gynecology & Obstetrics* 144 (March 1977): 425–31.

5. ENTIERROS

1. The quotations in this sketch are drawn from Francisco Tomás Hermenegildo Garcés, *A Record of Travels in Arizona and California, 1775–1776*, ed. John Galvin (San Francisco: J. Howell-Books, 1965), 69, 1–2, 70, 75, 15 (page numbers are cited in order of usage). On Pueblo and Hopi aesthetics, see Vincent Scully, *Pueblo: Mountain, Village, Dance* (New York: Viking, 1975), 309.

2. Puerto Rico suffered from epidemic smallpox in 1776. José G. Rigau-Pérez, "Smallpox Epidemics in Puerto Rico during the Prevaccine Era (1518–1803)," *Journal of the History of Medicine and Allied Sciences* 37 (October 1982): 429.

3. Donald B. Cooper, *Epidemic Disease in Mexico City, 1761–1813: An Administrative, Social, and Medical Study* (Austin: University of Texas Press, 1965), 56–69; and Alexander von Humboldt, *Political Essay on the Kingdom of New Spain*, trans. John Black (London: Longman, Hurst, Rees, Orme, and Browne, 1811), 1:111. On the 1760s epidemic in Baja California, see Jacob Baegert, *Observations in Lower California*, trans. M. M. Brandenberg (Berkeley: University of California Press, 1952), 77; and Robert H. Jackson, "Epidemic Disease and Population Decline in the Baja California Missions, 1697–1834," *Southern California Quarterly* 63 (Winter 1981): 321. On its impact elsewhere in northwestern New Spain, see Robert H. Jackson, *Indian Population Decline: The Missions of Northwestern New Spain, 1678–1840* (Albuquerque: University of New Mexico Press, 1994), 152–53; and Robert H. Jackson, "Causes of Indian Population Decline in the Pimería Alta Missions of Northern Sonora," *Journal of Arizona History* 24 (1983): 411–12.

4. Cooper, *Epidemic Disease*, 60–62. Sacramental records from churches in late-eighteenth-century Mexico City still need to be examined in detail. For one set of records in which some (but not all) smallpox victims are

identified with a "B" for *biruelas* (*viruelas*), see Iglesia Católica, San Cosme y San Damián (San Cosme, Distrito Federal), Registros parroquiales, 1598–1954, Archivo de la parroquia de San Cosme (microfilm, reel 0036303, FHL). On monetary equivalents, see Leslie Bethell, ed., *Colonial Latin America*, vols. 1 and 2, *The Cambridge History of Latin America* (1984; rpt., New York: Cambridge University Press, 1986), 2:xii.

5. Cooper, *Epidemic Disease*, 63–67; Ex-Ayun., "Policía, Salubridad, Epidemia Viruela," vol. 3678 (p. 255), tome I, exp. 3, fol. 6, quoted in Cooper, *Epidemic Disease*, 66–67.

6. Cooper, *Epidemic Disease*, 67; Cayetano Alcázar Molina, *Los virreinatos en el siglo XVIII* (1945; 2d ed., Barcelona: Salvat Editores, 1959), 70. The nine thousand estimate is from Humboldt, *Political Essay*, 1:111–12. The estimates are summarized in Cooper, *Epidemic Disease*, 68.

7. Humboldt, *Political Essay*, 1:112.

8. Peter Gerhard, *The North Frontier of New Spain* (Princeton: Princeton University Press, 1982), 7–9.

9. Bethell, *Colonial Latin America*, 1:420, 2:139–40.

10. Ibid., 1:422; 2:156 (map).

11. Herbert Eugene Bolton, "The Mission as a Frontier Institution in the Spanish Colonies," in David J. Weber, ed., *New Spain's Northern Frontier: Essays on Spain in the American West, 1540–1821* (1979; rpt., Dallas: Southern Methodist University Press, 1988), 51–65.

12. The statistics for central Mexico, the Pueblos, and Sonora are from Daniel T. Reff, *Disease, Depopulation, and Culture Change in Northwestern New Spain, 1518–1764* (Salt Lake City: University of Utah Press, 1991), 228–36; and Peter Gerhard, *A Guide to the Historical Geography of New Spain* (1972; rev. ed., Norman: University of Oklahoma Press, 1993), 24.

13. This argument is made persuasively in Reff, *Disease*, chap. 5.

14. Robert H. Jackson has already used these records for detailed demographic analysis of northwestern New Spain. His work is summarized in Jackson, *Population Decline*.

15. Iglesia Católica, Sagrario (Santo Domingo Tehuantepec, Oaxaca), Registros parroquiales, 1699–1967, Archivo de la parroquia (microfilm, reels 0604243 and 0604244, FHL).

16. Iglesia Católica (Santa Cruz, Tlaxcala), Registros parroquiales, 1686–1912, Archivo de la parroquia de Santa Cruz, Diócesis de Tlaxcala (microfilm, reels 0641484 and 0641485, FHL); Iglesia Católica (Tlacotepec de Benito Juárez, Puebla), Registros parroquiales, 1617–1909, Archivo de la parroquia de Tlacotepec de Benito Juárez, Diócesis de Tehuacán (microfilm, reels 0641376 and 0641377, FHL); and Iglesia Católica (Tlacotepec de Benito Juárez, Puebla), Registros parroquiales, 1617–1909,

Archivo de la parroquia de Tlacotepec de Benito Juárez, Diócesis de Tehuacán (microfilm, reel 0641378, FHL). On Oaxaca, see Iglesia Católica, Santo Domingo de Guzmán (Santo Domingo Tonalá, Oaxaca), Registros parroquiales, 1711–1965, Archivo de la parroquia de Tonalá, Diócesis de Huajuápan, Oaxaca (microfilm, reels 0676759 and 0676394, FHL); Iglesia Católica, Sagrario (Santo Domingo Tehuantepec, Oaxaca), Registros parroquiales, 1699–1967, Archivo de la parroquia (microfilm, reels 0604243 and 0604244, FHL); Iglesia Católica, Santo Domingo (Santo Domingo Yanhuitlán, Oaxaca), Registros civiles, 1721–1967, Archivo de la parroquia de Yanhuitlán, Arquidiócesis de Oaxaca, Oaxaca (microfilm, reel 0663255, FHL); Iglesia Católica (Santo Domingo Roayaga, Oaxaca), Registros parroquiales, 1657–1920, Archivos de la parroquia de San Ildefonso Villa Alta, Arquidiócesis de Oaxaca (microfilm, reel 1158080, FHL); and MS, *Memorial del teniente coronel Nicolás de Lafora para volver al servicio militar en el Cuerpo de Ingenieros. México, Julio 12 de 1788*, Archivo General de la Nación, ramo "Indiferente de Guerra," tomo 331, quoted in Nicolas de Lafora, *Relación del viaje que hizo a los presidios internos situados en la frontera de la America Septentrional*, ed. Vito Alessio Robles (México: Pedro Robredo, 1939), 20. On Colombia, see Juan A. Villamarín and Judith E. Villamarín, "Epidemic Disease in the Sabana de Bogotá, 1536–1810," in Noble David Cook and W. George Lovell, eds., *"Secret Judgments of God": Old World Disease in Colonial Spanish America* (Norman: University of Oklahoma Press, 1992), 128–31, Table 4.1. On Guatemala, see W. George Lovell, *Conquest and Survival in Colonial Guatemala: A Historical Geography of the Cuchmatán Highlands, 1500–1821* (Montreal: McGill-Queen's University Press, 1992), 154–60. On Ecuador, see Suzanne Austin Alchon, "Disease, Population, and Public Health in Eighteenth-Century Quito," in Cook and Lovell, eds., *"Secret Judgments of God*," 167, 179.

17. On the camino real, see Christine Preston (photographer), Douglas Preston, and José Esquibel, *The Royal Road: El Camino Real from Mexico City to Santa Fe* (Albuquerque: University of New Mexico Press, 1998). On travel networks of New Spain and their implications for infectious disease, see Reff, *Disease*, 119–24. On temperature, humidity, and smallpox, see *Smallpox and Its Eradication*, 115–16.

18. Iglesia Católica, San Juan Bautista (San Juan de los Lagos, Jalisco), Registros parroquiales, 1710–1957, Archivo de la parroquia (microfilm, reel 0220883, FHL); and Iglesia Católica (Asientos, Aguascalientes), Registros parroquiales, 1705–1941, Archivo parroquial (microfilm, reel 1156112, FHL).

19. Iglesia Católica (Santa Cruz de Juventino Rosas, Guanajuato), Registros

parroquiales, 1720–1966, Archivo de la parroquia de Santa Cruz (microfilm, reel 0641709, FHL); Iglesia Católica, Nuestra Señora de los Dolores (Teocaltiche, Jalisco), Registros parroquiales, 1627–1962, Archivo parroquiales (microfilm, reel 0639775, FHL); Iglesia Católica, San Sebastián (San Luis Potosí, San Luis Potosí), Registros parroquiales, 1651–1922, Archivo de la parroquia del barrio de San Sebastián, Diócesis de San Luis Potosí, San Luis Potosí (microfilm, reel 1156137, FHL); Iglesia Católica (Nochistlán, Zacatecas), Registros parroquiales, 1627–1959, Archivo de la parroquia (microfilm, reel 0226937, FHL); Iglesia Católica, San Juan Bautista (Pánuco, Zacatecas), Registros parroquiales, 1658–1936, Archivo de la parroquia (microfilm, reel 1092833, FHL); and Iglesia Católica, San Gregorio Magno (Mazapil, Zacatecas), Registros parroquiales, 1624–1980, Archivo de la parroquia (microfilm, reel 1164597, FHL); Iglesia Católica, Santiago (Tonalá, Jalisco), Registros parroquiales, 1652–1956, Archivo de la parroquia de Santiago de Tonalá, Guadalajara, Jalisco (microfilm, reel 0218298, FHL); and Iglesia Católica, San Juan Bosco (La Barca, Jalisco), Registros parroquiales, 1684–1958, Archivo de la parroquia (microfilm, reel 0281204, FHL).

20. Iglesia Católica, San Diego de Alcalá (Canatlán, Durango), Registros parroquiales, 1629–1905, Archivo de la parroquia (microfilm, reel 0654962, FHL).

21. For the arrival of smallpox in towns within one hundred miles of Canatlán, see Iglesia Católica, San Antonio de Padua (Cuencamé, Durango), Registros parroquiales, 1656–1963, Archivo de la arquidiócesis de Durango (microfilm, reel 1563156, FHL); Iglesia Católica, Santiago Apóstol (Santiago Papasquiaro, Durango), Registros parroquiales, 1643–1933, Archivo de la parroquia (microfilm, reels 0604830 and 0604831, FHL); Iglesia Católica, San Antonio de Padua (Cuencamé, Durango), Registros parroquiales, 1656–1963, Archivo de la arquidiócesis de Durango (microfilm, reel 1563156, FHL); Iglesia Católica, San Antonio de Padua (Cuencamé, Durango), Registros parroquiales, 1656–1963, Archivo de la arquidiócesis de Durango (microfilm, reel 1563156, FHL); and Iglesia Católica, San Francisco (Mezquital, Durango), Registros parroquiales, 1709–1956, Archivo de la arquidiócesis de Durango (microfilm, reel 1645702, FHL). On the rate of travel of caravans—approximately five to six Spanish leagues per day—see Reff, Disease, 121n. (One Spanish league equals 2.5699 miles.)

22. Iglesia Católica, Sagrario Metropolitano (Guadalajara, Jalisco), Registros parroquiales, 1599–1955, Archivo de la parroquia (microfilm, reel 0038420, FHL); Iglesia Católica, San José de Analco (Guadalajara, Jalisco), Registros parroquiales, 1666–1955, Archivo de la parroquia (mi-

crofilm, reel 0038711, FHL); Iglesia Católica, Nuestra Señora de Guadalupe de la Playa, San José (Bolaños, Jalisco), Registros parroquiales, 1739–1978, Archivo de la parroquia, Arquidiócesis de Guadalajara (microfilm, reel 1164243, FHL); Iglesia Católica, San José (Bolaños, Jalisco), Registros parroquiales, 1739–1978, Archivo de la parroquia, Arquidiócesis de Guadalajara (microfilm, reel 1164244, FHL); Iglesia Católica, San Juan Bautista (Sombrerete, Zacatecas), Registros parroquiales, 1678–1940, Archivo parroquial (microfilm, reel 0654990, FHL); Iglesia Católica, San Sebastián (San Luis Potosí, San Luis Potosí), Registros parroquiales, 1651–1922, Archivo de la parroquia del Barrio de San Sebastián, Diócesis de San Luis Potosí, San Luis Potosí (microfilm, reel 1156137, FHL). The Guanajuato statistic is from the *Gazeta de México*, December 29, 1784, *Colección Documenta Novae Hispaniae* (facsimile ed., Windsor, Mexico: Rolston-Bain, 1985), A-2:210.

23. Gerhard, *North Frontier of New Spain*, 200–01; Edward H. Spicer, *Cycles of Conquest: The Impact of Spain, Mexico, and the United States on the Indians of the Southwest, 1553–1960* (Tucson: University of Arizona Press, 1992), 28–29, 53; Iglesia Católica, Sagrario (Chihuahua, Chihuahua), Registros parroquiales, 1709–1957, Archivo de la diócesis de Chihuahua (microfilm, reel 0162698, FHL); Iglesia Católica, San Francisco Javier (Satevó, Chihuahua), Registros parroquiales, 1772–1955, Archivo de la diócesis de Chihuahua (microfilm, reel 0162607, FHL); Iglesia Católica, San Antonio (Julimes, Chihuahua), Registros parroquiales, 1719–1946, Archivo de la Catedral, Chihuahua (microfilm, reel 1222930, FHL); Iglesia Católica, Purísima Concepción (Guerrero, Chihuahua), Registros parroquiales, 1724–1948, Archivos de la parroquia de Ciudad Guerrero Prelatura de Madera, Chihuahua (microfilm, reel 1222896, FHL); Iglesia Católica, San Pablo (Balleza, Chihuahua), Registros parroquiales, 1747–1924, Archivo diocesano de Chihuahua (microfilm, reel 1222928, FHL); and Iglesia Católica, San Francisco de Borja (San Francisco de Borja, Chihuahua), Registros parroquiales, 1702–1939, Archivo de la arquidiócesis de Chihuahua (microfilm, reel 1222904, FHL). The 850 figure is based on the total burials for the six-month period less 180, or six times the average number of burials per month over the previous sixty-six months before the epidemic struck. On the Tarahumaras after the Jesuit expulsion, see Spicer, *Cycles of Conquest*, 37–39. For a general portrayal of Tarahumara population decline, see Reff, *Disease*, 206.

24. Smallpox is identified as cause of death in both the first and second waves of the epidemic. Iglesia Católica, San Francisco Javier (Temósachic, Chihuahua), Registros parroquiales, 1779–1957, Archivo de la prelatura de Madera, Chihuahua (microfilm, reel 1222869, FHL).

25. For smallpox in central Nueva Vizcaya in March 1780, see Iglesia Católica, Santiago Apóstol (Santiago Papasquiaro, Durango), Registros parroquiales, 1643–1933, Archivo de la parroquia (microfilm, reel 0604830, FHL). For the first reported smallpox fatalities in Sinaloa y Sonora, see Iglesia Católica, Sagrario de San Miguel (Culiacán, Sinaloa), Registros parroquiales, 1690–1967, Archivo de la parroquia, Culiacán, Sinaloa (microfilm, reel 0674051, FHL). Morfi's account is in Juan Agustín de Morfi, *Diario y Derrotero, 1777–1781*, ed. Eugenio del Hoyo and Malcolm Dallas McLean (Monterrey: Publicaciones del Instituto Tecnológico y de Estudios Superiores de Monterrey, 1967), 360–61.

26. Iglesia Católica, Nuestra Señora de la Asunción (Arizpe, Sonora), Registros parroquiales, 1740–1979, Parroquia de Arispe, Sonora, Archivo diocesano de Hermosillo (microfilm, reel 1389124, FHL). On Ati, see Jackson, *Population Decline*, 68. On San Ignacio and Magdalena, see Libro de entierros, San Ygnacio de Caburica Mission Records, 1697–1812 (microfilm, BANC MSS M-M 413, Bancroft Library, University of California, Berkeley [hereafter cited as RQE]); and Libro de entierros, Santa María Magdalena Mission Records, 1698–1825 (microfilm, BANC MSS M-M 414, RQE). On the decline of the missions after the Jesuit expulsion, see Spicer, *Cycles of Conquest*, 132. On the general population decline at Pimería Alta missions, see Jackson, "Causes of Indian Population Decline," 405–23; and Jackson, *Population Decline*, passim (esp. the graph on p. 56). For Pfefferkorn's account, see Ignaz Pfefferkorn, *Sonora: A Description of the Province*, trans. Theodore E. Treutlein (Albuquerque: University of New Mexico Press, 1949), 219.

27. On early Baja epidemics, see Harry W. Crosby, *Antigua California: Mission and Colony on the Peninsular Frontier, 1696–1768* (Albuquerque: University of New Mexico Press, 1994), 87, 106, 225. On the decline of three Baja mission populations, see Jackson, *Population Decline*, 69–83.

28. Teodoro de Croix describes the Yuma colonies in his general report of 1781. Alfred Barnaby Thomas, ed., *Teodoro de Croix and the Northern Frontier of New Spain, 1776–1783* (Norman: University of Oklahoma Press, 1941), 219–22. On Palma's disgust with the Spaniards, see Mark Santiago, *Massacre at Yuma Crossing: Spanish Relations with the Quechans, 1779–1782* (Tucson: University of Arizona Press, 1998), 111.

29. The events of the massacre are most thoroughly described in Santiago, *Massacre at Yuma Crossing*. For summaries, see also Elizabeth A. H. John, *Storms Brewed in Other Men's Worlds: The Confrontation of Indians, Spanish, and French in the Southwest, 1540–1795* (College Station: Texas A&M University Press, 1975), 562–72, 606–09; David J. Weber, *The Spanish Frontier in North America* (New Haven: Yale University Press, 1992), 256–58; and

Roberto Mario Salmon, *Indian Revolts in Northern New Spain: A Synthesis of Resistance (1680–1786)* (Lanham, Md.: University Press of America, 1991), 99–108. On the arrival of the overland colonists at San Gabriel, see Neve to Croix, San Gabriel, July 14, 1781, Archives of California, BANC MSS C-A 22:304–05, RQE.

30. On Loreto, see Luis Sales, *Observations on California, 1772–1790*, ed. Charles N. Rudkin (Los Angeles: Glen Dawson, 1956), 60–61; and Neve to Croix, San Gabriel, July 13, 1781, Archives of California, BANC MSS C-A 22:304, RQE. On the quarantine, see Neve to Croix, San Gabriel, October 29, 1781, Archives of California, BANC MSS C-A 22:306–07, RQE. Thomas Pearcy has challenged the long-standing conclusions of Sherburne Cook and Rosemary Valle regarding the efficacy of the quarantine at San Gabriel, but in the long run, the question may well prove unanswerable. See Thomas L. Pearcy, "The Smallpox Outbreak of 1779–1782: A Brief Comparative Look at Twelve Borderland Communities," *Journal of the West* 34 (January 1997): 26–37; San Gabriel Mission: Burial Records, 1774–1855, microfilm copy, HUV, 440:4; Rosemary Keuper Valle, "Prevention of Smallpox in Alta California during the Franciscan Mission Period (1769–1833)," *California Medicine: The Journal of Western Medicine* 119 (July 1973): 73–77; and Sherburne F. Cook, "Smallpox in Spanish and Mexican California, 1770–1845," *Bulletin of the History of Medicine* 7 (February 1939): 153–94.

31. Sales, *Observations on California*, 168–70.

32. Ibid., 60–61.

33. Ibid., 61; and Robert H. Jackson, "The 1781–1782 Smallpox Epidemic in the Baja California Missions," *Journal of California and Great Basin Anthropology* 3 (1981): 138–39.

34. Entierros, Registers of the Velicatá Dominican Mission, San Fernando de Velicatá, Baja California, 1769–1821, St. Albert's College, Oakland, California (microfilm, BANC MSS M-M 1766, RQE); Entierros, Registers of the Santísimo Rosario Dominican Mission, Baja California, 1744–1868, St. Albert's College, Oakland, California (microfilm, BANC MSS M-M 1768, RQE); Entierros, Registers of the Santo Domingo Dominican Mission, Baja California, 1775–1850, St. Albert's College, Oakland, California (microfilm, BANC MSS M-M 1769, RQE); and Registers of the San Vicente Ferrer Domincan Mission, Baja California, 1780–1828, St. Albert's College, Oakland, California (microfilm, BANC MSS M-M 1767, RQE).

35. Occurencias, diarias, pertenezientes á la Compañia del Rl. Preso. de Santa fee de Nuevo Mexico, February 28, 1781, Spanish Archives of New Mexico, 1621–1821, State of New Mexico Records Center, Santa Fe, New Mexico (hereafter cited as DV6 [SANM]) (microfilm, reel 11, f. 215

[Twitchell 817a], HUV); Catholic Church, Cathedral of San Francisco de Asis (Santa Fe, New Mexico), Church Records, 1726–1956, Bur-49, Archives of the Archdiocese of Santa Fe (hereafter cited as AASF) (microfilm, reel 0016906, FHL). Marc Simmons and Thomas L. Pearcy both have named smallpox as the cause of the early (1780) wave of mortality in New Mexico. Simmons has informed me that he believes he simply extrapolated backward from the later pestilence. However, Pearcy's identification of smallpox in the Santa Fe presidio in February 1780 appears to be a typographical error. As his own footnote indicates, the evidence he cites is dated February 1781, not February 1780. See Marc Simmons, "New Mexico's Smallpox Epidemic of 1780–81," *New Mexico Historical Review* 41 (October 1966): 321; Thomas L. Pearcy, "The Control of Smallpox in New Spain's Northern Borderlands," *Journal of the West* 29 (July 1990): 91; and Marc Simmons, letter to the author, January 10, 2001.

36. Reff, *Disease*, 121n; Antonio Acosta Rodríguez, *La población de Luisiana Española (1763–1803)* (Madrid: Ministerio de Asuntos Exteriores, 1979), 155; and Rudolph Matas, *The Rudolph Matas History of Medicine in Louisiana*, ed. John Duffy ([Baton Rouge]: Louisiana State University Press for the Rudolph Matas Trust Fund, 1958), 1:198–200.

37. Catholic Church, Entierros, St. Lawrence Mission (Picuris, New Mexico), Church Records, 1726–1867, Bur-20, AASF (microfilm, reel 0016869, FHL); and Catholic Church, Cathedral of San Francisco de Asis (Santa Fe, New Mexico), Church Records, 1726–1956, Bur-49, AASF (microfilm, reel 0016906, FHL).

38. Occurencias, diarias, pertenezientes á la Compañia del Rl. Preso. de Santa fee de Nuevo Mexico, February 28, 1781, DV6 (SANM) (microfilm, reel 11, ff. 215–16 [Twitchell 817a], HUV); Manuel de la Azuela, Extracto de revista, Real Preso. de la villa de Santa fee, March 1, 1781, DV6 (SANM) (microfilm, reel 11, f. 220 [Twitchell 818], HUV); Juan Bermejo, Certificado, Santa Fe, February 11, 1781, DV6 (SANM) (microfilm, reel 11, f. 222 [Twitchell 818], HUV); Manuel de la Azuela, Certificado, Santa Fe, February 11, 1781, DV6 (SANM) (microfilm, reel 11, f. 223 [Twitchell 818], HUV); Juan Bermejo, Certificado, Santa Fe, February 24, 1781, DV6 (SANM) (microfilm, reel 11, f. 221 [Twitchell 818], HUV); Manuel de la Azuela, Certificado, Santa Fe, February 25, 1781, DV6 (SANM) (microfilm, reel 11, f. 224 [Twitchell 818], HUV); Catholic Church, Santa Fe Castrense (Santa Fe, New Mexico), Burial Records, 1779–1833, Bur-51, AASF (microfilm, reel 0016906, FHL); Juan Bermejo, Certificado, April 6, 1781, DV6 (SANM) (microfilm, reel 11, ff. 237–40 [Twitchell 822], HUV); and [Manuel de la Azuela], Extracto de revista, Rl. Preso. de

la villa de Santa fee, May 1, 1781, DV6 (SANM) (microfilm, reel 11, ff. 237–40 [Twitchell 822], HUV).

39. Angélico Chávez, comp., *Archives of the Archdiocese of Santa Fe* (Washington, D.C.: Academy of American Franciscan History, 1957), 231–40.

40. Catholic Church, Entierros, St. Lawrence [San Lorenzo] Mission (Picuris, New Mexico), Church Records, 1726–1867, Bur-20, AASF (microfilm, reel 0016869, FHL).

41. Catholic Church, San Juan de los Caballeros (San Juan, New Mexico), Church Records, 1726–1956, Bur-28, AASF (microfilm, reel 0016982, FHL). On one-third of the Indians dying, see Alonso Ortiz, "San Juan Pueblo," in Alfonso Ortiz, ed., *Southwest*, vol. 9, *Handbook of North American Indians* (Washington, D.C.: Smithsonian Institution Press, 1979), 281. On Santa Clara, see Catholic Church, Santa Clara Mission (Santa Clara, New Mexico), Church Records, 1726–1880, AASF (microfilm, reel 0016975, FHL). On San Ildefonso, see Spicer, *Cycles*, 166; and Sandra A. Edelman, "San Ildefonso Pueblo," in Alfonso Ortiz, *Southwest*, 315. On Nambe and Pojoaque, see Catholic Church, Nambe, New Mexico, Church Records, 1707–1869, Bur-17, AASF (microfilm, reel 0016849, FHL); and Catholic Church, Nuestra Señora de Guadalupe (Pojoaque, New Mexico), Church Records, 1774–1851, Bur-22, AASF (microfilm, reel 0016870, FHL).

42. Catholic Church, San Buenaventura Mission (Cochiti, New Mexico), Church Records, 1736–1873, Bur-8, AASF (microfilm, reel 0016757, FHL); and Catholic Church, Santo Domingo Mission (Santo Domingo, New Mexico), Church Records, 1661–1869, Bur-37, AASF (microfilm, reel 0017004, FHL). On the February hunting dance, see Scully, *Pueblo*, 195. On Sandía, see Catholic Church, Entierros, Nuestra Señora de los Dolores (Sandía, New Mexico), Church Records, 1771–1864, Bur-46, AASF (microfilm, reel 0016998, FHL).

43. Frances Levine and Anna LaBauve, "Examining the Complexity of Historic Population Decline: A Case Study of Pecos Pueblo, New Mexico," *Ethnohistory* 44 (Winter 1997): 84, 87.

44. H. H. Bancroft, *History of Arizona and New Mexico, 1530–1888*, vol. 17, *The Works of Hubert Howe Bancroft* (San Francisco: History Co., 1889), 266.

45. Lafora, *Relación del viaje*, 102.

46. Ted J. Warner, ed., *The Domínguez-Escalante Journal: Their Expedition through Colorado, Utah, Arizona, and New Mexico in 1776*, trans. Angelico Chavez (Salt Lake City: University of Utah Press, 1995), 120.

47. Herbert Eugene Bolton, ed., *Pageant in the Wilderness: The Story of the Escalante Expedition to the Interior Basin, 1776* (1951; rpt., Salt Lake City:

Utah State Historical Society, 1972), 232; Eleanor B. Adams, "Fray Silvestre and the Obstinate Hopi," *New Mexico Historical Review* 38 (April 1963): 126; and Bolton, *Pageant*, 233.

48. Bolton, *Pageant*, 235. War between the Navajos and the Comanches has been documented in the 1720s and 1790s. The aggression may well have been continuous through the intervening period as well. John, *Storms Brewed*, 232, 234, 754.

49. Bolton, *Pageant*, 236, 237.

50. The Hopi disaster is described in John, *Storms Brewed*, 593–601. John identifies the early 1780 plague among the Hopis as smallpox but does not give a source (596). Juan Bautista de Anza's account refers to pestilence (*"Peste"* and *"abundancias de Pestes"*) but not to smallpox in particular. Juan Bautista de Anza, Diario de la expediccion que haze á la Prov[inci]a de Moqui, September 10–October 1, 1780, in Alphonse Louis Pinart, collector, Collection of documents concerning New Mexico, 1681–1841, BANC MSS P-E 54:6, RQE.

51. Anza, Diario, BANC MSS P-E 54:6, RQE.

52. For Domínguez's count, see Adams, "Fray Silvestre," 133–35. Anza's count is in his Diario, BANC MSS P-E 54:6, RQE. Scott Rushforth and Steadman Upham have argued that Anza's 1780 estimate is low, suggesting that he failed to understand that "most Hopis were in the fields" at harvesttime. While their argument may have merit, it is worth noting that Anza visited the Hopis after four years of drought, when there was little, if any, harvest to gather. Moreover, as Fray Garcés noted, agriculture in Hopi society was the work of men, not of families. Even if there was a harvest, only the men would have been in the fields, and the fact that Anza (like Domínguez before him) tallied whole families, not individuals, should have compensated for this. He counted 178 families at 6 members each. In addition, Rushforth and Upham appear to confuse Anza's 1780 census with Charles Bent's 1846 census in their work. See Scott Rushforth and Steadman Upham, *A Hopi Social History: Anthropological Perspectives on Sociocultural Persistence and Change* (Austin: University of Texas Press, 1992), 109; and Thomas Donaldson, *Moqui Pueblo Indians of Arizona and Pueblo Indians of New Mexico* (Washington, D.C.: U.S. Census Printing Office, 1893), 15. On gender roles in Hopi agriculture, see Garcés, *Record of Travels*, 70; and Edward A. Kennard, "Hopi Economy and Subsistence," in Ortiz, *Southwest*, 554, 557.

53. Anza to Croix, November 15, 1781, in Alfred Barnaby Thomas, ed., *Forgotten Frontiers: A Study of the Spanish Indian Policy of Don Juan Bautista de Anza, Governor of New Mexico, 1777–1787* (Norman: University of Oklahoma Press, 1932), 244–45.

54. Iglesia Católica, San Nicolás de Bari (Santa Fe de la Laguna, Arquidiócesis de Morelia, Michoacán), Registros parroquiales, 1751–1973, Archivo de la parroquia (microfilm, reel 0761728, FHL).
55. Iglesia Católica, San Francisco Javier (Satevó, Chihuahua), Registros parroquiales, 1772–1955, Archivo de la diócesis de Chihuahua (microfilm, reel 0162607, FHL).
56. Catholic Church, Santo Domingo Mission (Santo Domingo, New Mexico), Church Records, 1661–1869, Bur-37, AASF (microfilm, reel 0017004, FHL).
57. Catholic Church, Nuestra Señora de Guadalupe (Pojoaque, New Mexico), Church Records, 1774–1851, Bur-22, AASF (microfilm, reel 0016870, FHL).
58. Catholic Church, Nuestra Señora de Guadalupe (Pojoaque, New Mexico), Church Records, 1774–1851, Bur-22, AASF (microfilm, reel 0016870, FHL).
59. Iglesia Católica, Sagrario (Santo Domingo Tehuantepec, Oaxaca), Registros parroquiales, 1699–1967, Archivo de la parroquia (microfilm, reels 0604243 and 0604244, FHL).
60. Catholic Church, Santo Domingo Mission (Santo Domingo, New Mexico), Church Records, 1661–1869, Bur-37, AASF (microfilm, reel 0017004, FHL).

6. TRADERS

1. The material in this vignette is drawn from Matthew Cocking, York Factory Post Journal, June 10, 1782, B.239/a/80, fos. 63–64, 68–70, Hudson's Bay Company Archives (microfilm copy), National Archives of Canada (hereafter cited as NAC [HBC]).
2. For the events of 1716–17, see James Knight, York Factory Post Journal, June 3, 1716, B.239/a/2, fo. 36, NAC (HBC); and ibid., November 8, 1716, March 31, 1717, May 28, 1717, and June 11, 1717, B.239/a/3, fos. 10–11, 29, 53, 57, NAC (HBC). On trade for 1782, see Matthew Cocking, York Factory Account Book, 1781–1782, B.239/d/72, fo. 21, NAC (HBC).
3. These numbers refer to actual beaver skins, not Made Beaver. "Half parchment beaver" has been counted as one-half of a full beaver skin. Arthur J. Ray and Donald Freeman, *'Give Us Good Measure': An Economic Analysis of Relations between the Indians and the Hudson's Bay Company before 1763* (Toronto: University of Toronto Press, 1978), 171.
4. James Isham, York Factory Post Journal, February 9, 1738, B.239/a/20, fo. 23, NAC (HBC); and ibid., June 7, 1739, B.239/a/21, fo. 36, NAC (HBC).

5. For York Factory trade statistics, see Ray and Freeman, '*Give Us Good Measure,*' 171. (Here as above, I am counting actual beaver skins, not MB.) On French expansion, see Harold A. Innis, *The Fur Trade in Canada: An Introduction to Canadian Economic History* (1956; rpt. of rev. ed., Toronto: University of Toronto Press, 1970), 84–118.

6. On Indian preferences, trade manipulation, and complaints about inferior goods, see James Isham, "York Factory General Letter, 1739," and Rowland Waggoner and others, "Albany Fort General Letter, 1739," in K. G. Davies, ed., *Letters from Hudson Bay 1703–40* (London: Hudson's Bay Record Society, 1965), 279, 286; and Samuel Hearne, *A Journey from Prince of Wales's Fort in Hudson's Bay to the Northern Ocean in the Years 1769, 1770, 1771, and 1772*, ed. J. B. Tyrell (Toronto: Champlain Society, 1911), 285n. On the emergence of Indian middlemen, see Arthur J. Ray, *Indians in the Fur Trade: Their Role as Hunters, Trappers and Middlemen in the Lands Southwest of Hudson Bay, 1660–1870* (Toronto: University of Toronto Press, 1974), 51–71.

7. Eric W. Morse, *Fur Trade Canoe Routes of Canada/Then and Now* (1969; 2d ed., Toronto: University of Toronto Press, 1971), 30.

8. Cocking, York Factory Post Journal, July 2, 1782, B.239/a/80, fos. 74–75, NAC (HBC). The course of the 1780–82 epidemic in the western interior of Canada is outlined in detail in the work of Jody F. Decker. See Jody F. Decker, "Tracing Historical Diffusion Patterns: The Case of the 1780–1782 Smallpox Epidemic among the Indians of Western Canada," *Native Studies Review* 4 (1988): 1–24 (see esp. 12–24), and " 'We Should Never Be Again the Same People': The Diffusion and Cumulative Impact of Acute Infectious Diseases Affecting the Natives on the Northern Interior Plains of the Western Interior of Canada" (Ph.D. diss., York University, 1989), 55–86.

9. William Walker, "Hudson House Journal, 1781–82," in E. E. Rich, ed., *Cumberland and Hudson House Journals 1775–82*, 2d ser., 1779–82 (London: Hudson's Bay Record Society, 1952), 262–63.

10. Ibid., 261.

11. David Thompson, *David Thompson's Narrative 1784–1812*, ed. Richard Glover (Toronto: Champlain Society, 1962), 235–38.

12. Walker, "Hudson House Journal," 269–70. John Kipling, master at the inland post of Gloucester House on the Albany River, learned from two canoes of Rainey Lake Indians on June 22, 1782, "that the assineybols [Assiniboines'] Country is almost Depopulated." John Kipling, Gloucester House Post Journal, June 22, 1782, B.78/a/7, fo. 24, NAC (HBC). For more on Assiniboine mortality, see Matthew Cocking to Edward Jarvis, Thomas Hutchins, and Samuel Hearne, August 16, 1782, in Rich, *Cumberland and*

Hudson House Journals, 2d ser., 1779–82, 297–99; Alexander Henry, *The Journal of Alexander Henry the Younger, 1799–1814*, ed. Barry M. Gough (Toronto: Champlain Society, 1988), 2:374, 376; and Alexander Henry, "Ethnography of Fort Vermilion," in Elliot Coues, ed., *New Light on the Early History of the Greater Northwest: The Manuscript Journals of Alexander Henry and of David Thompson* (New York: Francis Harper, 1897), 2:516, 521, 523.

13. Thompson, *Narrative*, 236.
14. Walker, "Hudson House Journal," 265, 269.
15. William Tomison, "Cumberland House Journal, 1781–82," in Rich, *Cumberland and Hudson House Journals*, 223–24.
16. Walker, "Hudson House Journal," 269–70.
17. Tomison, "Cumberland House Journal," 225, 227.
18. Jody F. Decker examines the possibilities and implications of this case in "Tracing Historical Diffusion Patterns," 15–17, and " 'We Should Never Be Again,' " 63–67. She could probably state her conclusions even more forcefully than she does. Given *Variola*'s incubation period, there is almost no likelihood that the Indian lad picked up the virus from the Hudson House visitors who arrived at Cumberland House on December 17. It is almost certain that the Indian woman was the source of his infection. Tomison, "Cumberland House Journal," 223–24, 227–29.
19. An Indian woman died at Cumberland House on January 20, but the timing makes it unlikely that this was the same woman who took ill on December 26. Tomison, "Cumberland House Journal," 232.
20. Ibid., 240.
21. Ibid., 231, 229–56 (passim). The 9 percent figure represents the portion of cases that were either flat type or hemorrhagic type of smallpox—the two most severe clinical types and the two types associated with accelerated mortality. Since not all such cases resulted in rapid death, the actual percentage of cases in the twentieth century was probably well under 9 percent. *Smallpox and Its Eradication*, 5.
22. Tomison, "Cumberland House Journal," 234. See also Edward Umfreville, *The Present State of Hudson's Bay*, ed. W. Stewart Wallace (1790; Toronto: Ryerson, 1954), 49. On genetic circumstances, see Francis L. Black, "An Explanation of High Death Rates among New World Peoples When in Contact with Old World Diseases," *Perspectives in Biology and Medicine* 37 (Winter 1994): 292–307, and "Why Did They Die?," *Science* 258 (December 1992): 1739–40.
23. Tomison, "Cumberland House Journal," 233; and Cocking, York Factory Post Journal, July 3, 1782, B.239/a/80, fos. 75–76, NAC (HBC).
24. Tomison, "Cumberland House Journal," 231, 232, 233, 235, 239, 240, 241, 244, 264.

25. Walker, "Hudson House Journal," 289–90; Thompson, *Narrative*, 236. For other examples of this practice, see Cocking, York Factory Post Journal, July 4, 1782, B.239/a/80, fo. 77, NAR (HBC); and Tomison, "Cumberland House Journal," 233–35, 241–42, 244.

26. Tomison, "Cumberland House Journal," 240; and Thompson, *Narrative*, 236. Alexander Mackenzie likewise described "the putrid carcases which the wolves, with a furious voracity, dragged forth from the huts, or which were mangled within them by the dogs, whose hunger was satisfied with the disfigured remains of their masters." Alexander Mackenzie, *The Journals and Letters of Sir Alexander Mackenzie*, ed. William Kaye Lamb (Cambridge: Cambridge University Press for the Hakluyt Society, 1970), 75.

27. Decker, "Tracing Historical Diffusion," 14, 17–18, fig. 4, and " 'We Should Never Be Again,' " 61. On The Pas, see Alexander Henry, "The Saskatchewan Brigade of 1808," in Coues, *New Light*, 2:469n, 470. On January 2, 1782, Indians from the Pasquia region apparently remained unaffected by the smallpox, but by January 31, the disease was "rageing amongst" them "with its greatest Fury." They may have acquired the infection at Cumberland House in spite of Tomison's quarantine. Tomison, "Cumberland House Journal," 234. On the Indians encountered by the brigade, see William Tomison, Cumberland House Post Journal, June 15, 1782, B.49/a/12, fo. 15, NAC (HBC).

28. Ibid., June 22, 1782, B.49/a/12, fos. 16–17, NAC (HBC). In 1774–75, Bruce had apparently wintered northwest of the Red River near Dauphin Lake. In the spring of 1779 or 1780, he was at Fort des Trembles, but this may not have been his location in 1781–82. For more on Bruce's whereabouts, see Dale R. Russell, *Eighteenth-Century Western Cree and Their Neighbours* (Hull, Que.: Canadian Museum of Civilization, 1991), 337; and "The Red River, by John McDonnell of the North-West Company," in W. Raymond Wood and Thomas D. Thiessen, eds., *Early Fur Trade on the Northern Plains: Canadian Traders among the Mandan and Hidatsa Indians, 1738–1818* (Norman: University of Oklahoma Press, 1985), 82. On the impact of smallpox in the Red River–Assiniboine River region, see Mackenzie, *Journals and Letters*, 74–75; John Macdonnell, "The Diary of John Macdonnell," in Charles M. Gates, ed., *Five Fur Traders of the Northwest: Being the Narrative of Peter Pond and the Diaries of John Macdonnell, Archibald N. McLeod, Hugh Faries, and Thomas Connor* (St. Paul: Minnesota Historical Society, 1965), 112; and Thompson, *Narrative*, 235.

29. Cocking, York Factory Post Journal, June 23, 1782, B.239/a/80, fos. 68–69, NAC (HBC). Tomison, Cumberland House Post Journal, June 23, 1782, B.49/a/12, fo. 17, NAC (HBC).

30. Tomison refers to the lake currently known as Knee Lake as

"Maskech'eguan Lake." The two Indian men joined Cocking's party the following day. It is not clear if the women and children did the same. Tomison, Cumberland House Post Journal, June 24, 1782, B.49/a/12, fos. 17–18, NAC (HBC).

31. For the brigade's encounter with the Bungees on June 26, 1782, see Tomison, Cumberland House Post Journal, June 26, 1782, B.49/a/12, fo. 18, NAC (HBC). Although my own analysis differs slightly, the arrival of smallpox at York Factory is documented in detail in the excellent work of Jody Decker. See Decker, "Tracing Historical Diffusion," 13, 17–18. On the June 23 encounter, see Tomison, Cumberland House Post Journal, June 23, 1782, B.49/a/12, fo. 17, NAC (HBC).

32. Ibid., July 1, 1782, and July 2, 1782, B.49/a/12, fo. 20, NAC (HBC); and Cocking, York Factory Post Journal, July 10, 1782, B.239/a/80, fo. 81, NAC (HBC).

33. Ibid., July 2, 1782, B.239/a/80, fos. 74–75, NAC (HBC); Cocking to Jarvis, Hutchins, and Hearne, York Fort, August 16, 1782, in Rich, *Cumberland and Hudson House Journals*, 297–99. Cf. Decker, "Tracing Historical Diffusion," 17–18. On the fate of the man and child brought in by the Cumberland House brigade, see Cocking, York Factory Post Journal, July 10, 1782, B.239/a/80, fo. 81, NAC (HBC). The man's suffering was not unusual. In some cases the entire sole of the foot was shed. A. Ramachandra Rao, *Smallpox* (Bombay: Kothari Book Depot, 1972), 28, 36.

34. Cocking, York Factory Post Journal, July 11, 1782, B.239/a/80, fos. 81–82, NAC (HBC). On July 16, one of the Bungees returned to the factory and told Cocking "that his Brother (the Indian mentioned to be ill of the Head Ache the 11th Instant) whom he lives with, is now ill of the Small Pox." Ibid., July 16, 1782, B.239/a/80, fo. 84, NAC (HBC). On headache as a prodromal symptom of smallpox, see *Smallpox and Its Eradication*, 5, 37, 200. On the Lake Indians, see Cocking, York Factory Post Journal, July 14, 1782, B.239/a/80, fo. 83, NAC (HBC). On the plight of the little girl, see William Tomison, Hudson House (Lower) Post Journal, July 22, 1782, B.87/a/6, fo. 2, NAC (HBC).

35. Cocking, York Factory Post Journal, July 10, 1782, and July 11, 1782, B.239/a/80, fos. 81–82, NAC (HBC).

36. Ibid., July 25, 1782, and July 27, 1782, B.239/a/80, fos. 87, 88, NAC (HBC).

37. On the preservation of the home guard Indians, see William Falconer to Peter Wooldridge, York Fort, August 12, 1782, York Factory Correspondence Book, B.239/b/42, fo. 17, NAC (HBC). On the evolution of the home guard, see Dale R. Russell, "The Effects of the Spring Goose Hunt on the Crees in the Vicinity of York Factory and Churchill River in

the 1700's," *Proceedings of the 2d Congress of the Canadian Ethnology Society*, vol. 2, Mercury Series (Ottawa: National Museum of Man, 1975): 420–32.

38. Hearne, *Journey*, 200–01.

39. Cocking, York Factory Post Journal, August 8, 1782, B.239/a/80, fo. 92, NAC (HBC); Falconer to Wooldridge, York Fort, August 12, 1782, York Factory Correspondence Book, B.239/b/42, fo. 17, NAC (HBC); and John Hodgson, Severn Post Journal, April 14, 1783, B.198/a/28, fo. 15, NAC (HBC). (See also the journal entry for April 15.)

40. Thompson, *Narrative*, 259; Cocking, York Factory Post Journal, July 12, 1782, B.239/a/80, fos. 74–75, NAC (HBC); and Umfreville, *Present State of Hudson's Bay*, 47–49.

41. Walker, "Hudson House Journal," 264, 265.

42. Tomison, "Cumberland House Journal," 224, 275; and Samuel Hearne to John Thomas, Churchill, December 27, 1783, in E. E. Rich, ed., *Moose Fort Journals 1783–85* (London: Hudson's Bay Record Society, 1954), 225. On the close association of famine and epidemic disease on the plains, see Linea Sundstrom, "Smallpox Used Them Up: References to Epidemic Disease in Plains Winter Counts," *Ethnohistory* 44 (Spring 1997): 317 ff. On the mechanisms behind this phenomenon, see David Arnold, "Social Crisis and Epidemic Disease in the Famines of 19th-Century India," *Social History of Medicine* 6 (December 1993): 385–404.

43. *Smallpox and Its Eradication*, 47–48, 196; S. R. Duncan, Susan Scott, and C. J. Duncan, "The Dynamics of Smallpox Epidemics in Britain, 1550–1800," *Demography* 30 (August 1993): 418–20; and Hodgson, Severn Post Journal, April 14, 1783, B.198/a/28, fo. 15, NAC (HBC).

44. Humphrey Marten, York Factory Post Journal, June 29, 1780, B.239/a/78, fo. 37, NAC (HBC); Marten, ibid., July 21, 1780, B.239/a/78, fo. 41, NAC (HBC), and ibid., July 1, 1781, B.239/a/79, fo. 41, NAC (HBC); Robert Longmoore to Tomison, Hudson House, January 17, 1781, in Rich, *Cumberland and Hudson House Journals*, 134; and Walker, "Hudson House Journal," 261–62.

45. Cocking, York Factory Post Journal, June 10, 1782, B.239/a/80, fos. 63–64, NAC (HBC); and Mackenzie, *Journals and Letters*, 106–07. Although published editions of Thompson's *Narrative* make it appear that the account of animal depopulation is Thompson's, it is in fact attributable to Mitchell Oman. (I am grateful to Sean Peake for clarifying this issue for me.) Thompson, *Narrative*, 235–38; and Sean Peake, E-mail to the author, August 23, 1998.

46. Calvin Martin discusses this and similar animal die-offs in Calvin Martin, "Wildlife Diseases as a Factor in the Depopulation of the North American Indian," *Western Historical Quarterly* 7 (January 1976): 47–62 (see esp.

53–56), and *Keepers of the Game: Indian-Animal Relationships and the Fur Trade* (Berkeley: University of California Press, 1978), 131–34. On animal reservoirs and species susceptible to smallpox, see *Smallpox and Its Eradication*, 479–80, 1322–25.

47. Marten, York Factory Post Journal, August 19, 1782, B.239/a/80, fo. 96, NAC (HBC).

48. Ibid., August 20, 1782, B.239/a/80, fo. 96, NAC (HBC).

49. Ibid., August 21–August 22, 1782, B.239/a/80, fos. 96–97, NAC (HBC); and ibid., August 23, 1782, B.239/a/81, fos. 3–4, NAC (HBC).

50. Ibid., August 27, 1782, B.239/a/81, fo. 4, NAC (HBC); and ibid., September 1, 1782, B.239/a/81, fo. 5, NAC (HBC).

51. William Walker to [Master of Cumberland House], Hudson House, August 12, 1782, in Tomison, Cumberland House Post Journal, August 18, 1782, B.49/a/13, fos. 13–14, NAC (HBC); Tomison, Hudson House (Lower) Post Journal, January 14, 1783, B.87/a/6, fo. 19, NAC (HBC); John Kipling, Gloucester House Post Journal, May 24, 1783, May 26, 1783, and June 3, 1783, B.78/a/8, fos. 25–26; and Hodgson, Severn Post Journal, April 14, 1783, and April 16, 1783, B.198/a/28, fo. 15, NAC (HBC).

52. Marten, York Factory Post Journal, October 2, 1783, B.239/a/82, fo. 5, NAC (HBC); Samuel Hearne to Edward Jarvis, December 20, 1783, Fort Churchill Correspondence Book, B.42/b/26, fos. 3–4, NAC (HBC); and Samuel Hearne, Fort Churchill Post Journal, April 2, 1784, B.42/a/103, fo. 25, NAC (HBC).

53. Malcolm Ross and William Tomison, Cumberland House Post Journal, March 11, 1784, and March 19, 1784, B.49/a/14, fo. 25, NAC (HBC).

54. Umfreville, *Present State of Hudson's Bay*, 48; and Thompson, *Narrative*, 236.

55. "Red River," in Wood and Thiessen, *Early Fur Trade*, 82, 88; Thompson, *Narrative*, 245; Henry, *Journal of Alexander Henry the Younger*, 2:543–44; Thompson, *Narrative*, 236; Hearne, *Journey*, 200–01; Cocking to Jarvis, Hutchins, and Hearne, York Fort, August 16, 1782, in Rich, *Cumberland and Hudson House Journals*, 2d ser., 1779–82, 297–99; and Umfreville, *Present State of Hudson's Bay*, 49, 105.

56. Tomison, "Cumberland House Journal," 238; Walker, "Hudson House Journal," 285; Cocking, York Factory Post Journal, July 2, 1782, B.239/a/80, fos. 74–75, NAC (HBC); and Cocking to Jarvis, Hutchins, and Hearne, York Fort, August 16, 1782, in Rich, *Cumberland and Hudson House Journals*, 298.

57. On the North West Company's fur shipments, see Tomison, "Cumberland House Journal," 256 n. 1. For 1781 and 1782 data, see Humphrey

Marten, York Factory Account Book, 1780–1781, B.239/d/71, fo. 18, NAC (HBC); and Cocking, York Factory Account Book, 1781–1782, B.239/d/72, fo. 21, NAC (HBC). On 1784, see Marten, York Factory Account Book, 1783–1784, B.239/d/73, fo. 21, NAC (HBC). (N.B. There are two versions of this account book in the Hudson's Bay Company Archives. The second, B.239/d/74, also reports 2,832 Made Beaver in trade for the year [fo. 21].) In 1785, some 4,437 MB were shipped. Marten, York Factory Account Book, 1784–1785, B.239/d/75, fo. 20, NAC (HBC). A similar decline can be documented at Churchill, which shipped 13,290 MB in 1781, none in 1782 or 1783 thanks to the French attack, and then only 1,019 MB in 1784 after one year's reoccupation. In 1785, some 4,449 MB in furs were shipped, still a fraction of the trade before the epidemic. Samuel Hearne, Fort Churchill Account Book, 1780–1781, B.42/d/60, fos. 20, 21, NAC (HBC), and Fort Churchill Account Book, 1783–1784, B.42/d/61, fo. 18, NAC (HBC).

58. Mackenzie, *Journals and Letters*, 122.

7. CONNECTIONS

1. For an engaging appraisal of Thompson's life and work, see Jack Nisbet, *Sources of the River: Tracking David Thompson across Western North America* (Seattle: Sasquatch Books, 1994). For the material in this sketch, see David Thompson, *David Thompson's Narrative 1784–1812*, ed. Richard Glover (Toronto: Champlain Society, 1962), 3, 9–19, 21–36, 38–40, 45–51. Thompson gives two age estimates for Saukamappee. First, he says the old man was "near ninety," and later, he guesses he was "at least 75 to 80 years of age." Thompson, *Narrative*, 49, 240. On Thompson as an old man, see Nisbet, *Sources*, 257–58.

2. Matthew Cocking, York Factory Post Journal, June 23, 1782, B.239/a/80, fo. 70, NAC (HBC). Oman's account appears in Thompson, *Narrative*, 236.

3. Demitri Boris Shimkin, *Wind River Shoshone Ethnogeography*, vol. 5, *University of California Anthropological Records* (Berkeley: University of California Press, 1947), 245.

4. D. Fernando V, y Doña Isabel en Granada a 17 de Septiembre de 1501, in "Recopilacion de leyas de los reynos de las Indias," 1943, tomo II, libro VI, titulo I, 196, quoted in Frank Raymond Secoy, *Changing Military Patterns on the Great Plains* (1953; rpt., Lincoln: University of Nebraska Press, 1992), 2–5n (translation mine); and Gary Clayton Anderson, *The Indian Southwest, 1580–1830: Ethnogenesis and Reinvention* (Norman: University of Oklahoma Press, 1999), 169.

5. On Sioux expansion, see Richard White, "The Winning of the West: The Expansion of the Western Sioux in the Eighteenth and Nineteenth Centuries," *Journal of American History* 65 (September 1978): 319–43. On the Assiniboine-Sioux conflict, see Pierre Margry, *Découvertes et établissements des français dans l'ouest et dans le sud l'Amérique septentrionale (1614–1754)* (Paris: Imprimerie Jouaust et Sigaux, 1886), 6:82. For further discussion, see Secoy, *Changing Military Patterns*, 42, 67; Arthur J. Ray and Donald Freeman, *'Give Us Good Measure': An Economic Analysis of Relations between the Indians and the Hudson's Bay Company before 1763* (Toronto: University of Toronto Press, 1978), 43–44. On the *pays d'en haut*, see Richard White, *The Middle Ground: Indians, Empires, and Republics in the Great Lakes Region, 1650–1815* (New York: Cambridge University Press, 1991), 1–49. On contact with French traders and the availability of firearms, see Gary Clayton Anderson, *Kinsmen of Another Kind: Dakota-White Relations in the Upper Mississippi Valley, 1650–1862* (Lincoln: University of Nebraska Press, 1984), 32–36. A Lakota Sioux winter count denotes 1684 as the year "the very first White man they had ever seen came among them," a date reflecting the later arrival of French traders among the Yanktonais than among their Dakota kin to the east. See James H. Howard, "Yanktonai Ethnohistory and the John K. Bear Winter Count," *Plains Anthropologist* 20 (1976): 21; and Secoy, *Changing Military Patterns*, 67.

6. On Sioux fierceness without guns, see Nicolas Perrot, "Memoir on the Manners, Customs, and Religion of the Savages of North America," in Emma Helen Blair, ed., *The Indian Tribes of the Upper Mississippi Valley and Region of the Great Lakes* (Cleveland: Arthur H. Clark, 1911), 1:164. For a side-by-side comparison of many of the available winter counts, see James H. Howard, "Dakota Winter Counts as a Source of Plains History," *Bulletin* 173, Smithsonian Institution Bureau of American Ethnology, Anthropological Papers, no. 61 (Washington, D.C.: U.S. Government Printing Office, 1960): 335–416. On the Omahas and Arikaras or Pawnees, see Howard, "Yanktonai Ethnohistory," 21–23. For the Sicangu encounters, see Garrick Mallery, *Picture-Writing of the American Indians*, Tenth Annual Report of the Bureau of Ethnology to the Secretary of the Smithsonian Institution, 1888–'89 (1893; rpt. New York: Dover, n.d.), 1:295–305.

7. On the deadlock at the Missouri, see White, "Winning of the West," 323–24. The Mandans or Hidatsas may well have made the long journey to York Factory themselves as early as 1715. Soon thereafter, however, these Indians (if they were indeed Mandans or Hidatsas) appear to have decided that the trip was too difficult, for they disappear from the York Factory records after 1721. Thereafter, they probably relied upon second-hand goods acquired through Cree and Assiniboine traders. See Arthur J.

Ray, *Indians in the Fur Trade: Their Role as Hunters, Trappers and Middlemen in the Lands Southwest of Hudson Bay, 1660–1870* (Toronto: University of Toronto Press, 1974), 55–61. For a different point of view, see Dale R. Russell, *Eighteenth-Century Western Cree and Their Neighbours* (Hull, Que.: Canadian Museum of Civilization, 1991), 133–36. On French contacts with the Pawnees, see Richard White, *The Roots of Dependency: Subsistence, Environment, and Social Change among the Choctaws, Pawnees, and Navajos* (Lincoln: University of Nebraska Press, 1983), 189; and White, "Winning of the West," 323–24. On the value of the Missouri trade to St. Louis traders at the time of the American Revolution, see Pedro Piernas, Nations of the Missouri, May 19, 1775, in Lawrence Kinnaird, ed., *Spain in the Mississippi Valley, 1765–1794: Translations of Materials from the Spanish Archives in the Bancroft Library*, vol. 2, *Annual Report of the American Historical Association for the Year 1945* (Washington, D.C.: U.S. Government Printing Office, 1949), 1:228, 229. Sioux bands also benefited from the new St. Louis trade. See Francisco Cruzat to Luis de Unzaga y Amezaga, St. Louis, November 21, 1776, in Kinnaird, *Spain in the Mississippi Valley*, 233–34. For a general account of voyageur activity on the Missouri in this period, see the introduction to A. P. Nasatir, ed., *Before Lewis and Clark: Documents Illustrating the History of the Missouri, 1785–1804* (1952; rpt., Lincoln: University of Nebraska Press, 1990), 1:58–74.

8. Mallery, *Picture-Writing*, 1:306.

9. Colin G. Calloway, "Snake Frontiers: The Eastern Shoshones in the Eighteenth Century," *Annals of Wyoming* 63 (1991): 84–85; Alice B. Kehoe, *North American Indians: A Comprehensive Account* (Englewood Cliffs, N.J.: Prentice Hall, 1981), 287–88; and Demitri B. Shimkin, "Eastern Shoshone," in Warren L. D'Azevedo, ed., *Great Basin*, vol. 11, *Handbook of North American Indians* (Washington, D.C.: Smithsonian Institution Press, 1986), 308–09.

10. Calloway, "Snake Frontiers," 84–85.

11. Ibid., 86–87; and Thompson, *Narrative*, 240–41.

12. Thompson, *Narrative*, 242–45. The 1805 report is from François-Antoine Larocque, "A Few Observations on the Rocky Mountain Indians with Whom I Passed the Summer [of 1805]," in W. Raymond Wood and Thomas D. Thiessen, eds., *Early Fur Trade on the Northern Plains: Canadian Traders among the Mandan and Hidatsa Indians, 1738–1818* (Norman: University of Oklahoma Press, 1985), 220, cf. 247; and Calloway, "Snake Frontiers," 88.

13. John Canfield Ewers, "The Horse in Blackfoot Indian Culture, with Comparative Material from Other Western Tribes," *Bulletin* 159 Smithsonian Institution, Bureau of American Ethnology, (Washington, D.C.:

U.S. Government Printing Office, 1955): 3–4; and Secoy, *Changing Military Patterns*, 104.

14. On the acquisition of horses from the Utes, see Demitri B. Shimkin, "Introduction of the Horse," in D'Azevedo, *Great Basin*, 517. On 1706, see Thomas W. Kavanagh, *Comanche Political History: An Ethnohistorical Perspective, 1706–1875* (Lincoln: University of Nebraska Press in cooperation with the American Indian Studies Research Institute, Indiana University, Bloomington, 1996), 63; and Elizabeth A. H. John, *Storms Brewed in Other Men's Worlds: The Confrontation of Indians, Spanish, and French in the Southwest, 1540–1795* (College Station: Texas A&M University Press, 1975), 231–32.

15. On traveling in battle formation, see Pedro de Rivera, *Diario y derroterro de lo camionado, visto y observado en la visita que lo hizo a los presidios de la Nuevo España septentrional*, ed. Vito Allesio Robles (Distrito Federal, Mexico: Secretaria de la Defensa Nacional, 1946), 78–79, quoted in Kavanagh, *Comanche Political History*, 67. On the demand for slaves, see Anderson, *Indian Southwest*, 205–06. Seeking to curtail the flow of arms to their Comanche enemies, the Osages blockaded the Arkansas River and eventually forced the Wichitas to move south to the Red River. Willard H. Rollings, *The Osage: An Ethnohistorical Study of Hegemony on the Prairie-Plains* (Columbia: University of Missouri Press, 1992), 126–28; Anderson, *Indian Southwest*, 152–53; and John, *Storms Brewed*, 316–17. A June 1768 report indicated that seventeen loads of British guns had recently reached the Comanches. Alfred Barnaby Thomas, ed., *Forgotten Frontiers: A Study of the Spanish Indian Policy of Don Juan Bautista de Anza, Governor of New Mexico, 1777–1787* (Norman: University of Oklahoma Press, 1932), 61. On the Comanche gun trade, see Kavanagh, *Comanche Political History*, 128–29; Daniel H. Usner, Jr., *Indians, Settlers, & Slaves in a Frontier Exchange Economy: The Lower Mississippi Valley before 1783* (Chapel Hill: University of North Carolina Press for the Institute of Early American History and Culture, 1992), 133–36; and John, *Storms Brewed*, 378, 408, 412, 451.

16. Franchère's comments extended to the Spokanes as well. A North West Company trader named McTavish told Franchère "that he had seen among the Spokans an old woman who told him that she had seen men plowing the earth; she told him that she had also seen churches, which she made him understand by imitating the sound of a bell and the action of pulling a bell-rope; and further to confirm her account, made the sign of the cross. That gentleman concluded that she had been made prisoner and sold to the Spaniards on the Del Norte [Rio Grande]; but I think it more probable it was nearer, in North California, at the mission of San

Carlos or San Francisco." Gabriel Franchère, *A Voyage to the Northwest Coast of America* (Chicago: Lakeside, 1954), 203–05. The Larocque quotation is from his "Journal of an Excursion of Discovery to the Rocky Mountains by Mr. [François-Antoine] Larocque in the Year 1805 from the 2d of June to the 18th of October," in Wood and Thiessen, *Early Fur Trade*, 189, 220 (see also 170n). On the exchange of horses and goods for slaves, see Calloway, "Snake Frontiers," 87.

17. Thompson, *Narrative*, 244.

18. On the Blackfeet acquiring the horse, see Ewers, *The Horse in Blackfoot Indian Culture*, 15–19. For Hendey's report, see Anthony Hendey, York Factory Post Journal, August 21, 1754–February 10, 1755, B.239/a/40, fos. 11, 14, 18–19, 22, 27, NAC (HBC). Cocking's account is in Matthew Cocking, *An Adventurer from Hudson Bay: Journal of Matthew Cocking, from York Factory to the Blackfeet Country, 1772–73* (Ottawa: Royal Society of Canada, 1909), 106, 110.

19. On the Crow trade, see Ewers, *The Horse in Blackfoot Indian Culture*, 7–8; and Donald J. Lehmer, "The Other Side of the Fur Trade," in *Selected Writings of Donald J. Lehmer*, ed. W. Raymond Wood (Lincoln, Neb.: J & L Reprint Co., 1977), 96–97. In return for horses, the Crows gave the Shoshones metal arrow points they had probably obtained from the Missouri River tribes. Richard E. Hughes and James A. Bennyhoff, "Early Trade," in D'Azevedo, *Great Basin*, 242, 293–95. For the Indian with the cross, see Pierre Gaultier de Varennes, Sieur de la Vérendrye, *Journals and Letters of Pierre Gaultier de Varennes de la Vérendrye*, ed. Lawrence J. Burpee (Toronto: Champlain Society, 1927), 366–73. On the Mandan-Hidatsa villages as commercial hubs, see Ewers, *The Horse in Blackfoot Indian Culture*, 10. Lieutenant Governor Zenon Trudeau's comments were based on the reports of Jacques d'Église, a French trader working for Spain who spent time with the Mandans in 1790–91. Trudeau to Baron de Carondelet, St. Louis, October 20, 1792, in Kinnaird, *Spain in the Mississippi Valley*, 3:93.

20. On the destruction of the presidio, see Thomas, *Forgotten Frontiers*, 60. The Croix quotation is from his "General Report of 1781," *Teodoro de Croix and the Northern Frontier of New Spain, 1776–1783*, ed. Alfred Barnaby Thomas (Norman: University of Oklahoma Press, 1941), 111.

21. Diary of Governor Anza's expedition against the Comanche Nation, August 15–September 10, 1779, in Thomas, *Forgotten Frontiers*, 129–32, 376n. There may have been as many as three eighteenth-century Comanche chiefs known by the name of Cuerno Verde. On Cuerno Verde's identity, see John, *Storms Brewed*, 469; and Kavanagh, *Comanche Political History*, 92–93.

NOTES TO PAGES 211–213   337

22. Diary of Governor Anza's expedition, in Thomas, *Forgotten Frontiers*, 136. On the headdress, see Anza to Croix, Santa Fe, November 1, 1779, in Thomas, *Forgotten Frontiers*, 134–35, 142.

23. On the continuing hostilities in Texas, see Cabello to Croix, Béxar, September 19, 1780, Bexar Archives, 2C42, Center for American History, University of Texas at Austin (hereafter cited as IXA [CAH]); Cabello to Croix, Béxar, October 20, 1780, Bexar Archives, 2C43, IXA (CAH); Cabello to Croix, Béxar, December 6, 1780, Bexar Archives, 2C44, IXA (CAH). On the Comanches' disappearance, see Kavanagh, *Comanche Political History*, 95.

24. On Santander Jiménez, see Iglesia Católica, de los Cinco Señores (Santander Jiménez, Tamaulipas), Registros parroquiales, 1749–1911, Archivo de la parroquia de los Cinco Señores (microfilm, reel 0640389, FHL). The 15,674 population figure is from 1760–61. See Gerhard, *North Frontier of New Spain*, 171, 223. For mortality in Parras and Saltillo, see Iglesia Católica, Santa María (Parras, Coahuila), Registros parroquiales, 1627–1908, Archivo de la parroquia (microfilm, reel 0605294, FHL); and Iglesia Católica, Sagrario Metropolitano (Saltillo, Coahuila), Registros parroquiales, 1684–1906, Archivo del Sagrario Metropolitano (microfilm, reel 0605106, FHL).

25. On Monterrey, see Iglesia Católica, Catedral (Monterrey, Nuevo León), Registros parroquiales, 1667–1968, Archivo de la parroquia del Sagrario Metropolitano Catedral en Monterrey, Estado de Nuevo León (microfilm, reel 0605196, FHL). On the Rio Grande missions, see José David García, Estado actual de las misiones de la provincia de Coahuila y Río Grande de la misma jurisdiccion, año de 1786, March 3, 1786, Documents relating to the missions of New Spain, 1781–90, BANC MSS M-M 431, folders 3 and 34, RQE. Note that there are two copies of García's report in this collection.

26. On the cultivation of hostilities toward the Lipans, see Croix to Cabello, Chihuahua, August 16, 1779, Bexar Archives, 2C35, IXA (CAH); Cabello to Croix, Béxar, September 3, 1779, Bexar Archives, 2C36, IXA (CAH); and Croix to Cabello, Arispe, September 10, 1780, Bexar Archives, 2C42, IXA (CAH). Cabello's "pernicious" quotation is from Cabello to Croix, Béxar, October 20, 1780, Bexar Archives, 2C43, IXA (CAH). For more on Espíritu Santo, see Cabello to Croix, Béxar, November 30, 1780, Bexar Archives, 2C44, IXA (CAH).

27. The quotations are from the following: Cabello to Croix, Béxar, November 20, 1780, Bexar Archives, 2C44, IXA (CAH); Cabello to Croix, Béxar, December 6, 1780, Bexar Archives, 2C44, IXA (CAH); Domingo Cabello, Strength report and daily record of occurrences at San Antonio de Béxar

338 NOTES TO PAGES 213–214

Presidio for January 1781, Béxar, January 31, 1781, Bexar Archives, 2C44, IXA (CAH). The epidemic's impact is visible in the following two sets of records: Misión de San Antonio de Valero, San Fernando Cathedral Missions (San Antonio, Texas), Parish Registers, 1731–1860, Archdiocese of San Antonio, San Antonio, Texas (microfilm, reel 0025437, FHL); and Libro de entierros de la iglesia parroquial de la villa de San Fernando y presidio de San Antonio de Béxar, 1761–1801, San Fernando Cathedral (San Antonio, Texas), Parish Registers, 1703–1957, Archdiocese of San Antonio, San Antonio, Texas (microfilm, reel 0025450, FHL). Other San Antonio burial records are too incomplete to yield meaningful data. Smallpox and its attendant population loss are identified at the Texas missions in 1780 in José Francisco López, Informe, May 5, 1786, [Report on the Missions of the Province of Texas, copy], Documents relating to the missions of New Spain, 1781–1790, BANC MSS M-M 431, RQE. The population estimates from 1777 and 1783 are from Marion A. Habig, *The Alamo Chain of Missions: A History of San Antonio's Five Old Missions* (Chicago: Franciscan Herald Press, 1968), 270.

28. Domingo Cabello, Strength report and daily record of occurrences at San Antonio de Béxar Presidio for January 1781, Béxar, January 31, 1781, Bexar Archives, 2C44, IXA (CAH); and Cabello to Croix, Béxar, December 6, 1780, Bexar Archives, 2C44, IXA (CAH).

29. Pedro Vial and Francisco Xavier Chaves, "Inside the Comanchería: The Diary of Pedro Vial and Francisco Xavier Chaves," ed. Elizabeth A. H. John, trans. Adán Benavides, Jr., *Southwestern Historical Quarterly* 98 (July 1994): 35n, 37–38. See also Kavanagh, *Comanche Political History*, 97. The identification of La Zarca's location comes from Anderson, *Indian Southwest*, 212, 220. While Anderson's identification is almost certainly correct, it is conceivable (but extremely unlikely) that the infection came from Hacienda de la Zarca in the Mexican state of Durango, where the pox almost certainly struck around this time. For other possibilities, see Vial and Chaves, "Inside the Comanchería," 38n; Kavanagh, *Comanche Political History*, 500n; and Herbert E. Bolton, "French Intrusions into New Mexico, 1749–1752," in H. Morse Stephens and Eugene Bolton, *The Pacific Ocean in History; Papers and Addresses Presented at the Panama-Pacific Historical Congress* (New York: Macmillan, 1917), 394.

30. For references to the unnamed epidemic, see Herbert Eugene Bolton, *Athanase de Mézières and the Louisiana-Texas Frontier, 1768–1780* (Cleveland: Arthur H. Clark, 1914), 1:83–84, 2:231–32, 250; John C. Ewers, "The Influence of Epidemics on the Indian Populations and Cultures of Texas," *Plains Anthropologist* 18 (1973): 108; and Pat Ireland Nixon, *A Century of Medicine in San Antonio: The Story of Medicine in Bexar County, Texas*

(San Antonio: Lancaster Press for the author, 1936), 3. For parish records of Natchitoches, see Catholic Church, St. François (Natchitoches, Louisiana), Parish Registers, 1729–1796, Archives of the Immaculate Conception Church, Natchitoches, Louisiana (microfilm, reel 1026611, FHL). On the New Orleans City Council, see Records and Deliberations of the Cabildo, Book 1, 284–85, quoted in Rudolph Matas, *The Rudolph Matas History of Medicine in Louisiana*, ed. John Duffy ([Baton Rouge]: Louisiana State University Press for the Rudolph Matas Trust Fund, 1958), 1:198. On the identification as smallpox, see Antonio Acosta Rodríguez, *La población de Luisiana Española (1763–1803)* (Madrid: Ministerio de Asuntos Exteriores, 1979), 155–56. Rodríguez gives a different, vague accounting of the epidemic's arrival. On the New Orleans smallpox hospital, see Gilbert C. Din, "The Offices and Functions of the New Orleans Cabildo," in Gilbert C. Din, ed., *The Spanish Presence in Louisiana, 1763–1803* (Lafayette: Center for Louisiana Studies, University of Southwestern Louisiana, 1996), 150–51. The first Galveztown figure comes from Gilbert C. Din, *The Canary Islanders of Louisiana* (Baton Rouge and London: Louisiana State University Press, 1988), 35. The second (along with the 404 total) comes from Rodríguez, *Población*, 141.

31. William W. Warren, *History of the Ojibway Nation* (1885; rpt., Minneapolis: Ross & Haines, 1957), 261–62.

32. Alexander Mackenzie, *The Journals and Letters of Sir Alexander Mackenzie*, ed. William Kaye Lamb (Cambridge: Cambridge University Press for the Hakluyt Society, 1970), 74–75.

33. Georges-Henri-Victor Collot, *A Journey in North America* (1826; Firenze: O. Lange, 1924), 1:289–90. See also Pierre Antoine Tabeau, *Tabeau's Narrative of Loisel's Expedition to the Upper Missouri*, ed. Annie Heloise Abel (Norman: University of Oklahoma Press, 1939), 14n. For the appraisals of Lewis and Clark, see William Clark, "Estimate of the Eastern Indians," in Gary E. Moulton, ed., *The Journals of the Lewis and Clark Expedition* (Lincoln: University of Nebraska Press, 1983–93), 3:233, 402–03, 405.

34. Moulton, *Journals of the Lewis and Clark Expedition*, 3:233, 294–95, 312 (cf. 8:85–86). The map showing smallpox and Sioux depredations is in ibid., 1:map 28. On the Hidatsas fending off the Sioux, see Clark, "Estimate," ibid., 3:405. On the 1837 epidemic, see Michael K. Trimble, *An Ethnohistorical Interpretation of the Spread of Smallpox in the Northern Plains Utilizing Concepts of Disease Ecology* (1979; rpt., Lincoln, Neb.: J & L Reprint Co., 1986); and Trimble, "Epidemiology on the Northern Plains: A Cultural Perspective" (Ph.D. diss., University of Missouri, Columbia, 1985).

35. On abandoned Arikara villages, see Tabeau, *Tabeau's Narrative*, 123–24; Moulton, *Journals of the Lewis and Clark Expedition*, 3:161; and Henry M.

Brackenridge, *Views of Louisiana, Together with a Journal of a Voyage up the Missouri River in 1811* (Pittsburgh: Cramer, Spear, and Eichbaum, 1814), 242. Truteau's appraisal is from Jean-Baptiste Truteau, "Journal of Truteau on the Missouri River, 1794–1795," in Nasatir, *Before Lewis and Clark*, 1:299. William Clark describes Pawnees living with the Arikaras, perhaps seeking safety in numbers. Moulton, *Journals of the Lewis and Clark Expedition*, 3:161. On Arikaras taking refuge among the Mandans and Hidatsas, see Truteau, "Journal," in Nasatir, *Before Lewis and Clark*, 1:299; and White, "Winning of the West," 325.

36. On the Sioux attack on the Arikara village, see Linea Sundstrom, "The Destruction of Larson Village: A Possible Contemporary Lakota Account," *Newsletter of the South Dakota Archaeological Society* 26 (September 1996): 1–4. For High Hawk's count, see Edward S. Curtis, *The North American Indian*, ed. Frederick Webb Hodge (Cambridge, Mass.: University Press, 1908), 3:167. High Hawk was the son of Battiste Good, who also kept a winter count. Good refers to the same event in 1778–79. Mallery, *Picture-Writing*, 1:308. The incident ("Pennis body struck by wand") also appears in an Oglala winter count. Roger T. Grange, Jr., "The Garnier Oglala Winter Count," *Plains Anthropologist* 8 (May 1963): 76. For the Yanktonai count, see Howard, "Yanktonai Ethnohistory," 37–38.

37. Mallery, *Picture-Writing*, 2:589. These winter counts are summarized usefully in Linea Sundstrom, "Smallpox Used Them Up: References to Epidemic Disease in Plains Winter Counts," *Ethnohistory* 44 (Spring 1997): 330–40. The same essay addresses the linguistic designation of rashes by one word (310), the appearance of the epidemic over two successive winters (330–31), and date variations (307). Date variations are also addressed in Howard, "Yanktonai Ethnohistory," 2; and Howard, "Dakota Winter Counts," 339.

38. In several accounts, St. Louis residents assert that the town escaped smallpox entirely until 1801. Some even believed they were immune to the disease by virtue of their residence there. Nicolas de Finiels, *An Account of Upper Louisiana*, ed. Carl J. Ekberg and William E. Foley, trans. Carl. J. Ekberg (Columbia: University of Missouri Press, 1989), 68, 130–31; Joseph N. Nicollet, "Sketch of the Early History of St. Louis," in John Francis McDermott, *The Early Histories of St. Louis* (St. Louis: St. Louis Historical Documents Foundation, 1952), 152; and Auguste Chouteau, "Testimony before the Recorder of Land Titles, St. Louis, 1825," in McDermott, *Early Histories*, 93.

39. Larocque, "Journal of an Excursion," 206; James Mackay (Diego McKay), "Captain McKay's Journal," in Nasatir, *Before Lewis and Clark*,

2:494; Ewers, *The Horse in Blackfoot Indian Culture*, 7–8; and Larocque, "Journal of an Excursion," 213.

40. Thompson, *Narrative*, 245–47.

41. Saukamappee's account of both drowning and mortality is in Thompson, *Narrative*, 246. For other accounts of drowning, see Ross Cox, *The Columbia River: Or Scenes and Adventures during a Residence of Six Years on the Western Side of the Rocky Mountains among Various Tribes of Indians Hitherto Unknown; Together with "A Journey across the American Continent"* (Norman: University of Oklahoma Press, 1957), 169–70; Emmanuel Henri Dieudonné Domenech, *Seven Years Residence in the Great Deserts of North America* (London: Longman, Green, Longman and Roberts, 1860), 1:431; and Henry R. Schoolcraft, *Historical and Statistical Information Respecting the History, Condition, and Prospects of the Indian Tribes of the United States* (Philadelphia: Lippincott, Grambo, 1857), 1:234.

42. Offerings to the good spirit are described in Thompson, *Narrative*, 246; and Tomison, "Cumberland House Journal," in E. E. Rich, ed., *Cumberland and Hudson House Journals 1775–82*, 2d ser., 1779–82 (London: Hudson's Bay Record Society, 1952), 242. The "howlings of despair" quotation is from Thompson, *Narrative*, 245–47.

43. William Walker, "Hudson House Journal, 1781–82," in Rich, *Cumberland and Hudson House Journals*, 262–63; William Tomison, "Cumberland House Journal, 1781–82," ibid., 238; and Matthew Cocking to Edward Jarvis Chief at Moose Fort, Thomas Hutchins Chief at Albany Fort, and Samuel Hearne Chief at Churchill, York Fort, August 16, 1782, ibid., 298.

44. Matthew Cocking, York Factory Post Journal, July 2, 1782, B.239/a/80, fos. 74–75, NAC (HBC); and Anonymous, " 'Remarks' on the French Raids on Churchill and York, 1782," in Glyndwr Williams, ed., *Hudson's Bay Miscellany* (Winnipeg: Hudson's Bay Record Society, 1975), 87.

45. Walker, "Hudson House Journal," 262–63.

8. PASSAGES

1. This vignette draws upon a wide variety of sources. For the arrival of the two Indians, see "An Account of the *Tonquin*'s Voyage and of Events at Fort Astoria in 1811–12," translated from *Nouvelles annales des voyages de la géographie et de l'histoire*, 10 (Paris, 1821), 5–88, in Philip Ashton Rollins, ed., *The Discovery of the Oregon Trail: Robert Stuart's Narratives of His Overland Trip Eastward from Astoria in 1812–13* (New York: C. Scribner's Sons, 1935), 273. On the strange Indians' dress and the letter, see Gabriel Franchère, *Journal of a Voyage on the North West Coast of North America during the Years 1811, 1812, 1813 and 1814* (Toronto: Champlain Society,

1969), 85, 86. The letter is appraised in Claude Schaeffer, "The Kutenai Female Berdache: Courier, Guide, Prophetess, Warrior," *Ethnohistory* 12 (1965): 212–13. For Ross's account, see Alexander Ross, *Adventures of the First Settlers on the Oregon or Columbia River: Being a Narrative of the Expedition Fitted Out by John Jacob Astor, to Establish the "Pacific Fur Company"* (1849; rpt., n.p., 1966), 85. On Chinook and Clatsop enmity, see "An Account of the *Tonquin*'s Voyage," 273. For Thompson's arrival, see Franchère, *Journal*, 86–87. On his identification of the two women, see Ross, *Adventures*, 85; and Franchère, *Journal*, 88. For a brief account of the marriage to Boisverd, the sex change, and the ensuing marriages to women, see David Thompson, *David Thompson's Narrative 1784–1812*, ed. Richard Glover (Toronto: Champlain Society, 1962), 367. For oral accounts of Qánqon's transformation, see Schaeffer, "Kutenai Female Berdache," 195–216. Berdache is discussed in detail in Walter L. Williams, *The Spirit and the Flesh: Sexual Diversity in American Indian Culture* (1986; rpt., Boston: Beacon, 1992). On Kutenai displeasure, see Thompson, *Narrative*, 367. The 1930s descriptions are in Schaeffer, "Kutenai Female Berdache," 195, 200–01 (see also Jack Nisbet, *Sources of the River: Tracking David Thompson across Western North America* [Seattle: Sasquatch Books, 1994], 134–37). Accounts of the journey back up the Columbia River vary, but I am relying upon the following: Franchère, *Journal*, 88; Thompson, *Narrative*, 366–67; and David Thompson, *Columbia Journals*, ed. Barbara Belyea (Montreal: McGill-Queen's University Press, 1994), 160. For the death of Qánqon, see the interview with Simon Francis quoted in Schaeffer, "Kutenai Female Berdache," 216.

2. The arrival of smallpox on the Northwest Coast has received considerable scholarly attention. One historian has argued that the Northwest Coast outbreaks in this period were isolated local episodes and may not have been smallpox at all. Christon I. Archer, "Whose Scourge? Smallpox Epidemics on the Northwest Coast," in *Pacific Empires: Essays in Honour of Glyndwr Williams*, ed. Alan Frost and Jane Samson (Victoria: Melbourne University Press, 1999), 165–91. Other scholars agree that widespread epidemic smallpox occurred, but differ over the number of outbreaks and the most likely routes of infection. See Cole Harris, "Voices of Disaster: Smallpox around the Strait of Georgia in 1782," *Ethnohistory* 41 (Fall 1994): 591–626; Robert Boyd, *The Coming of the Spirit of Pestilence: Introduced Infectious Diseases and Population Decline among the Northwest Coast Indians, 1774–1874* (Seattle: University of Washington Press, 1999), 21–39; Robert T. Boyd, "Commentary on Early Contact-Era Smallpox in the Pacific Northwest," *Ethnohistory* 43 (Spring 1996): 307–28; Robert T. Boyd, "Smallpox in the Pacific Northwest: The First Epidemics," *BC Stud-*

ies (Spring 1994): 5–40; and Robert T. Boyd, "Demographic History, 1774–1874," in Wayne Suttles, ed., *Northwest Coast*, vol. 7, *Handbook of North American Indians* (Washington, D.C.: Smithsonian Institution Press, 1990), 135–48.

3. Nathaniel Portlock, *A Voyage round the World: But More Particularly to the North-West Coast of America* (London: John Stockdale and George Goulding, 1789), 271.

4. Portlock, *Voyage*, 272. For the Russian account, see Kyrill T. Khlebnikov, *Colonial Russian America: Kyrill T. Khlebnikov's Reports, 1817–1832*, trans. B. Dmytryshyn and E. A. P. Crownhart-Vaughan (Portland: Oregon Historical Society Press, 1979), 29.

5. George Dixon, *A Voyage round the World: But More Particularly to the North-West Coast of America* (2d ed.; London: George Goulding, 1789), 237; and Portlock, *Voyage*, 276.

6. Robert Haswell, "Robert Haswell's Log of the First Voyage of the 'Columbia,' " in Frederic W. Howay, ed., *Voyages of the "Columbia" to the Northwest Coast 1787–1790 and 1790–1793* (Boston: Massachusetts Historical Society, 1941), 34. The Indians are identified as Tillamooks in William R. Seaburg and Jay Miller, "Tillamook," in Suttles, *Northwest Coast*, 560.

7. John Boit, "John Boit's Log of the Second Voyage of the 'Columbia,' " in Howay, *Voyages*, 371; and John Hoskins, "John Hoskins' Narrative of the Second Voyage of the 'Columbia,' " ibid., 196.

8. Charles Pierre Claret de Fleurieu, *A Voyage round the World Performed during the Years 1790, 1791, and 1792, by Étienne Marchand* (London: T. N. Longman, O. Rees, and T. Cadell, 1801), 1:328, 438.

9. George Vancouver, *A Voyage of Discovery to the North Pacific Ocean and round the World, 1791–1795*, ed. William Kaye Lamb (London: Hakluyt Society, 1984), 2:540.

10. On villages overrun with weeds, see ibid., 2:516–17. For Manby's description, see Thomas Manby, "Voyage of H.M.S. Discovery and Chatham to the Northwest Coast of America," YUS (B), 2d part, 20–21. Vancouver's appraisal of the extant population as compared with the empty villages is in Vancouver, *Voyage of Discovery*, 2:538. The Spanish account is in John Kendrick, ed., *The Voyage of the Sutil and Mexicana, 1792: The Last Spanish Exploration of the Northwest Coast of America* (Spokane: Arthur H. Clark, 1991), 116. Both Cole Harris and Robert Boyd have examined and dismissed the possibility that the empty villages reflected seasonal migration patterns. Boyd, "Smallpox in the Pacific Northwest," 32; and Harris, "Voices of Disaster," 603.

11. Archibald Menzies, *The Alaska Travel Journal of Archibald Menzies,*

1793–1794 (Fairbanks: University of Alaska Press, 1993), 28–29; Peter Puget, "The Vancouver Expedition: Peter Puget's Journal of the Exploration of Puget Sound, May 7–June 11, 1792," ed. Bern Anderson, *Pacific Northwest Quarterly* 30 (April 1939): 198 (see also Menzies, *Journal,* 34–35); and *Voyage of Discovery,* 2:538–40.

12. Thompson, *Columbia Journals,* 134.

13. Thompson, *Narrative,* 358.

14. "Instructions from Empress Catherine Alekseevna to Captain Vitus Bering for the First Kamchatka Expedition," in Basil Dmytryshyn, E. A. P. Crownhart-Vaughan, and Thomas Vaughan, eds. and trans., *Russian Penetration of the North Pacific Ocean, 1700–1799: A Documentary Record,* vol. 2, *To Siberia and Russian America: Three Centuries of Russian Eastward Expansion* (Portland: Oregon Historical Society Press, 1988), 69.

15. On the voyage of Mikhail Gvozdev in 1732, see "The Report of the GeoDesist Mikhail Spiridonovich Gvozdev to Martyn Petrovich Spanberg Concerning his Voyage of Exploration to the Coast of North American in 1732," ibid., 161–67. Bering's voyages are summarized in Derek Pethick, *First Approaches to the Northwest Coast* (Seattle: University of Washington Press, 1979), 17–26.

16. On the Russian conquest of Siberia, see W. Bruce Lincoln, *The Conquest of a Continent: Siberia and the Russians* (New York: Random House, 1994), chaps. 1–17; Benson Bobrick, *East of the Sun: The Epic Conquest and Tragic History of Siberia* (New York: Poseidon, 1992), chaps. 1–9; and George V. Lantzeff and Richard A. Pierce, *Eastward to Empire: Exploration and Conquest on the Russian Open Frontier, to 1750* (Montreal: McGill-Queen's University Press, 1973). The description of *iasak* is from Heinrich von Füch, "An Eyewitness Account of Hardships Suffered by Natives in Northeastern Siberia during Bering's Great Kamchatka Expedition, 1735–1744," in Dmytryshyn, Crownhart-Vaughan, and Vaughan, *Russian Penetration,* 169. For the surgeon's quotation, see David Samwell, "Some Account of a Voyage to the South Sea's [*sic*] in 1776–1777–1778," in J. C. Beaglehole, ed., *The Journals of Captain James Cook on His Voyages of Discovery* (Cambridge, U.K.: Hakluyt Society, 1967), 3.2:1259.

17. Raymond H. Fisher, "Russia's Two Eastern Frontiers: Siberia and Russian America," *Pacifica* 2 (November 1990): 30–31; Raymond H. Fisher, "Finding America," in Barbara Sweetland Smith and Redmond J. Barnett, *Russian America: The Forgotten Frontier* (Tacoma: Washington State Historical Society, 1990), 29; "Translation of a Part of the Journal of One of Our Russian Officers while at Oonalashka in 1790," in Martin Sauer, *An Account of a Geographical and Astronomical Expedition to the Northern Parts of Russia* (London: T. Cadell, 1802), 56, 56n. The Aleutian Island

account is from "An Extract from the Journals of Captain Petr Kuzmich Krenitsyn and Captain Lieutenant Mikhail Dmitrievich Levashev," in Dmytryshyn, Crownhart-Vaughan, and Vaughan, *Russian Penetration*, 245. On shooting the Aleuts for entertainment, see "Translation of a Part of the Journal" in Sauer, *Account*, 56.

18. John Ledyard, *Journey through Russia and Siberia, 1787–1788: The Journal and Selected Letters*, ed. Stephen D. Watrous (Madison: University of Wisconsin Press, 1966), 75; and Füch, "An Eyewitness Account," 169.

19. On Catherine the Great, see W. J. Bishop, "Thomas Dimsdale, M.D., F.R.S. (1712–1800) and the Inoculation of Catherine the Great of Russia," *Annals of Medical History* 4 (1932): 324. For the Lesseps account, see Jean Baptiste Barthelemy Lesseps, *Travels in Kamtschatka during the Years 1787 and 1788* (London: J. Johnson, 1790), 1:128–29. David Samwell also reported that the smallpox had arrived in Kamchatka "from Ochotzk in Siberia," although he dated the outbreak to 1769. Samwell, "Some Account of a Voyage," in Beaglehole, *Journals of Captain James Cook*, 3, part 2:1252. On flight to the mountains, see Adam Brill, "A Report from Adam Brill, governor of Irkutsk," in Dmytryshyn, Crownhart-Vaughan, and Vaughan, *Russian Penetration*, 238. The 1780 figure is from William Coxe, *Account of the Russian Discoveries between Asia and America* (London: T. Cadell, 1780), 5. This number is repeated in Sauer, *Account*, 307. For the report given to Cook's men, see Samwell, "Some Account of a Voyage," in Beaglehole, *Journals of Captain James Cook*, 3, part 2:1252.

20. Grigorii I. Shelikhov, *A Voyage to America 1783–1786*, trans. Marina Ramsay, ed. Richard A. Pierce (Kingston, Ont.: Limestone, 1981), 55.

21. Writing of the Yakutis of Kamchatka, Martin Sauer says "great numbers were carried off in 1758 and 1774 by small-pox and measles." Neither of these dates corresponds with the known smallpox outbreaks reported by other writers and by Sauer himself elsewhere in the same work. Sauer, *Account*, 124, 307.

22. Portlock, *Voyage*, 271; and Boit, "Log," in Howay, *Voyages*, 371.

23. On Spanish anxieties, see Warren L. Cook, *Flood Tide of Empire: Spain and the Pacific Northwest, 1543–1819* (New Haven: Yale University Press, 1973), 47–55.

24. Tomás de la Peña, "Diary of Fray Tomás de la Peña Kept during the Voyage of the *Santiago*—Dated 28th August, 1774," in George Butler Griffin, ed. and trans., *The California Coast; A Bilingual Edition of Documents from the Sutro Collection*, re-edited and translated by Donald Cutter (1891; rev. ed., Norman: University of Oklahoma Press, 1969), 161, 181. On the spoons, see Estéban José Martínez, "Diario de la navegacion que yo el Alfz. de Navio de la Rl. Armda. Dn. Estevan Joséf Martinez, boy a exe-

cutar al pteo. de Sn. Lorenzo de Nuca, mandado la fragta. Princesa, y paquebot Sn. Carlos de Orne. del Exmo. sore. Dn. Manuel Anto. Florez Virrey Governor y Capitan Grale. de N.E. en el preste. año de 1789," [January 12–December 6, 1789], HM 529, 225, HUV.

25. Juan Crespi, "Journal of Fray Juan Crespi Kept during the Same Voyage—Dated 5th October, 1774," in Griffin, *California Coast*, 207, 209, 219, 243–45; and Peña, "Diary," in Griffin, *California Coast*, 155, 165–67.

26. Sherburne F. Cook, "Smallpox in Spanish and Mexican California, 1770–1845," *Bulletin of the History of Medicine* 7 (February 1939): 153–94; and Rosemary Keuper Valle, "Prevention of Smallpox in Alta California during the Franciscan Mission Period (1769–1833)," *California Medicine: The Journal of Western Medicine* 119 (July 1973): 73–77.

27. Peña, "Diary," in Griffin, *California Coast*, 193; and Crespi, "Journal," ibid., 268–70.

28. Specifications for these and other Spanish vessels visiting the Northwest Coast from 1775 to 1797 can be found in Cook, *Flood Tide*, 550 (cf. 71).

29. Francisco Antonio Mourelle, *Voyage of the Sonora in the Second Bucareli Expedition to Explore the Northwest Coast, Survey the Port of San Francisco and Found Franciscan Missions and a Presidio and Pueblo at That Port: The Journal Kept in 1775 on the Sonora*, trans. Daines Barrington (1781; rpt., San Francisco: Thomas C. Russell, 1920), 35–36.

30. Ibid., 35–36; Miguel de la Campa, *A Journal of Explorations Northward along the Coast from Monterey in the Year 1775*, ed. John Galvin (San Francisco: J. Howell-Books, 1964), 46; and [Francisco Antonio Mourelle], "Segunda exploracion de la costa septentrional de California hecha en 1775 con la fragata Santiago y goleta Sonóra mandádas por el Teniente de Navio Don Bruno de [H]ezeta, y el de fragata Don Juan de la Quadra, desde Sn. Blás hasta los 58 grs. de latitud N.," HM 161, HUV.

31. Cook, *Flood Tide*, 80–81; and Mourelle, *Voyage of the Sonora*, 58.

32. Boyd, "Smallpox in the Pacific Northwest," 23–24; Boyd, "Commentary," 314; and Boyd, *Coming of the Spirit of Pestilence*, 36–38; Portlock, *Voyage*, 271. I am following Warren Cook, who has examined many more manuscript sources for this voyage than I have, regarding illness aboard the *Sonora*. Cook, *Flood Tide*, 80–81.

33. Campa, *Journal of Explorations*, 58, 230, 232; and José García de León y Pizarro, "Extractos historicos y cronologicos de ordenes reales, y providencias para los descubrimientos actos y posesiones de costas y navegación del mar del sur especialmente la parte del norte y de Californias," June 18, 1790, HM 520, HUV. (While this last is not an eyewitness account, it is very likely derived from eyewitness reports.)

34. Benito de la Sierra, "Fray Benito de la Sierra's Account of the Hezeta Ex-

pedition to the Northwest Coast in 1775," *California Historical Society Quarterly* 9 (1930): 238.

35. Cook, *Flood Tide*, 85–86.

36. Charles Clerke to Admiralty Secretary, Plymouth, August 1, 1776, in Beaglehole, *Journals of Captain James Cook*, 3, part 2:1513.

37. See Rüdiger Joppien and Bernard Smith, *The Art of Captain Cook's Voyages* (New Haven: Yale University Press for the Paul Mellon Center for Studies in British Art, 1988), 3:80–98, 433–69.

38. On smallpox at Nitinaht, see Hoskins, "Narrative," in Howay, *Voyages*, 196; and Boit, "Log," ibid., 371. It is worth noting that Nathaniel Portlock had been aboard Cook's voyage and had visited Nootka with him in 1778.

39. Accounts vary, but the rendezvous was either on May 3 or May 4. Juan Antonio García Riobó, "An Account of the Voyage Made by the Frigates 'Princesa' and 'Favorita' in the Year 1799 [*sic*] from San Blas to Northern Alaska," *Catholic Historical Review* 4 (1918): 223; Juan Pantoja y Arriaga, "Extracto del diario," Western Americana Collection, YUS (B). On the meaning of the feather ceremony, see Stephen J. Langdon, "Efforts at Humane Engagement: Indian-Spanish Encounters in Bucareli Bay, 1779," in S. Haycox, C. Liburd, and J. Barnett, eds., *Exploration and Enlightenment in the North Pacific, 1741–1809* (Seattle: University of Washington Press, 1997), 189.

40. The events that took place at Bucareli Bay are described and analyzed from a bicultural perspective in Langoon, "Humane Engagement," 187–97. I have been unable to identify the plague in the following accounts: Riobó, "Account of the Voyage," 222–29; Juan Antonio García Riobó, "Diario que escrivio el P. P. Juan Riobó missionero apostólico de este colegio de San Fernando de Méjico en el viaje que hizo desde San Blas para el descubrimiento del Paso del Norte, año de 1779," Western Americana Collection, YUS (B); Juan Antonio García Riobó [erroneously attributed to Ignacio de Arteaga], "Relación del viaje hecho á la Alaska," Western Americana Collection, YUS (B); Pantoja y Arriaga, "Extracto del diario"; Francisco Antonio Mourelle de la Rúa, "Acaecimientos en el puerto de Bucareli (4 de Mayo–1 de Julio)," in Fernando Monge and Margarita del Olmo, eds., *Expediciones a la costa noroeste* (Madrid: Historia 16, 1991); and Francisco Antonio Mourelle [Maurelle], "Relación del viage que en el año de 1779 hizo el teniente de Nav. D. Bruno de Hezeta á las costas septentrionales de California," William Andrews Clark Memorial Library, Los Angeles, California. Warren Cook and Christon Archer have examined additional manuscripts and likewise cannot identify the disease. Cook, *Flood Tide*, 95; and Archer, "Whose Scourge?," 180–84.

41. Cook, *Flood Tide*, 80–81; and Langdon, "Humane Engagement," 192–93. The following records show smallpox within one hundred miles of San Blas from February through July 1780: Iglesia Católica, San José (Bolaños, Jalisco), Registros parroquiales, 1739–1978, Archivo de la parroquia, Arquidiócesis de Guadalajara (microfilm, reel 1164244, FHL); Iglesia Católica, Nuestra Señora de Guadalupe de la Playa, San José (Bolaños, Jalisco), Registros parroquiales, 1739–1978, Archivo de la parroquia, Arquidiócesis de Guadalajara (microfilm, reel 1164243, FHL); Iglesia Católica, Nuestra Señora del Favor (Hostotipaquillo, Jalisco), Registros parroquiales, 1690–1960, Archivo de la parroquia (microfilm, reel 0282482, FHL); Iglesia Católica (Amatlán de Jora, Nayarit), Registros parroquiales, 1677–1932, Archivo Diocesano de Guadalajara, Jalisco (microfilm, reel 1652668, FHL); and Iglesia Católica, Purificación (Guachinango, Jalisco), Registros parroquiales, 1682–1964, Archivo de la Parroquia (microfilm, reel 1156320, FHL).

42. "Expeditions in the Years 1775 to 1779 towards the West Coast of North America by Captain Juan Francisco Bodega y Quadra," anon. trans., *Anuario de la Dirección de Hidrografía*, Ano. III. 1865, Sección Historica, Miscelanea, p. 33, British Columbia Archives, Victoria, quoted in Langdon, "Humane Engagement," 21. The expedition's encounters with the Tlingits are described in detail in Francisco Antonio Mourelle [Maurelle], "Relación del viage," 28–103.

43. For the absence of known voyages from 1780 to 1784, see Cook, *Flood Tide*, 99–100, 551. On Prince William Sound, see Alexander Walker, *An Account of a Voyage to the North West Coast of America in 1785 & 1786*, ed. Robin Fisher and J. M. Bumsted (Vancouver: Douglas & McIntyre, 1982), 148. The accounts examined include the following: James Strange, *James Strange's Journal and Narrative of the Commercial Expedition from Bombay to the North-west Coast of America* (Madras: Printed by the superintendent, Government Press, 1928); Walker, *Account of a Voyage*; Jean-François de Galaup de la Pérouse, *The Journal of Jean-François de Galaup de la Pérouse 1785–1788*, trans. and ed. John Dunmore (London: Hakluyt Society, 1994); and *"New Fur Trade," an Article from the New World . . . Describing the Earliest Voyage to the Northwest Coast of America* (1788; rpt., San Francisco: White Knight Press, 1941).

44. Peña, "Diary," in Griffin, *The California Coast*, 181. On copper, see Cole Harris, ed., and Geoffrey J. Matthews, cartographer, *Historical Atlas of Canada: From the Beginning to 1800*, vol. 1 (Toronto: University of Toronto Press, 1987), plates 13 and 14. On iron implements among the Haidas, see Crespi, "Journal," in Griffin, *The California Coast*, 227–29; Cook, *Flood Tide*, 73; and Archer, "Whose Scourge?," 175.

45. Beaglehole, *Journals of Captain James Cook*, 3, part 1:321–22.

46. Martínez was clearly unaware of indigenous copper technologies, as he seems to attribute copper to European trade, albeit at a distance. Estéban José Martínez, "Diario de la navegación," HM 529, fos. 224–26, HUV. Manby's observations are in Manby, "Voyage," YUS (B), 2d part, 87 (see also 39). The Pacific Fur Company trader Gabriel Franchère also noted the extent of inland trade networks. Franchère, *Voyage*, 203–05.

47. Richard E. Hughes and James A. Bennyhoff, "Early Trade," in Warren L. D'Azevedo, ed., *Great Basin*, vol. 11, *Handbook of North American Indians* (Washington, D.C.: Smithsonian Institution Press, 1986), 239, 244–45.

48. Gregory Mengarini, *Recollections of the Flathead Mission*, ed. Gloria Ricci Lothrop (Glendale, Calif.: Arthur H. Clark, 1977), 193–94. On hemorrhagic type of smallpox, see *Smallpox and Its Eradication*, 5, 32, 37–38, 62–63.

49. Asa Bowen Smith to Reverend D. Greene, Kamiah, Oregon Territory, February 6, 1840, in Clifford Drury, ed., *The Diaries and Letters of Henry H. Spalding and Asa Bowen Smith Relating to the Nez Perce Mission, 1838–1842* (Glendale, Calif.: Arthur H. Clark, 1958), 136–37.

50. Smith to Greene, Kamiah, Oregon Territory, February 6, 1840, ibid., 136–37; and Franchère, *Voyage*, 203.

51. Both the Chinooks and the Nez Perces were known to trade at The Dalles. See William R. Swagerty, "Indian Trade in the Trans-Mississippi West to 1870," in Wilcomb E. Washburn, ed., *History of Indian-White Relations*, vol. 4, *Handbook of North American Indians* (Washington, D.C.: Smithsonian Institution Press, 1988), 352–54. For the comments of Ross, see Ross, *Adventures*, 98–99.

52. Gary E. Moulton, ed., *The Journals of the Lewis and Clark Expedition* (Lincoln: University of Nebraska Press, 1983–93), 7:64–66, 85–86.

53. Ibid., 6:285, 7:64–66, 86. On Puget Sound traditions, see Martin Sampson, *Indians of Skagit County* (Mount Vernon, Wash.: Skagit County Historical Society, 1972), 25.

54. Thompson, *Narrative*, 236; Ross Cox, *The Columbia River: Or Scenes and Adventures during a Residence of Six Years on the Western Side of the Rocky Mountains among Various Tribes of Indians Hitherto Unknown*, ed. Edward I. Stewart and Jane R. Stewart (1831; Norman: University of Oklahoma Press, 1957), 169–70. For a skeptical view of Cox's account, see Boyd, "Commentary," 309. For Stuart, see Rollins, *Discovery of the Oregon Trail*, 15.

55. On the *Tonquin*, see Franchère, *Journal*, 115–16, 23–27; Cox, *Columbia River*, 63–67; Ross, *Adventures*, 165–68. The story about McDougall is from Cox, *Columbia River*, 170.

EPILOGUE

1. Quoted in Colin G. Calloway, *The American Revolution in Indian Country: Crisis and Diversity in Native American Communities* (New York: Cambridge University Press, 1995), 282.

2. On age at marriage, see Ramón Gutiérrez, *When Jesus Came, the Corn Mothers Went Away: Marriage, Sexuality, and Power* (Stanford: Stanford University Press, 1991), 274–75. On mission contraction, see Caballero de Croix to Juan Bautista de Anza, Arispe, September 15, 1781, DV6 (SANM), reel 11, f. 324 (Twitchell 831); and Elizabeth A. H. John, *Storms Brewed in Other Men's Worlds: The Confrontation of Indians, Spanish, and French in the Southwest, 1540–1795* (College Station: Texas A&M University Press, 1975), 605. On conversion, see Gutiérrez, *When Jesus Came*, 155. Daniel Reff has shown how epidemic disease increased receptivity to Catholicism in the Pimería Alta. Daniel T. Reff, *Disease, Depopulation, and Culture Change in Northwestern New Spain, 1518–1764* (Salt Lake City: University of Utah Press, 1991), chap. 5.

3. For a summary of Comanche raids, see Thomas W. Kavanagh, *Comanche Political History: An Ethnohistorical Perspective, 1706–1875* (Lincoln: University of Nebraska Press in cooperation with the American Indian Studies Research Institute, Indiana University, Bloomington, 1996), 83–86, 94–95.

4. Jean-Baptiste Truteau, "Journal of Truteau on the Missouri River, 1794–1795," in A. P. Nasatir, ed., *Before Lewis and Clark: Documents Illustrating the History of the Missouri, 1785–1804* (1952; rpt., Lincoln: University of Nebraska Press, 1990), 1:299.

5. On the consolidation of Mandan, Hidatsa, and Arikara villages, see Michael K. Trimble, "Epidemiology on the Northern Plains: A Cultural Perspective" (Ph.D. diss., University of Missouri, Columbia, 1985), 36–53. Clark's comments are in Gary E. Moulton, ed., *The Journals of the Lewis and Clark Expedition* (Lincoln: University of Nebraska Press, 1983–93), 3:233, 8:85–86. See also Maximilian Alexander Philipp von Wied-Neuwied, *Travels in the Interior of North America, 1833–1834*, trans. H. Evans Lloyd (London: Ackermann, 1843), 1:334–36. It is conceivable but not likely that the Mandans also suffered in the 1801–02 epidemic. See Trimble, "Epidemiology," 46–47.

6. For the map and for Clark's comments, see Moulton, *Journals of the Lewis and Clark Expedition*, 1:map 28, 3:233. On the comparative impact of smallpox on the Sioux and the Missouri River tribes and on Sioux domination to the Yellowstone, see Richard White, "The Winning of the West: The Expansion of the Western Sioux in the Eighteenth and Nineteenth

Centuries," *Journal of American History* 65 (September 1978): 325, 327. On 1837, see Trimble, "Epidemiology," 268, 279.

7. For the sudden and marked increase in direct contact between traders and the Blackfeet, see William Tomison, Journal containing Transactions, Occurrences &c. from York Fort to Cumberland House, and from thence to Hudson's House, & to York Fort again, Hudson House (Lower) Post Journal, December 1, 1782, B.87/a/6, fos. 16ff., NAC (HBC). On Blackfoot domination of the Shoshones, see David Thompson, *David Thompson's Narrative 1784–1812*, ed. Richard Glover (Toronto: Champlain Society, 1962), 267; Frank Raymond Secoy, *Changing Military Patterns on the Great Plains* (1953; rpt., Lincoln: University of Nebraska Press, 1992), 51–61; and John Canfield Ewers, *The Blackfeet: Raiders on the Northwestern Plains* (Norman: University of Oklahoma Press, 1958), 29–30. Alexander Henry's observations are in his "Geography and Ethnography [of Rocky Mountain House]," in Elliot Coues, ed., *New Light on the Early History of the Greater Northwest: The Manuscript Journals of Alexander Henry and of David Thompson* (New York: Francis Harper, 1897), 2:737.

8. On the European and African American population of the British colonies in 1775, see Robert V. Wells, *The Population of the British Colonies in America before 1776* (Princeton: Princeton University Press, 1975), 284. For total population estimates for New Spain's northern frontier in 1750 and 1800, see Peter Gerhard, *The North Frontier of New Spain* (Princeton: Princeton University Press, 1982), 24. On central Mexico, see Peter Gerhard, *A Guide to the Historical Geography of New Spain* (1972; rev. ed., Norman: University of Oklahoma Press, 1993), 24.

9. The January 1775 report is in Extract of a letter from Boston, author unknown, *London Evening Post*, March 25–March 28, 1775, in Margaret W. Willard, ed., *Letters on the American Revolution, 1774–1776* (Boston and New York: Houghton Mifflin, 1925), 58. For July 1775, see Christopher Marshall, *Passages from the Remembrancer of Christopher Marshall*, ed. William Duane, Jr. (Philadelphia: James Crissy, 1839), 38. For sick and wounded among British and American troops, see Philip Cash, *Medical Men at the Siege of Boston* (Philadelphia: American Philosophical Society, 1973), 155–56. Unfortunately, it is impossible to ascertain the role of smallpox in these figures. For Boston figures from 1776, see John B. Blake, *Public Health in the Town of Boston, 1630–1822* (Cambridge, Harvard University Press, 1959), 244–45.

10. On the camp before Quebec, see Henry Caldwell, "The Invasion of Canada, Letter Attributed to Major Henry Caldwell," *Literary and Historical Society of Quebec, Historical Documents*, 2d ser., no. 5 (1887): 15. The estimates for prisoners of war can be found in Simon Fobes, "Narrative of

Arnold's Expedition to Quebec," in *March to Quebec*, 593; and Abner Stocking, "Journal of Abner Stocking," in *March to Quebec*, 566.

11. For a summary of troop returns and for notes regarding their enormous inaccuracies during the withdrawal, see Charles H. Lesser, ed., *The Sinews of Independence: Monthly Strength Reports of the Continental Army* (Chicago: University of Chicago Press, 1976), 17–31. From early June to mid-July 1776, estimates for the size of the American army ranged from eight thousand to roughly five thousand men. Benedict Arnold to Philip Schuyler, June 6, 1776, George Washington Papers, Library of Congress, quoted in *Papers of G. W.*, War Ser., 4:510n; Benedict Arnold to GW, June 25, 1776, *Papers of G. W.*, War Ser., 5:97; John Trumbull, *The Autobiography of Colonel John Trumbull, Patriot-Artist, 1756–1843*, ed. Theodore Sizer (New Haven: Yale University Press, 1953), 27–28; and Horatio Gates to GW, July 16, 1776, *Papers of G. W.*, War Ser., 5:338–39. For John Lacey's account, see John Lacey, "Memoirs of Brigadier-General John Lacey, of Pennsylvania," *Pennsylvania Magazine of History and Biography* 25 (1901): 203–04, 206. For Lewis Beebe's appraisals, see Lewis Beebe, "Journal of a Physician on the Expedition against Canada, 1776," *Pennsylvania Magazine of History and Biography* 59 (October 1935): 338, 339, 342, 345. Charles Cushing gave his estimate in a letter to his brother, July 10, 1776, in *Am. Arch.*, 5th ser., 1:131. For Gates, see Horatio Gates to GW, July 16, 1776, in *Papers of G. W.*, War Ser., 5:339. David's account is in his letter to Nicholas Brown, August 31, 1776, in Jeanette D. Black and William Greene Roelker, eds., *A Rhode Island Chaplain in the Revolution: Letters of Ebenezer David to Nicholas Brown, 1775–1778* (Providence: Rhode Island Society of the Cincinnati, 1949), 26–27. Beebe's 300 figure is in his "Journal," 345.

12. On Nova Scotia, see Allan E. Marble, "Epidemics and Mortality in Nova Scotia, 1749–1799," *Nova Scotia Historical Review* 8 (1988): 84; and Simeon Perkins, *The Diary of Simeon Perkins, 1766–1780*, ed. Harold Innis (Toronto: Champlain Society, 1948), 151. On the Iroquois in 1775–76, see Barbara Graymont, *The Iroquois in the American Revolution* (Syracuse: Syracuse University Press, 1972), 113; Barbara Graymont, "The Oneidas and the American Revolution," in Jack Campesi and Laurence M. Hauptman, eds., *The Oneida Indian Experience: Two Perspectives* (Syracuse: Syracuse University Press, 1988), 35; William L. Stone, *Life of Joseph Brant—Thayendanegea, Including the Indian Wars of the Revolution* (New York: Alexander V. Blake, 1838), 1:104; Calloway, *American Revolution in Indian Country*, 58–59; and Copy Colo: Bedels Defence, Crown Point, July 9, 1776, Timothy Bedel Papers, NL4, box 1, folder 1B. On the Oneidas and Senecas in 1780–82, see Philip Schuyler to the President of Con-

gress, Saratoga, December 2, 1780, NAR (PCC), M247, r173, i153, v3, p551; *Notices of Sullivan's Campaign* (1842; rpt., Port Washington, N.Y., 1970), 150; Campesi and Hauptman, *Oneida Experience*, 39–40; Graymont, *Iroquois in the Revolution*, 243; George H. Harris, "The Life of Horatio Jones: The True Story of Hoc-Sa-Go-Wah, Prisoner, Pioneer, and Interpreter," *Publications of the Buffalo Historical Society* 6 (1903): 433–34; and David Zeisberger to Daniel Brodhead, Schoenbrun, June 1, 1780, in Louise Phelps Kellogg, ed., *Frontier Retreat on the Upper Ohio, 1779–1781* (Madison: The Society, 1917), 189. On Yorktown and the contagion at the Hudson Highlands, see Morris H. Saffron, *Surgeon to Washington: Dr. John Cochran, 1730–1807* (New York: Columbia University Press, 1977), 191.

13. On the Wyoming Valley and New Concord, see Michel Guillaume Jean de Crèvecœur [J. Hector St. John de Crèvecœur, pseud.], "History of Mrs. B.," in Henri L. Bourdin, Ralph H. Gabriel, and Stanley T. Williams, eds., *Sketches of Eighteenth Century America: More "Letters from an American Farmer"* (New Haven: Yale University Press, 1925), 218; and John Beebe, Jr., "Excerpts from a Diary of John Beebe, Jr. (1727–1786)," Columbia County Historical Society, Kinderhook, N.Y. (typescript of original in the New York State Archives), 2 (photocopy kindly furnished by John L. Brooke, Tufts University). On the *Jersey*, see Silas Talbot, *An Historical Sketch, to the End of the Revolutionary War, of the Life of Silas Talbot, Esq., of the State of Rhode-Island* (New York: G. & R. Waite, 1803), 108–09.

14. On Dunmore's troops, see John E. Selby, *The Revolution in Virginia 1775–1783* (Williamsburg: Colonial Williamsburg Foundation, 1988), 126; and Particular Account of the Attack and Rout of Lord Dunmore, *Am. Arch.*, 1:151. For more Gwynn's Island numbers, see Purdie's *Virginia Gazette*, Friday, July 19, 1776, in *Nav. Docs.*, 5:1147–50; Deposition of John Emmes, a Delaware Pilot, ibid., 5:668; and Diary of Miguel Antonio Eduardo, ibid., 5:1344. For the deaths at Alexandria, see John Williams and John Crittenden, Declarations re a hospital at Alexandria, undated, NAR (PCC), M247, r73, i59, v3, p189.

15. For Natchitoches, see Catholic Church, St. François (Natchitoches, Louisiana), Parish Registers, 1729–1796, Archives of the Immaculate Conception Church, Natchitoches, Louisiana (microfilm, reel 1026611, FHL). The estimate of 58 is based on the number of deaths from October 1777 through April 1778 minus 1.4 deaths per month—the average over twenty-five months before the epidemic struck. The pestilence is not identified in the Natchitoches burial records, but in the spring of 1778, officials in New Orleans expressed concern that it was headed their way and later identified it as smallpox. Rudolph Matas, *The Rudolph*

Matas History of Medicine in Louisiana, ed. John Duffy ([Baton Rouge]: Louisiana State University Press for the Rudolph Matas Trust Fund, 1958), 1:198–99. On Galveztown, see Antonio Acosta Rodríguez, *La población de Luisiana Española (1763–1803)* (Madrid: Ministerio de Asuntos Exteriores, 1979), 140–41; and Gilbert C. Din, *The Canary Islanders of Louisiana* (Baton Rouge: Louisiana State University Press, 1988), 35. For the Pensacola numbers, see Muster Roll of Capt. Isaac Costen's Company of Maryland Loyalists Commanded by Lieut. Colonel James Chalmers, Pensacola, February 22, 1779, British Military and Naval Records, "C" Ser., RG 8 I, v. 1904, NAC; Muster Roll of Captain Caleb Jones's Company of the Maryland Loyalists Commanded by Lt. Col. James Chalmers Esqr., Pensacola, February 22, 1779, British Military and Naval Records, "C" Ser., RG 8 I, v. 1904, NAC; Muster Roll of Captain Philip Key['s] Company in the First Battalion of Maryland Loyalists Commanded by Lieutenant James Chalmers Esquire, Pensacola, February 22, 1779, British Military and Naval Records, "C" Ser., RG 8 I, v. 1904, NAC; Muster Roll of Capt. James Frisby's Company in the Maryland Loyalists—Jas. Chalmers Esqr. Lieut. Colonel Commandt., Pensacola, February 22, 1779, British Military and Naval Records, "C" Ser., RG 8 I, v. 1904, NAC; Muster Roll of the late Capt. Grafton Dulaney's Company [of] Maryland Loyalists, commencing 25th Oct. 1778 and ending the 23d. Feby. 1779, Pensacola, February 23, 1779, British Military and Naval Records, "C" Ser., RG 8 I, v. 1904, NAC; and Muster Roll of Captain Key's Company in the First Battalion of Maryland Loyalists commanded by Lieut. Colo. James Chalmers, [Red Cliffs], West Florida, April 26, 1779, British Military and Naval Records, "C" Ser., RG 8 I, v. 1904, NAC. On the Creeks, see *Pa. Gaz.*, October 27, 1779; and Alexander Cameron to Prevost, Little Tallassie, Creek Nation, October 15, 1779, Sir Guy Carleton Papers [Headquarters Papers of the British Army in America] (microfilm), DLC, P.R.O. 30/55, reel 7, item 2372. On the Moravians, see Adelaide L. Fries, ed., *Records of the Moravians in North Carolina* (Raleigh: State Department of Archives and History, 1922–69), 3:1286, 1304, 1312, 4:1659–60, 1778.

16. From Ralph Izard, June 10, 1785, Boyd, *Papers of Jefferson*, 8:199, cited in Sylvia R. Frey, *Water from the Rock: Black Resistance in a Revolutionary Age* (Princeton: Princeton University Press, 1991), 211n; Eliza Pinckney [?] to [?], Charleston, September 25, 1780, Charles Cotesworth Pinckney Family Papers, DLC, 1st ser., box 5.

17. Peter Fayssoux to David Ramsay, March 26, 1785, in Robert Wilson Gibbes, ed., *Documentary History of the American Revolution* (1853–57; rpt., New York: Arno Press, 1971), 117–21 (also quoted in David Ramsay, *The*

History of the Revolution of South Carolina [Trenton: Collins, 1785], 2:527–35); see also Chalmers Davidson, *Friend of the People: The Life of Dr. Peter Fayssoux* (Columbia: Medical Association of South Carolina, 1950), 42–46. Both yellow fever and smallpox began to appear even before prisoners were loaded aboard prison ships. Robert Stark to Nicholas Eveleigh, Charleston, July 28, 1781, NAR (PCC), M247, r102, i78, v21, p99. On Wilmington, see William Hooper to James Iredell, Wilmington, February 17, 1782, in Don Higginbotham, ed., *The Papers of James Iredell* (Raleigh: Division of Archives and History, Department of Cultural Resources, 1976), 2:327–28.

18. Leslie to Cornwallis, Portsmouth, July 13, 1781, Cornwallis Papers (microfilm), DLC, reel 4, P.R.O. 30/11/6, items 280–81; Charles O'Hara to Cornwallis, Portsmouth, August 9, 1781, Cornwallis Papers (microfilm), DLC, reel 45, P.R.O. 30/11/70, items 16–17; Martin, *Private Yankee Doodle*, 241–42; St. George Tucker, "St. George Tucker's Journal of the Siege of Yorktown, 1781," *WMQ* 3d ser., 5 (July 1948): 387; and Thomas Jefferson to William Gordon, July 16, 1788, in *Papers of T. J.*, 13:363–64.

19. Alexander von Humboldt, *Political Essay on the Kingdom of New Spain*, trans. John Black (London: Longman, Hurst, Rees, Orme, and Browne, 1811), 1:111–12; Archivo General de la Nación, "Epidemias," vol. XVI, exp. 6, fols. 79–79v, quoted in Donald B. Cooper, *Epidemic Disease in Mexico City, 1761–1813: An Administrative, Social, and Medical Study* (Austin: University of Texas Press, 1965), 68; and Gonzalo Díaz de Yraola, *La vuelta al mundo de la expedición de la vacuna* (Seville: Escuela de Estudios Hispano-Americanos de la Universidad de Sevilla, 1948), 108. On Guatemala, W. George Lovell, *Conquest and Survival in Colonial Guatemala: A Historical Geography of the Cuchmatán Highlands, 1500–1821* (Montreal: McGill-Queen's University Press, 1992), 158–59. The Guanajuato figure is from *Gazeta de México*, December 29, 1784, Colección documenta Novae Hispaniae (facsimile ed., Windsor, Mexico: Rolston-Bain, 1985), A-2:210.

20. The 18,053 figure is based on statistics in Elizabeth A. Fenn, "Pox Americana: The Great North American Smallpox Epidemic of 1775–1783" (Ph.D. diss., Yale University, 1999), appendix 2. From January 1775 through February 1779, the average number of burials per month in the records examined was 509. In March 1779, however, the number began to rise steadily, and it remained high through March 1781, an increase that reflected the impact of epidemic smallpox. The records examined chronicle some 30,778 fatalities in this twenty-five-month period. To allow for nonsmallpox-related mortality that would have occurred regardless of *Variola*'s arrival, I have subtracted 12,725 (25 months times the

nonepidemic average of 509) from this number, arriving at a total of 18,053 smallpox deaths. This probably underestimates the number of smallpox deaths, for those who would have died regardless of smallpox represented the weakest segments of the population—immunologically compromised individuals who very likely succumbed in disproportionate numbers when *Variola* arrived. On New Mexico, see Hubert Howe Bancroft, *History of Arizona and New Mexico, 1530–1888*, vol. 17, *The Works of Hubert Howe Bancroft* (San Francisco: History Co., 1889), 266.

21. Domingo Cabello to Teodoro de Croix, Béxar, December 6, 1780 [translation], Bexar Archives, 2C44, IXA (CAH); Pedro Vial and Francisco Xavier Chaves, "Inside the Comanchería: The Diary of Pedro Vial and Francisco Xavier Chaves," ed. and trans. Elizabeth A. H. John and Adán Benavides, Jr., *Southwestern Historical Quarterly* 98 (July 1994): 37–38, 49. An unnamed pestilence afflicted the Wichitas, Caddos, and Taovayas in 1777, also afflicting "Bejar, Bucareli and Nachitos." Herbert Eugene Bolton, ed., *Athanase de Mézières and the Louisiana-Texas Frontier, 1768–1780* (Cleveland: Arthur H. Clark, 1914), 2:231–32; and F. Todd Smith, *The Caddo Indians: Tribes at the Convergence of Empires, 1542–1854* (College Station: Texas A&M University Press, 1995), 74–75. Although this plague is not named as smallpox in the available sources, it is possible that this is what it was. Extensive mortality appears in the San Antonio (Béxar or "Bejar") burial records for January 1777. Misión de San Antonio de Valero, San Fernando Cathedral Missions (San Antonio, Texas), Parish Registers, 1731–1860, Archdiocese of San Antonio, San Antonio, Texas (microfilm, reel 0025437, FHL); and Libro de entierros de la iglesia parroquial de la villa de San Fernando y presidio de San Antonio de Béxar, 1761–1801, San Fernando Cathedral (San Antonio, Texas), Parish Registers, 1703–1957, Archdiocese of San Antonio, San Antonio, Texas (microfilm, reel 0025450, FHL). On the Shoshones, see Joy Leland, "Population," in Warren L. D'Azevedo, ed., *Great Basin*, vol. 11, *Handbook of North American Indians* (Washington, D.C.: Smithsonian Institution Press, 1986), 609.

22. Donald J. Lehmer, "Epidemics among the Indians of the Upper Missouri," in *Selected Writings of Donald J. Lehmer*, ed. Raymond Wood (Lincoln, Neb.: J & L Reprint Co., 1977), 107. See also Trimble, "Epidemiology," 29–35. On the Crows, see François-Antoine Larocque, "Journal of an Excursion of Discovery to the Rocky Mountains by Mr. [François-Antoine] Larocque in the Year 1805 from the 2d of June to the 18th of October," in W. Raymond Wood and Thomas D. Thiessen, eds., *Early Fur Trade on the Northern Plains: Canadian Traders among the Mandan and Hidatsa Indians, 1738–1818* (Norman: University of Oklahoma Press,

1985), 206. The Madras study is significant because it is one of the only studies of unvaccinated individuals. A. Ramachandra Rao, *Smallpox* (Bombay: Kothari Book Depot, 1972), 37.

23. The 25,000 figure is from Gary Clayton Anderson, *Kinsmen of Another Kind: Dakota-White Relations in the Upper Mississippi Valley, 1650–1862* (Lincoln: University of Nebraska Press, 1984), 15–16.

24. William W. Warren, *History of the Ojibway Nation* (1885; rpt., Minneapolis: Ross & Haines, 1957), 257–62.

25. Jody F. Decker, " 'We Should Never Be Again the Same People': The Diffusion and Cumulative Impact of Acute Infectious Diseases Affecting the Natives on the Northern Interior Plains of the Western Interior of Canada" (Ph.D. diss., York University, 1989), 86; and Jody F. Decker, "Depopulation of the Northern Plains Natives," *Social Science and Medicine* 33 (1991): 381, 391. On population recovery after smallpox epidemics, see Russell Thornton, Tim Miller, and Jonathan Warren, "American Indian Population Recovery Following Smallpox Epidemics," *American Anthropologist* 93 (March 1991): 37. On the increase in Cree and Blackfoot numbers, see Alexander Henry, *The Journal of Alexander Henry the Younger, 1799–1814,* ed. Barry M. Gough (Toronto: Champlain Society, 1988), 2:370, 381. On the Piegans, see Ewers, *Blackfeet,* 37.

26. Decker, "Depopulation," 382; and Decker, " 'We Should Never Be Again the Same People,' " 37.

27. Gregory Mengarini, *Recollections of the Flathead Mission: Containing Brief Observations, Both Ancient and Contemporary, Concerning This Particular Nation,* trans. and ed. Gloria Ricci Lothrop (Glendale, Calif.: Arthur H. Clark, 1977), 193–94; and Robert T. Boyd, "Demographic History, 1774–1874," in Wayne Suttles, ed., *Northwest Coast,* vol. 7, *Handbook of North American Indians* (Washington, D.C.: Smithsonian Institution Press, 1990), 136–38. The 83,832 figure is the sum of the following numbers, all from Suttles, *Northwest Coast* (page numbers in parentheses): Tlingits 14,820 (136); Haidas 14,427 (136); Nitinahts and Makahs 4,320 (136), Northern Coast Salish 4,057 (136); Central Coast Salish 20,000 (473); Southern Coast Salish 12,600 (501); Upper Chinookans 9,288 (136); and Tillamooks 4,320 (136).

28. Howard Henry Peckham, ed., *The Toll of Independence: Engagements & Battle Casualties of the American Revolution* (Chicago: University of Chicago Press, 1974), 130.

29. On ongoing outbreaks, see James H. Howard, "Dakota Winter Counts as a Source of Plains History," *Bulletin* 173, Smithsonian Institution Bureau of American Ethnology, Anthropological Papers, no. 61 (Washington, D.C.: U.S. Government Printing Office, 1960): 352; Garrick Mallery,

Picture-Writing of the American Indians, Tenth Annual Report of the Bureau of Ethnology to the Secretary of the Smithsonian Institution, 1888–'89 (1893; rpt., New York: Dover, n.d.), 1:313, 317; François Marie Perrin du Lac, "Extract from the Travels of Perrin du Lac, 1802," in Nasatir, *Before Lewis and Clark*, 2:710; Martha Warren Beckwith, "Mythology of the Oglala Sioux," *Journal of American Folklore* 43 (1930): 356, 361; James H. Howard, "Two Teton Winter Count Texts," *North Dakota History* 27 (1960): 71, 73; Garrick Mallery, *A Calendar of the Dakota Nation* (Washington, D.C.: U.S. Government Printing Office, 1877), 11; Edward S. Curtis, *The North American Indian*, ed. Frederick Webb Hodge (Cambridge, Mass.: University Press, 1908), 3:170, 172, 176, 178; and Ewers, *Blackfeet*, 64–66, 250, 252, 257–58.

30. Alexander Mackenzie, *The Journals and Letters of Sir Alexander Mackenzie*, ed. William Kaye Lamb (Cambridge: Cambridge University Press for the Hakluyt Society, 1970), 122; Henry, *Journal of Alexander Henry*, 1:21; and Peter Fidler, "Chesterfield House Journals 1800–1802," in Alice M. Johnson, ed., *Saskatchewan Journals and Correspondence* (London: Hudson's Bay Record Society, 1967), 264n.

31. Mackenzie, *Journals and Letters*, 74.

INDEX

abolitionists, 106
Absarokas, *see* Crows
Acoma, New Mexico, 158
Adams, Abigail, 34–37, 42, 53, 54
Adams, John, 33–35, 53, 74, 79, 84
Africans and African Americans, 29, 78,
    110, 268, 269; in Mexican silver mines,
    148; during Revolutionary War, 55–61,
    104–6, 126–33, 260, 267; *see also*
    slaves
Alabama, 114
Alamos, Mexico, 152
Alaska, 10, 28, 140, 227–30, 233, 235,
    238–40, 244, 249, 250, 258
Albany, New York, 70
Albuquerque, New Mexico, 156, 158
Aleuts, 235
Alexandria, Virginia, 80, 81, 94, 99–100,
    102
Allen, Ethan, 92
Allen, Joseph, 92
Alta California, *see* California
American Horse, 218, 219
American Revolution, *see* Revolutionary
    War
Amherst, Jeffery, 88–89
Antonio, Salvador, 242
Anza, Juan Bautista de, 135, 152, 162–63,
    210–11, 261, 324nn50, 52
Apaches, 29, 159, 207, 210, 212–14, 262, 270
Arikaras, 200, 201, 217, 262, 270–71

Arizona, 135, 151, 152–53, 160, 166
Arizpe, Mexico, 147, 151
Arnold, General Benedict, 62–63, 66–67,
    70–72
Arteaga, Ignacio de, 248–50
Asientos, Mexico, 146
Assiniboines, 169, 172, 176, 193–95, 200,
    201, 203, 204, 215, 263, 272, 333n7
Astor, John Jacob, 256
Astoria trading post, 224–26, 257
Athapaskans, 251
Atkins, Josiah, 129, 131
Atsinas, 173, 176, 193, 272
Augusta, Georgia, 115
Austin, George, 119
Awatovi Pueblo, 162
Aztecs, 6, 8, 137, 141, 203

Bagge, Betsy, 113
Bahamas, 86
Baja California, 24, 29, 151–52, 154–56,
    175, 186
Baldwin, Jeduthan, 75–76
Baltimore, Maryland, 40
Banks, James, 181
Baptist church, 105, 124
Barbados, 13–15
Bartlett, Josiah, 85, 91
Bayley, Frye, 73, 75
Baylor, Colonel George, 95
Bear, John K., 201

Bedel, Colonel Timothy, 72–73
Bedford, New Hampshire, 44, 76
Beebe, Lewis, 75–78, 266
Bent, Charles, 324*n52*
berdaches, 225–26
Bering, Vitus, 233
Bermejo, Juan, 157
Bethabara, North Carolina, 124
Bethania, North Carolina, 124, 125
Bethlehem, Pennsylvania, 94
biological warfare, 4; in Revolutionary
    War, 88–92, 131–33; threatened, 257–
    58
Birmingham, University of, 5
Black, Francis L., 26
Blackfeet, 173, 176, 197, 203, 204, 208,
    209, 220–22, 225–27, 253, 263, 272,
    275–76
blindness, 18, 22, 188
Bloods, 173, 197
Blue Salt, 104
Bodega y Quadra, Juan Francisco de la,
    243–45
Boisverd, 225
Boit, John, 229, 239
Bolaños, Mexico, 148
Boston, 21, 29, 31–33, 36, 37, 42, 57, 58,
    62, 84, 109, 135, 210; siege of, 14–15,
    42–44, 46–55, 69, 78, 82, 89–90, 107–
    8, 131, 243, 264–65
Boyd, Robert, 273, 343*n10*
Boylston, Zabdiel, 33, 36
Bracco, Lieutenant Bennett, 60, 293*n33*
Bradford, William, 18, 23
Braintree, Massachusetts, 37
Brandywine Creek, Battle of, 98
Brazil, 18
Britain, 335*n15*; African colonies of, 106;
    American colonies of, 29–30, 32–42,
    201, 264 (*see also* Canada); and emanci-
    pation of slaves, 55–56, 137; endemic
    smallpox in, 27–28, 83; inoculation in,
    36; Pacific Northwest interests of, 9–
    11, 228, 230–31, 233, 239, 245–46,
    248, 250, 252; Parliament of, 46, 210;
    in Revolutionary War, 44–52, 57–61,
    67–68, 72–78, 80, 82, 83, 88–94, 98–
    102, 105, 107–11, 113–35, 154, 160,
    175, 240, 243, 260, 261, 265, 267–69;

    wars between Native Americans and,
    29
British Columbia, 9, 10, 230–31, 239,
    240–42, 252, 257
Brookline, Massachusetts, 47
Bruce, William, 182, 216, 328*n28*
Bucareli, Antonio María de, 243
Bullen, Dr., 66
Bungee Ojibwas, 167–68, 183–84, 186,
    192, 329*n34*
Bunker Hill, Battle of, 44–45, 69
Burgoyne, General John, 92, 98
Burke, Thomas, 84–85
Butterfield, Major Isaac, 72–74

Cabello, Domingo, 211–13, 261, 270
Caddos, 219, 270
Caldwell, Henry, 265
California, 28, 135–36, 140, 152–54, 160,
    240; *see also* Baja California
Cambridge, Massachusetts, 14, 46, 48,
    53, 55, 78, 89
Camden, South Carolina, 120–22, 128,
    269; Battle of, 120
Cameron, Alexander, 115
camino real, 146, 147, 148, 157
Campa, Miguel, 244
Campbell, Archibald, 38
Campbell, General John, 114
Campbellton, North Carolina, 125
Canada, 28, 29, 229, 252, 264, 272;
    African Americans in, 106, 128; fur
    trade in, 167–200, 204, 207, 215–16,
    222, 232; inoculation in, 41; plains
    Indians in, 23, 199, 203, 215–16,
    220–22; during Revolutionary War,
    45, 51, 62–76, 86, 87, 92–93, 108, 127,
    189–91, 260 (*see also* Quebec, siege
    of)
Canatlán, Mexico, 147–48, 157
Carleton, General Guy, 66, 68, 89
Carroll, Charles, 69
Carter, Landon, 56
Carter, Robert, 61
case fatality rates, 20–24, 26, 43, 193–94;
    for inoculation, 32, 33
Cassacan, 229
Catawbas, 29
Catherine the Great, Tsarina, 237

Catholic Church, 136, 138, 141–43, 151, 158, 160, 242, 251, 270
Cedars, the, 72–74, 266
Chambly, Fort, 75
Charleston, South Carolina, 39, 105, 110–11, 113–20, 122, 127–28, 268–69
Charlestown, Massachusetts, 46
Chase, Samuel, 69
Chaves, Francisco, 213–14, 270
Chelsea, Massachusetts, 48–49
Cherokee Wars, 29, 110
Cherokees, 29–31, 114, 116, 126, 133, 260
Chesapeake Bay, 57–58, 60, 127
Chiapas (state), Mexico, 146
Chickasaws, 29
Chihuahua (state), Mexico, 148–49, 164
children, smallpox in, 20–21, 73, 113, 188
China trade, 229, 250
Chínipas, Mexico, 151
Chinooks, 224–26, 255, 273
Chipewyans, 23, 169, 186, 192, 193, 198, 272, 273
Choctaws, 29
cholera, 6
Chouteau, Auguste, 140
Christianity, conversion of Native Americans to, 141–42, 149, 156, 161–62, 261
Churchill Factory trading post, 185–87, 190, 191, 196, 222
Clanaham, Magdalen M., 61
Clark, William, 6, 216, 217, 232, 252–53, 255–56, 259, 262–63
Clarke, Gedney, 13, 15–16
Clarke, Mrs. Gedney, 15
Clatsops, 224–26, 256
Clerke, Captain Charles, 246, 248
Clinton, General Henry, 101, 102, 105, 117, 118, 120, 126, 127
Cloud Shield, 219
Coahuila (state), Mexico, 157, 211
Coahuiltecans, 28
Coast Salish, 25, 230–31, 243, 248, 273
Cochimis, 151, 155
Cochran, John, 94
Cocking, Matthew, 167–69, 174, 180, 182, 183, 185–87, 189, 193, 198, 208, 215, 222, 329nn30, 34
Codex en Cruz, 8

Codex Florentino, 8
Coercive Acts (1774), 46, 210
Cold War, 4
Colombia, 146
Colorado, 160, 199, 205
Columbia Redeviva (ship), 228–29
Columbus, Christopher, 21, 276
Comanches, 159, 161, 203, 205–7, 209–11, 213–15, 222, 253, 261–62, 270, 272, 324n48, 335n15
Concord, Massachusetts, 31; Battle of, 14, 28, 44, 46, 105, 243, 364
Conewago, Pennsylvania, 267
Connecticut, 40, 85, 87, 94, 95, 100, 108–10, 129, 266
Connecticut Gazette, 86
Constantinople, 32
Continental army, 53–55, 82, 107, 133–34, 161, 265–67, 275, 314n49; biological warfare against, 90, 131–33; Canadian campaign of, 62–76; establishment of, 14; expiration of enlistments in, 64, 66, 67, 99, 265; Fifteenth Virginia Regiment, 81, 97; Hospital Department, 50; mass inoculations of soldiers in, 80–82, 93–103, 107, 111, 117, 132–34, 260, 268; Ninth North Carolina Regiment, 80–81; Northern Army, 45, 66–78, 83, 92, 265–66; professional soldiers in, 80–81; Pulaski's Legion in, 111–13, 115, 116, 123–24, 268; recruitment difficulties of, 86–88; during siege of Boston, 42, 43, 45–48, 50–52; Southern Army, 113, 117, 123; Third North Carolina Regiment, 97; Thirteenth Virginia Regiment, 99; veterans of, 108
Continental Congress, 14, 45, 50, 53, 69, 84, 123; Medical Committee, 94; Secret Committee, 84
Continental fleet, 85–86
Cook, Captain James, 10, 11, 235, 237, 238, 245, 248, 251–52
Cook, Sherburne, 321n30
Cooper, Donald B., 140
Cornwallis, General Charles, 118, 120, 122–32, 154, 269, 222
Cortés, Hernán, 6, 137, 141, 203
Costen, Captain Isaac, 114

Cowpens, Battle of, 123
cowpox vaccination, 33, 260
Cox, Ross, 256–57
Crafts, Thomas, 89
Creeks, 29, 104, 114, 115, 126, 133, 260, 268
Crees, 167–70, 172, 173, 181, 184–86, 189, 192, 193–95, 197, 200, 201, 203, 204, 215, 224, 263, 272, 273, 333n7
Cresswell, Nicholas, 24–25, 95, 109
Croix, General Teodoro de, 210, 212, 261
cross-dressing, 225
Crown Point, New York, 77, 266
Crows, 220, 271, 336n19
Cuba, 138
Cuerno Verde (Green Horn), 210–11, 214, 261, 336n21
Cumberland House trading post, 168–69, 173–74, 177–82, 184, 187, 191, 192, 197, 198, 221–22
Cunningham, James, 91
Cushing, Charles, 266
Cussita, Georgia, 104
Cutler, Manasseh, 54

Dalgleish, John, 38
Danbury, Connecticut, 109
David, Ebenezer, 266
Decker, Jody F., 272, 327n18
Declaration of Independence, 76, 128, 137, 269
Delawares, 23
Denny, Ebenezer, 131
depopulation, 6, 260, 276–77; in Canada, 176, 186, 193; of Pacific Northwest, 9–11, 230–31; reported by Lewis and Clark, 216, 217, 255–56, 262–63; in Spanish colonies, 142, 163, 212
Detroit, 74
Dimsdale, Thomas, 36
diphtheria, 6
Discovery (ship), 245, 246
Discovery Bay, 9, 10
Dixon, Captain George, 227–28
dolores de costado (side pains), 149
Domínguez, Francisco Atanasio, 160–62, 324n52
Dominicans, 24, 151, 155, 175
Donkin, Robert, 132

Douglass, William, 36
Dring, Thomas, 121
Dudley, Dorothy, 53
Dumfries, Virginia, 94
Dunmore, John Murray, Lord, 45, 55–57, 59–61, 82, 91, 126, 267, 292n28
Durango (state), Mexico, 147, 148, 149, 157
dysentery, 78, 99, 121, 266, 268

Ecuador, 146
elderly, smallpox in, 20–21
El Paso, Texas, 140
Emmet, James, 125
England, 5, 21, 27–28, 35
Escalante, Silvestre Vélez de, 160–63
Ethiopian Regiment, 46, 56–60, 78, 82, 91, 109, 260, 267
Ewald, Johann, 130
Ewers, John, 272

Fairfax, Virginia, 94
famines, 21, 22, 114, 187–89, 191, 192
fatality rates, see case fatality rates
Favorita (ship), 248, 249
Fayssoux, Peter, 121
Ferguson, Major Patrick, 123
Fidler, Peter, 276
firearms, 275; plains tribes and, 199–201, 203, 204, 207–9, 220, 223; trade with Canadian tribes for, 169–70, 192, 199–200
Flatheads, 253, 254, 273
Flatt, William, 180
Fleurieu, Charles Pierre Claret de, 229–30
Florence, Italy, 21
Fobes, Simon, 65, 66
Forster, Captain George, 73–74
Fort Pitt, 88
Fort Union, 23
France: American colonies of, 140, 143, 172, 199, 200, 207, 209; Canadian trading posts attacked by, 190–91, 194; inoculation in, 41; Pacific Northwest interests of, 229–30, 233, 250; in Revolutionary War, 101, 104, 106–7, 129; in Seven Years' War, 29; territory ceded to Spain by, 239–40

Franchère, Gabriel, 207, 335*n16*
Francis, Thomas, 90
Franciscans, 23, 135, 151, 153, 160–62, 261
Franklin, Benjamin, 41, 69, 83, 132
French and Indian War, 83, 89
Frey, Peter, 124
Friedberg, North Carolina, 124
Füch, Heinrich von, 237
fur trade, 207, 216, 272–73, 275; Canadian, 167–200, 204, 207, 215–16, 222, 232, 255; in Pacific Northwest, 250, 254–55; Russian, 233, 235–39

Gage, General Thomas, 88–89
Galphin, George, 105, 115
Gandiaga, Pedro, 156
Garcés, Francisco Tomás Hermenegildo, 135–37, 152, 160, 161
Gates, General Horatio, 77, 78, 120, 266
George, David, 104–6, 115–16, 126–28, 133
George III, King of England, 107, 248
Georgetown, Maryland, 94, 100
Georgia, 29, 30, 103, 107, 111, 114–15, 126, 137, 268
germ warfare, *see* biological warfare
Germain, Lord, 101
Germantown, Battle of, 98
globalization, eighteenth-century, 106–7, 233
Gloucester House trading post, 191
Good, Battiste, 17, 201, 202, 219, 340*n36*
Goulding Harbor, Alaska, 227
Gray, Captain Robert, 228, 229
Greene, General Nathanael, 123–26
Greenman, Jeremiah, 63, 65
Green Mountain Boys, 71
Guadalajara, Mexico, 148
Guanajuato, Mexico, 141, 146, 148, 270
Guatemala, 146, 270
guerrilla warfare, 123
Guilford Courthouse, Battle of, 123, 125
guns, *see* firearms
Gwynn's Island, Virginia, 58–61, 91, 267

Hachijo-Jima, Japan, 21
Haidas, 240, 242, 251, 273
Halifax, North Carolina, 125

Halifax, Nova Scotia, 51
Hall, George Abbott, 268
Hamond, Captain Andrew Snape, 58, 59
Hancock, John, 48, 67, 86, 89, 93
Hardin, 219
Harris, Cole, 343*n10*
Harvard College, 54
Haskell, Caleb, 63, 64
Haswell, Robert, 229
Hearne, Samuel, 23, 185–87, 191–93
Heath, General William, 100, 133
Hendey, Anthony, 208
Henry, Alexander, 193, 263, 272, 276
Henry, John Joseph, 70, 90
Henry, Patrick, 85, 87
Hessians, 98, 102, 130
Hezeta, Bruno de, 243, 244
Hidalgo del Parral, Mexico, 148
Hidatsas, 173, 200, 201, 208–9, 215–17, 220, 262, 270–72, 333*n7*
High Hawk, 340*n36*
Hillsborough, North Carolina, 120, 125
Homans, John, 53
Hood Canal, 11
homosexuality, 225
Hooper, William, 128, 269
Hopis, 135–37, 153, 160–63, 210, 324*nn50, 52*
Hopkins, Commodore Esek, 85–86
horses, acquisition by Native Americans of, 201, 203–5, 207–9, 220, 222, 223
Hostotipaquillo, Mexico, 145
Howe, General William, 49–51, 82, 89, 98, 99
Hudson Bay, 23, 169, 172, 173, 180, 188, 190, 196, 198, 199, 208, 224, 252
Hudson Highlands, New York, 94, 95
Hudson House trading post, 174–77, 180, 187, 188, 191–94
Hudson's Bay Company, 24, 168, 170–72, 174, 175, 177, 179–80, 182, 185, 186, 188–92, 194–96, 200, 208, 215, 220–22, 254, 263
human immunodeficiency virus (HIV), 3–5
Humbolt, Alexander von, 140
Huntington, Samuel, 85
Hurons, 200

Île-aux-Noix, Quebec, 75–76
Illinois, 209
immune systems: compromised, 21; of Native Americans, 26, 27
immunity: acquired, 20, 23, 24, 28, 29, 43, 95, 271 (*see also* inoculation; vaccination); innate, 26
India, case fatality rate in, 21, 271
Indians, *see* Native Americans
infants, smallpox in, 20–21, 73
influenza, 6
inoculation, 31–43, 96, 133; in Anglo-American colonies, 32–41; of black loyalist soldiers, 58, 59; of British soldiers, 49, 75, 118; changes in procedure for, 35, 36; of civilians during Revolutionary War, 50, 61–62, 85, 265; cost of, 41, 42; dangers of, 33, 36–38, 47, 93; economic inequality in availability of, 66, 83–84, 87, 66; fatality rates for, 32, 33; mass, in Continental army, 47, 81, 93–103, 107, 111, 117, 132–34, 260, 268; of militiamen, 60; in New Spain, 139, 155; opposition to, 36, 38–39, 42; preparation for, 33–34, 95; process of, 34–35; restrictions on, 39, 41, 53–54, 70–71, 77, 84, 88; spread of smallpox by, 73, 84, 112; Suttonian, 35–36, 42, 95
Inquiry into the Causes and Effects of the Variolae Vaccinae (Jenner), 33
Iroquois, 72, 108, 133, 200, 260, 266–67, 307n3
irregular soldiers, *see* militiamen
Isham, Charles, 177
Isham, James, 170
Isleta, New Mexico, 158
isolation, 29–31; *see also* quarantine
Italy, case fatality rate in, 21

Jackson, Andrew, 122, 269
Jackson, Elizabeth, 122
Jackson, Robert, 122, 269
Jamaica, 107, 114
Japan, 232; case fatality rate in, 21
Jefferson, Thomas, 59, 83, 91, 131, 269
Jenner, Edward, 11, 20, 33, 260
Jersey (ship), 121, 267

Jesuits, 142, 149, 151, 253
John, Elizabeth A. H., 324n50
Jones, Captain Caleb, 114
Jordan, Reuben, 61

Kamchatka, 233, 235–38
Kansas, 205
Kansas Indians, 219
Kavanagh, Thomas, 211
Kendrick, Captain John, 228
Keowee, Georgia, 30, 31
Kickapoos, 200
King, Boston, 128, 133
King Jack, 104
King's Mountain, Battle of, 123
Kingston, New Hampshire, 91
Kipling, John, 326n12
Knight, James, 170n
Kutenais, 225–26

Labrador, 28
Lacey, John, 76, 266
Lady Washington (ship), 228
Laguna, New Mexico, 158
Lakotas, 16, 17, 200–201, 217, 219, 333n5
Lamb, William Kaye, 280n4
La Pérouse, Jean-François de Galaup, comte de, 190–91
Larocque, François-Antoine, 207, 220, 271
La Vérendrye, Pierre Gaultier de Varennes, sieur de, 172
Ledyard, John, 235, 237
Lee, Richard Henry, 56, 57, 59, 87, 99, 129
Lee, William, 129, 313n41
Leesburg, Virginia, 61
Le Havre, France, 107
Lehmer, Donald, 270
Leslie, General Alexander, 132, 269
Lesseps, Jean, 237
Lewis, Andrew, 56
Lewis, Meriwether, 6, 216, 217, 232, 252–53, 255–56, 259, 262–63
Lexington, Battle of, 14, 28, 44, 46, 105, 243, 364
Lincoln, General Benjamin, 111, 117, 119

Little Tallasee, Alabama, 115
Livingston, Robert, 131
London, England, 21, 32
Longmoore, Robert, 188
Loreto, Mexico, 151, 154
Los Angeles, 135, 152, 153
Louisiana, 24, 140, 157, 207, 214, 240
loyalists, 51, 57–59, 104–6, 110, 114, 118, 123, 126–31, 133, 260; see also Tories

Maalin, Ali Maow, 5
Macdonnel, John, 193
MacKay, James, 220
Mackenzie, Alexander, 188, 216, 276, 277, 328n26
Madras, India, 21, 271
Maine, 63
malaria, 6, 78, 118, 122
Manby, Thomas, 10, 230, 252
Mandans, 173, 200, 201, 208–9, 215–17, 219, 220, 262–63, 270–71, 333n7
Marblehead, Massachusetts, 38, 41
Marchand, Étienne, 229
Marion, Colonel Francis (Swamp Fox), 110, 119, 309n7
Marten, Humphrey, 189–91
Martin, Francisco, 159
Martin, Joachim, 159
Martin, Joseph Plumb, 95, 269, 305n32
Martínez, Estéban José, 252
Maryland, 40, 60, 94, 114
Maryland Council of Safety, 60
Mascoutens, 200
Massachusetts, 3, 38, 46, 51–54, 62, 71, 95, 100, 243
Massachusetts, Council of, 52
Massachusetts Bay Colony, 30
Massachusetts General Court, 52
Massachusetts House of Representatives, 48, 49, 89; Smallpox Committee appointed by, 50
Mather, Cotton, 32, 33, 36
Matonabbee, 192
McDougall, Duncan, 257–58
McGuire, John, 64
McNeal, Captain Hector, 90–91
measles, 6, 26–27, 219
Melvin, James, 65
Mendon, Massachusetts, 46

Mengarini, Gregory, 253–54, 273
Menzies, Archibald, 11, 231
Mescaleros, 212
Mexico, see New Spain
Mexico City, 137–44, 146–48, 155–57, 163, 211, 215, 269–70
Miamis, 200
Michilimackinac, 74, 108, 266
Michoacán (state), Mexico, 164
Middletown, Connecticut, 109
Mier y Trespalacios, Cosme de, 140
militiamen, 110, 117–25, 131
mines, Mexican, 141, 146, 148, 151, 270
missionaries, Spanish, 135–37, 141–42, 151–58, 160–62, 240, 275
Mobile, Alabama, 115
Mohawks, 72–73
Monmouth, Battle of, 102
Montagnais-Naskapis, 28
Montagu, Mary Wortley, 32
Montcalm, Marquis de, 62
Monterey, California, 242–44
Montgomery, General Richard, 63, 64, 66
Montreal, 63, 72–75, 93, 173, 200
Moravians, 111–13, 123–24, 268
Morel, Esteban, 139
Morfi, Juan Agustín de, 149
Morgan, General Daniel, 64, 65, 123
Morgan, John, 50, 53, 83
Morristown, New Jersey, 82, 92, 94, 98, 117
Morse, Moses, 54
Moultrie, General William, 117
Mourelle de la Rúa, Francisco Antonio, 244, 245
Mourning Dove, 25
mumps, 6
Murry, Lieutenant William, 97

Nacogdoches, Texas, 140, 211
Nahathaways, see Crees
Nakotas, 200
Nambe, New Mexico, 159
Narragansett Indians, 18
Nassau, Bahamas, 86
Natchez Indians, 104
Natchitoches, Louisiana, 214

Native Americans, 198–99, 237, 260–61, 264, 275–77; biological warfare against, 88–89; in Canada, 166, 170–98, 220–23, 272; case fatality rate among, 23, 43; famine among, 22; healing customs of, 24–25, 155; immune systems of, 26–27; and inoculation, 41; isolation strategies of, 30–31; in military campaigns, 29; Northwest Coast, 10–11, 224–33, 239, 242–44, 246, 248–58, 273; number of epidemics impacting, 28; plains, 200–15, 219, 270–73; during Revolutionary War, 72–74, 78, 108–10; slave ownership among, 104–5; in Spanish colonies, 140, 141, 151–63, 213–14, 270; virulence of *Variola* among, 16, 24; *see also specific tribes*
Navajos, 161–63, 324*n48*
Nelson, Thomas, 129
Nelson, William, 38
Neve, Felipe de, 154
New Bern, North Carolina, 111
New Concord, New York, 109, 267
New England, 39–40, 64, 70, 87, 91, 92, 228–29; *see also specific colonies and municipalities*
New France, 29
New Hampshire, 44, 69, 72, 76, 85, 91–92
New Jersey, 40, 82, 86, 87, 94, 101, 102
New Mexico, 136, 142, 156–62, 166, 203, 205–6, 209–11, 214, 261, 270
New Orleans, 107, 137, 140, 157, 214, 219, 268
New Orleans City Council, 214
New Spain, 3, 23, 29, 41, 42, 137–51, 162, 199, 209–11, 261, 269–70; Catholic Church in, 141–44; inoculation in, 139; silver mining in, 141, 146, 148, 151, 270; as source of horses for plains Indians, 204; Spanish conquest of, 6, 137; voyages to Pacific Northwest from, 240, 243, 249
Newtown, Pennsylvania, 94
New York, 29, 40, 52, 87, 94, 100, 108, 109, 131, 133, 200, 266–67
New York City, 36, 39, 60, 82, 92, 101, 109–10, 114, 132, 267

Nez Perces, 253–55, 273
Nichols, Lieutenant Francis, 66
Nitinahts, *see* Nootkans
Nootkans, 240, 246, 248, 257, 273
Norfolk, Virginia, 38, 57, 59, 91, 267
North Carolina, 84, 93, 95, 97, 100, 103, 104, 107, 111, 122–28, 134, 239, 268
North West Company, 23, 172, 180, 193, 194, 198, 216, 220, 224, 225, 232, 263, 335*n16*
Northwest Passage, 9, 230, 245–46
Nova Scotia, 51, 106, 128, 133, 266
Nuevo León (state), Mexico, 157, 211

Oaxaca (state), Mexico, 144, 146, 164
O'Hara, General Charles, 130*n*, 269
Ohio, 29
Ojibwas, 169, 181, 189, 191, 194, 215–16, 271–72; *see also* Bungee Ojibwas
Omahas, 200, 201, 219, 262
Oman, Mitchell, 175–76, 181, 188–89, 192–93, 198
Oñate, Juan de, 205
Oneidas, 108, 267
Onesimus, 32, 41, 285*n32*
Onondaga Iroquois, 108
Opatas, 151
Oraibi Pueblo, 135–37, 160, 161, 163
Oregon, 228, 245, 255
Osages, 219, 335*n15*
Oswegatchie, New York, 74
Otos, 219
Ottawas, 88, 108, 200

Pacific Fur Company, 224–25, 257
Page, John, 59
Palma, Salvador, 153
Paris, Treaty of, 207, 261
Parker, Janet, 5
Pasquia Indians, 198
Patten, John, 44, 69, 76, 77, 80
Patten, Matthew, 44–45, 76
Pawnees, 200, 201, 217
Pearcy, Thomas L., 321*n30*, 322*n35*
Pecos, New Mexico, 159
Pegogomew Indians, 193
Peña, Tomás de la, 242, 251
Pendleton, Edmund, 57, 87, 304*n29*

Pennsylvania, 30, 40, 87, 88, 94, 98–100, 108, 266, 267
Pennsylvania Gazette, 84, 131–32
Pensacola, Florida, 3, 107, 114
Pérez, Manuel, 156
Pérez Hernández, Juan José, 240, 243, 245, 250–52
Petra, María, 159
Petropavlovsk, Russia, 233, 235, 238
Pfefferkorn, Ignaz, 151
Philadelphia, 14, 29, 41–42, 46, 53, 62, 69, 82–86, 92–94, 98, 99, 101, 102, 137
Philipsburg, New York, 126
Phillips, Colonel James, 125
Phipps, James, 33
Pickens, Andrew, 119
Picuris Pueblo, 157, 158
Pierce, John, 64, 66
Pimas, 151
Pinckney, Eliza, 127, 268
plague, 6
Plains of Abraham, 62–64, 68, 70–72
Pojoaque, New Mexico, 159, 164
Pomeroy, Seth, 89
Pontiac, 88
Pontiac's Revolt, 29
Portlock, Captain Nathaniel, 227–29, 231, 239, 244, 248
Portsmouth, Virginia, 132, 269
Potawatomis, 200
pregnancy, smallpox during, 21
Prevost, General Augustine, 113, 116
Price, Ezekiel, 53, 54
Price, Major Thomas, 59
Prince Rupert (ship), 196
Princesa (ship), 248, 249
Princeton, Battle of, 82, 92
Provincetown, Massachusetts, 52
Pueblos, 142, 158, 159, 160, 205, 261
Puerto Rico, 138
Puget, Peter, 10, 231
Puget Sound, 3, 10, 11
Pulaski, General Casimir, 111–13, 115, 116, 123–24, 268
Puritans, 18, 30, 32

Qánqon, 225–26, 257
Quakers, 83
Quapaws, 219

quarantines, 29–31, 36, 40, 83; at Canadian trading posts, 178–79, 185; during Revolutionary War, 47–52, 64, 68, 70, 77–79, 92, 100, 128; in Spanish colonies, 154, 214
Quebec, 28, 74, 134, 186; siege of, 45, 46, 62–68, 70–72, 82, 88, 90–91, 134, 260, 265

Randolph, Richard, 97
Reed, Joseph, 90
Reide, Thomas Dickson, 92–93
Resolution (ship), 245, 246
Revolutionary War, 6, 9, 29, 41, 76–79, 84, 86–88, 141, 153–54, 160–61, 199, 201, 239, 259, 264–69; African Americans in, 55–61, 78, 104–6, 126–33, 260, 267; biological warfare in, 88–92, 131–33; British surrender ending, 127, 129–31, 133, 175; Canadian campaign of, 62–76, 265; France in, 101, 104, 106–7, 129, 189–90; inoculation of Continental army during, 80–82, 93–103, 107, 111, 117, 132–34, 260, 268; Native Americans during, 72–74, 78, 108–10; outbreak of, 44–45, 264; siege of Boston in, 42, 44, 46–55, 78, 264–65; southern campaign of, 110–30, 133–34, 248, 268–69
Rhode Island, 30, 63, 84
Richmond, Virginia, 129, 133
Rickman, William, 81, 95, 97–98
Ridgely, Frederick, 50–51
Rivera y Moncada, Captain Fernando Xavier de, 152, 154
Roberts, Captain Lemuel, 68–69
Roebuck (ship), 58
Rosario, Texas, 211
Ross, Alexander, 224, 255
Ross, George, 180
Roxbury, Massachusetts, 46
Rush, Benjamin, 83, 85, 94
Rushforth, Scott, 324*n52*
Russia: and Pacific Northwest, 228, 233, 235, 237–40, 251; repository of *Variola* in, 4

Sabedra, Francisco Xavier Davila, 157
Sabin, Josiah, 71

Sacagawea, 253
St. Augustine, Florida, 60, 119
St. Inigoes, Maryland, 60
St. Jean, Quebec, 75
St. Louis, 140, 201, 219
St. Lucia, 101
St. Malo, France, 107
Salem, Massachusetts, 38, 48
Salem, North Carolina, 111–13, 123–25, 268
Sales, Luis, 154, 155
Salisbury, North Carolina, 124
Salish Indians, see Coast Salish
San Antonio, Texas, 140, 211–13
San Blas, Mexico, 240, 242, 248, 249
San Diego, California, 242, 243
San Francisco, 140, 240
San Gabriel, California, 135, 152, 153, 154
San Juan de los Lagos, Mexico, 146
San Juan Pueblo, 158–59
San Luis Potosí, Mexico, 146, 148
San Miguel Culiacán, Mexico, 149, 151
Sandia, New Mexico, 159
Sandusky, Ohio, 23
Santa Fe, New Mexico, 137, 140, 146, 156, 157–60, 210
Santiago (ship), 240, 242–46
Santo Domingo, 138
Santo Domingo, New Mexico, 159, 164
Santo Domingo Tehuantepec, Sanctuary of, 144
Saratoga, Battle of, 98, 120
Sauer, Martin, 345n21
Saukamappee, 197–98, 203, 204, 208, 220–21, 225, 227, 332n1
Saunderson, James, 181
Savage, Lieutenant Abijah, 295n46
Savannah, Georgia, 104, 105, 113–16, 126–28, 248
scarlet fever, 6
Schöpf, J. D., 25
Schumacher, Eva, 112
Schuyler, General Philip, 70, 75, 78, 87, 108, 307n3
Scotland, case fatality rate in, 21
scurvy, 242–45
Senecas, 109, 267
Senter, Isaac, 68, 70

Seven Years' War, 29, 62, 192, 239
Severn trading post, 186, 188, 191
Shelikhov, Grigorii Ivanovich, 235, 238
Sherburne, Major Henry, 74
Shippen, William, 62, 93, 305n33
Shoshones, 199, 203–9, 215, 220–22, 226, 227, 253, 254, 257, 263, 270, 271, 336n19
Siberia, 233, 235, 237
Siberians, indigenous, 233, 235–36
Sierra Leone, 106, 128, 133
Silver Bluff, South Carolina, 105, 115
silver mines, Mexican, 141, 146, 148, 151
Simmons, Marc, 322n35
Simons, Keating, 118
Singleton Mills, South Carolina, 119
Sioux, 16, 198, 200–201, 209, 216–17, 219, 254, 262, 263, 271, 275–76, 334n7; see also Lakotas; Nakotas
Six Nations, see Iroquois
slaves: inoculation of, 40; during Revolutionary War, 55–56, 62, 104, 105, 112, 126, 128–29, 137, 269 (see also Ethiopian Regiment); in Spanish colonies, 148, 207
smallpox: and biological warfare, 4, 88–92, 131–33, 257–58; blindness from, 18, 22, 188; in children, 20–21; complications of, 187–88; confluent, 18; control of spread of, 29 (see also isolation; quarantine); course of, 16, 18, 20; deaths from, 18; destruction of, 4; early epidemics of, 28, 192; in elderly, 20–21; endemic, 27–28, 82–83; eradication of, 3–5, 27; fatality rates of, see case fatality rates; fear of, 24, 31, 37, 52, 67, 87–88, 112–13, 132, 187, 257–58; hemorrhagic, 16, 253; hospitals for, 38–41, 47–48, 50–51, 53, 64–67, 75, 95, 138, 139, 214; immunity to, 20, 23, 24, 26, 28, 29, 32, 39, 43, 53, 65, 86, 87, 99, 114, 179; incubation period for, 15–16, 31, 35, 146, 178, 179, 250; infectiousness of, 16, 20; inoculation against, see inoculation; laboratory outbreak of, 5; nutritional status and, 21, 22, 63, 187–89; during pregnancy, 21; repositories of virus causing, 4; scarring from, 11, 18, 20, 188, 218, 227,

229–31, 256; symptoms of, 16; transmission of, 5–7, 15, 27; treatment of, 24–25; vaccination against, 11, 20, 32–33, 260; virgin soil epidemics of, 22–23, 193; vulnerability to, 20–21, 25–26, 31, 62, 82, 93, 110, 124, 138, 179
Smith, Asa Bowen, 254–55
Smith, John, 38
Smith, Josiah, 119
Snake Indians, *see* Shoshones
Society for Inoculating the Poor, 42
Somalia, smallpox in, 5
Sombrerete, Mexico, 148
Sonora (ship), 243, 245
Sonora (state), Mexico, 142, 149–51, 154
Sorel, Quebec, 69–70, 75
Soulés, François, 91
South Branch House trading post, 197
South Carolina, 29–31, 86, 103–5, 107, 110–23, 125–27, 134, 268
Southington, Connecticut, 109
Spain, 56; American colonies of, 135–37, 152–66, 175, 199, 203–5, 207, 209, 210–14, 219, 261–62, 264 (*see also* New Spain); inoculation in, 41; Pacific Northwest interests of, 9, 228, 230, 231, 233, 239–40, 242–46, 248–52
Spokanes, 335*n16*
Steamboat, 219
Stevenson, Henry, 40
Stone Indians, *see* Assiniboines
Stuart, Robert, 257
Sullivan, General John, 77, 109
Sumner, General Jethro, 125
Sumter, Thomas, 119
Suttonian inoculation, 35–36, 42, 95
sweat baths, 24–25

Taitt, David, 114
Tamaulipas (state), Mexico, 211
Taos, New Mexico, 157, 158
Taovayas, 213, 270
Tarahumaras, 148–49
Tarelton, Colonel Banastre, 119
Tejas, 212
Temósachic, Mexico, 149
Tennessee, 116
Texas, 28, 29, 199, 203, 205, 209, 211–15, 261, 270

Thacher, James, 37, 131
Thetford, Vermont, 51
Thomas, General John, 67–71, 74–75
Thompson, David, 175–76, 186, 189, 193, 196–98, 203, 204, 208, 220–21, 225–26, 232–33, 256, 257, 332*n1*
Thompson, General William, 74
Thornton, Matthew, 85
Ticonderoga, 77, 92, 94
Tillamooks, 228, 273
Tilton, James, 305*n33*
Tlacotepec, Mexico, 146
Tlaxcala, Mexico, 146
Tlingits, 227–29, 231, 238, 244, 249, 273
Tomison, William, 168–69, 173–74, 177–84, 187, 191, 193, 194, 222–23, 328*nn27, 30*
Tonkawas, 212
Tonquin (ship), 257
Tories, 47, 51, 52
Townshend Acts, 201
Trenton, Battle of, 82, 92, 161
Trumbull, John, 77
Trumbull, Jonathan, 87, 98, 108
Truteau, Jean-Baptiste, 216, 217, 262
Tucker, St. George, 130, 269
Tucker's Point, Virginia, 58, 59
Tucson, Arizona, 152
typhus, 6, 127, 245

Umfreville, Edward, 192
United States, repository of *Variola* in, 4
Upham, Steadman, 324*n52*
Utah, 160
Utes, 205

vaccination, 11, 20, 32–33, 260
Valle, Rosemary, 321*n30*
Valley Forge, Pennsylvania, 98–100, 102, 111*n*
Vancouver, Captain George, 9–11, 230–31, 251, 280–81*n4*
Variola, see smallpox
variolation, *see* inoculation
venereal disease, 237, 248
Veracruz, Mexico, 144, 146
Vermont, 51, 91
Vial, Pedro, 213–14, 270

Virginia, 30, 38, 39, 55–65, 80–81, 85–88, 91, 94, 95, 99, 103–5, 107, 109, 117, 124, 126–35, 154, 222, 267–69
Virginia Gazette, 40
Virginia House of Burgesses, 39

Wakashan Indians, 229, 251; *see also* Nootkans
Waldeckers, 114
Walker, Jacob, 97
Walker, William, 175–77, 187, 221
Wallace, Richard, 51
Walpi Pueblo, 161
Ward, General Artemas, 54
Ward, Samuel, 63, 84
Warner, Colonel Seth, 71, 88
Warren, James, 84
Warren, Joseph, 33, 34
Warren, William W., 272
Washington, George, 33, 46, 48, 54–56, 67, 70, 78, 83, 86–88, 161, 266; and British biological warfare attempts, 89, 90, 132–33; and inoculation of Continental army, 47, 81, 92–95, 98–103, 134, 260; during siege of Boston, 42, 43, 45, 47–48, 51; slaves owned by, 62, 106; smallpox infection of, 13–16, 20, 35, 64
Washington, Harry, 106
Washington, John Augustine, 88
Washington, Lawrence, 13–14
Washington, Lund, 55
Washington, Martha, 62, 83
Wass, James, 180
Waterhouse, Benjamin, 39
Webber, John, 236, 247, 251

Wells, Bayze, 76
Wells, Thomas, 97
West Florida General Assembly, 114
West Point, New York, 133
Whigs, 47, 48, 52, 56, 58, 109, 115, 119, 131
Whipple, William, 91
White, Richard, 263
White Bull, 219
whooping cough, 6
Wichitas, 207, 213, 219, 270, 225n15
Williams, Colonel John, 81, 97
Williams, William, 88
Williamsburg, Virginia, 30, 38, 39, 61, 131
Wilmington, North Carolina, 126, 128, 269
Wilson, Joseph, 55
Winchester, Virginia, 30
Winthrop, Hannah, 54
Wolfe, General James, 62
Women of the Army, 102
World Health Organization (WHO), 3

Yanktonais, 219, 333n5
Yaquis, 151
yellow fever, 6, 122, 266, 268
York Factory trading post, 167–74, 180–91, 193, 194, 196, 198, 215, 222
Yorktown, Virginia, 38, 154, 267, 269; British surrender at, 127, 129–33, 175
Yuma, Arizona, 137, 152–53, 160
Yumans, 137, 151–53, 155, 175

Zacatecas, Mexico, 146
Zúñiga, Lieutenant José de, 152, 154
Zunis, 162